Ma

MA EI

Education, Cultures, and Economics

REFERENCE BOOKS IN INTERNATIONAL EDUCATION
VOLUME 48
GARLAND REFERENCE LIBRARY OF SOCIAL SCIENCE
VOLUME 1152

Education, Cultures, and Economics

Dilemmas for Development

Edited by
Fiona E. Leach
Angela W. Little

RoutledgeFalmer
New York London

Published by
RoutledgeFalmer
29 West 35th Street
New York, New York 10001

Published in Great Britain by
RoutledgeFalmer
11 New Fetter Lane
London EC4P 4EE

RoutledgeFalmer is an imprint of the Taylor & Francis Group.

10 9 8 7 6 5 4 3

Library of Congress Cataloging-in-Publication Data

Education, cultures, and economics : dilemmas for development / edited by Fiona E. Leach, Angela W. Little.

p. cm. — (Garland reference library of social science : vol.

Includes bibliographical references and index.

ISBN 0-8153-2783-8 (alk. paper)

1. Educational sociology—Developing countries Cross-cultural studies. 2. Education—Economic aspects—Developing countries Cross-cultural studies. I. Leach, Fiona E. II. Little, Angela.

III. Series: Garland reference library of social science : v. 1152.

IV. Series: Garland reference library of social science. Reference books in international education ; vol. 48.

LC191.8.D44E38 1999

306.43'09172'4—dc21 99-32544

CIP

Printed on acid-free, 250-year-life paper

Manufactured in the United States of America

Contents

Acknowledgments		viii
Series Editor's Foreword		ix
About the Contributors		xi
Part I	**Introduction**	
Chapter 1	Development and Education: Cultural and Economic Analysis *Angela Little*	3
Chapter 2	Economics and Culture: Towards an Anthropology of Economics *R. L. Stirrat*	33
Chapter 3	Meanings of Culture in Development: A Case Study from Literacy *Brian V. Street*	49
Chapter 4	Different Eyes: Schooling and Indigenous Education in Tonga *Konai Helu-Thaman*	69
Part II	**The Economic and Cultural Goals of Development: Whose Goals Matter?**	
Chapter 5	Learning versus Development: A Palestinian Perspective *Munir Fasheh*	81

Chapter 6 Alternative Development and Education: Economic Interests and Cultural Practices in the Amazon 95
Sheila Aikman

Chapter 7 Local Accountability to Rural Communities: A Challenge for Educational Planning in Africa 111
Robert Serpell

Part III The Costs of Culture and the Culture of Costs

Chapter 8 Language Policy in Ethiopian Education: Implications for the Costs of Textbook Production 143
Christine McNab and Peter Stoye

Chapter 9 The Costs of Culture: Some Dilemmas for Educational Investment in Mauritius 159
Keith Lewin

Chapter 10 Community Financing of Education: Cultural Variations and Policy Dilemmas in Less Developed Countries 183
Mark Bray

Chapter 11 Educational Financing Strategies in Developing Countries: The Case of Cameroon and Uganda 203
Mercy Tembon

Chapter 12 Educating Girls in Pakistan: Tensions Between Economics and Culture 225
Iffat Farah and Kazim Bacchus

Part IV Cultures of Knowledge and Learning

Chapter 13 Alternative Cultures of Knowledge in Higher Education in the Australia-Pacific Region 241
J. I. Teasdale and G. R. Teasdale

Chapter 14 Cultural Ambiguity and the Primary School Teacher: Lessons from Rural Mozambique 261
Mikael Palme

Chapter 15 Economic Imperatives and Cultural Discontinuities in Science Education: A View from the Solomon Islands 283
John Lowe

Chapter 16 Cultural Perceptions of the Role of Mathematics and Mathematics Education in Economic Development: Examples from Kenya 301
Florence Kiragu Nyamu

Chapter 17 Women and Mathematics: Ignoring a Majority? 315
Mary Harris

Chapter 18 Education, Social Identity, and Occupational Aspirations in Brazil: Reasons for (Not) Learning 327
Terezinha Nunes and Antonio Roazzi

Part V Dilemmas for Educational Aid

Chapter 19 Whose Rules Apply? Educational Project Management in Less Developed Countries: Cultural Considerations 347
Michael Delens

Chapter 20 Dilemmas Between Economics and Culture in Educational Aid: Lessons for Donors 371
Fiona Leach

Index 395

Acknowledgments

Many of the chapters in this book were presented initially in 1995 at a conference held at the Institute of Education, University of London. After the conference, all chapters were substantially revised, while others were commissioned anew. We are grateful to all who participated in the conference, to those who offered critical comment, and to those who agreed to revise their work for this volume.

Conferences that bring together an international audience and books that bring together an international authorship require organization and resources. We are grateful to Dr. Carew Treffgarne, formerly a colleague at the Institute of Education, who co-organized the conference with us; to Yana Krizka and Rajee Rajagopalan, who provided administrative support to it; and to Nicolette Castle for her artwork. We are also grateful to the Department for International Development (previously the Overseas Development Administration) and a range of other institutions that provided financial support for conference participants. For assistance in the editing of this volume and for keeping us on track, we are especially grateful to Dr. Felicity Rawlings.

Series Editor's Foreword

This series of scholarly works in comparative and international education has grown well beyond the initial conception of a collection of reference books. Although retaining its original purpose of providing a resource to scholars, students, and a variety of other professionals who need to understand the role played by education in various societies or world regions, it also strives to provide accurate, relevant, and up-to-date information on a wide variety of selected educational issues, problems, and experiments within an international context.

Contributors to this series are well-known scholars who have devoted their professional lives to the study of their specializations. Without exception these men and women possess an intimate understanding of the subject of their research and writing. Without exception they have studied their subject not only in dusty archives, but have lived and traveled widely in their quest for knowledge. In short, they are "experts" in the best sense of that often overused word.

In our increasingly interdependent world, it is now widely understood that it is a matter of military, economic, and environmental survival that we understand better not only what makes other societies tick, but also how others, be they Japanese, Hungarian, South African, or Chilean, attempt to solve the same kinds of educational problems that we face in North America. As the late George Z. F. Bereday wrote more than three decades ago: "[E]ducation is a mirror held against the face of a people. Nations may put on blustering shows of strength to conceal public weakness, erect grand façades to conceal shabby backyards, and profess peace while secretly arming for conquest, but how they take care of their children tells unerringly who they are" (*Comparative Methods in Education*, New York: Holt, Rinehart and Winston, 1964, p. 5).

Perhaps equally important, however, is the valuable perspective that studying another education system (or its problems) provides us in understanding our own system (or its problems). When we step beyond our own limited experience and our commonly held assumptions about schools and learning in order to look back at our system in contrast to another, we see it in a very different light. To learn, for example, how China or Belgium handles the education of a multilingual society; how the French provide for the funding of public education; or how the Japanese control access to their universities enables us to better understand that there are reasonable alternatives to our own familiar way of doing things. Not that we can *borrow* directly from other societies. Indeed, educational arrangements are inevitably a reflection of deeply embedded political, economic, and cultural factors that are unique to a particular society. But a conscious recognition that there are other ways of doing things can serve to open our minds and provoke our imaginations in ways that can result in new experiments or approaches that we may not have otherwise considered.

Since this series is intended to be a useful research tool, the editor and contributors welcome suggestions for future volumes, as well as ways in which this series can be improved.

Edward R. Beauchamp
University of Hawaii

About the Contributors

Sheila Aikman is a Lecturer in Education and International Development at the Institute of Education, University of London, where she gained her doctorate. She has carried out extensive field work in the Madre de Dios region of Peru into relations between indigenous peoples' informal educational practices and those of the formal education system. She is currently involved in research on interculturalism and intercultural bilingual education.

Kazim Bacchus was formerly Professor of Education and Director, Centre for International Education and Development, University of Alberta. He was also the first Director of the Institute for Educational Development, the Aga Khan University, Pakistan. He has taught at the universities of London, Guyana, West Indies, Alberta, and Chicago, and has been consultant with CIDA, UNESCO, the World Bank, the Government of Papua New Guinea, and the Commonwealth Secretariat. He is author of numerous books and journal articles.

Mark Bray is Director of the Comparative Education Research Centre and Professor at the University of Hong Kong. He has taught in secondary schools in Kenya and Nigeria, and at the Universities of Edinburgh, Papua New Guinea, and London. He has also undertaken numerous consultancy assignments for such agencies as the Asian Development Bank, UNESCO, UNICEF, and the World Bank. Among these assignments has been extended collaboration with the Government of Bhutan, focusing on the processes of educational planning and on assessment of the costs and financing of education.

Michael Delens is an adviser in teacher training management at the Ministry of Education, Youth and Sport, Cambodia. He has participated in various English for Specific Purposes projects in the Middle East and Africa, as a curriculum developer, materials writer, and teacher trainer. At the National University of Ivory Coast, he established and managed a post-graduate programme in Applied Linguistics. He gained his Masters from the Institute of Education, University of London.

Iffat Farah is Assistant Professor at the Institute for Educational Development, Aga Khan University, Karachi, Pakistan. She earned her doctorate from the University of Pennsylvania. She has conducted research in the areas of women and literacy in rural Pakistan and positive change in rural schools. Her present interest is in the area of community and parental participation in children's schooling in Pakistan.

Munir Fasheh is the Director of the Tamer Institute in Palestine. Born in Jerusalem, Palestine, he gained his doctorate in education from Harvard University. He was Visiting Scholar at the Center for Middle Eastern Studies, Harvard. Previously he was Assistant Professor of mathematics and education, and Dean of Students at Birzeit University. He has had extensive involvement in community education and has published numerous articles and six books on mathematics, education, religion, and social issues.

Mary Harris was formerly a Visiting Fellow in the Department of Mathematics, Statistics and Computing at the Institute of Education, University of London. Her work in mathematics education in many countries has ranged from special needs to secondary mathematics curriculum development, with emphasis on the development of teacher-made, environmentally sourced learning materials.

Konai Helu-Thaman, a Tongan national, is currently Professor of Pacific Education and Culture and Head of the School of Humanities at the University of the South Pacific, Suva, Fiji. She has conducted several educational consultancies and has published widely in the areas of curriculum development and teacher education and, more recently, in indigenous education and in women and university management. She is also a widely read poet in the Pacific region; five volumes of her poetry have been published.

Fiona E. Leach is Senior Lecturer in Education at the University of Sussex Institute of Education. Prior to joining the University of Sussex in 1996, she was lecturer at the Institute of Education in London and a teacher and curriculum developer on British aid projects in Africa. Her current professional and academic interests are: project management and implementation; the cross-cultural transfer of knowledge and skills; alternative forms of education; gender, education, and development; and women and the labour market.

Keith M. Lewin is Professor in Education at the University of Sussex and Director of the Centre for International Education. He has worked widely in Asia and southern Africa over the last 25 years for governments, donors, and lending agencies. His research interests focus on educational policy, planning, and assessment and science education. His recent books include studies of the implementation of basic education policy in China, primary school assessment in Africa, and science education and development.

Angela W. Little is Professor of Education (Developing Countries) at the Institute of Education, University of London and Head of the Education and International Development Group. She has extensive research and teaching experience in Asia, Africa, and Europe, with specialised knowledge of Sri Lanka. Her disciplinary interests embrace development studies, social psychology, and sociology and their applications in basic and primary education, qualifications, jobs, and assessment. She gained her doctorate from the University of Sussex.

John Lowe is a Lecturer in the Centre for the Study of Education in an International Context, at the School of Education, University of Bath. He gained his doctorate at the Institute of Education, University of London. He has experience in Africa, the Pacific, and Eastern Europe. He has a broad interest in all matters relating to science education, particularly its impact on the everyday lives of learners and, through them, on social and economic development.

Christine McNab has worked in the Education Division of the Swedish International Development Cooperation Agency, SIDA, since 1989. The research for her doctoral dissertation, from the University of Stockholm, examined language planning and implementation dilemmas in formal and nonformal education in Ethiopia.

Terezinha Nunes is Professor of Education in Child Development and Learning at the Institute of Education, University of London and Head of the Child Development and Learning Group. She gained her doctorate from City University of New York. Her research interests include social influences on cognitive development and uses of mathematics and literacy in everyday life.

Florence Kiragu Nyamu is Programmes Manager at the regional secretariat for the Forum for African Educationalists (FAWE) based in Nairobi, Kenya. She has conducted research in mathematics teaching and learning and has extensive experience in the training of mathematics teachers. She has coordinated capacity-building workshops in several African countries. Her interest is to develop strategies that will increase girls' access to mathematics and science courses and encourage their participation in science-related careers.

Mikael Palme is Team Leader for a capacity-building programme of educational research at the National Institute of Educational Development, Mozambique, in association with the Stockholm Institute of Education. He has written extensively on Swedish higher and secondary education from a Bourdieuan perspective and has also been engaged in educational research in Mozambique, Ethiopia, and Guinea-Bissau. He is currently completing his doctoral thesis, which entails a sociological study of the Mozambican primary school teacher. He is based at the Stockholm Institute of Education.

Antonio Roazzi is Associate Professor at the Department of Psychology, Universidade Federal de Pernambuco, Recife, Brazil. He gained his doctorate from the University of Oxford. His research interests include cognition and culture, and social influences of cognitive development.

Robert Serpell is Professor and Director of Applied Developmental Psychology at the University of Maryland Baltimore County. He received his doctorate from the University of Sussex, UK. Formerly Professor of Psychology and Director of the Institute for African Studies (1977–1983) at the University of Zambia, and a naturalised citizen of Zambia, he has conducted research on children's development, socialization, and education in rural and urban Zambian communities and in the American city of Baltimore.

R. L. (Jock) Stirrat is a Senior Lecturer in Social Anthropology at the University of Sussex. While most of his field research has been concerned with Sri Lanka, he has also carried out consultancy work in Asia, Africa, and Latin America. He has published two monographs and a series of articles concerning economic anthropology, religion, and development and is presently writing a monograph on the development industry in Sri Lanka.

Peter Stoye has been manager of Esselte Print Consult (now known as Graphium Consult) since 1978, where he has been working with various printing and textbook projects in developing countries. He holds a master of science degree from the Royal Institute of Technology in Stockholm and a master of business administration from the Stockholm School of Economics. While working at the Ministry of Education, Sweden, he was responsible for the establishment of the University of Linköping. He has managed various graphic subsidiaries in Sweden and Germany.

Brian V. Street is Professor of Language in Education in the School of Education at King's College, University of London, and Visiting Professor of Education in the Graduate School of Education, University of Pennsylvania. He has written and lectured extensively on literacy practices from both a theoretical and an applied perspective. He undertook anthropological fieldwork in Iran during the 1970s, and has since worked in the United States, Britain, and South Africa.

G.R. (Bob) Teasdale is based at the Flinders University of South Australia where he teaches international, comparative, and cross-cultural studies in education, and is Director of the Centre for International Education. He has worked extensively in development assistance programmes in the South Pacific region, and also has a long-standing interest in the education of Indigenous peoples.

J.I. (Jennie) Teasdale currently lectures part-time in Sociology in the School of Theology at the Flinders University of South Australia, and is research coordinator for the Adelaide College of Divinity. She has a background in educational research and development programmes with Indigenous Australian peoples. She also has extensive experience in the field of teacher education, most recently as a teacher education adviser in a major development assistance project in the South Pacific.

Mercy Miyang Tembon is a Research Officer at the Institute of Development Studies, University of Sussex, where she has been working on the Gender and Primary Schooling Project since 1995. She gained her doctorate from the Institute of Education, University of London. Her primary research interests are gender issues and funding in the education sector of developing countries.

PART I
INTRODUCTION

CHAPTER 1

Development and Education

Cultural and Economic Analysis

ANGELA LITTLE

DEVELOPMENT AND EDUCATION

The analysis of the relationship between development and education in developing countries has been dominated over the past three decades by goals that are primarily economic in character. Alternative goals (e.g., human development, cultural development, and empowerment) have tended to remain at the level of description or advocacy and have rarely found their way into well-formulated educational policy, planning, and practice.

Analyses depend in part on the interests and locus of those who offer them; and in part on the nexus of economic, social, and political character of the specific contexts of analysis. Most formal analyses of the relationship between education and development in developing countries have been offered by "outsiders" generated from contexts beyond those to which they were subsequently applied. In the case of human capital theory, the initial empirical grounding of the thesis was the economic development of the United States between 1920 and 1950; in the case of social reproduction theory, the initial empirical grounding was the failure of educational expansion to diminish social and economic inequalities in the 1960s and 1970s, again in the United States.

This is not to imply that analyses of the relationship between education and development are necessarily irrelevant for contexts beyond those that generate them. The strength of abstract concepts resides in their transferable nature. But some abstract concepts are more context-bound than others, and those who transfer and apply concepts across contexts need to address at least three questions. Which development concepts and forms of analysis are sufficiently context-free to be used without revision? Which concepts and forms of analysis need fundamental or adaptive revision before they can aid both descriptive analysis of the past and prescriptive analysis for the future? Are economic concepts of development and of education's role in it transferred across cultures by outsiders "blind"?

The cultural aspirations of the "users" of education cannot be ignored. However, development policymakers and planners tend to perceive culture as an obstacle to economic progress. Bowing to pressures for "cultural relevance" in education often implies additional costs (e.g., a differential curriculum, textbooks produced in multiple languages). Excessive sensitivity to cultural relevance is also seen as endangering national unity. Parents and communities may perceive education not just as irrelevant to cultural reproduction but also as a way of undermining or even destroying it, whether culture is defined by the markers of ethnicity, religion, territory, or race. Students may well drop out of school if they or their parents see it as having an adverse impact on prevailing cultural values. Yet, while parents may doubt the value of schooling as a cultural preparation, they continue to see it as a gateway to economic security.

The global context within which the relationship between education and development is explored has changed over the past two decades. The shift in composition of the control of many domestic economies, away from national and towards global and regional, raises questions about whose economic and cultural goals and interests are being served by education. The growth of information technology raises questions about the language of communication and education, about the creation of people's aspirations, about the tolerance for linguistic, cultural, and economic diversity, and about the selection of knowledge for educational curricula. The growth in some countries towards de-centralised control of funding for education, combined with increasing demands for political participation among communities hitherto marginalised, raises questions about the balance between local, national, and transnational forces for change and the implications for educational policies and practice.

This introductory chapter explores ideas about the relationships between education, culture, and economy as presented by some of the classic writers in sociology, economics, anthropology, and development studies. This is intended to help the reader relate the chapters in this volume, most of which are located within the more specific field of education and development, to the broader discourse on culture, economy, and social change.

The title of the book, "Education, *Cultures,* and *Economics,*" requires a little explanation. In the opening paragraph of this chapter, the strong influence hitherto of economics on our understanding of the relations between development and education was highlighted. The contributions to this book acknowledge and extend that influence. But they identify also the importance of understanding interactions between economy and culture on the one hand, and between economic and cultural modes of thought on the other. Our title also identifies *cultures* in the plural rather than singular. Notwithstanding the plea of one of our contributors to construct *culture* as a verb, rather than a noun (*cf.* Chapter 3), we seek to highlight the plurality of cultures that impinge on education. On the one hand, education reproduces, worldwide, a variety of mainstream cultures. On the other hand, several layers of culture impinge on and determine the educational process. For example, we may speak of cultures of knowledge and their interactions, of the cultures of classrooms, of the cultures of home learning environments, of the cultures of social groups within mainstream society, and of donor and host cultures in the transaction of educational aid for development. In general terms, our title reflects our hope that this book, with its international authorship, will lead to an enhanced communication between economic and cultural analysts of education and development.

This chapter also sets out the broad structure of our volume, and some of the key issues raised by our authors. Part I, led by this chapter, is introductory. It raises questions about the ways of thinking about culture and economy in relation to education, the plurality of those views, and the cultural determination of ways of viewing and studying the economy. Part II, comprising Chapters 5 through 7, examines the economic and cultural goals of development and the role of education and schooling in realising them. All three chapters highlight the plurality of goals present in all development contexts and the diversity of views of how education might serve their realisation. Part III, comprising Chapters 8 through 12, brings together questions of costs and culture. Two of the chapters explore the cost implications of educational policies determined primarily by cultural considerations. Three explore how cultural considerations generate the material resources available for financing the costs of education. Part IV, comprising Chapters 13 through 18, explores cultures of knowledge and learning in some detail. While some may be related to economic considerations, they are not determined solely by them. Cultures of knowledge and learning may not be reduced to economic analysis. Finally, Part V, comprising Chapters 19 and 20, is titled "Dilemmas for Educational Aid." In it, we focus on the particular role of external development agencies in the practice of development and on the dilemmas for this practice posed by cultural and economic analysis.

CULTURE AND ECONOMY

Many ideas about the relationship between economy, culture, and education derive from a broad set of ideas about economic and social change in the West. The overriding concern of the founding fathers of sociology—among them Karl Marx, Emile Durkheim, and Max Weber—was the nature of relations between the economy and other social institutions, especially in periods of change. The changes which influenced the writings of the founding fathers of sociology most were the late 18th and 19th century industrial revolutions of Europe and North America, the transitions from domestic work to factory work, and the shift from family and religious group–based education to school-based education.

Marx's materialist conception of history posited the economy and associated social relations of production as the primary driving forces of society in all stages of history. Together these constituted the modes of economic production, the substructure or base of society. They determined social structures, cultures, and ideologies, the superstructure of society. Education was viewed as part of this cultural and ideological superstructure.

For Durkheim, the relationship between the economic, social, and cultural depended on the degree of complexity of society. In simple societies with a limited division of labour, the values and norms of people were construed as homogeneous and embedded within the economic production system. In more complex societies with a greater division of labour and occupational specialisation, the economic and cultural aspects of society become separated. This separation resulted for some individuals and groups in a state of anomie—i.e., behaviour unregulated by social norms and values. Education played an important role in the allocation of individuals to the differentiated structure of labour. In contrast with Marx, Durkheim viewed education as having the potential to both influence and be influenced by culture and broader social transformations.

Weber's interest in the relationship between the economic and cultural has at least two aspects. In common with Marx and Durkheim, Weber was interested in the impact of industrial capitalism on culture. In his essay "Capitalism and Rural Society in Germany," Weber contrasted capitalist economy with the economy of the rural peasantry:

> Under the conditions of old civilised countries, the differences caused by capitalism assume the character of a *cultural contest*. Two social tendencies resting upon entirely heterogeneous bases thus wrestle with each other. The old economic order asked: How can I give, on this piece of land, work and sustenance to the greatest possible number of men? Capitalism asks: From this given piece of land how can I produce as many crops as possible for the market with as few men as possible? (translated by Gerth and Mills 1948, 363ff)

Weber's interest lay not only in the conditioning of cultures by the economic order, but also in the reaction of the economic order to the social and cultural, a relationship expressed most clearly in his *Protestant Ethic and the Spirit of Capitalism*. Weber's central concerns with the growth of modern rational bureaucracies, monetised economies, free markets, legal systems, and the expansion of modern state administrations influenced his writings on education and training. Weber's ideal-typical form of rational bureaucracy referred to organisations in which domination was based on impersonal, written rules and a hierarchy of offices, recruitment to which was based on qualifications acquired through academic merit. Educational institutions of the European continent, he said, were "dominated and influenced by the need for the kind of 'education' that produces a system of special examinations and the trained expertness that is increasingly indispensable for modern bureaucracy" (Weber in Gerth and Mills 1948, 240–244). The acquisition of certificates and qualifications through these specialised examinations made possible the achievement of status and lifestyle. Trained expertise and success in special examinations provided access not only to class group membership, based on economic position, but to membership of status groups and their associated cultures.

The influence of the founding fathers of sociology is clearly visible in many writings about education and schooling in the West. Several excellent readers based on reviews of this work are available (e.g., Cosin 1972; Halsey, Floud, and Anderson 1961; Karabel and Halsey 1977). The most recent, *Education: Culture, Economy and Society*, edited by Halsey, Lauder, Brown, and Stuart Wells (1997), questions many assumptions commonly held in the West about the role of education in economic, cultural, and social transformation. These include the power of the nation-state to drive national economy, of bureaucratic organisation to deliver mass education and industrial efficiency, and of a common culture as the basis of social solidarity. With the exception of Kumar (1997) all contributors to the latest Halsey et al. collection write from an urban, industrialised, and "developed" country standpoint. In contrast, the majority of contributions to this volume are written from the standpoint, if not always the nationality, of less urban and less industrialised developing countries.

CULTURES AND ECONOMIES: PLURALITY, DIVERSITY, AND ALTERNATIVES

Notwithstanding their different cultural and economic bases, studies of education in the West have influenced many of those conducted in the so-called developing countries. But authors of studies of education in developing countries have also recognised that many national economies and education systems have emerged only relatively recently from European colonial domination, that European cultures represent but one set among the population of world cultures, and that the degrees of embeddedness of economic, cultural, and educational forms vary across societies.

In *The Great Transformation,* Karl Polanyi (1957) argued that in "primitive" societies economic institutions were "embedded" in social institutions and that economic and social organisation and culture were fused. Polanyi was critical of the application of concepts drawn from conventional economic theory and Western economy to non-Western economies and economic institutions. In Chapter 2 of this volume, Jock Stirrat describes how Polanyi's work provided the basis for the "substantivist" school of economic anthropology which argued that the application of formal economics was valid only in societies where economies were *not* embedded in social and cultural forms. Stirrat contrasts the "substantivists" with the "formalists" who suggest that the concepts, categories, and methods of economic analysis had universal validity. In education studies, similar distinctions between forms of educational analysis do not appear to have emerged. Rather, writers on schooling in contemporary Western societies and on indigenous learning systems in non-Western societies have co-existed, with relatively little reference to each other. On balance, the former have been trained in educational sociology, with its roots in European industrial societies, and the latter in educational anthropology, with its roots in colonial societies.

In this volume, Konai Helu-Thaman echoes most nearly Polanyi's plea for different analytical treatments of societies in different contexts. Writing on education in Tonga in Chapter 4, Helu-Thaman defines "culture" as an all-inclusive term to describe society, the values it embodies, learning systems, and all other "systems," including those which determine the production of goods and services. She suggests that in the analysis of *indigenous* education it is inappropriate to separate discussion of culture from that of economy. The Tongan economy is part of culture and can be distinguished from neither it nor from indigenous education. To speak of tensions between the economic and cultural goals, processes, or conditions of education is to pose a false dichotomy.

However, as Helu-Thaman points out, the contemporary educational, cultural, and economic realities in Tonga are more complex. Education, culture, and economy have been influenced greatly by colonialism and the cultures of the West. Among the otherwise diverse cultures of the peoples of the Pacific Region, the imposition of these colonial forces has generated a common British or French colonial history. At best, this imposition has generated a coarse blend of traditional and modern educational and economic forms. Modern formal schooling offers the means of access to the modern sector of development, marked by its monetised economic character. At worst, the imposition of the "capitalist/imperialistic forces" of global economy have generated a process of destruction of Tongan culture, requiring "counteraction" by it. The dilemma which faces educators and "development" planners, Helu-Thaman suggests, is the extent to which they should be promoting the individualistic economic values of the market through formal schooling and the socially oriented cultural values of teachers, students, parents, and their communities. Where indigenous cultures and economies were once fused, their penetration by external economic, cultural, and political forces has led to their separation and to tensions between the indigenous and modern forms of economy, culture, and education.

It is this interaction of indigenous and Western forms of education, culture, and economy which limits in practice (though not in principle) the generation and application of universal models of education and development. The generation is limited in practice by the restricted knowledge of each potential analyst of the diversity of education, cultural, and economic systems worldwide, and by the social, political, and economic arrangements that constrain the cultures of production and exchange of this knowledge of diversity.

DEVELOPMENT THEORY AND EDUCATION

Attempts to develop branches of economic and sociological theory which recognised the distinctive nature of colonial and post-colonial societies gained momentum in the period of reconstruction and decolonisation after World War II. Development economics, development studies, development sociology, and the economics of education emerged alongside the major efforts *for* development driven by the business of international finance. Models *of* change and transition, developed by political economists and sociologists interested mainly in history, were now supplemented by models *for* change and transition, encapsulated by the term *development.* These new models attempted simultaneously to (1) describe and analyse economic and social change and (2) prescribe and advocate economic and social change.

The first major strand of development theory was advanced by the school of modernisation. The modernisation school of development theory emerged after World War II, in the late 1950s, and presented an optimistic model for development of those societies which were not yet modern and industrialised. Although modernisation theory attracted the attention of researchers from several social science disciplines, it was of particular interest to sociologists and social psychologists. McClelland's early work (1961) focused on the values held by the majority of people in a society and the implications of these for economic and technological growth. The value attached to and the motivation for achievement were central to McClelland's explanation of modernising societies. Where Max Weber had focused attention on the role of ideas and religion in setting the conditions for the rise of capitalism, McClelland focused on early socialisation and child rearing practices.

Inkeles and Smith (1974) drew from both sets of ideas. They accepted the logic of modern values leading to modern behaviour, modern society, and economic development. In contrast to McClelland, however, they stressed the role of modern institutions such as the formal school and the factory in the formation of modern values and attitudes. While Inkeles and Smith's work provided empirical support for the link between schooling and the development of modern values, empirical support for the consequent links in the causal chain have been more difficult to establish (Fägerlind and Saha 1992).

If sociologists were prominent among those who advanced modernisation theory, economists were, as we shall see later, active in promoting a parallel, economic theory—human capital theory. This theory suggested that people invest in themselves through education and generate increases in their future incomes through greater lifetime earnings. The policy advocacy which drew from the theory was that investment in human capital through education was a priority for governments keen to reap economic benefits for both individuals and societies.

In the late 1960s and 1970s both modernisation and human capital theory were challenged by a set of ideas which came to form the school of dependency. Marxian ideas on exploitation of the proletariat by the bourgeoisie and Lenin's writings on imperialism were developed by Andre Gunder Frank (e.g., 1967) and Galtung (e.g., 1971). Dependency theory focused on the extent to which poor countries were dependent on rich countries and the mechanisms through which economic dependency was maintained. Thus, the unit of analysis of economic development and underdevelopment shifted and embraced economic, political, and social relations *between* countries as well as those within. While most of the work focused on economic dependency, a few writers extended the analysis to the maintenance and development of relations of cultural dependency (e.g., Carnoy 1974). Formal schooling in dependent economies played a key role in the furtherance of a cultural and economic dependency of peripheral on central economies.

These early theoretical debates in development studies were economic in character. Whether as a goal, process, or condition for "development," the meaning of development generally stressed the economic over the cultural. "Indicators" of development were economic—for example the per capita Gross National Product or the distribution of income. The emphasis on economic development was accompanied by the notion that culture was separate from economy and impeded economic development. Culture was often invoked as an explanation of past failure rather than success, of present problems rather than achievements, and of likely future difficulties rather than possibilities (Little 1990). Culture was treated frequently as a fixed and enduring endowment responsible for continuities and inhibiting change. In his article "Cultural Endowments and Economic Development: What Can We Learn from Anthropology?" Ruttan suggests that:

> to the extent that cultural endowments are considered at all by economists, they tend to be subsumed under the concept of tastes. And tastes, even more so than technology and institutions, are traditionally regarded as not subject to economic analysis. (Ruttan 1988, S250)

Citing a handful of studies from Japan and China, Ruttan provides examples of cultural resources facilitating economic change. More often, however, cultural endowments are viewed as obstacles to economic change.

The notion of culture as a fixed endowment is explored in some detail in Brian Street's chapter in this volume (Chapter 3). Street confirms

Ruttan's view that for many anthropologists the notion of culture has had a fixed and enduring character in which it is assumed that all people in the same culture share the same inner meanings. More recently, anthropologists including Street have begun to describe culture as a "process" rather than a set of "essential meanings." No longer a set of a people's inner, fixed meanings, ways of life and ideas, culture is now a "contested process" in which questions about how particular meanings get onto the agenda and how particular meanings come to be powerful are explored (pages 53–54 this volume). Applying this notion of culture to the practice of literacy, Street contrasts the "autonomous" model—in which illiterate people are assumed to come from a backward culture which acts as a barrier to both "progress" and literacy—with an "ideological" model—in which literacy is assumed to be a social practice rooted in conceptions of knowledge, identity, and a particular world view. The meanings and practices of literacy are contested by different social groups. Particular versions of literacy are "always rooted in a particular world view and a desire for that view of literacy to dominate and to marginalise others" (page 59 this volume).

Nonetheless, whether as a set of endowments restricting the spread of literacy, or as an ideological process promoting different types of literacy, culture has been seen by most as a *means to the economic end of* development.

EDUCATION AND LEARNING

In the context of education and learning I have suggested that the notion of culture may be treated as an interactive and dynamic social process between learner and educator. A learner's culture is the stock of knowledge, attitudes to knowledge, and ways of learning new knowledge which he or she brings to bear on each new experience and learning activity (Little 1990, 1992). An educator's culture is the stock of knowledge, attitudes to knowledge, and ways of teaching new knowledge that he/she brings to bear on new teaching activities. The culture of the learner and the educator may be more or less remote from each other. These cultures are negotiated within *learning arenas*—the home, the classroom, the on-line and interactive computer, the field, the temple, the factory. To the extent that learning occurs within any of these arenas, then the cultural base for future learning changes.

In all societies, whether industrialised or nonindustrialised, there are gaps between the cultures of learners and educators. It is these gaps which are negotiated within learning arenas. When learning occurs, then gaps are bridged to a degree. But the size of that gap can vary. In static societies which reproduce themselves completely, and where the educator shares the language of the learner and the values to which the learner aspires, the gap between the culture of the learner and the educator may be relatively narrow. Although the gap may appear wide to the learner, the educator can apprehend readily the language, pre-existing knowledge, the orientations, and strategies of the learner. The educator can build from the learner's culture in a way which makes learning effective, and which in turn changes the learner's culture. In rapidly transforming societies, where the learner and educator share language but where the educator subscribes to values and goals that diverge from those of the parents of the young learner, then the gap may be large and the effectiveness of learning compromised. In rapidly transforming societies where learner and educator use different mother tongues and subscribe to different values and goals, or where learner and educator are required to learn and teach in a language foreign to both, then the gap may become very wide. In such conditions the process of learning and teaching may be so meaningless for both parties that it assumes the character of an ineffective ritual (cf. Mikael Palme in Chapter 14). That people learn from and teach others in more or less formal ways throughout life renders a dynamic quality to the idea of culture. The recognition that in all processes of learning and teaching there is a gap between what the learner and educator bring to their social interaction lends a negotiated quality to the idea of culture.

However, it is important to recognise that in most educational settings the negotiation of knowledge occurs between partners of unequal power. The educator generally conducts his/her negotiation from a position of power over the learner. That power resides in the status accorded the role of educator by the culture in which he/she educates and in his/her role in the process of educational assessment and selection.

Economy complements culture by producing the material and human resources for learning—the space, the time, the materials, the educators. Various stake-holders generate these resources, for example, individuals, families, communities, nation-states, and the international community of "donors." The nature of the economy also influences the goals of learning, for example, the acquisition of a job in society or skill outcomes that feed directly into the economy. Power relations between individuals, families, communities, and nation-states are reflected in differential access to the material resources for learning. And differential access to material resources for learning generates differential access to power, both economic and cultural, in the future.

Economics complements economy and culture by specifying *ways of thinking about* education and learning. Using the discourse of economics, economists of education have sought, *inter alia*, (1) to achieve the maximum output for the minimum input of material resource, (2) to compare the cost of material inputs for alternative educational policies, (3) to understand the decisions made by the "consumers" of education, and (4) to assess the contribution of education to economic development.

The gaps between the cultures of learners and educators in terms of knowledge, attitudes, and ways of learning and teaching are to be found in many learning arenas. The idea may be applied at all levels of the educational and development process, a process that involves multiple levels of social interaction and negotiation of meaning. For example, there may be gaps between parents and teachers, between educational planners and teachers, between presidents and planners, between donor agency officials and policymakers, between external consultants and counterparts, between teacher educators and teachers, between economic planners and education planners. Social interactions at each level carry implications for learning arenas, both in terms of the cultural aspirations for learning and teaching and in terms of the resources available for their interaction and negotiation.

Wide cultural gaps between any or some of these sets of actors can lead to a progressive reinterpretation of intent and aspiration which in turn compromises what is possible in the classroom. Where the chain of actors in the planning of education becomes so extended that the control of the material resources for learning is vested with those who have little apprehension of the culture of either learners or educators, then the potential for gaps between educational plans and practice is magnified. Magnified, too, is the potential for the process of learning and teaching to become a "meaningless ritual," a term used some years ago to describe classrooms where the instrumental goals of learning dominated the intrinsic, a symptom of societies gripped by the "Diploma Disease" (Dore 1976, 1997).

THE CULTURE OF ECONOMICS

One aspect of the culture of those who plan development and education is the knowledge they bring to their work as a result of their own formal education. For many development and education planners this includes a formal knowledge of economics. In Chapter 2, Jock Stirrat proposes an anthropology of economics. Drawing from the work of Stephen Gudeman (1986), Stirrat questions the claim of neoclassical economics to embody a form of rationality which is not itself culturally determined. Economics may be treated both in terms of what economists do and in terms of what they normally study (production, exchange, and consumption). For Stirrat culture refers to "what people produce." Because economics is produced through an endeavour of human activity, then economics is as cultural as religion, art, or music. It is one of several ways through which people comprehend and act on the world.

Stirrat's views are echoed by other social scientists. Perelman (1996), an economist, has argued recently in *The End of Economics* that the discipline of mainstream economics as taught and practised at the end of the 20th century is a product of 19th century economic realities and the cultural need of economists to identify and distinguish themselves as a profession. Galtung, writing from the perspective of peace studies (1996), has described the influence of economics on the *culture of homo economicus*. This culture focuses on the individual person as the unit to be satisfied, on the material satisfaction of man's needs by goods and services, and the use of cost-benefit analysis as a guide for individual choice. And, in his assessment of the contribution of economic analyses to our understanding of the education "black box," Heyneman (1995) concludes that economists of education have yet to make a "significant dent." Economists of education make ungrounded assumptions about the behaviour of educational stakeholders and fail to specify assumptions behind data and conclusions. Arguing that the education community has a responsibility to demand better economic evidence on a wider variety of educational questions, Heyneman suggests that "past questions in the economics of education were driven less by a search for insight and more by an adherence to disciplinary tradition" (Heyneman 1995, 573).

VOICES OF DEVELOPMENT

Even within the economics discourse, speakers construct their understandings of the "same" development project in ways that depend on their location within a global economic and social system. Using an example from an irrigation and river development project in Sri Lanka, Stirrat illustrates how different stakeholders in development projects perceive their goals differently. Specifically, he contrasts the voices from a World Bank team with those from the implementing authority, the Maheveli Authority of Sri Lanka (MASL):

(World Bank) . . . the "rate of return" from the project was too low . . . MASL was not following "free market" principles. The result was the inefficient allocation of resources and the failure of farmers within the project to produce high value crops . . . the World Bank advocated the wholesale privatisation of functions presently carried out by the MASL and the creation of free markets which would both force farmers to shift to higher value crops by allowing cheap staple food imports and encourage them in this shift by allowing new markets for high value products to develop.

(MASL) Rather than judge the project in terms of the narrow rationality of "rates of return," the MASL attempted to move the discussion to the broader question of the role of the project for the social and political future of Sri Lanka. Thus the MASL saw issues such as landlessness, education and housing as crucial, issues which were at best marginal to the World Bank.

Although Stirrat does not spell out similar contrasts with respect to the different stakeholders in education and schooling, one may imagine the following:

(Lending Bank) The proportion of costs of education borne by the Sri Lankan state is high by international standards. Because parents make only small contributions to the costs of formal schooling, and because, in principle, school places are rationed by residence, there is little incentive for schools to improve their quality and efficiency. School fees should be introduced. Moreover, the student:teacher ratio is very favourable compared with other countries in the region and the proportion of costs spent on salaries extremely high, reducing the resources available for quality improvements.

(Parents' Association) In Sri Lanka parents spend a high proportion of their consumable income on education, through the costs of private tuition followed *after* school hours, and the "facilities" fees paid to the school. The culture and tradition of "shramadana," the voluntary labour of parents and older school children, ensures that school buildings are maintained, school grounds made attractive and playgrounds constructed. Parental contribution to all aspects of their children's' education is high, not low. Moreover the cost of the national education system, as a proportion of GDP and public expenditure, is low, when

> compared with countries elsewhere in the region. Our children are going to school to *get* a job. That is part of our culture. Many of them hope to become teachers. If you reduce the number of teachers you reduce the jobs available to our young people in the future.

THE MEANS AND ENDS OF DEVELOPMENT

Within the dominant discourse of development the *ends of development* have been questioned only rarely. Improvements in material wealth and its distribution dominated the development discourses of the 1960s through the end of the 1990s. However, by the early 1990s there were signs that the major players in the international business of development finance began to display a diversity of views of the *means* and *ends* of development.

The discourse on the role of education in development over the past three decades illustrates the shift (Little 1992). In the 1960s schools and education constituted part of the "human investment revolution in economic thought" (Bowman 1966). In one of the most influential writings on the role of education in development in the 20th century, Theodore W. Schultz explored the idea of education as a form of capital and introduced the notion of education as a form of human capital (Schultz 1961, 1–17). The propositions of human capital theory were that the skills and knowledge which people acquire are a form of capital, that this capital is a product of deliberate investment, that it had grown in Western societies at a rate faster than "conventional" (nonhuman) capital, and that its growth has been the most distinctive feature of the economic system of the mid-20th century.

Schultz's work was especially influential in the 1960s and 1970s among those who allocated money to development projects and those who promoted the growth of formal education worldwide. The production of an educated labour force was perceived by both economists and development planners as a means to the end of the growth of the national economy, and hence, development. This, combined with the *idea* of education as a form of capital, and the subordination of this idea to the broader idea of development as economic growth, rendered subordinate supplementary and alternative ideas about the goals of learning and education—education as empowerment, education as enculturation, education as liberation.

By the 1970s, however, the benefits expected of education had not always materialised, or had not materialised sufficiently fast. Faith in educational investment as an engine of development began to decline. Social and cultural explanations were invoked. The function of schools, it was argued, is not to change the lives of people, nations, and societies; rather it is to reproduce the social divisions and culture of the wider society. When schools were seen as a means to the end of economic development, education was construed in a positive light. When schools seemed not to be producing the economic ends, they were viewed by economists in a negative light.

By the end of the 1980s and early 1990s, education had returned to the forefront of the development discourse. In the written documents of development agencies the role of education in development was presented in a positive light. It was vital that all governments invest in it heavily in order that each maintain its economic competitiveness. It was also seen as a vital ingredient in meeting global, as distinct from national, challenges, such as worldwide economic stagnation, environmental degradation, civil war, and population growth.

I have suggested elsewhere that this renewed faith in education did not represent a complete return to human capital theory, described above (Little 1992). The dominant conception of development showed signs of a shift away from economic growth and income redistribution, and towards the development of people. More significantly, economic growth began to be posited as *a means to the end of human development*, rather than as an end in itself (e.g., UNDP 1990). The shift was consistent with the promotion of cultural awareness and cultural development throughout the world's decade for cultural development (1988–1997).

The concept of human development, pitched at the level of a national or international project, emphasised the growth of human potential as well as the growth of income, the quality of life, the participation of people in their own development, and human freedom. The authors of the UNDP report urged that neither economic growth nor income distribution be construed as ends in themselves. They asserted that economic growth and the redistribution of income serve human development as much as human development serves them. Education was seen as serving all three—human development, economic growth, and income redistribution. Moreover, the notion of education in the relationship between education and human development, economic growth, and income redistribution was itself redefined. The redefinition involved a closer attention to learning and the quality of learning, as distinct from enrolment in school. It involved an appreciation of the means of communication and social action additional to formal schooling by which learning may be imparted. And it involved a particular focus on social groups which have been excluded from formal learning—girls, the poor, street and working children, remote and rural populations, migrant workers and nomads, indigenous peoples, ethnic, racial, and linguistic minorities, refugees, and those displaced by war.

A consideration of the means-ends relationships between human development, economic growth, income distribution, and education is not new. In the West it draws on ideas as old at least as those of Adam Smith in 1776 and John Stuart Mill in 1848. As Schultz suggested, a consideration of means and ends lay at the root of a longstanding resistance by mainstream economists to the treatment of education as investment rather than as consumption.

> Although economists are seldom timid in entering on abstract analysis and are often proud of being impractical, they have not been bold in coming to terms with this form of investment. . . . Deep-seated moral and philosophical issues are ever present. Free men are first and foremost the end to be served by economic endeavour; they are not property or marketable assets. . . . Our values and beliefs inhibit us from looking upon human beings as capital goods, except in slavery, and this we abhor . . . to treat human beings as wealth that can be augmented by investment runs counter to deeply held values. It seems to reduce man once again to a mere material component, to something akin to property. And for man to look upon himself as a capital good, even if it did not impair his freedom, may seem to debase him. No less a person as J.S. Mill at one time insisted that the people of a country should not be looked upon as wealth because wealth existed only for the sake of people. But surely Mill was wrong; there is nothing in the concept of human wealth contrary to his idea that it exists only for the advantage of people. By investing in themselves, people can enlarge the range of choices available to them. It is one way free men can enhance their welfare. (Schultz 1961, 313)

THE ECONOMIC AND CULTURAL GOALS OF DEVELOPMENT: WHOSE GOALS MATTER?

The plea for a shift in the definition of the ultimate goal or "end" of development is made in Munir Fasheh's chapter in this volume (Chapter 5). In a stark and passionate counterposition of economy and culture, Fasheh objects to the subordination of education to the goal of economic rather than cultural development, and, more particularly, to a definition of economic development which is generated by "cultural outsiders." For Fasheh, culture is about human values, such as human respect for nature, the value of every human being, and cultural resources (e.g., language, family, and civilisations). These, he claims, in the context of Palestine, are currently ignored in "grand development plans" which are primarily economic in character, and are driven by powerful external forces. The plans, he asserts, lead to permanent economic debt and cultural impoverishment. Fasheh's alternative conception of development places cultural products and cultural producers at the centre of development. Such products and producers build from the existing culture, do not build a spiral of debt, and are more resilient than development products imposed from outside.

Alternative definitions *of* development, or even alternatives *to* development, lie at the heart of Sheila Aikman's chapter on economic interests and cultural practices in the Amazon (Chapter 6). Aikman contrasts perspectives on development, and the relationship of education to it, of three social groups in a region of lowland tropical rainforest in the southeast of Peru, the Madre de Dios. The *mestizos,* people of mixed racial descent, are settlers from impoverished coastal towns and are mainly urban-based. As pioneers building better futures for themselves and their families, they see themselves as "opening up" the rainforest, of "bringing development" to the area. They support economic policies designed to break the area's economic isolation through the "extractive" activities of trade and mining, and through improved communication links. Within this conception of development parents view schooling as an investment in the future: education is a means of progressing up the social and economic ladder, a meritocratic means to a better chance in life. Aikman characterizes this perspective as "economic modernisation." The *serranos* in the Madre de Dios are people from the Andes, who have come to the area in search of land. In Madre de Dios they live isolated lives along the river banks and they clear forest to grow maize. Their identity is based on their relationship with the land. They have already experienced a shortage of land in the highlands and are now exploiting the rainforest in search of survival. Development revolves around the notion of taming the wild and antisocial rainforest. Within this conception there is little demand for a formal schooling which neither reinforces the values of the social group nor provides access to a useful body of knowledge. Aikman characterises this perspective as "dependency." The *Arakmbut* are people indigenous to the region. Hunting and fishing in the rainforest form the economic means of survival of the people. Although the Arakmbut have legally titled areas of land, colonists and extractive companies penetrate their land, destroying the Arakmbut's relationship with a territory and its physical and spiritual resources. The Arakmbut do not speak in terms of development. Nor do they speak of children's futures in terms of progress. But they do have schools, want to participate in the wider society, and welcome formal education. In particular, they welcome the opportunity to learn Spanish, which they need to defend and protect their lands and to communicate with traders. At the same time they want an education which respects their own educational practices and processes. Aikman characterises this model as "community self-development."

To some extent the competition between the alternative goals of development and learning derives from the relative power of different stakeholders located at different vantage points, the use of different "units of analysis," and the use of alternative discourses and vocabularies of analysis. For the officials of governments, discussions of development focus on national economies and national education systems, or the economic and educational development of regions or institutions within the nation-state. For the officials of international development agencies the focus on national and intra-national development is frequently, nowadays, supplemented by concerns of a global nature (e.g., global environment, or global communication systems) and the implications of these for national economies and national education systems. For the officials of nongovernmental agencies the focus may be grassroots community or school development. But for many, especially teachers, the most pressing "unit" of and for development is the individual child or person.

In Chapter 7, Robert Serpell illustrates the different units of analysis employed by different stakeholders in the discussion of development. For some, development means economic growth, for others social progress and the transmission of culture, and for still others individual and personal development. Schools and education are expected to contribute to all three. While the goals of development may be complementary in principle, "their demands often run into competition" (page 107 this volume) in practice. Serpell focuses on the role of schooling in its cultivation of individual development in its sociocultural context. This, he suggests, is the most fundamental strand of the multiple agenda of schooling, contributing indirectly to economic progress and the intergenerational transmission of culture. The sociocultural context within which individuals develop is structured by "a set of historically evolving cultural resources, including a particular language and technology, as well as particular political *and* economic structures" (page 108 this volume; editors' emphasis).

This view of how personal development takes place contrasts, Serpell suggests, with the view of national educational planners working with a notion of development at the level of the nation-state. At this level planners consider personal development only very indirectly. The impact of schooling on the nation, viewed in largely economic terms, is constructed as homogeneous, discontinuous, and mechanistic. The view invokes principles which are locally invisible, or at least unseen and largely inscrutable. The notions of cost-effectiveness at the macro level contrast with the variety of meanings which schooling carries at the micro level, in the lives of different individuals. Schooling "contributes in various, strikingly different ways to their life-journeys" (page 116 this volume).

THE COSTS OF CULTURE AND THE CULTURE OF COSTS

The language in which people learn lies at the heart of at least three of the levels of development discussed above—personal learning and identity, national development, and international development. The issue is particularly pressing in multilingual societies where the planner's dilemma is: How does a nation facilitate personal learning and cultural identity through the mother tongue while simultaneously promoting (1) a language and cultural identity of national unity, and (2) a language of international communication? This dilemma, familiar in multilingual societies, is explored in Chapter 8 by Christine McNab and Peter Stoye in the context of contemporary Ethiopia.

The chapter by McNab and Stoye is also important for the ways it links cultural identity with the question of costs. Ethiopia is in the process of changing from a monolingual to a multilingual system of primary education. This has implications for the costs and organisational complexity of teacher training, teacher appointments/transfers, materials development, and materials production. A similar issue is explored in Keith Lewin's chapter (Chapter 9) on the tensions between economic and cultural priorities in the education system of Mauritius, a country characterised by high levels of cultural diversity. Lewin's underlying argument is that culturally based decisions have costs which can affect efficiency and effectiveness and will reflect the interests of some stakeholders at the possible expense of others. Educational policies and strategies that may be considered culturally desirable may have costs which exceed their likely benefits. Lewin examines the tensions between economic and cultural considerations in relation to language provision, repetition, and organisational practice.

Both chapters underline the general point, often overlooked by those who adopt a purely cultural analysis of education, that all education policies, irrespective of their location (local, national, or international) and orientation (cultural or economic), carry implications for material resources. Culture needs material resources for its reproduction and production. Culture implies costs.

Conversely, the realisation of material resources is culturally determined. Mark Bray (Chapter 10), Mercy Tembon (Chapter 11), and Iffat Farah and Kazim Bacchus (Chapter 12) explore how different communities organise material resources for education and how parental decisions about their children's schooling is based on an interplay of material and cultural considerations.

Mark Bray's central concern is with community variation in the scale, form, and mechanisms of the financing for education. In his discussion of community financing, or the contribution of communities to the costs of providing education, Bray distinguishes monetary from non-monetary costs. The latter may include contributions of land, labour, and materials by the community. In many countries these types of cost may be substantial. In many economic analyses of education, such costs are usually invisible.

In her discussion of educational finance strategies in Cameroon and Uganda, Mercy Tembon explains how educational policies predicated on a monetised cash economy, especially policies on the introduction of school fees, can undermine the abilities of some parents to send their children to secondary school. Although many parents are able and willing to contribute to the costs of their children's schooling in kind, through, for example, foodstuffs which could be used by residential hostels, the insistence on payments in cash prevents many from sending their children to school. Moreover, in economic contexts where family incomes, in both cash and kind, are declining, parents employ cultural considerations in choosing which of their children be given the opportunity of continuing with their schooling. In both countries, attitudes to female children and to female work mean that parents are more likely to invest in their sons' than daughters' education. Iffat Farah and Kazim Bacchus' chapter continues this theme, in the context of Pakistan. They contrast the writings of those who claim that economic poverty is the most critical obstacle to girls' schooling with those who focus on social and cultural norms about the inferior status of girls and women. They suggest that there is a "subtle interplay," what some researchers would call an "interaction effect," between economic and sociocultural factors in decisions about sending girls to school. Cultural considerations come into play when economic resources are constrained.

Tembon, and Farah and Bacchus write about the economic and cultural bases of educational decision making in patriarchal societies that reinforce beliefs about the inferior economic and social status of women. When economic resources are limited, then parents prefer to invest in their sons' education. To invest in a girl's education can be wasteful, since, in patriarchal societies girls generally join their husband's families upon marriage. However, as Mikael Palme explains in a later chapter (Chapter 14), the cultural preference for boys' education is not limited to patriarchal societies. In the rural, matrilineal community in Nampula in Mozambique, where Palme focuses his study, a major accomplishment in the social career of a woman is to become a respected and influential "senior" woman. An educated girl is not expected to marry a man with less education than herself, nor is she expected to move away from her family of origin. The parents of the man who moves into the family as the girl's husband retain his economic value, as he is expected to provide not only for his wife's family, but also for his own lineage, in his role as brother, uncle, or nephew. Educating a son is to educate "an organic member of the group and a means for the group to secure its future well-being" (page 263 this volume).

CULTURES OF KNOWLEDGE AND LEARNING

Culture, whether as a noun or a verb, to use Street's distinction (Chapter 3), inheres inside as well as outside learning spaces. Cultural goals may give direction to educational policy and cultural considerations may influence how material resources are mobilised for the realisation of the policy. But the organisation, content, and process of education are also central to the process of cultural transmission. Some of the best known work on the organisation, transmission, and evaluation of educational knowledge is by Bernstein (e.g., 1977) and Bourdieu and Passeron (e.g., 1977). Though generated in Britain and France respectively, this work has had a substantial impact on the discourse of education internationally. Its common focus is the relationship between forms of social control and the organisation, transmission, and evaluation of knowledge.

For Bernstein, the educational curriculum involves the organisation or "classification" of knowledge into more or less bounded domains, and the transmission of that knowledge through more or less teacher-controlled "frames." Based on empirical studies in Britain, Bernstein suggested that the classification and framing of knowledge are realised in two types of knowledge code, each with consequences for social order and control. The collection code, with strongly bounded domains of knowledge content, consists of clearly defined subjects (e.g., chemistry, history) and is transmitted through didactic teaching and learning methods with a strong emphasis on facts. The integrated code, with weakly bounded domains of knowledge content, consists of contents with a more open relationship (e.g., social studies) and is transmitted through teaching and learning methods based more on the self-regulation of the learner. These broader concepts embraced Bernstein's earlier work on language codes of working- and middle-class children at home and in school. The collection code embraced the "restricted" language code of working-class homes and classrooms; the integrated code embraced the "elaborated" language code of middle-class homes and classrooms.

Bourdieu and Passeron (1977) link a similar set of ideas about social control and reproduction to the discourse of economics, through the concept of "cultural capital." Those who possess cultural capital enjoy a similar power to those who possess economic capital. They use their cultural capital to exert power over other social groups, to gain access to better occupations, and in turn to legitimate their claims to control over economic capital. Dominant groups establish hegemony over the language, ideas, and culture in society at large as well as within schools. The mechanisms of success and failure in education systems, and especially the processes of selection and certification, ensure that those with the greatest cultural capital succeed, while simultaneously preserving the ideals of equality and meritocracy.

Though none adhere strictly to the theoretical frameworks of Bourdieu, Passeron, and Bernstein, our authors of Chapters 13 through 18 explore some of their central concerns—the organisation, transmission, and evaluation of knowledge and learning. This is what we describe in this volume as "Cultures of Knowledge and Learning." Chapters 13 through 16 explore the cultures of knowledge and learning in the context of societies recently independent of colonial rule. While Western knowledge systems have been strongly associated with the occupations and cultures of work of the colonising powers in these societies, indigenous knowledge systems continue to have significance for the cultural identity of learners.

Drawing on earlier research in this area (e.g., Nabobo and Teasdale 1995; Teasdale and Little 1995), Jennie and Bob Teasdale focus on the process of knowledge analysis and transmission in higher education in Chapter 13. Their geographical focus is the Australia-Pacific region, where, until relatively recently, societies had been isolated and cultures intact and coherent. The content, process, and context of knowledge and knowledge transmission constitute a crucial aspect of any culture. Where cultures have been colonised, tensions between cultures of knowledge arise. While those tensions were apparent from the onset of the colonial period, they are now exacerbated by contemporary economic developments. Higher education institutions are expected to focus, externally, on narrow, vocationally oriented goals and, internally, on improved economic efficiency and profit. The Teasdales conceive these tensions and differences as obstacles to neither cultural identity nor economic development. Rather, the emergence of indigenous cultures of knowledge within a Western-dominated higher education is conceived as a dynamic process of creation and recreation, as part of the continuous search by people for cultural continuity and identity. The use of indigenous processes of knowledge analysis and transmission is seen as compatible with effective economic functioning. The Teasdales speak of a blending rather than separation of different cultural processes and practices, a reconciliation with rather than a rejection of the economic goals of contemporary Western higher education, and a future marked by a reversal of power relations in which indigenous perspectives influence Western knowledge cultures and economic arrangements. While the focus of their chapter is the interaction between alternative cultures of learning, the link with economic considerations is forged through "a new wave of economic rationalism that is sweeping through the region" (page 234 this volume) in this final decade of the 20th century and is affecting the goals and organisation of educational institutions. People are thinking about education in ways which are economic.

In Chapter 14 Mikael Palme leads us to the cultures of knowledge and learning at the opposite end of the educational system, the primary school. Based on extensive observations and interviews in Mozambique, he describes the typical classroom in terms of its strong "ritualisation." Teachers ask questions and organise exercises; pupils listen to the teacher, answer questions, and do exercises. The content of what is said or done is less important than the ritual of the interaction. Pupils learn that much of what the teacher says is incomprehensible; teachers learn that pupils rarely understand and even more rarely seek clarification.

Teaching continues even where the conditions for teaching and learning are absent. As a result, as the child moves through the school, there is a growing discrepancy between what is taught and what is understood. Palme suggests that if schooling is to have a substantial impact on learning, then a greater awareness of the cultural aspects of teaching and learning is needed at every level, not least among the urban middle classes who dominate the state administration and donor agencies.

The role of science education in the process of development is explored by John Lowe in Chapter 15. The importance placed by development planners on science in national curricula has been driven by economic imperatives. Both industrialisation and modern agriculture were seen to be dependent on science-based technology. Science, seen by many as a-cultural, has escaped the critiques of Western development as cultural imperialism. Based on research with science students in Solomon Islands, Lowe's chapter suggests that although students achieve scientific literacy and accept the practical power of science, the application of this literacy is limited because it does not penetrate the "world view" of the students. The world view of students comprises sets of beliefs deriving from religion and "custom," as much as from science. Students' ideas and explanations reside in "domains" of knowledge, applicable in specific social and physical contexts. The application of scientific understanding may be confined to the culture of the classroom.

Mathematics and mathematics education provide the focus for the next two chapters. In Chapter 16 Florence Kiragu Nyamu explores some of the disillusionment with the formal education system. Using examples from mathematics education in Kenya she suggests that part of the disillusionment with education resides in the lack of congruence between cultural and economic considerations. She also draws attention to alternative arenas for learning and education in the home and community. Picking up on this theme, Mary Harris leads us from the learning arena of the classroom to that of the workplace in Chapter 17. Like the subject of science, the subject of mathematics carries an authority that appears to transcend cultures. As a tool, mathematics is highly visible, useful, and prestigious within the practice of economics, education, and development planning. It is assumed to be abstract and culture-free. Harris challenges this assumption and suggests that mathematics is itself a social construct, the invention of people, in social, historical, and cultural context. Moreover, mathematics is cultured by gender. It has frequently been assumed to be a male activity, both within education and within work. Harris challenges this assumption by exploring the mathematics which women apply in needlework and suggests that if we are to understand how effective mathematics learning can occur, then we need to identify the specific cultures of work within which learning occurs.

Terezinha Nunes and Antonio Roazzi lead us to the learning arena of the home and associated learning contexts in Chapter 18. Several analyses of the economic outcomes of educational experience and of the intergenerational transmission of educational status have attributed the greater access to education of the children of richer rather than poorer families to the economic conditions of the latter. They draw from a recent study conducted in Brazil by Barros and Lam (1996), which suggested that income differences between families explained only part of the intergenerational transmission of educational status. Using a term reminiscent of Ruttan's discussion of cultural endowments and economic development, presented earlier in this chapter, Barros and Lam (1996) suggest that household characteristics, such as "taste for schooling," are important for our understanding of the intergenerational transmission. Nunes and Roazzi explore this idea in relation to processes of socialisation in urban Brazil. They demonstrate how young people from different socioeconomic backgrounds build different consensual worlds "that give middle-class children reasons for learning and working-class children reasons for not learning in school" (page 321 this volume). They suggest that children from different cultural backgrounds differ in the ways they represent social and educational stratification, in the ways they construct their personal identity within this represented social world, and in how they attach value to different types of knowledge. These are integral aspects of the processes of socialisation that occur outside the school and that influence the interaction of school and home cultures for learning.

DILEMMAS FOR EDUCATIONAL AID

In the final part of the book we move to the organisation, transmission, and evaluation of development practice and to the present and future role of economic and cultural analysis in it. We focus on the particular role of external development agencies in this practice.

In the early 1990s, a noneconomist working in the World Bank made a plea to his economist colleagues to employ social and cultural analysis in the planning of development projects for rural development (Cernea 1991). Cernea's plea was couched in the language of economics. His case rested on the proposition that people lie at the core of all development processes and that technocratic or econocratic (*sic*) models generally overlook social and cultural variables. The penalty for ignoring these can be "costly." In a study of the relation between the "sociocultural fit" of project designs and the estimated economic rate of return at project completion, 30 were judged to have a design compatible with prevailing cultural and social conditions, while 27 did not. Significant, from an economic point of view, was the much higher average rate of return of the "compatible" projects, and the lower average rate of return of the "incompatible." Neglect of sociocultural aspects of development projects carries economic costs. Cernea's general plea is for the involvement of noneconomists at all stages of development project cycle work. Their involvement in the formulation of development policies grounded in social knowledge and the development of methods for social action is vital.

This theme is developed in the final two chapters of this book. Michael Delens (Chapter 19) explores the cultural dilemmas intrinsic to educational management when "donor" and "host" cultures interact in the planning and implementation of donor-funded education "projects," a familiar scene in the education and development landscape. Drawing from his own experience of educational development projects in Cote d'Ivoire and a literature informed by management theory, Delens suggests that donor-funded development projects tend to be planned in accordance with donor cultural values. The cultural values of those who will implement the project in the recipient institution are often ignored, increasing the likelihood of project failure. The challenge for project managers, especially expatriate managers, is the bridging of the cultural gap between donor values and the values of the "target community." Educational project management in alien cultures requires a set of skills different from those required in familiar settings. Delens goes on to propose a process of mediation or negotiation that encompasses the cultural values of both "donor" and "beneficiary."

Finally, in Chapter 20, the co-editor of our book, Fiona Leach, reflects on the contributions, draws together dilemmas between economic and cultural considerations in educational aid, and draws some general lessons for donor agencies. She suggests that bilateral and multilateral donor agencies have reinforced the economic analysis of education in development to guide their interventions. Many of these interventions have failed because they were themselves culture-bound and inappropriate to the contexts of introduction. She also suggests that donors move away from analysing educational provision in largely economic and product-oriented terms, relying on universal models, towards a more varied and complex portfolio of forms of support which assist governments and social groups to produce their own tailor-made solutions.

In conclusion, the chapters in this book identify the value of both economic and cultural analyses of education in development. They suggest that both economic and cultural considerations define the goals and conditions for education and learning, but that different social groups draw on these to varying degrees. Social groups with economic resources and power have tended to overrely on an economic analysis of education and learning and have disregarded the potential of cultural analyses of the goals, processes, and conditions of learning and education. This overreliance has been accompanied by educational projects and reforms that have often been disappointing in implementation and outcome. At the same time several of the chapters have underlined the value of economic analyses of educational programmes that are driven mainly by cultural considerations. Material resources for education are scarce and all educational stakeholders must address questions about their efficient, equitable, and effective use in the realisation of cultural aspirations. By bringing together voices which employ different languages and often different premises in the understanding of education and learning, we attempt to build bridges of communication between economic and cultural analysts, and to raise economic and cultural dilemmas for those who participate, and those who wish to participate, in the development process.

REFERENCES

Barros, R., and D. Lam. 1996. "Income and Educational Inequality and Children's Schooling Attainment." In *Opportunity Foregone: Education in Brazil*, eds. N. Birdsall and R. H. Sabot. Washington, DC: Inter-American Development Bank.

Bernstein, B. 1977. *Class, Codes and Control*. Vol. 3. London: Routledge.

Bourdieu, P., and J.P. Passeron. 1977. *Reproduction*. London: Sage.

Bowman, M.J. 1966. "The Human Investment Revolution in Economic Thought." *Sociology of Education* (Spring): 111–137.

Carnoy, M. 1974. *Education as Cultural Imperialism*. London: Longman.

Cernea, M.M. 1991. "Knowledge from Social Sciences in Development Projects." In *World Bank Discussion Paper No.114*. Washington, DC: World Bank.

Cosin, B.R., ed. 1972. *Education: Structure and Society*. Harmondsworth: Penguin Books.

Dore, R.P. 1976. *The Diploma Disease*. 1st ed. London: George Allen and Unwin.

Dore, R.P. 1997. "Reflections on the Diploma Disease Twenty Years Later." *Assessment in Education* 4 (1): 189–206.

Fägerlind, I., and Saha, L. 1992. *Education and National Development.* 2nd ed. London: Butterworth Heinemann.

Frank, A.G. 1967. *Capitalism and Underdevelopment in Latin America.* New York: Monthly Review Press.

Galtung, J. 1971. "A Structural Theory of Imperialism." *Journal of Peace Research* 8 (2): 81–117.

Galtung, J. 1996. "Social Costs of Modernisation. Social Disintegration, Atomie/Anomie and Social Development." *Development and Change* 27: 379–413.

Gerth, H., and C.W. Mills, eds. 1948. *From Max Weber: Essays in Sociology.* London: Routledge.

Gudeman, S. 1986. *Economics as Culture: Models and Metaphors of Livelihood.* London: Routledge.

Halsey, A.H., J. Floud, and J. Anderson, eds. 1961. *Education, Economy and Society.* New York: Free Press.

Halsey, A.H., H. Lauder, P. Brown, and A. Stuart Wells, eds. 1997. *Education: Culture, Economy and Society.* Oxford: Oxford University Press.

Heyneman, S. 1995. "The Economics of Education: Disillusions and Hopes." *Prospects Quarterly Review of Comparative Education* 25 (4): 611–642.

Inkeles, A., and D. Smith. 1974. *Becoming Modern: Individual Change in Six Developing Countries.* London: Heinemann Education Books.

Karabel, J., and A.H. Halsey, eds. 1977. *Power and Ideology in Education.* New York: Oxford University Press.

Kumar, K. 1997. "The Post Modern Condition." In *Education: Culture, Economy and Society*, eds. A.H. Halsey et. al. Oxford University Press.

Little, A.W. 1990. *Understanding Culture: A Pre-Condition for Effective Learning.* Paris: UNESCO.

Little, A.W. 1992. "Education and Development: Macro Relationships and Micro-Cultures." *Institute of Development Studies Silver Jubilee Papers No. 4*, Sussex.

McClelland, D. 1961. *The Achieving Society.* New York: The Free Press.

Nabobo, U., and J. Teasdale. 1995. "Education for Cultural Identity: A Fiji Case Study." *Prospects Quarterly Review of Comparative Education* 25 (4): 695–706.

Perelman, M. 1996. *The End of Economics.* London: Routledge.

Polanyi, K. 1957. *The Great Transformation.* Boston: Gower Beacon Press.

Ruttan, V.W. 1988. "Cultural Endowment and Economic Development: What Can We Learn from Anthropology?" *Economic Development and Cultural Change* 36 (3): 5247–5271.

Schultz, T.W. 1961. "Investment in Human Capital." *American Economic Review* 51: 1–17.

Teasdale, G.R., and A.W. Little, eds. 1995. "Education and Culture." *Prospects Quarterly Review of Comparative Education* 25 (4): 587–784.

UNDP. 1990. *Human Development Report 1990*. New York: Oxford University Press.

Weber, M. 1930. *The Protestant Ethic and the Spirit of Capitalism*. London: Allen and Unwin.

CHAPTER 2

Economics and Culture

Towards an Anthropology of Economics[1]

R. L. STIRRAT

This chapter explores the relationship between "culture" and "rational technical knowledge," specifically that form of knowledge known as economics. I am not an economist and write from outside the discipline. My recent experience of economics has been dominated by the economists of the "development" agencies. When I write of "economists" and "economics" it is this context to which I am referring. But besides my own experience, I also draw on the growing body of anthropological writing plus other literature both within and outside the tradition of economics which problematises the opposition of "culture" to "economics" and questions the claim of neoclassical economics to embody a form of rationality which is not culturally determined.

The argument I present in this paper is a version of an emerging anthropological orthodoxy: that the distinction between economics and culture is analytically false—*from an anthropological point of view.*[2] Economics, both in terms of what economists do (theoretical economics, economic analysis, etc.), and in terms of what they normally study (production, exchange, and consumption), is a cultural activity. For my purposes, culture is what people produce, and because economics is a product of human activity, then it is as much cultural as, for instance, religion, art, or music. Following from this, economics ceases to have a privileged status but rather becomes one of many ways of comprehending and acting on the world.

THE HEGEMONY OF ECONOMICS AS A DISCIPLINE

To understand how anthropological approaches to "the economy" have developed, it is essential to recognise the hegemonic role of economics and economists in the social sciences. This has been true throughout the present century (Friedland and Robertson 1990, 5), but has become much more marked since World War II. The "ubiquitous rise of economists" has been traced by Markoff and Montecinos (1993), who point out that by the mid-1970s around 75 percent of all social scientists in high-level civil service posts in the United States were economists. Throughout Europe, particularly Britain, economists have increased in number and influence in government. This is also true for the "less developed countries" and institutions such as the World Bank, the International Monetary Fund, and the regional banks such as the Asian Development Bank.[3]

Markoff and Montecinos (1993) argue that the rise of economists is not simply a matter of their technical knowledge or technical skills; rather it is a matter of their role as legitimators of policies. They increasingly perform a "sacerdotal" rather than a "technical" role. The language or discourse of economics has become dominant in government and a "transnational political culture" dominated by a common language of economics has emerged. The intellectual hegemony of economics within the social sciences has steadily increased.

The hegemonic position of economics relative to anthropology is easily seen. If one looks for the influence of anthropology on economics the list of references would be short indeed. It has generally consisted of misunderstandings of the ethnographic record, as in the common economists' argument which sees barter as a precursor of money (Humphrey and Hugh-Jones 1992). The flow of ideas and influences has been much greater in the opposite direction.

As far as anthropology is concerned, the status and power of economics has been such that throughout this century the issues and questions which have dominated "economic anthropology" have been framed in terms derived from, or in opposition to, economics. The first major work in economic anthropology, Malinowski's *Argonauts of the Western Pacific*, was written explicitly in the context of economists' ideas about *homo economicus*. Ever since, anthropologists have worked under the shadow of a larger, more powerful, and more prestigious discipline. This is perhaps most clearly seen in the context of the debate which dominated economic anthropology in the 1950s and 1960s between the so-called formalists and the substantivists.

The formalists in effect accepted the economists' assertion that the methods of economic analysis were universally valid, and thus claimed there was no qualitative distinction between the economies of the capitalist West and "traditional" or "primitive" societies. Human nature was essentially the same. People everywhere were involved in decision-making activities in which the goal was to maximise utilities. Even if the forms might look bizarre, social life was essentially an elaboration of market principles. Thus, transfers of goods or labour at marriage were represented in terms of the marketplace rather than in cultural terms of exchange and interdependency. Culture, if mentioned in the formalists' analyses, became little more than a schedule of preferences.[4]

The substantivists, on the other hand, held a radically different position. For them, the methods of formal economics were only valid in societies where the economy was not embedded in social and cultural forms. They argued, following Karl Polanyi, for a "great divide" between those societies ("traditional," "premodern," "primitive") where production, exchange, and distribution were determined by social and cultural factors, and those societies ("modern," "monetised," "capitalist") where the processes of production, exchange, and distribution were separated out from the cultural and social; where the "economy" or the "economic" had an autonomy of its own (Dalton 1968). In the former, the logic through which the production, exchange, and distribution of goods were organised was in terms of cultural factors: kinship relations, political structures, religious ideology. Only in the latter, where the economy is an autonomous sphere instituted around the market principle, are the methods of economics valid. Only here can the distinction be made between culture and society on the one hand and economics on the other.[5]

To a large extent the debate was an exercise in futility. The two sides tended to use different definitions of economics, the formalists focusing on economics as the analysis of decision making; the substantivists on economics as the material processes of production, exchange, and consumption. Furthermore, by accepting the validity of economic analysis in modern societies, the substantivists in effect accepted that their analyses were limited to fast-disappearing entities. And both sides of the debate were overtaken by the rise of Marxist analysis in anthropology within which "culture" became subservient to what Sahlins (1976) was to call, practical reason.

Yet the divisions mapped out in the formalist/substantivist debate linger on. Many contemporary anthropologists use what amounts to a traditional/modern dichotomy, although this is often disguised in various ways. Thus Gregory's important treatment of exchange in New Guinea deals in terms of a hard distinction between market exchange (the market: the future) and gift exchange (culture: the past) (Gregory 1982). Another example is Taussig's influential analysis of commoditisation in Latin America where culture is invoked in the battle against invading capitalism (Taussig 1980). And in the field I know best, the practice of development, anthropologists frequently collude with economists in defining modern sectors ruled by the market and traditional sectors still dominated by the laws of culture rather than economics. Here the anthropologists' primary role is to deal with those distressing and troublesome social and cultural factors which are seen as external to economics.

ECONOMIC THEORY AS CULTURAL ARTEFACT

Although I suspect that many anthropologists have felt for a long time that the status of economics and economists was perhaps overrated, it is only in the last 20 years that there has been an attempt to view the discipline of economics as a cultural construct. In effect this has amounted to a critique of the claims made by many economists that economics is a science and that the truths of economics are universally valid.

One of the first to do so was Marshall Sahlins in his rather unfortunately titled *Culture and Practical Reason* (1976). The main thrust of this book was directed at Marxist analyses of society. What Sahlins argued for forcibly was the autonomy of culture; that culture is in no way dependent on what the Marxists called material forces. Rather than see people as producers of material objects, Sahlins stressed their role as makers of meaning. Through this process, Sahlins began a critique of the epistemological bases of economics, most significantly the model of maximising man.

Perhaps of greater importance is Stephen Gudeman's *Economics as Culture: Models and Metaphors of Livelihood* (1986). Gudeman is perhaps the first writer since Polanyi to tackle head on the problem of how anthropologists and anthropology should relate to economic theory, and his general conclusion is that the latter has to be seen as culture rather than as science. "Any set of economic constructions is a kind of mystification or ideology" (Gudeman 1986, 154). Rather than one "science of economics" there are for Gudeman many economics or, as he prefers to call them, "models of livelihood." And this approach is further developed in his more recent book, *Conversations in Colombia* (Gudeman and Rivera 1990), in which he elaborates the distinction between the "house" and the "corporation" as two distinct ways of modelling and organising forms of livelihood.

I shall return to Gudeman's work, but first I want to elaborate a little on what is meant by his claim that "any set of economic constructions is a kind of mystification or ideology," a claim similar to that made by Friedland and Robertson that "the discipline of economics is itself a cultural artefact, an unselfconscious victim of its own narrow discourse" (Friedland and Robertson 1990, 38). How do economists construct their object of study? In what way does this differ from anthropologists' objects of study? Are the claims of economists to be producing a "scientific" analysis of society valid? And what are the implications of this sort of approach?

Economics and anthropology are heirs to two rather different intellectual traditions. While economics has tended to follow the models of the physical sciences, and more recently the mathematical sciences, anthropology at one time drew its inspiration from the biological sciences (the importance of functionalism) and, more recently, has allied itself to history, literature, and the nebulous area of "cultural studies." While economics has stressed a search for what is universal, anthropology has tended to stress cultural relativism and reflexivity: "Anthropology is essentially discourse upon social and cultural values based on materials about others" (Thomas 1991, 14). Whereas anthropology has always been somewhat eclectic in its methods and forms of analysis, economic theory, or at least neoclassical economic theory, has based itself on a set of axioms from which a series of logical inferences are drawn.

Perhaps the most succinct formulation of these axioms was produced by Jevons writing over a century ago, but they still appear to be fundamental to all neoclassical thought:

> The science of economics . . . is in some degree peculiar, owing to the fact . . . that its ultimate laws are known to us immediately by intuition. . . . That every person will choose the greater apparent good; that human wants are more or less quickly satiated; that prolonged labour becomes more and more painful, are a few of the simple inductions on which we can reason deductively with great confidence. From these axioms we can deduce the laws of supply and demand, the laws of that difficult conception, value, and all the intricate results of commerce, so far as the data are available. The final agreement of our inferences with *a posteriori* observations ratifies our method. (Jevons 1871, 18, quoted in Gregory and Altman 1989, 25)

To an anthropologist, what is striking about these "ultimate laws" of the "science of economics" is that they depend on intuition, and thus necessarily involve assumptions about the nature of the person. Yet in the anthropological and historical literature, it is clear that the concept of the person is problematic (e.g., Carrithers, Collins, and Lukes 1985; Dumont 1977, 1986; Morris 1972). In different cultures the "person" is constructed in different ways, yet in the tradition of neoclassical economics there is little if any room for such variety. As Preston in a critique of neoclassical economics puts it:

> Orthodox economists deploy a quite particular philosophical anthropology: rational economic man is deployed as the route to rendering coherent states of persons whose behaviour is then amenable to scientific treatment and evaluation via the notion of efficiency. This model presents humankind as centrally rational and calculative, and thereafter to be understood only in less reliable or subjective ways. (Preston 1992, 65)

"Rational economic man," which according to Jevons is known to us by our intuition, becomes "modernist" man, the heir to enlightenment thought. "Economic man" is not "cultural man" but rather the true essence of man, which is realised when the "nonrational," the "cultural clothing" is stripped away. Furthermore, economics supplies the means, the models for action, through which this modernist goal can be achieved. Neoclassical economics presents itself as the epitome of modernity in the social sciences, to such an extent that the great economist Samuelson could claim in the late 1940s that "economics studies behaviour that was rational while sociology [and by implication anthropology] studied that which was not" (Friedland and Robertson 1990, 6, quoting Swedberg 1987, 101).

It is upon the axiom of the "rational man" that the edifice of neoclassical economics is constructed. Rational man exercises choice, and by allowing the free play of individual choices through the free exchange of goods and services—the market—resources are rationally allocated so as to minimise costs and maximise benefits. Admittedly in practice there are commodities which do not directly enter the market and there are markets which are not "free." Yet through metaphorical extensions of the market principle (e.g., the concept of externalities and the creation of regulatory bodies which function as simulacra of the market) the same goals of efficient resource allocation can be achieved.

The discourse which emerges is ultimately unquestionable because it is axiomatic, the axioms being known to us through "intuition." These axioms define the terms of the debate; what can and cannot be said, what is and what is not relevant. They define what can and cannot be understood—the limits of rationality. Implied by claims that economics is a science, it is not surprising that measurement plays a crucial role in the practice of economics. Put crudely, if it can't be measured it is either unimportant or irrelevant. Once it is decided that it is relevant (e.g., the environment), then it has to be measured.[6]

The result is that economics, or at least neoclassical economics, tends to become tautologous and the arguments circular. One example of this is the recent World Bank document on the "East Asian Miracle" (World Bank 1993) which attempts to identify the lessons which can be learnt from the experience of the HPAEs (high-performing Asian economies). Given the dominance of neoclassical economic thought in the World Bank, it is not surprising that the rapid rates of economic growth in these countries are, according to the report writers, linked to the market. Furthermore, faced with evidence of state involvement in these economies, the authors claim that these were successful when they were "market friendly." Yet it is difficult to see how they could have come to an alternative conclusion. By definition the market is the motor of growth and state intervention is antithetical to the market because it runs counter to the freedom of choice for the rational individual. Therefore, as growth has taken place, state involvement must have been market friendly. Yet as the authors admit, it is impossible to produce a "rigorous counterfactual scenario." In other words, the analysis does not approximate to the demands of the scientific method and we have to be content with what Keynes called an "'essay in persuasion,' based on analytical and empirical judgements" (World Bank 1993, 6).

At this point it is worth returning to Markoff and Montecinos' remark that the role of economists is often "sacerdotal"—ritual rather than technical.

One of the most influential essays in anthropology is Clifford Geertz's "Religion as a cultural system" in which he characterises religion as being both a "model of" and a "model for" (Geertz 1966). By this he means that religion provides both an explanation of the world, existence within the world and what happens in the world, and a model for practice within the world—a code for behaviour, a set of moral standards, and so on.

To an anthropologist a striking feature of economics (or perhaps more correctly economics as practised in the world of development) is that it too provides "models of" and "models for." It purports to explain why things have happened as they have (why certain economies grow and others don't) and provides prescriptions as to what actions should be taken in the future (what policies should be pursued). But perhaps more significantly, there are other aspects of economics which can be compared with those of religion.

- As I have already mentioned, the basic axioms of economics are above question, just as the basic assumptions of religion are above question. To deny the concept of rational man is similar to denying the existence of God. Without rational man the edifice of economics collapses; without God the existence of religion collapses.
- Both religion and economics are incapable of disproof. To a believer, whether or not a prayer is answered does not prove or disprove the "truth" of religion. As Evans-Pritchard (1937) pointed out in his famous work on the Zande, belief in oracles is not threatened by events: failures simply show that the oracle is being interfered with by magic, sorcery, or whatever. Similarly, as Markoff and Montecinos have noted, what is rather striking about economists is how "little the policy failures of economists have reduced their collective influence amongst political elites" (Markoff and Montecinos 1993, 55, quoting Nettle and Robertson 1968). And they go on to remark that "on the contrary, policy failures have enhanced the tendency to define political problems as economic—and therefore to search for other economists." Again, economics retains its legitimacy despite its failures.
- Both religion and economics appear to exist as if they were outside humanity. Both appear as part of nature, as outside the control of humanity, no matter that they are constructed by people. Thus, just as a believer cannot question the laws of God or His will, so we are extolled to accept the laws of economics: "You can't buck the market." To do so is as irrational as to question the existence of God in a fundamentalist theocracy.

Thus, there is at least a metaphoric relationship between religion and economics. Neoclassical economics claims many of the same qualities as religion, and just as in their heyday theologians attempted to determine the nature of the economy and define the nature of the family, so now neoclassical economists attempt to employ their methods based on the revealed truths of economics to understand areas of life previously seen as external to the economy: for instance, politics and the family. And one could even claim that today's economic theorists are comparable to theologians.[7]

It is precisely because economics epitomises the modernist approach to social phenomena that it has the power and prestige—the hegemonic position in the social sciences—obvious today. Based as it is on the axiom of the individual endowed with rational powers of decision making which exist independent of culture, economics is in many ways immune to challenge. Any effective alternative has to start from different preconceptions about the nature of humanity. Because anthropologists on the whole have always been somewhat suspicious of modernity and have harboured a rather romantic view of "traditional," "premodern," and "nonrational" societies, they have always been prone to what one formalist called the "obsolete anti-market mentality." A more effective challenge to the position of economics as a discipline (and economists as a profession) will probably come from the world of post-modernism. What anthropologists have done, however, is to trace the contours of alternative ways of organising the economy, of alternative theories of how the economy works.

ALTERNATIVE CONSTRUCTIONS OF THE ECONOMY

If, as I have been arguing in the last section, the models of neoclassical economics are cultural constructions, then are there alternatives? Is it possible to recognise other modes of economic analysis which are not based on the axiom of the individual ceaselessly engaged in maximising activity?

Within contemporary anthropology, the most comprehensive and far-reaching attempts to explore alternative forms of economic models have been those of Stephen Gudeman (Gudeman 1986, 1992; Gudeman and Rivera 1990).[8] At the most general level, Gudeman argues that economies and economic theories are social constructions and that the central processes of making a livelihood are culturally modelled (1986). More specifically, Gudeman and Rivera have produced detailed analyses of two forms of economic organisation, "the house" and "the corporation," focusing primarily on Colombian data.

According to their analysis, there is a distinct "peasant" model of economic activities in rural Colombia. Here, it is the relationship between the household and the earth which is stressed. The house has two main purposes: to reproduce itself and to increase what Gudeman and Rivera translate as its "base": land, stock, and implements. The logic of the "house" is not to engage in market exchanges, which are associated with a reduction in the freedom of manoeuvre and autonomy of the house, but rather to minimise relations with the market. In contrast, "the corporation" is akin to the commercial company of the market economy, and the rules of conduct are broadly those recognised by neoclassical economics.

Besides presenting a detailed analysis of the contemporary situation in rural Colombia, they also argue that much of what became modern economics arose in 18th century European contexts, where the two models of house and corporation were brought into conjunction. In other words, what became a technical and rational discourse of "experts" had its origins in the practices and reflections of practical people. As Escobar notes, "The implications of this view are enormous. Not only does the idea of a universal model of the economy have to be abandoned, it becomes necessary to recognise that forms of production are not independent from the representations (the 'models') of social life in which they exist" (Escobar 1995, 97–98).

Similar stories are to be found in the literature on development projects in Africa. Here too, the "development agents" and the people whose lives are to be "developed" often have radically different ideas about the nature of their modes of livelihood. What de Sardan describes as "peasant logics" are often more akin to the "house" economy analysed by Gudeman than to the constructs of neoclassical economics (Crehan and Oppen 1988; de Sardan 1988; Long and Long 1992).

While research on alternative discourses of "making a livelihood" have tended to stress a two-tier model—popular versus scientific knowledge; peasants versus experts; the house versus the corporation—anthropologists on the whole have ignored the various other discourses of the economy. In most ethnographic situations it appears that the total picture is much more complex. Rather than just two contrasting models, there are usually a number of alternative models competing with one another. Furthermore, these alternative discourses are not limited to remote marginal rural areas, as discussed by Gudeman, but also exist at the heart of national entities.

ONE DEVELOPMENT PROJECT, TWO ECONOMIC DISCOURSES

Recently, I participated in a meeting in Colombo, the capital of Sri Lanka. The meeting involved a team of economists from the World Bank and a team from the Mahaweli Authority of Sri Lanka (MASL), the managers of the largest single development project ever undertaken in the country. At stake was the proposed restructuring of the project, and within the meeting, two basic economic discourses based on differing sets of axioms were apparent.

- As far as the team from the World Bank was concerned, the project had to be seen in narrow economic terms in which other issues were irrelevant. The basic problem was that the "rate of return" from the project was too low. The reason for this was that MASL was not following "free-market" principles. The result was the inefficient allocation of resources and the failure of farmers within the project to produce high-value crops. Therefore, the World Bank advocated the wholesale privatisation of functions presently carried out by the MASL and the creation of free markets, which would both force farmers to shift to higher value crops by allowing cheap staple food imports and encourage them in this shift by allowing new markets for high-value products to develop.
- As far as the MASL was concerned, the World Bank was starting off from much too narrow a view of the project. Rather than judge the project in terms of the narrow rationality of rates of return, the MASL attempted to move the discussion to the broader question of the role of the project for the social and political future of Sri Lanka. Thus, the MASL saw issues such as landlessness, education, and housing as crucial, issues which were at best marginal to the World Bank.[9]

The debate became an attempt by each party to impose its particular discourse on the other. Both were working with models of the "economic," but while the World Bank team used one derived directly from the postulates of neoclassical economics, the MASL speakers drew theirs from a much broader nationalist discourse concerning the role of small-scale agriculture in Sri Lanka. The debate became most intense when the MASL introduced topics which the World Bank team thought irrelevant; for instance, the "second generation" problem and how to create enough jobs in the project area for settlers' children.

Yet even though these were the only two parties present, there are others centrally involved in the Mahaweli project, with their own models of economic activity and modes of livelihood that contrast with both those of the MASL and the World Bank. First, there are the small farmers, frequently mentioned in the discussions between the Bank and the MASL, but never present. They, too, have their own "economics," akin in broad terms to the "house" described by Gudeman. Second, there are the small traders of the area who run their businesses and conceive of them in ways very different from those of the farmers on the one hand or the idealised entrepreneurs of the World Bank on the other. Third, there are the relatively small number of so-called commercial farmers, whose interests and modes of economic activity contrast with both the mass of small-scale rice producers and the activities of the traders. And there may well be others with their own distinct economic practices and distinct ways of constructing and representing the economy.

To fully map this constellation of differing discourses would be a major task, but if anthropology is to fulfil its own project, then at some time the research will have to be done. For what is clear is that much of the confusion displayed by the World Bank experts (and, it has to be said, by MASL staff as well) was based on misreadings of the activities undertaken within the Mahaweli area. Put crudely, neither farmers nor traders do what is expected of them. The models for action put forward by both parties ignored the culture, or the alternative rationalities, of small-scale agricultural producers and traders.

Such a situation is, of course, not unique to Sri Lanka. Throughout the less developed countries, the "discourse of development" systematically imposes its own set of categories, its own set of models, as means of understanding and changing the world. Yet as the two most important books from an anthropological perspective on this discourse of development make clear, this discourse involves a fundamental misunderstanding of the nature of societies which are to be "developed" (Escobar 1995; Ferguson 1990). The implication of this work is not just that for developmental interventions to be more effective, more notice has to be taken of indigenous models, but that these interventions are in themselves part of a struggle for hegemony, for dominance over ways of thinking about the world.

NOTES

[1] This paper is partly based on research funded by the British Economic and Social Research Council (grant no R 000235423) to whom I am grateful.

[2] I stress the anthropological point of view. This does not mean to belittle the work of theoretical economists, just as later comments on religion are not meant to belittle the work of theologians. Rather, it is to point out that there are different ways of approaching the same phenomena, and to accept that theologians and economists may well have uncomfortable things to say about the traditional domains of anthropology.

[3] It is claimed that around 70 percent of the World Bank professional staff are economists (Escobar 1995,165).

[4] See Barth (1959) for an example of formalist analysis of political processes.

[5] There is a vast literature on the formalist/substantivist debate. The two main collections of essays are those edited by LeClair and Schneider (1968), which adopts the formalist position, and George Dalton (1967) which presents the substantivist position.

[6] One of the more bizarre manifestations of this process is the attempt to put values on the aesthetic importance of natural phenomena such as waterfalls.

[7] For parallel comments about developmentalism as being, "not merely a matter of reason and logic [but also] at heart, the performance of a religious duty," see Pieterse 1991, 16–17.

[8] *Conversations in Colombia* is probably the most important book to be published in economic anthropology over the last two decades, not only for the way in which it deals with the traditional subject matter of economic anthropology, but also for what it has to say about the practice of anthropology.

[9] The MASL also pointed out a rather basic error in the World Bank calculations. Rather than judge the rate of return at constant prices, actual prices had been used. Much of the difference between the rate of return at appraisal and at evaluation could be explained through the fall in the price of rice, the basic crop in the project area, over the lifetime of the project.

REFERENCES

Barth, Fredrik. 1959. *Political Leadership Among Swat Pathans*. London: Athlone Press.

Carrithers, Michael, Steven Collins, and Steven Lukes. 1985. *The Category of the Person: Anthropology, Philosophy, History*. Cambridge: Cambridge University Press.

Crehan, Kate, and Achim von Oppen. 1988. "Understandings of 'Development': An Arena of Struggle." *Sociologia Ruralis* 28: 113–145.

Dalton, George, ed. 1967. *Tribal and Peasant Economies: Readings in Economic Anthropology*. Garden City, NY: The Natural History Press.

Dalton, George, ed. 1968. *Primitive, Archaic and Modern Economies: Essays of Karl Polanyi*. New York: Anchor Books.

de Sardan, Jean Paul Olivier. 1988. "Peasant Logics and Development Project Logics." *Sociologia Ruralis* 28: 216–226.

Dumont, Louis. 1977. *From Mandeville to Marx: The Genesis and Triumph of Economic Ideology*. Chicago and London: Chicago University Press.

Dumont, Louis. 1986. *Essays on Individualism: Modern Ideology in Anthropological Perspective*. Chicago and London: Chicago University Press.

Escobar, Arturo. 1995. *Encountering Development: The Making and Unmaking of the Third World*. Princeton: Princeton University Press.

Evans-Pritchard, E.E. 1937. *Witchcraft, Oracles and Magic among the Azande*. Oxford: Clarendon Press.

Ferguson, James. 1990. *The Anti-Politics Machine. "Development," Depoliticisation and Bureaucratic Power in Lesotho*. Cambridge: Cambridge University Press.

Friedland, Roger, and A.F. Robertson, eds. 1990. *Beyond the Marketplace: Rethinking Economy and Society*. New York: Aldine de Gruyter.

Geertz, C. 1966. "Religion as a Cultural System." In *Anthropological Approaches to the Study of Religion*, ed. M. Banton. London: Tavistock.

Gregory, C.A. 1982. *Gifts and Commodities*. London: Academic Press.

Gregory, C.A., and J.C. Altman. 1989. *Observing the Economy*. London: Routledge.

Gudeman, Stephen. 1986. *Economics as Culture: Models and Metaphors of Livelihood*. London: Routledge.

Gudeman, Stephen. 1992. "Remodelling the House of Economics: Culture and Innovation." *American Ethnologist* 19: 141–154.

Gudeman, Stephen, and Alberto Rivera. 1990. *Conversations in Colombia: The Domestic Economy in Life and Text*. Cambridge: Cambridge University Press.

Humphrey, Caroline, and Stephen Hugh-Jones, eds. 1992. *Barter, Exchange and Value: An Anthropological Approach*. Cambridge: Cambridge University Press.

Jevons, W. 1871. *The Theory of Political Economy*. Harmondsworth: Penguin, (1970).

LeClair, E.E., and H.K. Schneider, eds. 1968. *Economic Anthropology: Readings in Theory and Practice*. New York: Holt, Rinehart and Winston.

Long, Norman, and Ann Long. 1992. *Battlefields of Knowledge*. London: Routledge.

Malinowski, Bronislaw. 1932. *Argonauts of the Western Pacific: An Account of Native Enterprise and Adventure in the Archipelagoes of Melanesian New Guinea*. London: Routledge and Kegan Paul.

Markoff, John, and Veronica Montecinos. 1993. "The Ubiquitous Rise of Economists." *Journal of Public Policy* 13: 37–66.

Morris, Colin. 1972. *The Discovery of the Individual: 1050–1200*. London: Society for the Propagation of Christian Knowledge.

Nettle, J.P., and R. Robertson. 1968. *International Systems and the Modernization of Societies: The Formation of National Goals and Attitudes.* New York: Basic Books.

Pieterse, Jan Nederveen. 1991. "Dilemmas of Development Discourse: The Crisis of Developmentalism and the Comparative Method." *Development and Change* 22: 5–29.

Preston, Peter. 1992. "Models of Economic-Theoretical Engagement." In *Contesting Markets: Analyses of Ideology, Discourse and Practice,* ed. Roy Dilley. Edinburgh: Edinburgh University Press.

Sahlins, M. 1976. *Culture and Practical Reason.* Chicago: Chicago University Press.

Swedberg, R. 1987. *Economic Sociology; Past and Present.* Newbury Park, CA: Sage.

Taussig, M. 1980. *The Devil and Commodity Fetishism in South America.* Chapel Hill: University of North Carolina Press.

Thomas, Nicholas. 1991. *Entangled Objects: Exchange, Material Culture, and Colonialism in the Pacific.* Cambridge and London: Harvard University Press.

World Bank. 1993. *The East Asian Miracle: Economic Growth and Public Action.* Oxford: Oxford University Press.

CHAPTER 3

Meanings of Culture in Development

A Case Study from Literacy

BRIAN V. STREET

I would like to address some of the issues that have arisen in discussions about the concept of culture as it is used, particularly in development contexts, and some of the contestations around that term. I will illustrate these issues with a case study from my own work in the area of literacy. I look first at some of the history of ideas from an earlier period that I think underlie some contemporary uses of the concept of culture. At first sight these may not appear to be the obvious ideas that one would consider when thinking about culture, but I argue that in fact they often underlie contemporary usage. Second, I discuss contemporary work, particularly in anthropology and in social linguistics, concerning the concept of culture as a process rather than the more reified sense of the earlier usage. I then use my own literacy research as a case study to illustrate some of the contemporary theoretical debates in the "new literacy studies" and consider how they relate to development discourse. I conclude with a brief reference to a recent project in South Africa, to try to link academic research with practical applications in the Cape Town area (Prinsloo and Breier 1996). This will serve as an example of some current directions in literacy work which may also have implications for the way we think about culture and development. The chapter represents a contribution to our reconceptualisation of the relationship between culture and development on the one hand, and economics on the other, by emphasising just what is involved in coming to a more complex understanding of the former domain of the relationship.

THE CONCEPT OF RACE

I want to start where in fact my own doctoral research began more than 20 years ago by looking at some of the intellectual history of European representations and conceptions of diversity (Street 1975). The term is important in this context, because if we start by looking at the 18th century and then continue to the 19th century in Europe, one of the major problems confronting European society was, indeed, how to handle the issue of diversity (Cairns 1965; Curtin 1965). Travellers reported back from different places in the world, indicating diversity internally—within the society being observed—and externally—between those groups and the travellers' own society. These observations challenged previous ideas about what it was to be human at that time (Kiernan 1969). I suggest that three key concepts emerged to handle this challenge, linked to scientific discourse: the concepts of classification, evolution, and hierarchy (Burrow 1966; Gates 1986; MacKenzie 1995; Mitter 1977).

In traditional Western science, the first response to experience that is difficult to understand is to classify it, to create a typology of some kind. So travellers, for instance on Cook's voyages, took with them scientists who could describe all the flora and fauna that they encountered in all those exotic parts of the world and reproduce them with the help of artists trained in scientific observation (Smith 1960). The accounts of the peoples of the world were likewise inserted into the same framework as were physical and natural phenomena: the same discursive strategies, the same intellectual devices and strategies for handling diversity in nature, were used for human beings (Hodgen 1964). I put it in this way in order to address the issue from a slightly different angle than, for instance, Edward Said, who focuses mainly on the political dimension of this process (Said 1978). I do not want to underplay the political dimension—in fact, I will give it much emphasis when ideology is discussed later—but I think it is important to try to understand the roots of ideas at that period.

There was, then, a pressure and a desire to make sense of disorder by creating order out of it. One of the dominant methods of doing so was the concept of "type," and in the case of the peoples of the world, type was to be described in the same way as objects in the natural world—through physical appearance. So external characteristics such as head shape, colour, pigmentation, hair, and various other features of people appeared to be a perfectly natural way, in scientific terms, of making a typology and an ordering. Michael Banton (1967), an anthropologist who has researched this period, argues that the word "race" emerges at that period meaning "type"; it didn't have the connotations that it has now and that it had in, for instance, Hitler's use of it, and in contemporary "racist" discourse. At that time race as type was a supposedly scientifically founded subconcept within general typology that provided a way of making sense of diversity.

Scientists such as Blumenbach, Cuvier, and Linnaeus arrived at different numbers of "races" in this sense of the term, and also at different ways of inventing words for them (Banton and Harwood 1975; Street 1975). It is interesting to recognise how invented these terms are, and yet they are considered "natural" today. For instance, the word "Caucasian" was invented by Blumenbach to refer to that race of people who live in the shadow of Mount Caucasus. Whatever its geographical reference, which was somewhat vague and imprecise, it was a useful term to signify difference. Other terms included "Mongoloid" and "Negroid," which occasionally find echoes in today's language. There were, of course, disputes—are there two types or races, are there three, are there five, are there six? At the time these appeared to many to be scientific debates about the nature of the typology rather than political decisions about the nature and quality of the people being described (Greene 1954; Lyons 1970; Stepan 1982; Street 1992).

From a contemporary perspective, of course, these concepts seem less natural than they were claimed to be at the time. This is partly because of the role played by another of the dominant conceptions of the time, historically derived from a much earlier period, namely hierarchy, whereby the human types or races were placed in a rank order with one above the other. In earlier periods, religious discourse had used the concept of a "great chain of being" to make sense of diversity (Hodgen 1964; Irvine 1955). The concept represented the whole of the universe as linked in a single chain that was also a hierarchy: from the lowest orders of flora, fauna, up through animals and mammals, from human beings to the angels, and eventually to God, there was a universe with an ordered chain. Given that intellectual history, the scientific expansion of religious discourse and the development of typologies characteristic of 18th- and 19th-century Europe made use of that notion of hierarchy. Embedded in the representation of peoples in the world, then, were a notion of race and a notion of hierarchy, with some races being in some way higher, nearer to God, in the way of the old "great chain of being," and others closer to the lower orders (Stocking 1968).

Finally, another concept developed at that time to make sense of diversity—evolution. Evolution derives not simply from Darwin, as might appear with hindsight. In fact Darwin crystallised what had been going on for at least a hundred years in terms of scientific theories. The concept of evolution emerges in this context to give a time dimension to the hierarchy and typology of scientific attempts to make sense of diversity. It argues that the whole of the human and of the natural condition is in a process of change and development, from the simple to the complex, from lower orders to higher orders, and ultimately to human beings as the highest level. Darwin did not include angels in his account, although at the time there was considerable debate about where angels begin and apes end (Irvine 1955). There were, inevitably at a time of classification and taxonomising, many debates about boundaries as well as about types. The concept of evolution in this context becomes a supposedly scientific device for asserting the degree of what we might now call "development" among societies—in other words, social evolution.

There is, then, in 19th-century accounts of diversity, a typology of races, embedded in a hierarchy, and with an evolutionary component that suggests that in some way those "higher up" have actually evolved further and those "lower down" have not evolved so far. This complex of ideas, rooted in science and validated by science, with a history of religious ideas behind it, was reinforced by travellers as they explored Africa, India, and Asia, and reinforced as well by novelists grounded in the same theoretical debates. My own earlier research (Street 1975, 1984) on novelists aimed to demonstrate how they used these ideas: Rider Haggard, John Buchan, Rudyard Kipling, Joseph Conrad—all used the ideas of race, hierarchy, and evolution in order to make sense of diversity, to ask the questions: Where does this society that we are representing stand in the rankings? Where is it in the process of evolution? Does it represent an earlier version of what we went through, the "we" being modern civilised urban European society? This involved, for instance, talking about Bushmen societies and hunter-gatherer societies as though, in some way, we can learn about our past by studying them.

The idea of social evolution linked to hierarchy and race has, then, been a very powerful ordering device for dealing with diversity. Most of these ideas have now been rejected as unsound, particularly through the work of social as well as natural scientists and anthropologists (Banton 1967; Barzun 1937; Montague 1964). For most social scientists the concept of race is no help at all in making sense of diversity. There are too many variations. You cannot read from external characteristics into internal—one of the major intellectual devices of that period. It seemed easy to observe somebody's shape and size as indicative of where they stand in the rankings of evolution and hierarchy; that is now deemed intellectually unsound and of no use in serious research. Moreover, there are also moral and ethical problems with this reasoning. I cite it here because a number of contemporary authors argue that in rejecting it and moving to other concepts, we have in fact smuggled a lot of early 19th-century ideas back in under apparently more neutral terms (Gates 1986; Said 1978).

CONCEPTS OF "CULTURE"

I move now to the second part of the paper, focused on concepts of culture. I begin with a quote from Paul Gilroy, one of the main writers in the fields of difference, diversity, culture, and discrimination in contemporary societies (Gilroy 1987, 1990). He argues that in contemporary Britain, at least—and, I would now argue, maybe more broadly—the concept of culture has come to stand for the underlying conceptions that "race" previously stood for. It is no longer considered appropriate, morally or intellectually, to use the word "race" in any kind of positive sense, given the problems I have cited above. But, he argues, race remains at the centre of contemporary British politics:

> The politics of race in this country is fired by conceptions of national belonging and homogeneity, which not only blur the distinction between race and nation, but rely on that very ambiguity for their effect. The new racism is primarily concerned with mechanisms of inclusion and exclusion; it specifies who may belong to the national community, and simultaneously advances reasons for the segregation or banishment of those whose origin, sentiment or citizenship assign them elsewhere. (Gilroy 1987, 53)

The issue of inclusion and exclusion is one of the dominant themes that runs through the discussions of how the concept of culture is used. For Gilroy and a lot of other contemporary writers, the word "culture" is being used as code for race. There is not space here to document that, but one could look at political speeches and newspapers today and find people using the word "culture" in ways which carry forward many of those earlier ideas. One of the dominant themes is the notion of culture as some kind of fixed inventory of characteristics, a list of things that belong to a set of people. That, of course, is exactly how the word *race* emerged as "type," which then had fixed characteristics that in the discourse of the time were biologically, or later genetically, fixed. Gilroy and others argue that these characteristics have now been transferred to "culture." Even though the concept of culture appears to be not rooted in biology, it is in fact very often premised on assumptions about fixity and permanence: the idea that somebody, for instance, might come from Nigeria and settle in England, somehow bringing along a bag with Nigerian culture in it, with which he or she is then stuck. Looking at some of the accounts of cultural movement, migrations, and diversities, one finds that the built-in assumption is very often of this fixity; a person belongs to a given culture, that is how they are, they must think that way, and behave that way.

This discourse on culture, then, is coding many of the ideas that derive from that earlier period, including references to hierarchy and to social evolution. I argue that the ways in which culture has been used in development very often draws on that same tradition. For instance, in development work it is common for anthropologists to be asked the question: What can we do about culture? We are going into this society and trying to persuade women to manage fertility, people to take their babies to health clinics, nonliterate people to attend literacy classes, and they resist: their culture is getting in the way. Culture is a barrier. Some of the development documents concerned with health, agriculture, or, as we shall see below, literacy, that ask consultants to help improve conditions in these domains employ the concept of culture as though it were a barrier to progress. The fixed, rooted, almost biological inventory of characteristics previously associated with race is very often what comes to mind, implicitly if not explicitly, when agencies and documents are talking about culture.

Contemporary anthropology has had a hand both in reinforcing that particular set of ideas and also in challenging it. Anthropologists, in some periods, have tended to look for what Talal Asad has called "essential meanings," to assume that one could go to another place and study those people's inner, fixed meanings, as though that was what constituted culture (Asad 1980). The traveller or researcher finds a set of people, identifies their customs, their fixed meanings, their ways of life, their ideas, and because they belong to that culture, that is what their characteristics are. These features can then be applied to their "stage" of development.

Asad (1980), writing about the history of the use of the concept of culture in anthropology, criticises this conception on a number of levels.

First, there is the question of power. "The anthropological tendency," he says, "to accord a critical priority to systems of human meaning leaves un-posed the question of how different forms of discourse come to be materially produced and maintained as authoritative systems" (Asad 1980). The use of culture as the frame for studying peoples and diversity begs the question of how a particular set of meanings that you are describing and then inscribing as you study these people, got on to the agenda in the first place. Use of the concept also disguises contestation; some of those early studies of culture assumed culture was just sitting there and you simply described it as you might the flora and fauna of an environment. Very often, too, the anthropologists and others would be talking to particular categories of people in society—men, chiefs, those in control of land—and it may be that other people have quite different conceptions of, for instance, gender behaviour, spacing of children, or what writing and reading were about—but their conceptions did not get onto the agenda because they were marginalised by the dominant version. That version, often articulated by leaders or by observers, then became what Asad calls the "essential meaning" of that culture: it was assumed that this was what everyone meant when they talked about these things, that there was a common core of meaning, rather than the varied accounts of different groups competing to represent the whole culture. In recent years many anthropologists, critiquing this more fixed notion of culture, have started to describe culture as a process rather than in the earlier reified sense (Clifford 1988; Street 1993b).

I will provide just one brief but rather fraught example from South Africa to illustrate this point. About four or five years ago, a number of anthropologists were preparing to go to court to challenge the way certain politicians were using the concept of culture in order to justify the carrying of cultural weapons on the streets. That weapons could be considered "cultural" was being justified on the grounds that Zulus were a "culture"; it served the interests of the political party Inkhata to represent the whole Zulu nation as a culture, which then had rights in law to cultural artefacts, including *assegai*—spears. So Zulu members of Inkhata could go out on the streets with these weapons of intimidation, whereas ANC members could not parade with weapons. There is a contest here over the conception of culture, in the way that Inkhata was using it, and the way the anthropologists were using it. They were going to court precisely to make the point that I have been making in this chapter; that in contemporary intellectual discourse, culture is a contested process rather than a fixed inventory of characteristics. Use of the definite or the indefinite article to say "a culture," "the culture," "cultures" implicitly reproduces the reified sense of "culture." This "nominalisation" (Fairclough 1992)—the use of "culture" as a noun—in the South African context, then, facilitated the claim that all Zulus must be the same, and must also, of course, be under a single leader, Buthelezi, separate from other groups in the country as a whole. This is itself a political statement, not a neutral statement about culture at all; it is using culture as a resource in a political conflict. In fact, of course, Zulu people varied considerably; they took up different political positions, and the vast majority of them were ANC supporters, not Buthelezi supporters. It was in Buthelezi's interest to disguise that political dimension underneath the reified, nominalised conception of culture, but that is no reason for analysts and researchers to do likewise. The anthropology department at the University of Witwatersrand, with the help of "struggle" lawyers, in adopting a more processual view, referred to "cultural processes"—to what culture does rather than what culture is (Thornton 1988), a usage I have referred to as "culture is a verb" (Street 1993b).

That, then, is just a very brief example of the way in which in contemporary discourse anthropologists would look at culture as much more contested, and ask the questions that Asad was asking: How did that particular meaning get on the agenda? How did that particular meaning come to be powerful, and how did it marginalise other meanings, and what are the other meanings and how can we find out? What does it mean to conceptualise culture as a process where it is being used in a reified sense for political purposes?

CULTURE IN DEVELOPMENT: LITERACY AS A CASE STUDY

I have laid out two sets of concepts—culture as fixed, race-like, and culture as a process—to provide a background against which we can view some of the contemporary uses of culture in the field of development. I want to use the example of literacy to illustrate this and I begin with some of my own experiences doing anthropological fieldwork in Iran during the 1970s under the rule of the Shah. For various reasons I found myself working in villages in the area of Mashhad on the border with Afghanistan. I had gone, in fact, to study migration patterns and the rural-urban movement, because that was the sort of thing anthropology students studied in those days, but I found myself drawn into looking at literacy activity in the village. I sat at a village table with the local school textbooks to help me learn Farsi, and people would ride past on their donkeys on their way up to orchards where they had fruit that they were selling to the city. As they rode by, they would stop and talk to this strange foreigner, help me learn the language, and discuss the books I was using. Some interesting discussions began to emerge in which older men, in particular, would say, "Isn't it terrible, the kids in the schools today aren't learning anything, standards are falling. The teachers don't bother, this school is no use really, it's not like in our day." So I explored this further, and the "our day" turned out to be a reference to the fact that, before the state schools arrived in this village, there were Islamic schools, Koranic schools, *Maktabs*. I explored this a bit further and discovered that what people thought about reading and writing and what they did with it, and their identities associated with text, were quite different for those who had been in these *Maktab* schools.

This challenges, I believe, many dominant stereotypes regarding Islamic learning as merely rote learning, mindless, uncritical, backward, as it is often represented. One of the interesting things in this village was the way in which local mullahs would go around to different men's houses for dinner parties, at which a number of men would gather to discuss a theme. They might discuss the Sura of Maryam in the Koran, partly generated by my presence, I think, because it has references to different interpretations between Islam and Christianity regarding Mary and virgin birth. Having been brought up as a Catholic, I got quite interested in these theological debates, and we had some interesting discussions. But this is quite different from the dominant Western stereotype of Islamic schooling as mindless rote learning, a myth still perpetrated in many development programmes.

The other thing that I learned from these encounters was that the kind of literacy that people were learning from these texts was different from that represented in the dominant image of literacy in development. The literacy of the Koranic school was actually deployable in other contexts. While development stereotypes suggest Koranic literacy was not proper literacy because the pupils were "simply" memorising the words, a closer look at some of the texts indicates more complex and interesting ways in which they were being used. For instance, the texts did not necessarily employ the conventions familiar in dominant academic discourse (such as the book in which this chapter appears), with neat, straight lines on the page all the way down, empty margins, and so forth (Street 1996). Instead, books of Islamic commentary used at the Koranic school would have texts at an angle across the page with bullet points and little inserts and commentaries down the side of the page at different angles: the whole text was juggled around much more. I began to realise that what people were learning implicitly if not explicitly was the nature of text, the nature of meaning being constructed not only semantically in the actual units, the words, the grammatical structures, but actually through the text type; the positioning of words, positioning of sentences was actually part of meaning, and pupils were learning that and on occasion transferring it to other contexts.

One such context was the selling of fruit to the cities. This was the time of the Shah, the early 1970s oil boom in the cities that led to great demand for products. This village was well known as a rich village and was cashing in very well. In selling the fruit down to the nearby city of Mashhad, it was necessary to develop various forms of organisation which involved literacy: individual farmers would bring the fruit down from the orchards and sell it to a *tajer*, a middle-man, who would then put it into a store and send it off later at an appropriate time for sale at the urban markets. In order for that transaction to take place, as farmers sold their fruit to a *tajer*, people had to fill in bills of sale, names had to be written, quantities, accounts, places, times, and dates recorded, and cheques written—there was a branch of a bank in the village. So there was a lot of literacy going on. The *tajer* would send the crates down to the city and write "Mohammed Amini" on the crate; the driver had to know where he was taking it, who it belonged to. So I began to recognise a different literacy to that going on in the *Maktab*, and yet that built on this traditional literacy to provide a new form relevant to the needs of modern commerce. For it was the older men who had been trained in the *Maktab* who were acting as *tajers*. I have suggested elsewhere (Street 1984) that it was their social authority and knowledge, linked with their Koranic literacy, that facilitated this new literacy: children trained in the *Dabastan* or the state school may at first seem to be the most likely people to develop this commercial literacy, but in practice, the form of literacy they learned at school and their lack of authority in social circles in the village countered this possibility. It was the social practices of literacy, not simply the decoding skills that mattered.

There are a number of reasons why the state school did not provide the basis for such literacy practices. The teachers who taught there often came from urban areas and were not very interested in the village; as in many such contexts, they focused upon an urban hierarchy and career progress, and they saw the village as a backward place they had to put up with for a short while, so they were not really interested in the lessons.

On the other hand, there was an ambivalence; the parents wanted to send at least one child to the city, because then they could get out of the village and into the white-collar urban work of the cities. In order to achieve this they had to send their sons to the village school—but at the same time they did not really respect it. What was happening in schools was not, then, providing pupils with the kind of literacy that would be useful in the village: it did not give them the social authority or the skills to actually do the *tajer* work, to do this middle-man buying and selling; the school pupils were looking outside, not inside. So gradually I began to do my own classification and developed the notion that in this village there were three literacies, not one: *Maktab* literacy, commercial literacy, as I call the work of buying and selling, and *Dabastan* school literacy.

But this ran counter to the dominant classification of those working in education and in the literacy programmes. For instance, the *Sepayeh Danesh*, the Shah's army of knowledge, was founded on the principle of sending people into the rural areas to overcome illiteracy; the soldiers for education would come into the village and say, "Isn't it sad, all these mindless villagers living in the dark, illiterate." This appeared in direct contrast with the complex literacies with which I found myself surrounded in such villages. It was, indeed, true that few of the villagers probably would have passed the various tests and exams set by agencies and educational institutions. Most of them, for instance, had not been through the third or fourth grade of the *Dabastan*, and very often those are the bases for the figures on literacy that countries send to UNESCO, that is, years of schooling. So I thought, if this is the case here, maybe it's the case elsewhere; these international conceptions of illiteracy may not correspond to what's actually happening on the ground. Here I was living in a place with a variety of intellectual, social, and material, economic processes going on, with three different kinds of literacy, yet the villagers were all being dismissed at the centre, both in Tehran and in international agencies such as UNESCO, as being illiterate.

Development discourse about illiteracy has traditionally associated it with living in darkness, with mindlessness, lack of cognitive skills, lack of progress, inability to think in a modern way. Colin Lankshear (1987) in *Literacy, Schooling, and Revolution*, sums up some of these issues well: "The association of literacy with a modernisation syndrome, the conception of modern man [*sic*], and the development of attitudes and dispositions of flexibility, adaptability, empathy, willingness to accept change, proneness to adopt innovations, all of these were guiding assumptions behind the trend to literacy campaigns in the Third World"

(Lankshear 1987, 42). Another writer, Hagerstrand, claims that "The demand for education is at times an innovation which must be introduced to a society in order to open it to further innovation. Literacy and other new skills eventually transform social communication and resistance into patterns more susceptible to innovation and the progress that comes with it" (*ibid.*). The word "progress," familiar from the account above of 19th-century discourse, recurs here unselfconsciously. Again the belief is that culture and the culture of illiteracy are holding people back; their cognitive processes are not as developed as those of Western educated people. Illiterate people are presumed to come from "backward" cultures—indeed their illiteracy is a distinguishing mark of backwardness. Their "culture" is a barrier to progress and to literacy. Culture, in the fixed sense referred to earlier in this chapter, is then linked with what I have come to call the "autonomous" model of literacy (Street 1984)—a similar reification of literacy and reduction of its dynamic, varied, and contested nature to a single "thing."

All of this seemed quite at variance with my experience in this and other villages. So I then turned to the academic literature to see what it had to say about literacy. And there I discovered a similar adherence to the autonomous model of literacy. Here, too, literacy was being conceptualised as a single thing that is the same everywhere, and it was assumed that without it people were in cognitive, social, and cultural deficit. Literacy in this view is the same across the world, with a big L, little y—a singular noun. Yet, I had already come across three different sets of literacies in one village. The argument from this autonomous model suggests that the acquisition of literacy has consequences for social progress, cognitive development, democracy, and economic take-off. Anderson and Bowman (1966), for instance, suggest a 40 percent literacy level is necessary for economic take-off, a threshold figure. This idea still appears occasionally in the development discourse. Illiteracy and literacy are treated as two terms in a complete binary system: you are either one or you are the other. The people in the Iranian villages where I was living might well not pass the tests for literacy and yet were using reading and writing all the time. So the dominant assumptions about literacy, both in development circles and in academic discourse, did not seem to me to work. The conceptions involved reification, treating literacy as unitary; they were probably ethnocentric as well, because the conceptions of literacy were actually derived from developers' and academics' own society. The model of literacy seemed to have the same character as the model of culture.

So an alternative model was necessary. As it happens, around the world various academics, researchers, and practitioners working in literacy were beginning to come to the conclusion that the autonomous model did not work, that it was not an appropriate intellectual tool for looking at the diversity of reading and writing around the world, and its meanings (Barton and Ivanic 1991; Besnier 1988; Heath 1983). So we developed what I have come to call an ideological model of literacy (Street 1984). This model starts from different premises—from the premise that literacy is a social practice, not simply a technical and neutral skill, and that it is always embedded in socially constructed epistemological principles of one kind or another. It is about knowledge: the ways in which people address reading and writing are themselves rooted in conceptions of knowledge, identity, being. Literacy, in this sense, is always contested, both its meanings and its practices; hence, particular versions of it are always "ideological"; they are always rooted in a particular world view and a desire for that view of literacy to dominate and to marginalise others (Besnier and Street 1994; Gee 1991).

These conceptions themselves are, of course, rooted in cultural practices and cultural processes, of the kind indicated above within the dynamic model of culture. One example, to bring home the significance of this argument concretely, comes from an article in *Cross-Cultural Approaches to Literacy*—a collection of articles by anthropologists who have worked in literacy around the world and have attempted to apply dynamic models of culture to dynamic models of literacy (Street 1993a). Kulick and Stroud (1993) conducted anthropological research in New Guinea villages and began with the question that developers ask: What is the impact of literacy? However, they soon noticed that literacy was being added to the communicative repertoire in more complex ways than the concept of "impact" conveyed. They noted that the things that people did with that literacy were rather different than the people who had brought it had imagined. Missionaries had brought it and wanted to use it for conversion and for control and discipline; this is similar in many contexts where missionary groups have brought reading, but not writing, for precisely that purpose of control—if people can write, they actually can write their own things down, whereas if they can read, they can only read what you provide them. They can still reinterpret it, but the providers have rather more control. Kulick and Stroud, being social linguists as well as anthropologists, were interested in what happens to the communicative repertoire when this missionary literacy arrives: they argued that instead of talking about the "impact" of literacy, we should ask the question: How do people "take hold of" literacy? What they saw happening was that people were using literacy in the way that they had used oral interaction. There were precise conventions for making a speech, the dominant one being that you must not appear to put anyone else down when you make it. It is inappropriate to put someone down, it is inappropriate to speak in a braggardly way about yourself, and yet at the same time you want to get your own way. So a variety of clever political discourses and conventions emerged. Kulick and Stroud discovered when they looked at the texts people were writing, that they were using the same social linguistic conventions, the same discourse strategies as in this speech making. They were inserting the written into their oral. So instead of talking about impact, the researchers here talk about taking hold, they talk about the way people have made use of literacy. There are now many such examples from around the world that indicate how the communicative repertoire varies, from people simply taking literacy and doing with it what they had already done, to people discovering new functions to do with it which may be quite different from what the school teachers or the missionaries had in mind.

A further example comes from research among young adolescents in schools in Philadelphia (Camitta 1993; Shuman 1986). In a high school, the students were producing blank pages and resisting the teacher's blandishments to write. While at first the teacher was very upset, she quickly discovered that beneath the desks all kinds of documents were circulating. The teacher's first response was, this was a discipline issue, she must clamp down on this—the students were meant to write above the desk, on school-validated paper, not below the desk on their own materials. But, being an anthropologist as well, she thought, this is interesting, this is a social fact, this is an example of the social practice of literacy. What are they doing with it? And what she discovered was that people were writing notes, setting down rap songs that they then edited and developed when they met outside. They were making huge collections of cuttings from newspapers, cuttings from each other's writing, development of stories, editing of various kinds. Suitcases full of these materials were kept under pupils' beds; in a sense they contained their identity, an identity they kept away from their parents and their teachers, but which was inscribed in writing. One of Shuman's (1986) arguments about that was that this form of writing has exactly the opposite qualities to the dominant conception of writing. The dominant conception of writing is that it is separate, individualised, cognitively removed from immediate interaction; it is distanced, detached, scientific, objective. While oral is interactive and personal, in this context it was the written that was interactive and group oriented: people were working together designing their rap songs, working together on texts. Once this has been said, it is obvious: we know there are lots of contexts where people work together on text; we know that our identities are bound up with inscriptions on paper. We all have some version of writing that inscribes our sense of who we are. And yet the dominant model continued to represent it as though writing was "out there," detached and separate, and oral communication is the interactive channel. The great divide between oral and literate persists within this autonomous model of literacy, which suggests that oral language has one set of features, written another, and the two are quite different. So this kind of research—that of Kulik and Stroud in New Guinea, Camitta and Shuman in Philadelphia, and various other examples—is challenging an autonomous model of literacy and looking at cultural processes, epistemological issues in literacy acquisition, taking hold, identity.

I call this alternative approach an ideological and not a cultural model because I want to ensure that we attend to the power dimension of these reading and writing processes. The example of the missionaries and of the teachers makes that clear. The concept of "impact," then, is not just a neutral developmental index to be measured, but already part of a power relationship. These are issues about power, assumptions about one particular set of ideas, conceptions, cultural group, being in some way taken on by another group. What is the power relation between them, what are the resources, where are people going if they take on one literacy rather than another literacy, how do you challenge the dominant conceptions of literacy? It seems to me quite impossible to address the issue of literacy without addressing also the issue of power (Street 1996). A cultural model of literacy, particularly the reified view of culture rather than culture as process, leads one to fall back into the old reifications: a particular group of people become associated with a particular literacy; another group of people are associated with another literacy. The contestation over what counts as literacy and whose literacy is dominant gets lost. So we call it an ideological model of literacy in order to highlight the power dimension of literacy (Foucault 1969; Street 1996).

Finally, I would like to outline a project in South Africa called the Social Uses of Literacy, that rejects the autonomous approach and attempts to build a new conception of culture and development in the field of literacy (Prinsloo and Breier 1996). This project was based at the Universities of Cape Town, and of the Western Cape, which came together to research the actual meanings and uses of literacy on the ground prior to the development of policy. As an anthropologist this seems to me a truism, but I keep being naively astonished to discover that development is often done the other way round; the policy on, say, adult education and literacy is developed without reference to research on what people are doing with literacy.

The programme is quite challenging in the context of the needs for redress, reconstruction, and redevelopment in South Africa at the moment. There are large numbers of people without any schooling; the apartheid state marginalised and ignored them, and the new government needs to quickly get things in place to help them. It needs to develop an adult literacy policy and adult education policy. It is doing so very often on the basis of models derived from European countries. A lot of NGOs on the ground are concerned that the local nature of literacy teaching, literacy learning, and literacy practice may get lost in this central process. This research project has to be seen in terms of that current tension. The project involves a dozen or so researchers going into different sectors or domains of South Africa—Namaqualand; rural areas; Marconi Been; a settlement in Cape Town; among taxi drivers in Cape Town; Belleville South, a coloured settlement; and Site 5, where people had been forcefully uprooted and settled, and then tried to make a kind of living and develop resources. The researchers also did some study on the ways in which a mass electoral process could be successfully implemented for a population without majority literacy.

Different sites were chosen on the premise, contradicting that of dominant educational and development discourse, that literacy means different things in different contexts, and that if you are designing literacy programmes you may have to design them differently according to where people are. I will give one example of what this might mean. A Xhosa-speaking woman called Elizabeth on Site 5 has been working for the last decade to create resources in the settlement such as paved roads and running water. In her house she has lots of different documents; she has worked with and across and around documents; she goes to meetings all the time. Some of those documents are in English, some in Xhosa. It is probably doubtful whether she would pass many exams in literacy in either of those languages or literacies, but she used them effectively in political action for the last decade, with meetings and pressure groups, to get these things done in the settlement. Now in the new dispensation, the ANC is setting up classes for local people to give them literacy, while at the same time there is a new bureaucratised hierarchy of relationship between local people and the local state. In this context Elizabeth has now become marginalised; with respect to educational institutions, she is told she is illiterate, her children laugh at her and say, "You're illiterate, you must go to classes." She goes to classes, and the classes employ neo-Freireian discourse which involves not contestation but rote repetition of syllables—*bah-be-bo.* The class all chant it. So Elizabeth is sitting there finding it not much help in relation to her political practice. Likewise, with respect to the new political institutions, meetings have now been taken over by besuited men who are speaking in English, and Elizabeth sits at the back in silence. So she is being marginalised and silenced in both domains. Ironically, she is being made illiterate by the arrival of the literacy class and silenced by the arrival of democracy.

So the question the researchers are posing to the ANC and to the organisers of adult literacy practices in South Africa (and elsewhere) is: What kind of literacy class or support, not just necessarily classes, might one provide for someone like Elizabeth, to enable her to enhance the skills she has already got, to build on what she is doing and what she has done for the last ten years, and not to marginalise her and treat her as nothing? Good pedagogy, according to these researchers and practitioners, builds upon where people are and acknowledges the contestation involved in change both for the learners and the facilitators. There are an increasing number of examples like this that are currently being documented in different parts of the world (Hornberger 1997; Street 1995).

If one looks closely at contemporary literacy programmes in the light of some of the conceptual tools I have been putting forward here, I would argue that you would find the dominant, the majority, subscribing to the autonomous model of literacy and to the fixed, "race" model of culture, and just a few here and there beginning to talk about local cultural processes and local literacies. The practical implications of such a shift are immense, ranging from the need for educators to take account of local meanings before designing programmes and curricula, to the importance of developers noting local variation in beliefs and practices before introducing Western-oriented health, agricultural, and economic programmes. The relationship between these cultural processes, including literacy practices, on the one hand and economic processes and change on the other, represent the central theme of this book. I hope that this article has contributed to some elaboration of the former and it now remains to pursue in greater depth its implications for the latter.

REFERENCES

Anderson, C.A., and M. Bowman, eds. 1966. *Education and Economic Development.* London: Frank Cass.

Asad, T. 1980. "Anthropology and the Analysis of Ideology." *Man*, 14: 607–627.

Banton, M. 1967. *Race Relations*. London: Tavistock.

Banton, M., and J. Harwood. 1975. *The Race Concept*. London: David and Charles.

Barton, D., and R. Ivanic, eds. 1991. *Writing In The Community*. London: Sage.

Barzun, J. 1937. *Race—A Study in Superstition*. New York: Harper and Row.

Besnier, N. 1988. "The Linguistic Relationship of Spoken and Written Nukulaelae Registers." *Language* 64(4): 707–736.

Besnier, N., and B. Street. 1994. "Aspects of Literacy." *Companion Encyclopedia of Anthropology*, ed. T. Ingold. London: Routledge.

Burrow, J. 1966. *Evolution and Society*. Cambridge: Cambridge University Press.

Cairns, H. 1965. *Prelude to Imperialism*. Oxford: Oxford University Press.

Camitta, M. 1993. "Vernacular Writing: Varieties of Literacy among Philadelphia High School Students." In *Cross-Cultural Approaches to Literacy*, ed. B. Street. Cambridge: Cambridge University Press.

Clifford, J. 1988. *The Predicament of Culture*. Cambridge, MA: Harvard University Press.

Curtin, P. 1965. *The Image of Africa*. London: Macmillan.

Fairclough, N. 1992. *Discourse and Social Change*. London: Polity Press.

Foucault, M. 1969. "What Is an Author?" In *The Foucault Reader* (1984), ed. P. Rabinow. London: Penguin Books.

Gates, L. Jr., ed. 1986. *"Race," Writing and Difference*. Chicago: University of Chicago Press.

Gee, J. 1991. *Social Linguistics: Ideology in Discourses*. London: Falmer Press.

Gilroy, P. 1987. *There Ain't No Black in the Union Jack*. London: Hutchinson.

Gilroy, P. 1990. "The End of Anti-Racism." In *Race and Local Politics*, eds. W. Ball and J. Solomos. Basingstoke: Macmillan.

Greene, J. 1954. "Some Early Speculations on the Origins of the Human Races." *American Anthropologist* 56(1): 31–41.

Heath, S.B. 1983. *Ways with Words*. Cambridge: Cambridge University Press.

Hodgen, M. 1964. *Early Anthropology in the 16th and 17th Centuries*. Philadelphia: University of Pennsylvania Press.

Hornberger, N., ed. 1997. *Language Planning from the Bottom Up: Indigenous Literacies in the Americas*. Berlin: Mouton de Gruyter.

Irvine, W. 1955. *Apes, Angels and Victorians*. London: Readers' Union.

Kiernan, V.G. 1969. *The Lords of Human Kind*. London: Wiedenfeld & Nicholson.

Kulick, D., and C. Stroud. 1993. "Conceptions and Uses of Literacy in a Papua New Guinean Village." In *Cross-Cultural Approaches to Literacy*, ed. B. Street. Cambridge: Cambridge University Press.

Lankshear, C. 1987. *Literacy, Schooling and Revolution*. London: Falmer Press.

Lyons, A. 1970. "The Genesis of Scientific Racism." *Journal of the Anthropological Society of Oxford* 1(2): 91–100.

MacKenzie, J. 1995. *Orientalism: History, Theory and the Arts*. Manchester: Manchester University Press.

Mitter, P. 1977. *Much-Maligned Monsters*. Chicago: University of Chicago Press.

Montague, A. 1964. *The Concept of Race*. London: Free Press.

Olson, D. 1994. *The World on Paper*. Cambridge: Cambridge University Press.

Prinsloo, M., and M. Breier, eds. 1996. *The Social Uses of Literacy*. Amsterdam: J. Benjamins.

Said, E. 1978. *Orientalism*. London: RKP.

Shuman, A. 1986. *Storytelling Rights: The Uses of Oral and Written Texts by Urban Adolescents*. Cambridge: Cambridge University Press.

Smith, B. 1960. *European Vision and the South Pacific*. Oxford: Clarendon Press.

Stepan, N. 1982. *The Idea of Race in Science*. London: Macmillan.

Stocking, G. 1968. *Race, Culture and Evolution*. London: Free Press.

Street, B. 1996. "Literacy and Power?" *Open Letter: Australian Journal for Adult Literacy Research and Practice* 6(2): 7–16.

Street, B. 1995. *Social Literacies: Critical Perspectives on Literacy in Development, Ethnography and Education*. London: Longman.

Street, B., ed. 1993a. *Cross-Cultural Approaches to Literacy*. Cambridge: Cambridge University Press.

Street, B. 1993b. "Culture Is a Verb." In *Language and Culture*, eds. D. Graddol, L. Thompson, and M. Byram. Clevedon: Multilingual Matters.

Street, B. 1992. "Representations and Images of 'Primitive' Peoples." In *The Colonial Viewfinder*, ed. E. Edwards. New Haven: Yale University Press.

Street, B. 1984. *Literacy in Theory and Practice*. Cambridge: Cambridge University Press.

Street, B. 1975. *The Savage in Literature*. London: RKP.

Thornton, R. 1988. "Culture: A Contemporary Definition." In *Keywords*, eds. E. Boonzaeir and J. Sharp. Cape Town: David Philip.

CHAPTER 4

Different Eyes

Schooling and Indigenous Education in Tonga

KONAI HELU-THAMAN

From the perspective of a person who has been educated in a small Pacific Island kingdom, culture is the way of life of a discrete group of people, which includes their language, a body of accumulated knowledge and skills, beliefs and values. Culture is central to understanding all human endeavours. Education can be understood as an introduction to worthwhile learning and in so doing a distinction can be made between formal, nonformal, and informal education. Formal education is organised and institutionalised worthwhile learning; nonformal education is organised but noninstitutionalised worthwhile learning; and informal education is unorganised and noninstitutionalised worthwhile learning.

My perception of culture is inclusive of the education system as well as of all the other "systems" which might be discernible in a particular society. Pacific peoples, variously described by Western scholars as Melanesian, Polynesian, and Micronesian, have their own cultures and associated cultural identities that they perceive to be unique. Their worldviews are closely linked to their *vanua/ples/fonua* concepts, which are inadequately translated to mean "land" or "place," but which embody social and spiritual as well as physical dimensions.

While the Pacific Island region is characterised by cultural diversity, the people share common colonial histories and hence, also the consequences of colonialism, whether it be French, English, or American. Formal education, such as Christianity, has been embraced by all Pacific Island nations as the main tool of modern development, yet it continues to reflect the tensions between Western and indigenous knowledge, values, and understandings, creating challenges to educators as well as development planners.

SCHOOLING AND CULTURAL CHANGE

The introduction of formal education in the last century meant that the dominant ideologies of the cultures of Europe (England and France in particular, and Australia, New Zealand, and the United States more recently) were introduced to Pacific societies through both the overt and the hidden curriculum. Early European missionaries, as well as colonial administrators, brought with them varying notions of education in their quest to civilise and convert Pacific Islanders and taught them to reject many aspects of Pacific cultures that were regarded as detrimental to the foreigners' purposes. Consequently, important aspects of Pacific cultural traditions, including those relating to learning and knowledge, as well as to subsistence living, were at best devalued and at worst destroyed. Goldsmith (1993, 285) is harsh in his description of the situation:

> The colonial powers sought to destroy the cultural patterns of traditional societies largely because many of their essential features prevented traditional people from subordinating social, ecological and spiritual imperatives to the short-term economic ends served by participation in the colonial economy. There is no better way of destroying a society than by undermining its educational system.

ECONOMIC DEVELOPMENT

The other legacy of formal education is well known; from primary to tertiary, education continues to be concerned mainly with training young people for a career in the urban/industrial sector and the cash economy. It is not concerned with cultural development. In the context of the Pacific Islands, there are several manifestations of this, not least of which is urban drift. Primary school leavers go to towns; secondary school leavers go to capital cities; and graduates of tertiary institutions choose to stay in the metropolitan countries where they received their education. Formal education, instead of providing Pacific Island societies with the means for cultural renewal, has provided them with a means of ensuring their cultural demise.

Since political independence in the 1960s and 1970s, Pacific Island leaders have looked to formal education as the main tool of economic development and the key to success in the global market economy. Island cultures are seen as having little contribution to make towards the achievement of monetary economic goals. Only those elements of these cultures which are regarded as potentially important for economic development are valued, such as some rituals, ceremonies, crafts, and certain types of performing arts. One of the unfortunate results of this is the increasing number of Pacific Islanders who are unable to renew themselves culturally. Many are doomed to become isolated and alienated in Pacific towns or metropolitan cities.

There are, however, other less visible signs of the impact of formal education on Pacific societies. One is the way it has changed peoples' notions of what constitutes education and the educated person. I wish to illustrate by reference to three basic Tongan educational ideas: *ako, 'ilo,* and *poto*. But first, a brief summary of the development of schools is offered.

SCHOOL LEARNING

Although societies differ as to what they might consider worthwhile to transmit to the young, most seem to share the view that education should aim at ensuring cultural continuation, transmitting knowledge, skills, and values from the mature to the immature, either informally through the social milieu or formally through the school (Gutek 1972, 11). Such worthwhile patterns and values of a culture are reflected in its language and the meanings it denotes or conveys. This is certainly true of Western European cultures.

In Tonga, as in most Pacific Island societies, schools developed not because the social organisation had become complex, as in Europe (Shipman 1971), but because European missionaries wanted to convert the Tongan people to Christianity and thus "civilise" them. Later, as the missions and colonial governments needed clerks, teachers, nurses, and other types of workers, the school came to serve the function of mobilising labour and providing for the needs of the colonial economy.

As in other indigenous island societies, most early Tongan education was informal and aimed at the continuation of the social order and the maintenance of the status quo, what Shipman called "cultural continuity" (Shipman 1971, 70). For over 3,000 years, education prepared Tongans for their societal roles, and kept their desires and knowledge within limits appropriate to their social position and environment. Where learning was organised, as in the case of the education of some members of the aristocracy, the values taught did not conflict with those of the wider society; in fact, they reflected the nature of that society. People were instructed in specific knowledge, skills, and (appropriate) behaviour that were deemed to be necessary for survival and cultural continuation.

The largely informal type of education was provided within the *'api* (household) and to some extent in the wider community of kinsfolk. This education was mainly effected through a variety of means such as myths, legends, poetry, song, proverbs, and some rituals, for example the *'inasi* (the annual presentation of first fruits to the Tu'i Tonga or "divine ruler"). However, this pragmatic approach to learning had to be broadened in order to accommodate the new knowledge and way of learning, that is, European knowledge gained from books and the institution of the school.

In the school, education was associated with "learning" those things that the missionaries considered important and worthwhile in line with their perceptions of what was good, pious, and economically productive. The emphasis of learning shifted from the here and now and the practical to the there and then and the abstract. As can be expected, there was a real conflict between the values promoted by the school and those of the students' home cultures. Such conflicts have continued to the present day, not only among a large proportion of students in Tonga but in other island communities as well, thus creating what Little calls the "learning gap" (Little 1990, 4). The Tongan values that underpinned traditional Tongan education included emphases on the supernatural, formal conformity, rank and authority, kinship relationships, *'ofa* (compassion), restrained behaviour, and *faka'apa'apa* (respect). Most of these were not the major concerns of school education.

TONGAN NOTIONS OF EDUCATION

One of the main aims of analysis is to seek clarification. In my study of Tongan educational concepts, cultural values, and teachers' role perceptions (Thaman 1988), I undertook an analysis of educational concepts that involved four simple tasks: examining the word in which the idea is expressed; examining how the word is used in different contexts; determining whether the meaning is educational or noneducational; and determining what the meaning implies or presupposes.

The terms *ako*, *'ilo*, and *poto* and their derivatives are commonly used within the context of Tongan education. Accepting that there was no one standard use of words in ordinary language and that some philosophers tend to stress certain uses rather than others (Langford 1973, 92), as many types of uses as possible for each term were identified (Thaman 1988, 172–205). Brief summaries follow for each of the three main terms mentioned above.

Ako

The earliest written reference to the meaning of "aco" (*sic*) was by Martin in 1827, who said it meant "to teach or to learn" (Martin 1827, lix). *Ako* was used to denote teaching and learning in a society where everyone was expected to perform certain roles in accordance with their various statuses, which were predetermined and expressed through a complicated network based largely on kinship relationships. A person learned mainly through observing, listening, and imitating others, and when the need arose, specific knowledge and skills were taught by those who were responsible for imparting them.

Current uses of *ako* provide some clues about the evolution of the use of the term and how social and cultural changes might have affected and broadened its meaning. Today *ako* is variously used to mean: to learn, to study, to practise, to receive instruction, the learning process, instruction, training, and the formal education system itself. A derivative of *ako* is *faiako*, used to refer to a teacher or instructor. (The prefix *fai* is commonly used to denote making something happen; in the case of *faiako* it implies making learning happen or bringing about learning.) *Faiako* is closely associated with formal education, since in informal contexts, people learn mainly through imitating, observing, and listening to those who possess desired skills and knowledge. Today, however, the term *faiako* is used almost exclusively to refer to a schoolteacher.

'Ilo

Koskinen (1968,12) claims that *'ilo* was used widely among Polynesian peoples to denote what he called "seeing." In Tonga, *'ilo* is used in a variety of ways; as a verb meaning to find, to recognise, to discover, to know, experience, or to understand; and as a noun meaning information or different types of knowledge and skills. We may say, therefore, that in Tonga, *'ilo* refers both to the process of knowing and knowledge itself.

Koskinen (1968, 26) also suggested that *'ilo* might be obtained naturally or through active searching, studying, and/or learning. Tongans distinguish between *'ilo* which is public and passed on from adults to young people and *'ilo* which is more restrictive and personal. To say that someone has *'ilo* is to imply that she or he has gone through a process of searching, learning, or studying. Hence *'ilo* may be said to be the end result or product of *ako* (learning).

Poto

Poto is the fundamental idea of Tongan education (see McCrae 1986, 125; and Thaman 1988, 195–205, for a detailed analysis). It appears that the precontact meaning of "boto" (*sic*) denoted skill or cleverness. Churchward suggested that the meaning of *poto* was "to be clever or skillful; to understand what to do and be able to do it" (Churchward, 1959, 125). Schneider, a linguist, agrees. Among his suggested meaning are knowledgeable, intelligent, wise, clever, and skillful (Schneider 1977, 60).

Like most Tongan terms, *poto* is used in a variety of ways and contexts. In relation to educational uses, various types of *poto* states are often identified, such as *atamai poto* (intelligent), *nima poto* (clever hands), and *anga poto* (appropriate behaviour). Mamae'apoto, a well-known poet, used *poto* to denote using one's knowledge and skills to survive difficult conditions, such as when encountering an enemy (Colcott 1928, 125). In such situations, one definitely had to know what to do and be able to do it well; in short, one had to be *poto*.

RELATIONSHIP BETWEEN *AKO*, *'ILO*, AND *POTO*

Poto in the context of *ako* (Tongan education) is achieved through the appropriate use of *'ilo* (knowledge), that is, its positive application. The educated person, therefore, is one who applies *'ilo* with positive and successful results. Kavaliku referred to the educated person or *poto* as "a man (*sic*) of wisdom, an ideal, a thing of value" (Kavaliku 1966, 13). One who is not *poto* is *vale*; she or he cannot apply *'ilo* (knowledge) positively. *'Ilo* therefore may be said to be a precondition of *poto*, but it is through its positive application that one becomes *poto*.

Over the past 100 years, the school has come to be closely associated with all three concepts. It has been regarded as the major source of *'ilo* and hence *poto*. Most students would say that the purpose of schooling is to become *poto*. Formerly, in order to become *poto* one had to learn to read, write, and perform simple arithmetic. By the turn of the century those who were successful in school, judged by the passing of various examinations, were known as the *kau poto* (the educated ones). *Poto* was thus reconceptualised to include the new type of learning carried out in schools.

The reconceptualisation of *poto* did not go unnoticed. In 1931 for instance, Havea, a well-known schoolmaster and a *poto* person, compared the old and the new meaning of *poto* in a poem in which readers were reminded of the passing of the (old) meaning of *poto,* which was rooted in the value of maintaining good relations and helping one another, and was not related to attending school (Havea 1931, 3).

In my study (Thaman 1988) I found that the majority of Tongan teachers believed that the school was a place where children could become *poto*. Most also emphasised the need for students to use the *'ilo* (knowledge) gained in school wisely, especially to help others, whether in the family or community or nation. One teacher put it aptly: "What is the use of a degree if a person is only looking at herself?" (Tu'itupou 1981, personal communication). Modern education, therefore, is valued in Tonga not so much because it is a human right or that it is good in itself, but because it is seen as a means of acquiring knowledge and skills necessary to find jobs that pay well and help Tongans fulfil their social obligations within the various groups in which they interact. This, of course, is a utilitarian view of education, but it is consistent with Tongan perceptions of the purpose of education—to become *poto*, to be able to learn what to do and do it well.

Given the above, it is perhaps important to begin to question the value underpinning modern education that emphasises the dominant paradigm of scientific materialism and individual achievement. Beare and Slaughter (1994, 59–61) have suggested that the scientific-industrial worldview that has dominated education in the Western world for the past 300 years is now questionable, even for Western societies. However, most Pacific schools and tertiary institutions continue to promote a scientific-industrial view, where indigenous holistic views yield to the reductionist view in which knowledge has to be compartmentalised and only people with specialised knowledge can teach it in schools (Beare and Slaughter 1994, 60). For too long Pacific educators have promoted and continue to promote such a view, characterised by an overemphasis on individual gain and competition and not necessarily on maintaining good relationships; where the status of schools and teachers are judged by the number of students who pass external examinations and not whether such learning relates to their cultures. What is ironic, perhaps, is the fact that most Tongan teachers had perceived their role to be the nurturing of Tongan values and teaching appropriate Tongan *'ulungaanga* (behaviour) (Thaman 1988, 223–225).

Despite the fact that formal education is premised on a Western industrial and scientific worldview, most teachers do not fully appreciate the nature and/or meaning of the scientific paradigm nor its manifestations. Today, in the Pacific Islands in general and in Tonga in particular, people may be aware of the impact of formal education on their economic and political developments, and even their ecosystems, but its impact on themselves as individuals and as unique cultural groups, particularly on their labour and their minds, is less understood and certainly not well documented.

CONCLUSION

There is no doubt that formal education has greatly affected Tongan indigenous notions of education, as it has other aspects of Tongan life. This is inevitable. What is perhaps unfortunate is the fact that many Pacific educators have failed to appreciate the tensions between the values underpinning the education that they have been providing and those of the cultures that they and their students share. There is a need for all teachers today to critically examine the (Western) social-psychological theories and philosophies that have informed their work in schools and other institutions of learning. For example, theories which rely on a biological model of interaction and a view of a person as comprising a distinct, physically bounded, and genetically determined self-actualising individual (Strauss 1977) are in conflict with the view that is still prevalent in most Pacific Island societies: that of a person defined through his or her placement in particular social settings (Linnekin and Poyer 1990, 7).

Pacific Island educators need to examine more closely their different indigenous notions of education in order to better enable them to bring about the kind of synthesis required of the old and the new, thus bringing about the kinds of educational change that incorporate those values that have helped nurture Pacific cultures for millennia; values which may go a long way toward counteracting the forces of globalisation (which in the context of the Pacific Islands means a revisit of Western capitalist/imperialistic forces), and thus assist Pacific people to maintain to some extent their cultural uniqueness and identities.

REFERENCES

Beare, H., and Slaughter, R. 1994. *Education for the Twenty-first Century*. London: Routledge.

Churchward, C.M. 1959. *Tongan Dictionary*. London: Oxford University Press.

Colcott, E.E.V. 1928. *Tales and Poems of Tonga*. Bulletin 46. Honolulu: Bishop Museum.

Goldsmith, E. 1993. *The Way: An Ecological World View*. Boston: Shambhala.

Gutek, G.L. 1972. *History of Western Educational Experience*. New York: Random House.

Havea, S. 1931. "Ko e Mau kuo fakapale'i." *Tohi Fanongonongo* 4 (1): 3.

Kavaliku, S.L. 1966. "Educational Reorganisation for National Development in Tonga." Unpublished Ph.D. thesis, Victoria University, Wellington.

Koskinen, A.A. 1968. *Kite: Polynesian Insight into Knowledge*. Helsinki: FSME.

Langford, G. 1973. "The Concept of Education." In *New Essays in the Philosophy of Education*, eds. G. Langford and D.J. O'Connor. London: Routledge.

Linnekin, J., and Poyer, L., eds. 1990. *Cultural Identity and Ethnicity in the Pacific*. Honolulu: University of Hawaii Press.

Little, A. 1990. "Understanding Culture: A Precondition for Effective Learning." Special Study for the UNESCO World Conference on Education for All, Thailand.

Martin, J. 1827. *An Account of the Natives of Tonga Islands in the South Pacific Ocean*, Vol. 2. London: Constable and Company.

McRae, C.J. 1986. "Problems in Educational Development in the Kingdom of Tonga." Unpublished Ph.D. thesis, University of London Institute of Education, London.

Schneider, T. 1977. *Functional Tongan-English, English-Tongan Dictionary*. Suva: Oceania Printers.

Shipman, M.D. 1971. *Education and Modernisation*. London: Faber and Faber.

Strauss, A.L. 1977. *Mirrors and Masks: The Search for Identity*. London: Martin Robinson.

Tu'itupou, L. 1981. Personal Communication. Nuku'alofa, Tonga.

Thaman, K. 1988. "Ako and Faiako: Educational Concepts, Cultural Values and Teacher Role Perceptions in Tonga." Unpublished Ph.D. thesis, University of the South Pacific, Suva.

PART II

The Economic and Cultural Goals of Development: Whose Goals Matter?

CHAPTER 5

Learning versus Development

A Palestinian Perspective

MUNIR FASHEH

ON DEVELOPMENT, EDUCATION, AND LEARNING

The challenges of the real world that are of greatest human concern are far messier, more complex, more ambiguous and uncertain, and more unpredictable than the problems that educational institutions, development agencies, educators, and development experts are, in general, able and ready to tackle or want us to believe are important and crucial. Such challenges may include: balancing economic growth with spiritual values (such as respecting nature and the value of every human being); balancing freedom with justice; balancing individual growth with community interests; protecting children and youth from the "junk culture" that is invading the world; cultivating wisdom and not only knowledge; dealing with the fragmentation at the individual, family, and community levels; managing limited natural resources such as water; balancing urgent needs with long-term interests; connecting thought with action; seeing the "whole picture" rather than being drowned in the flood of detailed information; and keeping hope and faith alive in the face of current disastrous trends and increasing absurdities.

Such complex needs and problems obviously require a completely different set of abilities, skills, and attitudes than those usually taught in schools and universities. This does not mean that schools and universities do not have a role to play in addressing these issues but, rather, that their role has to be more honestly related to the *real* world and to people's *real* needs.

Formal education with its ready-made curricula, its standardized tests and measures, its stress on competition more than cooperation, its fragmentation of knowledge, its equation of teaching with telling and learning with recalling, its separation of means from ends, theory from action, and research from implementation, and its perception of knowledge as value-free, culture-free, and context-free is an education ill-equipped to deal with the problems of greatest human concern that people experience in their daily lives, such as those referred to earlier.

Development, at least since World War II, has been the grand "dream" which controlled the discourse, the conceptions, and the actions of many academicians, community workers, and policy makers, especially in the so-called Third World. The dream, however, has turned out to be a false hope. In fact, it has been the Trojan horse through which societies have been dismantled, diversity killed, and global monopolies allowed to flourish. In short, development, like education, has moved in many people's minds from being a saviour into being a false messiah.

In order to deal with the real problems in the world today and to create a viable and human response to the trends towards chaos, dismemberment, dependency, hypocrisy, control, greed, destruction, and insecurity, and to the monopolies that dominate the world today, a shift of mind is needed. Central to this shift of mind is learning.

Learning embodies acquiring abilities at a less visible but more fundamental level than is offered through schooling: reflective writing, working and dialoguing within teams, constructing meaning and understanding, having a vision, obtaining necessary information, and recognizing thinking patterns that control our words and behaviour as well as our perceptions of other people's words and behaviour. Learning also embodies a vision which revolves around respecting nature and the human body, as well as embodying a strategy which revolves around planting "seeds" for the future and finding leverages that help shake and build at the same time.

DEVELOPMENT WITHIN THE PALESTINIAN CONTEXT

The Palestinian tragedy started with the British mandate early this century. Today, at the end of the century, the World Bank is given a new "mandate" over Palestine, to finish, seemingly, the job of dismantling the social, economic, and cultural fabric of Palestinian society and moving it further along the tragic path of increasing dependency, fragmentation, and debt. The development plans currently imposed on Palestinians avoid talking about natural resources (such as land and water); ignore completely cultural resources (such as the Arabic language, the Arab family, the Arab-Islamic civilization with all its diversity and richness); and ignore crucial human treasures (such as people's experiences and expressions). Dominant development plans have no room for dreams, visions, and values (such as spirituality, wisdom, cultural production, respecting nature and the human body, and having community feelings, compassion, and love for one another). They suppress seeing the whole picture, whether in terms of seeing the New World Order with its alliances, monopolies,[1] policies, and strategies or in terms of finding new points of departure or leverages for creating a human response. Development plans currently imposed on the Palestinians avoid talking about the increasing restrictions on movement and access to relevant information, where such movement and access are crucial for the healthy growth of individuals and the community. It is difficult to speak of the development of Palestinians when access to Jerusalem is forbidden for Palestinians living in the West Bank and the Gaza Strip; it is like talking about the development of England and closing London off to the English living around it! Just like London for the English, Jerusalem is the heart of the Palestinian economy, culture, and information as well as the center of social, recreational, and religious activities. It is worth mentioning also that the World Bank refuses to engage in any project within Arab Jerusalem, an area which was extended by Israel to comprise, geographically speaking, a big portion of the West Bank, and which is still internationally recognized as occupied Palestinian land. Moreover, it is difficult to speak of the development of Palestinians while we have no access to any water resources (except rainfall).

One can summarise the Palestinian situation today as a continuation of confiscation of land and water, denial of rights and lack of protection, as well as continued dehumanization. These have been at the root of the problem since the inception of Israel. We cannot hope for a lasting solution and for a better future for everybody without dealing with these issues.

DEVELOPMENT: A SUBTLE AND EFFECTIVE FORM OF CONTROL

In February 1948, George Kennan, then a senior official in the U.S. State Department, wrote of the United States:

> We have about 50 percent of the world's wealth but only 6 percent of its population. . . . Our real task in the coming period is to devise a pat-

> tern of relationships which will permit us to maintain this position of disparity without positive detriment to our national security. To do so, we will have to dispense with all sentimentality and daydreaming; and our attention will have to be concentrated everywhere on our immediate national objective. We need not deceive ourselves that we can afford today the luxury of altruism and world benefaction. We should cease to talk about vague and . . . unreal objectives such as human rights, the raising of living standards, and democratization. The day is not far when we are going to deal in straight power concepts.[2]

Kennan was fired immediately, not because his statement was criminal, but because he failed, it seems, to internalize the hypocrisy which was needed to carry on the job.

The power of colonial rulers has steadily declined since the end of World War II. However, the control of resources and markets continues, mainly through development discourse, plans, policies, and projects. Although development is always presented as if it were a neutral idea, driven by good intentions and noble aims, and supported by "scientific and statistical studies," it has been the Trojan horse through which our minds have been conquered.

The development business has survived throughout the past 50 years by continuously shifting from one theme or "fad" to another. As soon as one fad ran its course and turned "sour," that is, turned into a crisis and reached a dead end, another was created. The fads that the World Bank has used since its establishment have followed more or less the following sequence: social progress with economic growth; rural development; unemployment and inequality; eradication of poverty; fighting ignorance and hunger; meeting basic needs; environmental and ecological concerns; advancement of women and human rights; civil society and democracy; institutional development; social development; and, finally, development for peace. Other terms that have been in use in recent years include: human-centred development, sustainable development, empowerment, strengthening institutional capacity, and so on. What was the role of "experts" in all of this? Development experts were experts in turning a crisis into a problem, devising a new strategy to resolve it, and assigning themselves to the new jobs, at least until the next development crisis appeared.

Determining priorities, choosing and defining terms, stressing certain problems, imposing certain solutions and deciding who is allowed to implement them, are all forms of control that are more subtle and less visible, but are more effective and go much deeper and stay much longer than more overt forms. The Chinese discovered controlling people's minds and perceptions through the choice of words and determining their meanings more than 3,000 years ago when they said, "He who defines the terms wins the argument." Controlling the meaning of words such as development, underdevelopment, progress, poverty, human rights, violence, democracy, terrorism, and intellectual and moral superiority has played a crucial part in determining our perceptions, priorities, and the options in our imaginations. When civilisations as rich as those of China and Egypt are measured along the path of progress in terms of a single number such as per capita income, or when a family that lives happily and produces all that it needs is considered below the poverty line, it is very hard to imagine a worse distortion and hypocrisy in controlling human beings and human communities and determining the direction they should follow. It is very hard to imagine a more criminal act in killing diversity in human life and controlling resources and markets. Contracting some individuals, with indigenous names and looks and high formal credentials, to legitimise policies and plans is a practice central to this hypocrisy.

The claim that the goal of development is to raise the standard of living of people (another phrase commonly used by developers) is usually translated in practice into drinking Coca-Cola instead of water, watching TV instead of conversing with family members and friends or playing with one's children, eating junk food instead of fruit and vegetables, caring for symbolic gains instead of ways that sustain life and enjoying what it naturally provides, running after individual wants rather than community needs, and being satisfied with small expectations instead of having visions and dreams that sustain life; in short, becoming better consumers of junk goods, junk information, junk entertainment, and junk interactions. At the deeper level, "raising the standard of living" is translated into dismantling our society and ignoring (often degrading) our civilisation and culture. What characterises development and the occupation of minds is not so much the imposing of a certain model as preventing our ways of living, thinking, and relating to one another and to nature from surviving and flourishing.

Another subtle form of control and of determining outcomes is stressing changes and improvements at the symbolic, superficial, or technical level while allowing conditions to deteriorate at a deeper and more real level. Building universities that are not involved in the creation of knowledge (in its broad and diverse sense) is one example. Establishing governing or administrative bodies (which is happening right now in Palestine) that have no resources, no information, and no power to make decisions over fundamental issues is another example. The West Bank and Gaza are currently flooded with programmes to upgrade institutional development and managerial skills, none of which takes learning as an integral part of that development. These programs are being undertaken by UN agencies, European and North American government and non-government organisations, and donor agencies. The construction boom taking place right now in some cities in the Gaza strip and the West Bank (which does not reflect economic activity or production) is a third example.

A third form of subtle control that development plans often use is limiting the options and alternatives in people's minds. Schools, for example, severely limit our imagination and sense of possibilities in the field of education and learning. In most societies today (especially in Third World countries), schools almost completely monopolise the resources allocated to education and learning. Building learning centres for teachers (and other adults), experimenting with innovative ideas and projects, building communication networks among people, establishing facilities that increase people's access to relevant information (such as libraries), all belong to the broad area of education and learning, and yet they hardly receive any attention or resources (or even recognition). Moreover, many, under the drug of schooling, have forgotten that conversation, walking, reading, writing, playing, and doing, form some of the most wonderful ways of learning. Most of us cannot think of an alternative to the extremely wasteful, rigid, and ineffective education system that takes up a decade or so of a young person's life.

A fourth means of controlling minds, determining outcomes, and killing diversity has been the dominance of linear thinking and technological rationality. This is linked to the almost fanatical adherence to technique (with its emphasis on such values and norms as control, distancing, precision, neutrality, and objectivity); and to the various forms of "separation" which plague people's perceptions and practices (separating knowing from doing, means from ends and consequences, and theory and research from practice and implementation). Science and mathematics, as they have been perceived and practised, play a central role in this form of control[3] (cf. Chapters 15 and 16).

A fifth form of control is television. A television permanently occupying a corner (or corners) in one's home is much worse than a soldier occupying that same home. A soldier is never invited, welcomed, or paid to enter homes. A television is welcomed with open arms and is often paid for with needed and scarce money. In addition, the harm of the soldier is obvious and his control is limited to some visible forms. The harm of television is subtle and far-reaching. It slowly robs us of our health, money, time, sense of existence and belonging, and sense of surroundings. It invites the whole world into our homes and expels our families. Moreover, television, like schools, helps in producing conformity and kills diversity and richness in human life and communities.

These subtle forms are part of the slow but far-reaching dangers in today's world. Coca-Cola does not kill you instantly. And development is, at best, similar to unnecessary antibiotics: it may make things feel better for a short period but, in the long term, it slowly kills the natural immune system (i.e., the internal strength) that exists in human beings, communities, and cultures, leaving them susceptible to all kinds of "diseases." A statement issued by the All Africa Conference of Churches marking the 50th anniversary of the World Bank and IMF and launching the movement "Fifty years is enough" carries these words: "Every child in Africa is born with a financial burden which a lifetime's work cannot repay. The debt is a new form of slavery as vicious as the slave trade."[4]

To summarise, development, like any other major ideology or world view, rests on a certain "mythology" with some basic myths, assumptions, or beliefs. One set of myths suggests that:

- Development assumes that progress moves along a specific linear path controlled mainly by technical experts and implemented by trained professionals; a path along which societies are judged in comparison to others.
- There is a direction, a single progressive track, to be followed by all peoples and societies.
- There are developed nations and underdeveloped nations and it is the duty of the former to assist the latter.
- Progress is the result of planned action.
- Education is the key to development.
- There is a sense of universality embedded in development, which gives the "right" to "experts" to impose it on peoples around the world.
- Development usually starts with the assumption that people are the problem, and it usually stresses what societies lack and ignores the richness and wisdom that they have.
- Development is built on a concept and practice of science that embody contradictions detrimental to the creation of meaningful knowledge and to the healthy growth of human societies.[5]

- Development usually focuses on visible and usually superficial, if not even harmful, changes and ignores those less visible and more fundamental.

It is exactly these beliefs, characteristics, and forms of control which make me believe that development cannot be compatible with fostering human life or with nature's "wisdom." Development in the way it has been practised has all too often been like trying to put legs on a snake, something which is both unnatural and undesirable.

In short, talking about alternative development is like talking about alternative Coca-Cola: the problem is in development and not in the brand or adjective attached to it. The disease has been in the medicine prescribed. The dream was really a nightmare. We seem to be reaching the end of the tunnel. Development is a dying concept, even within the circles that created and benefited from it. The real dangers and trends we face today are common to all societies; they endanger human communities and the human race as a whole. Pollution of both human and physical nature is taking place everywhere. What children and youth are exposed to today (such as drugs, guns, junk food, junk information, junk relationships, and junk entertainment) and the basic needs they lack (such as human warmth, compassion, deep communication with others, feelings of security, etc.) are becoming increasingly prevalent in most societies. A new vision is obviously needed.

Once we admit that development is a bankrupt idea, we are on our way to building a saner and happier world. The basic need is to start talking about a whole new way of perceiving the world, new terminology and meanings that are more in tune with current realities and needs, new priorities and relationships, new values and beliefs, and new "mythology" and attitudes.

A short poem depicting the wisdom of the Cree Indians in Canada aptly and concisely captures what I want to say:

When the last tree is cut down
the last river poisoned
the last fish caught,
then only will man discover
that he cannot eat money.[6]

WHAT IS THE ALTERNATIVE TO DEVELOPMENT?

Proposing a full-fledged and ready alternative is contrary to life, to human communities, and to the spirit of this paper. In matters related to human life and human communities, prescribing such a solution is inappropriate, even harmful. What I will do here, therefore, is point to some guiding principles and some "seeds" that I see as both appropriate and "ripe." The key ideas or seeds in building a new vision and a more human and viable alternative are learning and respecting the human body and nature. Creating learning environments in harmony with the human body and spirit and with nature is the basis for building a saner world.

The basic convictions in building such an alternative, thus, are:

1. People are the solution and not the problem; that is, people are the creators and not the receivers of alternative visions.
2. Creating learning environments is the strategy; that is, we should stress means rather than the provision of ready-made products and solutions.
3. Respecting human and physical nature is the basis for creating a saner and more sustainable world.

Those convictions embody a spiritual dimension within them. Life within this vision revolves around the relationship of people to people rather than of people to manufactured things, as is the case in current development thinking and practice. Two thousand years ago a Palestinian with the name of Jesus Christ articulated this spiritual dimension and these convictions, and built his "way," on two simple principles: "man cannot live by bread alone" and "love one another." Another man from the same region, with the name of Muhammad, articulated a third principle, *al-ijtihad*, which means making an effort to understand in the light of current conditions whatever is presented to us; in other words, it puts the responsibility on the individual to reflect and understand. I do not see why these same principles cannot be part of our guide for an alternative vision today—at least for us as Arabs.

One important aspect of building an alternative to development is to stop the mind and rational planning from overriding and overruling the body and nature, and ignoring or abusing them. (In this sense, emotional development, in contrast to only intellectual and physical development, is central.) It is important to respect the wisdom of the body and of nature at least as much as the wisdom of the mind. Mind and language can create verbal worlds and mental empires that completely ignore, distort, or destroy the real world. Mind and language have to be contextualized and driven by a dream which respects nature and the body. Respecting nature is the basis of respecting other human beings, including future generations.

The "raw material" in building learning environments is people's experiences and their creative and honest expressions of these experiences. Reflective writing of individual and shared experiences is the basis for meaningful learning, for revitalizing culture, for producing culturally, and for ensuring diversity, creativity, freedom, and communication. Reflective writing of personal experiences is a fundamental activity in integrating language, thinking, and doing. It is the basis of building new meanings and understandings (i.e., knowledge). This is done through dialogue within small groups sharing a common experience or engaging in a common activity and working within a common vision, and who write reflectively about their experiences. An integral part of the work of any team is learning how to tackle thinking patterns that determine our actions and our understanding as well as our perceptions of others. All of these form the basic components of learning environments.

Unlike ending the occupation of our lands (which is characterised by whom we are against), ending the occupation of our minds is characterised by asserting who we are. We assert who we are not by verbal declarations but through daily practices: in our conversations, dialogues, interactions, leisure activities, cultural expressions, and cultural products. A people that does not produce culturally and intellectually ends up being dependent, wasteful, disintegrated, and unable to deal with its needs and challenges. Ending the occupation of our minds means rediscovering ourselves, our voices, and the internal strength in our people and our communities. It means seeing the value of our experiences and our culture. It means revitalizing again our ways of solidarity, community bonding, and the various forms of mutual help. It means ending fragmentation, factionalism, cultural dependency, and competing with one another over small and symbolic gains. It means refusing to fall victim to the patterns of perception and behaviour that work against us. It means being honestly and authentically ourselves; for Palestinians, feeling happy and proud of being Arabs and disregarding the racist and poisonous messages that American TV, journalists, academicians, and experts try to spread around the world against Arabs and Muslims. Ending the occupation of our minds means defining ourselves as Palestinians, as Arabs, and not as underdeveloped or as developing. Ending the occupation of our minds, however, also means seeing the real needs and weaknesses in ourselves and doing something about them.

MANIFESTATIONS OF THE ALTERNATIVE: THE HUMAN CULTURAL ECONOMIC LINK

In many instances, being a visionary does not mean seeing something in the distant future but, rather, seeing something that is there but made invisible. If we look with a magnifier, so to speak, at the reality of the Palestinians today, we clearly see that the solution lies within. The only long-term investment lies in the human treasure (mainly children and youth) and the cultural treasure. Under the prevailing conditions, where Palestinians are denied control over their natural resources and offered only loans to live on, our only hope lies in revitalizing these two treasures. Cultural products and cultural producers should, and could, be the basis of our economy. We have almost all the ingredients necessary to excel in this type of production. Such products and producers are much harder to destroy, they are built on what we have, and they do not produce a spiral increase of debt, which current development plans are designed to do.

As for revitalizing teaching in schools, we can, and should, depend on what we have rather than on expensive and ineffective experts and on big budgets and big plans. In our case, and in the light of the above discussion, writing can form the pivotal skill in revitalizing teaching in schools, and at a very minimal cost. I am talking about writing here as a reflective process that combines several aspects of the reality which one lives: cultural, social, psychological, and mental. I am talking about writing within groups or teams as a process that links expression with thought and action and, thus, is crucial in constructing knowledge and seeing holistic "maps" of what is happening. Writing could be very effective in combining the teaching of an academic discipline with other disciplines as well as with experiences, events, and phenomena related to learners. In addition, it is an important source of producing primary information. It forms a convenient way of articulating shared visions as well as discovering thought patterns that control our behaviours and perceptions. In short, writing could be very effective in creating the components of a learning environment as articulated above, a process which depends mostly on our own efforts rather than on big budgets and plans. Moreover, language in the Arab culture is pivotal; most Arabic arts, for example, are related to the Arabic language and to geometric designs.

THE EXAMPLE OF A SMALL INSTITUTION: THE TAMER INSTITUTE FOR COMMUNITY EDUCATION

The Tamer Institute is a Palestinian nonprofit organization which was established in Jerusalem in 1989 as a natural and necessary response to the needs and realities of the Palestinian community. Its philosophy and work revolve around creating learning environments, working mainly with youth, and producing culturally. This is crucial for the healthy growth of individuals and for building community.

Both individual growth and community building take place at two levels: the visible and mainly technical level, and the less visible and mainly "growth" learning level. Much of the effort thus far in helping Palestinian society survive in the face of systematic attempts to destroy it has focused on the visible level, such as relief and service activities and building factories and schools. All of these are important, but without building at the more fundamental but less visible level, what we build at other levels will eventually fall apart. An analogy with trees is helpful here. We see the visible part of a tree, we enjoy its branches, its shade, the sound and colours of its leaves, its delicious fruit, and so forth. But all of this is possible only if we nurture its roots, the invisible part. This is exactly what we try to do at the Tamer Institute in relation to individuals and groups.[7]

CONCLUSION

One way to begin creating an alternative that is in tune with the above "mythology" is to start telling our own stories and encourage others to tell theirs. In a very short time, we will have a wealth of information reflecting the human spirit and the cultural treasures that peoples and communities have, as well as reflecting the connectedness that exists among ordinary peoples everywhere. By telling our stories in each community we help enhance that community; and by telling our stories across countries and cultures, we help build a world community. Moreover, telling stories helps us to live in the real world again (as opposed to the ideological world to which most of us are exposed daily through mass media and official systems), as well as helping us formulate a common vision and create learning environments, in the sense discussed in this paper.

Telling our own stories honestly, and trying to knit them within a coherent whole, is a creative act. It is constructive, it integrates language with thinking and action, and it usually embodies great truths. Telling stories is very effective in preserving diversity and combatting hegemony, with all its myths and in all its forms.

Telling stories is as beautiful as the flourishing of the wild flowers in the Palestinian landscape in the spring. Since I was a little boy, I have always been fascinated by how thousands of flowers—of all kinds, colours, and shapes—grow next to each other, with no one trying to control or suppress others. The beauty of each is enhanced by being a whole in itself and at the same time part of a larger whole. There is always enough room for all. Our main role today is to try or protect our human flowers from the bulldozers that are trying to crush them in the name of progress and development. Helping human beings and communities to flourish is the central challenge we face today.

NOTES

[1] According to Samir Amin, the New World Order is characterised by five monopolies: flow of information, flow of capital, natural resources, lethal weapons, and new technologies. Amin, S. "Globalisation and Polarisation" (paper presented at a conference on Arab NGOs, organized by the Arab Resource Collective in Cyprus, 8–10 April 1994).

[2] P. 223 in Gaddis, *Strategies of Containment*, pp. 226–227. Source: Foreign Relations of the United States 1948, I (part 2) pp. 523–526, February 1948.

[3] For further details concerning the characteristics of the dominant model in education and science, see Fasheh, 1990. "Community Education: To Reclaim and Transform What Has Been Made Invisible," *Harvard Educational Review* 56 (1): 19–35.

[4] "Fifty Years is Enough." Factsheet produced by the Inter-Church Coalition on Africa (a Canadian ecumenical coalition of eight national churches in Canada): Toronto.

[5] For more details concerning the role of the dominant model in science and research, see Argyris, C. 1980. *Inner Contradictions of Rigorous Research*. San Fransisco: Jossey-Bass.

[6] This wisdom is taken from a Swedish book, 1993. *I denna Vida Varld*. Stockholm: En Bok for Alla.

[7] For more details concerning the philosophy and work of the Tamer Institute, see Fasheh. 1995. "The Reading Campaign Experience Within Palestinian Society: Innovative Strategies for Learning and Building Community," *Harvard Educational Review* 65 (1): 66–92.

CHAPTER 6

Alternative Development and Education

Economic Interests and Cultural Practices in the Amazon

SHEILA AIKMAN

This chapter is concerned with different perceptions of development according to different cultural and philosophical traditions. It examines a new education policy in the southeastern Peruvian Amazon that is expected to foster intercultural dialogue, participatory processes, human resource development, and respect for the environment as a means of encouraging new alternatives for the development of the region. The chapter examines alternatives for development as they are expressed by different cultural groups in terms of their relationships with their environment and their aspirations for their children's education and their future. Despite its aims, the new education policy remains bound to an economic development discourse which fails to acknowledge that other cultural groups' aspirations for education are based on broader perceptions of development and qualitatively different relations with the environment.

THE NEED FOR A NEW EDUCATION POLICY

In September 1991, in Cuzco, Peru, the Inka regional government approved a proposal for a new education policy for the department of Madre de Dios, an area of tropical rainforest within the otherwise Andean Inca region. The education policy had been drawn up by state and civil organisations and included criticism of the exploitative nature of the development process in Peru, and Madre de Dios in particular, and the irrelevance of formal education for the peoples of the region (CAAAP 1992).

The education policy states its aim as being to shape the potential of the youth of Madre de Dios to enhance the development of new, less ecologically destructive and more sustainable economic practices based primarily on the natural resources of the department. Moreover, it stresses the need for the development not only of a sound economic basis for the future but of an alternative approach to development based on more equitable relations between the diverse linguistic and cultural groups living there (CAAAP 1992).

The education policy proposal reflects changing agendas not only within Madre de Dios but at continental and global levels. In the 1990s the governments of Mexico, Bolivia, Chile, the Dominican Republic, Ecuador, and Peru began a process of national consultation and cooperation with nongovernmental organisations, social institutions, and religious orders to promote the greater pertinence and relevance of educational programmes, as well as to act as new sources of funding in a climate of economic recession and structural adjustment policies. At an intergovernmental meeting in Quito in 1991 it was agreed that, after the quantitative expansion of education in previous decades, new radical strategies were needed to respond to new demands for social equality, political democratisation, and the transformation of production (Rivero 1993). By the late 1980s several South American governments had legislated for intercultural bilingual education for the indigenous peoples of their countries to foster "unity within diversity" (Chiodi 1990). Meanwhile, this was a time of preparation for the United Nations Conference on Environment and Development (the "Earth Summit") at Rio de Janeiro in June 1992, which produced Agenda 21, an intergovernmental blueprint for sustainable development.

THE MADRE DE DIOS: CULTURAL DIVERSITY AND GEOGRAPHICAL MARGINALISATION

The Madre de Dios is a region of lowland tropical rainforest situated in the southeastern corner of Peru, bordering the Bolivian, Brazilian, and Central Peruvian Amazon to the north, south, and east and with the steep Andes mountains to the west, that provide a forbidding mountainous barrier between the Amazon and the Peruvian coast. The Madre de Dios remained largely isolated until the end of the 19th century, when its natural resources, particularly rubber, attracted the first wave of colonisation. This colonisation led to huge loss of life for the indigenous peoples who followed a hunting, gathering, fishing, and horticultural lifestyle in their respective territories. Today there are some 10,000 indigenous people in Madre de Dios belonging to seven different linguistic families and 19 different ethnolinguistic groups.

The 1970s was a period of increasing gold mining activity on riverine and inland areas of alluvial deposits. By the end of the decade this "gold rush" reached its peak as the price of gold soared on the international market (Gray 1997). Much of the gold production, which still continues today, relies on cheap labour in the form of underemployed and landless *serranos* (predominantly highlanders from the Cuzco area, many of whom are monolingual Quechua speakers). The total population of the region today is estimated to be around 49,000, of which the majority is concentrated in the department capital of Puerto Maldonado. However, there are increasing numbers of permanent settlements along the banks of the main rivers. Today 70 percent of the gold exploitation is by transitory *serrano* and *mestizo* (mixed descent) migrants using artisan methods, and 30 percent by Peruvian and transnational companies using mechanisation in the form of bulldozers and river dredgers (CAAAP 1992).

The price of gold declined through the 1980s, forcing the migrants to search for complementary sources of income. Successive governments have promoted the Madre de Dios as an area of huge potential for colonisation and agriculture in attempts to ease urban and rural poverty on the coast and in the Andes. This has been a widespread policy for the Amazon which, as living conditions in Madre de Dios testify, is not synonymous with "development" in the sense of material improvement. Migration from the Andean region to both the coast and the rainforest was fuelled by the failure of the land reform in the 1970s, increasing oppression by both the Shining Path guerilla movement and the military, and drug trafficking-related violence.

Governments see the natural resources of Madre de Dios—timber, cattle, gold, and oil—as sources of revenue for servicing the international debt.[1] In 1996 Mobil began oil exploration in two areas of Madre de Dios, one inhabited by voluntarily isolated peoples and the other on the indigenous territory of the Arakmbut people.[2]

Increasing demand in rural areas throughout the 1980s led to a quantitative expansion in the provision of primary schooling in Madre de Dios, though secondary schools remained concentrated in the urban centres. The existing system is characterised by authoritarian and bureaucratic relations between levels of the educational hierarchy (e.g., inspectors/teachers and teachers-pupils/parents). The majority of teachers are mestizos who have a high turnover rate in rural areas where those with least experience are sent and often work in multigrade or single-teacher schools. They closely follow the national curriculum using standard textbooks which have an urban focus and make no reference to the rainforest in general or Madre de Dios in particular. Teaching methods are teacher-centred and learning very passive, with end-of-year grade promotion exams leading to a high rate of repetition and drop-out (Aikman 1994).

In 1991, concern for qualitative improvement in education brought together a range of interest groups: the local education and health authorities; continuing education institutions, secondary schools, and health services run by Dominican Catholics; the Catholic lay-missionary education service for indigenous communities; indigenous and environmental support nongovernmental organisations; and the representative indiginous federation of Madre de Dios. They deplored the numbers of young people who were acquiring educational qualifications but were not being equipped for any of the jobs available in the region or who were without the appropriate training to allow them to benefit from the productive potential of the rich natural resources of Madre de Dios (CAAAP 1992).

The new education policy calls for an education system that promotes education for work and intercultural dialogue. Education for work is interpreted as training for existing occupations in the region (such as mechanics, shopkeepers, or small-scale entrepreneurs) and the provision of competencies, skills, and attitudes to design and implement transformational industries. The policy calls for schooling that promotes communal dialogue, planning, and decision making so as to contribute to economic development and increased economic returns and investment in Madre de Dios. It is hoped that in turn this will have a positive effect on the quality and provision of social services and facilities. The policy appears to set great store by intercultural dialogue based on more equitable and democratic practices between the indigenous Amazonian, serrano, and mestizo populations (as well as between these and the state) and sees it as the key to an active and creative search for new alternatives for the economic development of the region (CAAAP 1992).

THE NATURE OF DEVELOPMENT IN MADRE DE DIOS

Considering Madre de Dios in relation to Peru as a whole, the region bears many of the hallmarks of what Casanova and Stavenhagen term internal colonialism: "a metropolis-satellite structure within countries [that] constitutes a kind of internal colonialism which is strengthened by the political power structure and, in some nations, by the inter-ethnic relations between different segments of the population" (cited in Kay 1989, 75). The relations between the resource extraction in Madre de Dios and the urban metropolis of Lima reflect the dynamics of internal colonialism, while the relations between social and ethnic groups are characterised by the "domination of one ethno-cultural group by another largely through extra-economic coercion" (Kay 1989, 75). Social and economic relations in Madre de Dios reflect the ethnic hierarchical relations between mestizo, serrano, and indigenous Amazonians.

The serranos who form the main labour force for gold production, receive wages below subsistence level, have no political participation or labour rights, and have restricted access to health provision. Others are involved with noncapitalist forms of colonial relations: many of these labourers, or *peones*, become indebted to mestizo *patrones* (bosses) and find themselves enmeshed in debt bondage[3] (*enganche*). The indigenous Amazon peoples suffer discrimination, human rights abuses, the destruction of their territory by illegal settlers, gold panners, and loggers, and the consequent depletion of forest and river resources on which they depend. Their rights to their legally titled territories are flouted by serranos and mestizos alike and they are denied access to their rivers at gunpoint. They do some gold panning on their lands, but work in kin groups, not for *patrones*.

Of the economic wealth produced through primary resource extraction, little has been reinvested in the Madre de Dios. Thus development in Madre de Dios is hierarchical, authoritarian, and extractive, characteristics reflected in the education system. Fortunes have been made during the booms of natural resource extraction in Madre de Dios by people from outside who move in when economic opportunities abound and move out again when opportunities dry up. Similarly, the economically and politically powerful elites use the education facilities in Madre de Dios as they suit them. Those with the economic power "extract" their children from the local education system and send them for secondary and higher education to Lima, where it is considered of higher quality and status. For the people whose lives are rooted in Madre de Dios, the indigenous peoples and landless migrants, moving away is not an option; they must live with the consequences of the economic exploitation and with schooling which is nothing but a poor reflection of the urban, middle-class mestizo education provided in Lima.

DEVELOPING THE HUMAN RESOURCE POTENTIAL OF MADRE DE DIOS

Today, destructive natural resource exploitation continues, as do the abuses of human rights and indigenous rights and contraventions of the Peruvian constitution. Since the 1970s, however, there have been changes in the guise of the capitalism which promotes this "development." At the beginning of the 1980s, after a decade of revolutionary socialism, the Peruvian government embarked upon a trajectory of monetarist economic policy and free-market principles. Foreign bank lending and foreign and private investment soared, although raw material prices dropped (Poole and Renique 1992).

Puerto Maldonado was a frontier town in the early 1980s; the main street was lined with timber-built stores selling sacks of rice, dried Andean potatoes (*chuna*), and picks and shovels. At that time the natural resources were exploited by a primarily serrano labour force. After an economic dip in the mid–late 1980s, it is thriving again, as witnessed in the plastic-clad fast-food restaurants and growing numbers of hi-fi and computer shops. As a growing administrative centre, it has a flourishing finance sector and both a fast growing urban middle class and fast growing slum areas inhabited by unemployed or underemployed mestizo migrants, a reflection of the dramatic influence on the poor of neoliberal public spending cuts. Today relations between different indigenous, ethnic, and social groups in Madre de Dios present a complex picture, although the exploitation of serrano *peones* by Quechua urban elites in gold production in the 1970s indicates that these were never clear-cut homogeneous groups and, conversely, that debt peonage and child slavery continue (CODEH-PA 1983).

Over the last few years new alliances and relationships have been established between different sectors of civil society, for example, between indigenous and agriculturalists' organisations. The spread of municipal government has produced, on the one hand, new opportunities for democratic representation and, on the other, new levels of political corruption and hegemony. New horizontal relationships are being forged, for example, between indigenous and nonindigenous Brazil nut gatherers and rubber tappers, to fight a common exploitation and injustice.

The next section investigates the contributions of the mestizos, serranos, and indigenous Amazon peoples to the new education policy call for alternative developments. Their perspectives on education and development will be examined in terms of the way they perceive their relations with the natural environment, their vision for the future, and the place of formal education in their lives.

MESTIZOS—BRINGING DEVELOPMENT TO THE RAINFOREST

Mestizo means "mixed" and is a residual category applied to people of mixed racial descent who do not consider themselves serranos (from the Andes) and are not indigenous to the rainforest. The mestizo population is ethnically heterogenous, but is predominantly urban based. While the mestizo middle and lower classes are growing rapidly in Puerto Maldonado, there is also an expanding mestizo migrant population of dynamic, individualistic, enterprising individuals who have been influential in establishing growing settlements in the "outback." These settlers see themselves as pushing forward the frontiers of a modern world in a pioneering attempt to build better futures for themselves and their families than seem possible in the economically depressed coastal towns of Peru whence they came. The success of the trading, agriculture, and timber extraction in which they are involved hinges on improving communications and achieving support for infrastructural facilities. In the municipal centre of Boca Colorado, mestizo settlers are lobbying for a new road link with the main gold extraction area of Huaypetue in order to market agricultural produce, and for electricity, solid cement housing, sewage, sanitation, and running water to bring a permanence and dignity to their new settlement and lives.

They are "opening up" the rainforest, "bringing development" to the area. While central government lack of efficiency and local government corruption frustrates them, the majority support President Fujimori's neoliberal aims for the spread of a free market and foreign investment (Gray 1997). Breaking the economic isolation of Madre de Dios from the rest of Peru is a priority for most mestizo inhabitants, be they urban or rural. Plans for a transamazon highway linking Pacific and Atlantic coasts has long been a goal of the main extractive companies and traders, a goal which may become a reality with outside investment. Consequently, mestizo development plans (be they individual settler, private sector investor, or government official) focus on the development of the economic extractive potential of Madre de Dios.

In Boca Colorado, schooling is one of a range of institutions that symbolise the arrival of development (civilisation) to the rainforest and is considered an investment by mestizo parents so that their children can "improve themselves" and aspire to the urban middle-class values and material wealth promoted in the classroom. The hierarchy of the education system reflects the hierarchies in society; education is to help their children progress up the social and economic ladder, a meritocratic means to a better chance in life. To this end mestizo parents have clubbed together to supplement teachers' salaries and to contribute towards their board and lodgings to encourage them to stay in this insanitary settlement perched on the edge of the forest and river.

SERRANOS—COLONISATION IN AN ANTISOCIAL JUNGLE[4]

The serranos' relationship with the environment is embedded in their relations as indigenous peoples with land and identity. The rainforest has always been part of the Quechua world; the Incas called it Antisuyu and there is evidence throughout history of a widespread trade between the Andes and the lowland forests. For the serranos in the Andes or the rainforest, the environment is sacred and animated and "frames life" (Skar 1994). The serranos in the rainforest are part of a whole identity and wider territory that is bound together by ties of ritual kinship and shared identity. However, the rainforest is associated with wild, antisocial, subterranean forces competing with the orderliness of agriculture. The natural environment of the rainforest is something that has to be conquered and tamed because its natural forces sap physical strength and have a corroding effect on health.

In the Madre de Dios, serranos who manage to break free of *patrones,* or who arrive in the region independently in search of land, clear the forest to grow maize and tend some animals and perhaps pan some gold. Some clear land on indigenous titled territory, usually unaware of the status of the land or because they do not consider the *chunchos* to be farmers, but rather people who "live off the forest like animals" (Skar 1994, 157).Thus, the serranos define their lives in the rainforest in terms of their relationship with the sierra and mother earth, *Pachamama*. Their identity as Quechua comes from their relationship with their kin and their Andean highland environment, which is for them a sacred landscape in which agriculture is the epitome of a well-ordered and functioning world (Skar 1994).

Many of the serranos have had no schooling and come originally from small isolated highland communities. In the Madre de Dios, they continue to live relatively isolated lives in small shacks along the river banks. If there is a nearby settlement, they may send their children to school there, but many consider the schools in indigenous communities as inferior (Wahaipe Pukiri 1992, personal communication). In general, there is not a great demand for schooling, because it is not seen as reflecting their Quechua values or providing access to a useful body of knowledge. Moreover, those who can, send their older children to live with their extended families in the Andes and to attend school there.

THE INDIGENOUS PEOPLES—PROTECTING THE LAND FOR FUTURE GENERATIONS

One of the largest original peoples in the region, the Arakmbut provide an illustration of another relationship with the rainforest environment and aspirations for the future. The Arakmbut number 1,000 and live in five communities situated at large distances from each other over their traditional territory. Their communities have legally titled areas of land for their hunting, gathering, and gardening pursuits, but the official piece of paper offers no protection from incursions by colonists or companies denuding the land of its profitable hardwoods, deforesting for cattle ranching, or from the work stations and depots of large national and international oil exploration companies.

The indigenous peoples are deeply troubled by the destruction of the rainforest because it implies not only a destruction and loss of resources such as wild meat (peccary, tapir, monkey, large rodents), fish stocks, building materials, and edible forest fruits and plants, but it signifies a breakdown of their relationship with a territory and its resources, both physical and spiritual. Hunting and fishing are fundamental activities for the Arakmbut, not simply in terms of the source of food they provide, but because of the relations that the hunters and fishers establish with the animal species and, through them, with the invisible world of the spirits (Aikman 1994).

For the Arakmbut their territory *(wandari)* binds the visible and spirit worlds. For the Arakmbut it is not only the law which legitimises their collective ownership of the land, but the invisible spirit world (Gray 1996). The Arakmbut consider themselves the guardians of their *wandari,* which they hold in trust for future generations. They have no word for "development" and they do not talk of their children's futures in terms of "progress" or economic growth. They do not focus on productive activities without reference to their social and spiritual dimensions, dimensions which give gardening, hunting, and fishing meaning.

They want to be able to participate in the wider society and welcome formal education and Western medicine to help them combat change imposed from outside. They have schools that, above all, give them status in the eyes of the serranos, mestizos, and missionaries, and official recognition as "native communities" by the state. They see the schools as providing their children with Spanish, which they need in order to help defend their lands and to negotiate with traders. In order to have their own educated people (e.g., sociologists, economists), they have supported several youths in studies in Lima. They are supportive of the development of an intercultural education which is qualitative and relevant and provides them with access to higher tiers of formal education. But they want it also to respect and reinforce their own educational practices and processes (Aikman 1994).

EDUCATION FOR DEVELOPMENT—CULTURAL PERCEPTIONS OF THE ECONOMY

The Arakmbut and indigenous peoples of the Amazon have a relationship with the environment that is intrinsically different from that held by both the mestizos and the serranos. We could discuss whether this indigenous relationship implies an "alternative development" by those on the periphery in search of visibility, participation, and justice (Hettne 1992) or an "alternative to development" that rejects the entire development paradigm, is critical of established scientific knowledge, and focuses on local autonomy, culture, and knowledge (Escobar 1995). However, the Arakmbut talk in terms of the need for their "self-development." This is a total phenomenon which cannot be defined only in terms of economics, politics, or culture. As with all indigenous sociocultural formations, indigenous self-development has to be seen as a whole, covering many different areas. Unless the terms of development are defined by the people themselves, then there is no self-development (Henriksen 1989).

Indigenous Amazonian self-development is respectful of the environment and knowledgeable of its diversity and fragility. The spirit world regulates the use of its resources, bringing sickness to individuals, families, and communities if transgressed. Relations with the land and its resources are not governed by competition and individualism, but based on collective access and use. The Arakmbut are not "owners" of the land; they have legal communal title to their territory and maintain it as its guardians for future Arakmbut generations.

The serranos, trying to reproduce Andean agricultural patterns in the rainforest, do not present a model for sustainable development in Madre de Dios, nor do they relate to the environment in capitalist economic terms. As Gose (1994) explains, when a body is buried, energy is released from the soul, which travels to the mountains where it provides water, enabling crops to grow. Through the "death" or soul-loss that arises from hard labour, men provide the energy to plant or bury seeds irrigated by water from the mountains. Their relationship with the land is a complex spiritual relationship in which their identity is embedded. However, their taming of the lowland forest and its "wild antisocial forces" is ultimately destructive of the forest.

While we acknowledge the lack of attention to the heterogeneity of the category of mestizo, we can, nevertheless, identify in this group a broad adherence to capitalism, the inevitability of progress, and of economic development as the means of achieving it. From the company director or bank manager in Puerto Maldonado to the pioneer at Boca Colorado, "getting ahead" and "doing well" are common goals achieved, or at least aspired to, through the capitalist economic system. Economic development is the route to improved social conditions and material comfort.

The three relationships exemplified by the indigenous, serrano, and mestizo groups with the environment and its development can be termed self-development, dependency, and modernisation, respectively. The mestizo modernisation is an economic model in which formal education has an important part to play in terms of acquiring certificates and qualifications that allow access to higher rungs of the hierarchy. The new education policy's emphasis on education for work and developing local human resources, as well as greater local relevance of the curriculum, is completely compatible with their capitalist aspirations. The policy's focus on breaking hierarchical ethnic and social relations through participation and intercultural dialogue, however, is not a mestizo priority.

The serrano model of development is embedded in a structural shortage of land in the highlands and, for the *peones*, in an exploitative dependency in the rainforest. Formal education is not central to realising their aspirations for the future or an understanding of their own philosophy of relations between the natural and spiritual world. Serranos in search of a humble subsistence are following a path that will ultimately lead to the destruction of the environment, the direct exploitation of which is at present the basis of their existence, and where the rainforest itself is seen as the problem to be overcome (Norgaard 1990). Nevertheless, there are some nonformal educational efforts being directed at overcoming this contradiction. The federation of agriculturalists (FADEMAD) is providing training for serrano settlers to introduce them to alternative agricultural practices that are more suited to the rainforest soils than their traditional Andean horticulture. These practices use local crop varieties and are not aimed at monoculture for commercialisation, but at using the biodiversity to facilitate a sustainable subsistence agriculture. The majority of land-seeking serranos aspire to a well-ordered and functioning subsistence agriculture, which is only possible in the rainforest through agricultural practices suited to the region.

Conversely, the indigenous peoples want formal education to facilitate and strengthen their participation and representation in institutions in mestizo society, but primarily to be able to use these institutions and processes to break their own dependency on outsiders and for their own ends, which are the realisation of self-development and the future integrity of the rainforest. However, formal education alone will not lead to self-development. It is not taught in schools, but learned and practised through informal indigenous learning practices and the knowledge of the elders.

TENSIONS BETWEEN ECONOMIC DEVELOPMENT AND CULTURE

The new education policy states that it rejects the authoritative and hierarchical education system oriented to the maintenance and preservation of a development that is exploitative of both the environment and people. On the contrary, it promotes equality, social justice, and participation and has a strong faith in the contribution that formal education can make to the development of appropriate skills and knowledge. Education is seen as the means of fostering a development for and by the people of Madre de Dios themselves.

But what kind of development is this? To what extent is it an alternative to the modernisation paradigm currently prevalent and reinforced through the school system? The new education policy talks of respect for the environment, alongside maximising economic growth which is potentially destructive of the same environment. What of the potential of intercultural dialogue for producing alternative developments? In a region rich in cultural diversity, the new education policy advocates intercultural dialogue, yet denies the possibilities for this to happen. The policy is based on a misconception that economic growth is the universal basis of all development. Economic development is taken unquestioningly as a neutral, culture-free baseline common to all societies and their philosophies, yet, as we have seen, the serranos and indigenous peoples have alternative relations with the land, that derive from very different epistemologies and not from an economic relationship with the environment based on individualism and profit-making. Both serranos and indigenous peoples have a multidimensional relationship with the land that cannot be reduced to economics and to economic exploitation. Neither are maximising the land's potential and neither talk of progress. Consequently, there is no common ground for intercultural dialogue.

For the mestizos, the new education policy for Madre de Dios details proposals that are coherent with their perception of the role of education as improving human resources and economic activities within an encompassing capitalist growth model of development. The same policy, however, is limited in what it can offer the serranos, who do not confront the world around them in terms of maximising production and progress. Nevertheless, like the indigenous peoples, the serranos are making increasing use of the formal education system embedded in a capitalist model in order to acquire skills and knowledge with which to break out of a dependency on neoliberal economic development. For the indigenous peoples the new education policy will remain ultimately subordinate to their own "informal" learning practices until they acquire the self-determination they desire to develop an intercultural education that addresses the nature of the intercultural lives they lead.

The serrano population did not participate in the education policy-making discussions, as they have no representative political organisation in Madre de Dios.The indigenous peoples, with their representative organisation, FENAMAD, did take part, and we may assume that references to the educational needs and situation of the indigenous peoples and the proposals for intercultural dialogue in the policy are, to some degree, a reflection of their participation. But what is the future potential of intercultural dialogue if it takes place in an unequal and hierarchical society in which neoliberal economics determine the distribution of power?

To consider the implementation of the new education policy, a seminar on "Methodology for the Design of an Alternative Curriculum" was convened in December 1991 in Puerto Maldonado. The meeting was organised and controlled by members of the Madre de Dios mestizo educational establishment. In the course of the three-day meeting, the indigenous representative organisation, although represented and participating in the meeting, was sidelined and there was only one fleeting reference made to the educational needs and aspirations of the indigenous peoples.

CONCLUSION

This chapter has illustrated that in the Madre de Dios, people's aspirations for education are intimately bound up with the nature of the development in which they believe. Thus, for the mestizo population, development is perceived in terms of economic progress and improved social conditions, where education has an important role to play in access to higher social strata through qualifications and certificates. The serrano population provides a different perception of development, deriving from their complex and contradictory relationship with the land in the "hostile" rainforest environment. Formal education is not central to achieving their aims, which are to practise a well-ordered and functioning subsistence agriculture. However, without nonformal educational interventions in alternative agricultural practices, they are embarked on an ultimately destructive course. The indigenous peoples, on the contrary, are knowledgeable of the forest's diverse resources and base their self-development on collective access and use. Their own educational practices promote a respectful sustainable management of the environment, but they are increasingly in need of formal education that can support them in their struggle to protect the territories from the ravages of both mestizo maximising exploitation and serrano agricultural practices.

This examination of the Madre de Dios education policy proposal has illustrated how education systems and their aims and objectives do not stand "above" theories of development. On the contrary, the new education proposal itself is embedded in a particular development theory; it calls for alternatives to an extractive development which is exploitative and destructive, but it limits new development possibilities to those available within a neoliberal economics discourse. For the proposal to lay the foundations for alternative developments in Madre de Dios, there must also be a recognition of the validity of alternative conceptions of education based on different ways of perceiving the relations with the natural environment and different epistemologies. Before the education system can be the focus for alternative developments, policy makers must be aware of the ideological and paradigmatical bases of the development discourse in which they are immersed. Alternative education practices and aims are thus intimately linked with different conceptions of development, not independent of them.

In Madre de Dios, alternatives to economic development are practised by the least powerful groups in society, the serranos and the indigenous peoples. We are left pondering the possibilities for a meaningful participation of these peoples in future education policy-making processes, given that their alternatives hold no legitimacy in Madre de Dios discourse. The old internal colonial hierarchy has undermined the promise of intercultural dialogue and the monologue of economic development has swept away any real possibilities of an alternative development in Madre de Dios for the time being.

NOTES

[1] The multilateral banks have played a key role in influencing the economic and political dynamics of development in rainforest regions by promoting cattle projects, capital-intensive agriculture, and colonisation projects (Rich 1990).

[2] For details of the environmental effects of ranching, agro-forestry, cash cropping, and oil exploration in the Amazon, see Gelber 1992; Johnson et al. 1989; and Kimerling 1993.

[3] The form this takes in the Amazon can be termed *coercive peonage,* which relied on the existence of semi-autonomous pockets controlled by companies that scarcely acknowledge the national political regime, which allows abuses to go unchecked and unreported (Knight 1988).

[4] This section relies heavily on the work of Skar (1994), whose investigations into Quechua colonisation in the rainforest, unlike many other studies, approaches an understanding of Quechua conceptualisation of the rainforest.

REFERENCES

Aikman, S. 1994. "Intercultural Education and Harakmbut Identity: A Case Study of the Community of San Jose in Southeastern Peru." Unpublished Ph.D. thesis, University of London.

Aikman, S. 1995."Territory, Indigenous Education and Cultural Maintenance: The Case of the Arakmbut of Southeast Peru." *Prospects* 25(4): 665–681.

Centro Amazónico de Antropología y Aplicación Practica (CAAAP). 1992. *Propuesta de Politica Educativa: Sub-region de Madre de Dios.* Lima: Centro Amazónico de Antropología y Aplicación Práctica.

Chiodi, F., compiler. 1990. *La Educación Indígena en America Latina: México, Guatemala, Ecuador, Perú, Bolivia.* 2 vols. Santiago: Abya-Yala.

Comite de Defensa de lso Derechos Humanos de las Provincias Altas (CODEHPA). 1983. *La Selva y su Ley: Lavaderos de Oro.* Sicuani: Comite de Defensa de los Derechos Humanos de las Provincias Altas.

Escobar, A. 1995. "Imagining a Post-Development Era." In *Power of Development,* ed. J. Crush. London: Routledge.

Gelber, G. 1992. "Land Rights and Land Reform." In *Poverty and Power: Latin America after 500 Years,* ed. G.Gelber. London: Cafod.

Gose, P. 1994. *Deathly Waters and Hungry Mountains: Agrarian Ritual and Class Formation in an Andean Village.* Toronto: Anthropological Horizons.

Gray, A. 1997. *Indigenous Rights and Development: Self-Determination in an Amazonian Community.* Oxford: Berghahn.

Gray, A. 1996. *Mythology, Spirituality and History: The Arakmbut of Amazonian Peru.* Oxford: Berghahn.

Henriksen, G. 1989. "Introduction." In *Indigenous Self-Development in the Americas.* Amsterdam: International Work Group for Indigenous Affairs.

Hettne, B. 1992. *Development Theory and the Three Worlds.* 2nd ed. Harlow: Longman.

Johnston, C., R. Knowles, and M. Colchester. 1989. *Rainforests: Land Use Options for Amazonia.* London: Oxford University Press and WorldWide Fund for Nature, UK, in association with Survival International.

Kay, C. 1989. *Latin American Theories of Development and Underdevelopment.* London: Routledge.

Kimerling, J. 1993. *Crudo Amazonico.* Quito: Abya Yala.

Knight, A. 1988. "Debt Bondage in Latin America." In *Slavery and Other Forms of Unfree Labour,* ed. L. Archer. London: Routledge.

Norgaard, R. 1990. "The Development of Tropical Rainforest Economics." In *Lessons of the Rainforest,* eds. S. Head and R. Heinzman. San Francisco: Sierra Club Books.

Poole, D., and G. Renique. 1992. *Peru: Time of Fear.* London: Latin American Bureau.

Rich, B. 1990. "Multilateral Development Banks and Tropical Deforestation." In *Lessons of the Rainforest,* eds. S. Head and R. Heinzman. San Francisco: Sierra Club Books.

Rivero, J. 1993. *Educación de Adultos en América Latina: Desafíos de la equidad y la modernización.* Lima: Tarea Asociación de Publicaciones Educativas.

Skar, S. 1994. *Lives Together—Worlds Apart: Quechua Colonization of Jungle and City.* Oslo Studies in Social Anthropology. Oslo: Scandinavian University Press.

CHAPTER 7

Local Accountability to Rural Communities

A Challenge for Educational Planning in Africa

ROBERT SERPELL[1]

THE MULTIPLE AGENDA OF SCHOOLING

The local primary school has become a familiar institution in many rural communities across the world. The fashionable ideal that the school and the community should form a partnership requires a recognition that their joint endeavour has a multiple agenda: "the promotion of economic progress, the transmission of culture from one generation to the next, and the cultivation of children's intellectual and moral development" (Serpell 1993a, 1). Although these three agendas are complementary in principle, in practice their demands often run into competition. In Africa, perhaps even more than other regions of the Third World, formal education holds an ambiguous position, as a vehicle of technological progress and as a symbol of alien culture.

The expression *human development* is often used so loosely in the discourse of educational planning that important distinctions are obscured between "individual development," "social progress," and "economic growth." Indeed, the case for provision of public education as an investment in development often appears to rest on the simplistic premise that schooling adds value to the economy by increasing the level of competence of many individual members of the labour force: the more competent an individual is, the more productive she or he will be; and the more such competent individuals there are, the greater will be the cumulative level of economic production in the society. Implicit in this line of reasoning is a conception of individual development as isomorphic with economic development, as if the latter could be computed by simply adding together many instances of the former. In reality, however, a wide variety of different contributions are expected from (and made by) different individuals to a society's economy, so that the economy stands to benefit more from a differentiated spectrum of individual developmental outcomes than from an accumulation of cases of any single prototype of educated persons. Furthermore, most politicians and planners now agree that measuring the growth of an economy in terms of increasing productivity overlooks other important aspects of planned societal development, such as the quality of life afforded to individuals by the conditions of production, and the equitable distribution of wealth across various sectors of society. In my view, the most fundamental strand of the multiple agenda of schooling is the pedagogical activity of cultivating individual development in sociocultural context, which indirectly contributes both to economic progress and to the intergenerational transmission of culture.

PERSONAL DEVELOPMENT IN SOCIOCULTURAL CONTEXT

The psychological development of an individual involves growth along several dimensions, including social responsibility, personal identity, and skills, knowledge, and understanding. The developmental process arises from the individual's exploratory interaction with a physical and social context. The context is structured by a set of historically evolving cultural resources, including a particular language and technology, as well as particular political and economic structures (see Figure 7.1). The interaction between context and development has been theoretically conceptualised in recent decades in several related ways (Serpell 1993b). Context has been characterised as a set of nested and overlapping social systems (Bronfenbrenner 1979), and as a mutually interdependent system of cultural practices, artefacts, and meanings (Scribner and Cole 1981; Shweder 1990).

The values attached to various indicators of an individual's development can thus be understood as reflecting his or her adaptation to the demands of an ecologically, socially, and culturally defined developmental niche (Super and Harkness 1986; Gallimore et al. 1989). The niche has several interrelated components: a restricted range of physical and social settings; a particular set of child-rearing practices; and a system of meanings, informing a cultural model or ethnotheory of child development and socialisation (D'Andrade 1984; Harkness & Super 1992a; Serpell

Figure 7.1. Complementary Resources Perspective on Education for Personal Development

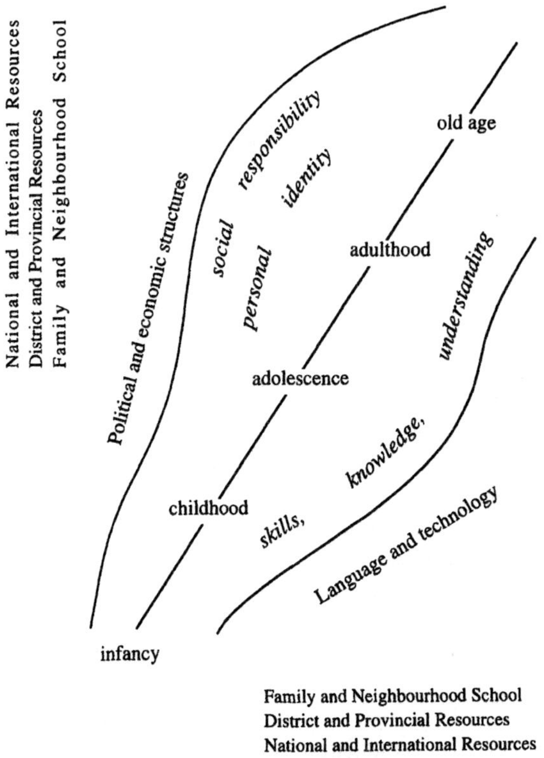

1993a), shared among those responsible for the upbringing of children in a given sociocultural group. Thus, "the cultural organization of context includes systematic patterns of social relationships, of recurrent activities, and of meanings. Over the course of their socialization, children gradually appropriate this complex system, becoming part of it, and by the same token coming to regard it as their own" (Serpell and Boykin 1994, 400).

The paradigmatic relationship between parenting and universal primary schooling is often presented by contemporary educators as one in which a population of primary caregivers agrees on the need to organise some parts of their children's socialisation on a collective basis, building on and extending developmental processes initiated at home. This ideological premise gives rise to the proposal that schools and the communities they are designed to serve should be regarded as partners in a joint endeavour. Historically, however, this kind of cultural attunement, which allows for continuity in the child's socialisation, seems to have been a rather late and incidental arrival among the various defining characteristics of formal education. Schools as institutions arose initially as mechanisms for transmitting specialised bodies of knowledge to learners of various ages (Cole 1990; Serpell 1993a).

When a school curriculum is designed in a manner that is alien to the cultural assumptions informing other socialisation practices to which its students have been exposed, discrepancies are liable to arise between the goals of that curriculum and the cultural goals of the social group. Religion and language are often cited as crucial dimensions of socialisation that call for explicit harmonisation across the school- and home-based facets of the eco-cultural niche of an individual's development. In general, the greater the degree of alienation between the culture of a child's socialisation at home and the culture of schooling, the greater the resulting discrepancy between their goals. But discrepancy is only part of the story: economic power attracts social prestige, with the result that the cultural practices of economically powerful groups often become a target of emulation by less powerful groups. In situations where economic power is controlled by a social group that differs systematically in culture from the group of which a child is raised as a member, the project of acquiring economically empowering cultural understanding at school easily becomes associated in the minds and practices of both teacher and student with devaluing the alternative culture of the child's family and home community (Howard and Scott 1981).

Nevertheless, in the second half of the 20th century, an increasingly standardised model of institutionalised public schooling has begun to emerge across many parts of the world (Serpell and Hatano 1997). In this model, schooling is organised as a sequence of tiers, with a primary, or basic, programme of instruction designed to afford opportunities for the foundational acquisition of basic literacy skills, followed by a secondary programme designed to build on that foundation while introducing students to various domains of cultural knowledge, such as the natural sciences, humanities, and social studies.

Superimposed on this two-tier conceptualisation of literacy, education, and schooling, and ultimately serving to legitimate it, we find a set of assumptions regarding the appropriate stages of human development for enrolling students in each successive phase: primary schooling is prescribed for children between the initial mastery of linguistic communication and the onset of puberty, whereas secondary education is reserved for the period of adolescence, and tertiary education for young adults. Preschool education is principally designed to prepare children for primary schooling, and is reserved for young children.

This congruence of developmental stages with types of educational provision has come to appear natural. Indeed, it informs the *paradigmatic* conception of the relationship between basic education in schools and parenting cited above. According to some analysts the trend toward international acceptance of this paradigm represents a convergence of wisdom based on experience (Kagitcibasi 1996). In my view, however, this model has taken on board unquestioningly a great deal of cultural baggage accumulated by the Western paradigm in the course of its unique historical evolution, much of which is extrinsic to the basic functions of pedagogy.

THE NARROWING STAIRCASE MODEL OF SCHOOLING

The narrowing staircase model of schooling, which informs the prototype of what Hatano and I have termed *institutionalised public basic schooling* (IPBS) (Serpell and Hatano 1997), combines a metaphor of the individual's developmental progress as climbing a staircase with a conception of the social function of schooling as the recruitment of an elite by gradually extracting them from humble origins into a privileged upper class (see Figure 7.2).

The Age-Graded Curriculum

"The gradation of the curriculum into a sequence of steps, each of which must be mastered before the student may embark on the next . . . has now become a crucial tenet of modern educational orthodoxy. Two historical factors appear to have been critical in generating this pedagogical pattern: the formalization of didactic process, and the stepwise matching of instruction with age" (Serpell 1995, 25).

A general fascination with explicit methodology pervaded many fields of cultural activity in Europe during the historical epochs of the Renaissance and the Enlightenment (Berlin 1956). Within this context, Comenius first published *Great Didactic* in 1657, which survived in multiple editions right into the 19th century as an authoritative statement of the paradigm of effective pedagogy as "a mechanical operation . . . a suitable environment must be provided and materials prepared, impedi-

Figure 7.2. Extractive Recruitment Model of Schooling

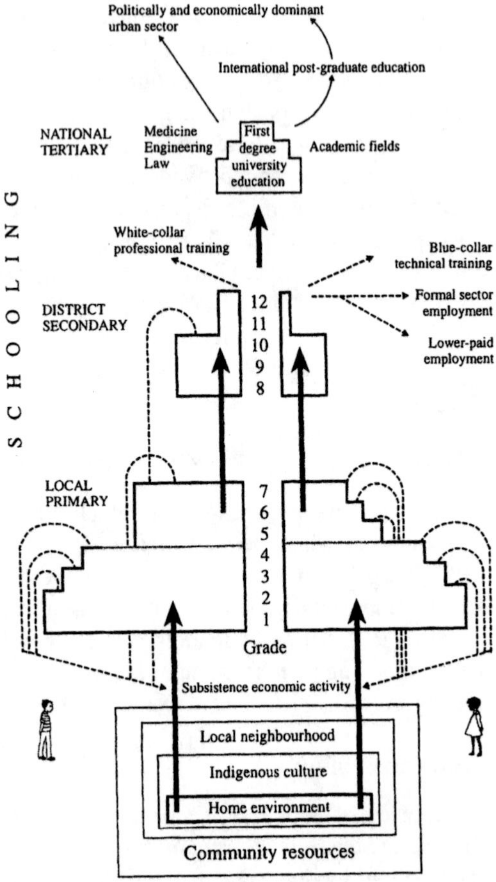

ments must be removed, difficulties avoided and assistance given where required. Then the timing must be right and the programme must advance through the simplest steps possible, with everything necessary for success and nothing irrelevant" (Sadler 1966, 202).

Initially, this stepwise methodology was not closely linked to the age of the student. But concerns arising from the residential arrangements at colleges gradually gave rise to the idea that students of a wide range of ages should not be enrolled together in the same class. It was not until the early 19th century that: "the regularization of the annual cycle of promotions, the habit of making all the pupils go through the complete series of classes instead of only a few, and the requirements of a new system of teaching adapted to smaller, more homogeneous classes, resulted . . . in an increasingly close correspondence between age and class" (Aries 1962, 239–240). This projection of the curricular gradation onto teachers' and parents' expectations of children at different ages has since become a Western cultural theme of great importance, influencing both the conception of education and that of child development. On the one hand, it serves to legitimate the organisation of knowledge into a hierarchy of elements best taught and learned sequentially, working up from the basics to higher and advanced stages. And on the other hand, it has come to inform the notion that a child's maturation is incomplete in the absence of specifiable learning experiences that follow a natural progression in the school curriculum.

The endurance of this age-by-grade matching as an integral feature of public education around the world underpins the metaphor of educational progress as climbing a staircase: a unilinear sequence of somewhat arduous movements along a predetermined path with a known set of discrete intervals and a specific, exalted destination (see Figure 7.2). Several peculiar consequences have flowed historically from this conceptualisation. First, "adult education, widespread in the 15th and 16th centuries, disappeared in the 17th century and its place was taken by an education confined to children" (Aries 1962, 300–301). Concomitantly, the role of *learner* became institutionalised as intrinsically suited to an immature mind. As a result, since adult education was reinvented in the 19th century, it has had to struggle to throw off an image of education as a condescending process in which the teacher has an obligation to control and direct the student along a predetermined path. The implications of this theme of condescension include an asymmetry in the flow of information between teacher and student, such that the timing of class activities will be strictly controlled by the teacher and any deviation by a student from prescribed forms of behaviour is subject to authoritarian correction by the teacher.

Second, this asymmetry has become available as a legitimating ideology for the stigmatisation of whole sections of adult society, such as women, the poor, and foreigners, who for social and political reasons have not had access to the socialisation institutionalised in "our" kind of schooling. Rather than seeing these out-groups as different but equal, the equation of schooling with normal child socialisation has encouraged the "products" of Western schooling to look down on them as incomplete human beings, either to be pitied for their deprivation or else to be despised as not deserving this essential ingredient of becoming fully human.

This stigmatisation of the unschooled as incomplete also found fertile ground in the Christian missionaries' project of evangelisation. The recipients of schooling in Africa were not only perceived by these exogenous teachers as needing "civilisation," but as lost souls in danger of perdition (Snelson 1974). Schooling was conceived as an effective instrument for deliberately inducing a process of cultural change. Not only were the missionaries uncompromisingly committed to a particular religious interpretation of social and moral behaviour, but they were also deeply and for the most part unquestioningly attached to the principles of contemporary Western civil life, including commerce and administration. As a result they generally saw little or no conflict between their evangelising objectives and the imperialistic expansion of their governments' sphere of influence. In Central Africa they were thus, at best unwittingly, often instrumental in paving the way for colonial occupation.

The Extractive Recruitment of Human Capital

Most political leaders and social planners of Third World nations in the 20th century have explicitly rejected the hegemonistic ideas of early Western missionaries and colonial administrators. But the project of "universal primary education" has captured their imagination as a major contribution to national development. Indeed, the World Declaration on Education For All, formulated at the international conference in Jomtien (1990) and endorsed by representatives of 155 governments, explicitly endorses the premise that "education is an indispensable key to, though not a sufficient condition for, personal and social improvement." Although the declaration embraced the concept of a broad-based education that would equip young people with skills for life, in practice it is most often cited as justification for the expansion of a rigidly structured system of primary schooling.

Given the conspicuous discrepancies between the culture of many Third World children's socialisation at home and the culture of schooling offered in their local neighbourhoods, this unquestioning endorsement is quite paradoxical. It appears to reflect what Cherns (1984) has termed "uncovenanted cultural transmission," underwritten by the enduring influence of two lines of social scientific interpretation, classically formulated as modernisation theory (McClelland 1961; Inkeles and Smith 1974) and human capital theory (Barnum and Sabot 1976; Harbison and Myers 1964). According to modernisation theory, the moving force of economic development is a certain kind of individual, equipped with a coherent package of skills, values, motives, and attitudes uniquely well adapted to the tasks of building, expanding, and maintaining a modern, industrialised society. Moreover, the argument goes, the recipe for moulding individuals into exemplars of this prototype is known, and it has been incorporated (with varying degrees of accuracy) in the design of various types of school curriculum.

According to human capital theory, development programmes should therefore invest public resources in the creation of a stock of such individuals by exposing the younger generation to appropriate school curricula. An elitist perspective on education, which is often expressed among those who have reached the top of the educational staircase in Africa, adds to these premises a couple of "common sense," "good husbandry" assumptions: that, given limited resources for public schooling, it is wiser to do the job properly for a small section of the population than to do it poorly for everyone; and that it is wiser to select for the "full treatment" those individuals who show promise of internalising its message efficiently.

Thus, in most contemporary African societies, the national government has invested heavily in public education since the mid-1960s, when many of these states achieved political independence, expanding the scale and accessibility of provision by building new schools in rural as well as urban areas. For the state as a whole, this investment is widely regarded as contributing significantly to economic progress by generating a stock of human capital with essential technical, administrative, and managerial knowledge and skills for a "modern" society. Yet, at the level of a single school with a catchment area in which most children are born into low-income families engaged in subsistence farming, the project is confronted with a moral trap. Such schools are responsible for delivering the bulk of the primary educational provision administered by governments in sub-Saharan Africa: they are the prototype on which the project of universal primary education in Africa is based, the elementary cogs on whose operation the nationwide machinery depends. Stated in its simplest form, the trap is that the school finds itself in the business of producing failures.

When we examine the profile of children going through a rural primary school over a period of years, what we see is that the vast majority of those who set foot in that institution leave school feeling that they are failures. Parents, teachers, and students all regard admission to a secondary school as the sole criterion of whether an individual's schooling was worthwhile. And yet, given the scale of educational resources provided by the state, this particular achievement is *automatically* denied every year to the majority of aspirants. Figure 7.2 represents schematically the planning model for public education that informs this situation. At each of the selection junctures, only a minority of students can proceed to the next step on the narrowing staircase (or educational pyramid).

The rationale of this model is that the national economy is thereby selectively recruiting the most able individuals to enter the ranks of the elite, whose role it is to manage the higher echelons of the society. Indeed, those members of the rural community who do not progress to higher levels of the educational staircase, nevertheless sometimes claim vicarious pride in the achievements of those who do. Many attribute the failure of those who do not qualify for a place in secondary school to personal rather than systemic inadequacies. Meanwhile, many young people emerge from school with a sense of frustration and lowered self-esteem. The remainder of this paper is addressed to what might be done to generate more positive outcomes for this majority of students enrolling in rural African primary schools.

Economists engaged in educational planning at the level of the nation-state tend to construe the impact of schooling as homogeneous, discontinuous, and mechanistic, and to invoke a set of principles that are locally invisible, or at least unseen and largely inscrutable. Their logic is characterised by adherence to the dictates of a macro-system that only has reality for those few people who familiarise themselves with the national-level statistics. Their policy recommendations are often formulated in terms of cost-effectiveness, as if education were a commodity whose contributions to the developmental niche and consequences for personal development can be specified as quantifiable inputs and outputs. In reality, however, young people who enrol in school in rural African communities do so with a sense of purpose and make eclectic use of it as a resource in the pursuit of their personal life-journey's independent agenda. Schooling carries a variety of meanings in the lives of different individuals and contributes in various, strikingly different ways to their life-journeys.

In the sections that follow, I shall first describe some educational activities that lie mainly outside the scope of institutionalised public basic schooling (IPBS) as it is currently conceived in many Third World countries. Each of these educational programmes defines successful outcomes in less extractive terms than the prevailing model of IPBS by explicitly linking its curriculum to ostensible local practices, as well as to widely valued social goals. I shall argue that IPBS, by excluding these types of educational endeavour from its mandate, misses some important opportunities to respond to felt needs in the local communities it aspires to serve. On the other hand, some of the extracurricular service functions already performed by rural schools represent glimmers of hope that some of the psychological and social goals successfully addressed by nonformal educational programmes are compatible with the mainstream of IPBS. In conclusion I will suggest that educational planners might profitably include the notion of schools as nodes in their planning models, in order to build local accountability into the public legitimation accorded by central administrative authorities to the activities of rural schools.

ALTERNATIVE DEFINITIONS OF EDUCATIONAL SUCCESS

Each of the three types of educational activity I have selected for analysis in this section places a high priority on the linkage of curriculum content with students' ongoing lives in the local community. As a result, each defines success in more intrinsic and less extractive terms than the model of IPBS described above. Furthermore, each of them has encountered resistance within the framework of IPBS, with the result that they typically occur outside the context of IPBS and are widely regarded as something less than "real education."[2] Figure 7.3 summarizes nine pedagogical characteristics that should be central to the design of basic education, according to the contextualised theory of personal development outlined earlier. In practice, however, they tend to be largely neglected in the model of IPBS designed to serve the function of extractive recruitment already discussed (pp. 111–114). It is probably no accident that some of the most effective applications of these general principles are found in the context of educational activities that are regarded as "special" or residual by the administrators of IPBS.

Home-Based Learning Programmes for Children with Disabilities

One of the most influential concepts in Vygotsky's (1978) sociocultural perspective on development has been the "zone of proximal development" (ZPD), defined as the level of proficiency which an individual is able to attain with assistance, and which (all being well) he/she will soon be able to perform without assistance (see Figure 7.3a). Educators within this tradition formulate optimal instruction as providing assistance to the learner within his/her ZPD (e.g., Tharp and Gallimore 1988). The socio-

Figure 7.3. Pedagogical Characteristics of Some Educational Activities Excluded from the Standard Model of IPBS

a. Individualized instruction within the student's zone of proximal development (ZPD)
b. Emphasis on ecological validity in the definition of curricular tasks
c. High premium on parent–professional collaboration for implementation of the educational program
d. Focus on authentic tasks that elicit high levels of intrinsic motivation to learn
e. Presentation of technical skills as integrally connected with social and moral responsibility
f. Explicit acknowledgement of the socially distributed nature of cognition
g. Use of appropriate technology
h. Integration of learning with economic productivity
i. Incorporation of the learner as a legitimate participant within a social system that displays the full range of desirable outcomes of the learning process

cultural aspects of this assistance have been further emphasised in recent years by conceptualising cognitive socialisation as a form of apprenticeship (Rogoff 1990) or as legitimate peripheral participation (Lave and Wenger 1991). The child's growing proficiency is thus contextualised as the appropriation of a system of meanings that informs a cultural practice (Serpell and Boykin 1994).

The principle of individualising instruction[3] within the student's zone of proximal development (ZPD) is assuredly relevant to everyone's education. But it has been especially valuable as a guide for the instruction of students with special needs, perhaps because a teacher's intuitions of how best to present a new task to a learner benefit most from careful observation of the student's behaviour in those cases where the student is constrained by factors of which the teacher lacks first-hand experience, such as sensory, motor, or cognitive impairment. The construction of an individual programme plan (IPP) or individual educational programme (IEP) begins with observation, analysis, and assessment of the individual's behaviour in one or more tightly specified domains. Each domain is analysed in terms of its task demands, and these two structured bodies of information (behavioural assessment and task analysis) are combined to prescribe a particular set of activities, often in a scheduled sequence, for promoting increases in the individual's proficiency in that domain. Well-known examples are the backward chaining programmes for instruction in self-help such as dressing and feeding, and the graded mastery of grapheme-phoneme correspondence rules in early phases of reading. Behavioural assessment is repeated periodically in order to determine progress toward the stipulated goals of the programme. If insufficient progress is found or if the student has achieved an adequate level of proficiency, new activities are prescribed, and the IPP thus evolves over time, providing a sensitively adjusted guide to the individual's education.

Because most of the research that gave rise to this systematic approach was conducted in highly controlled laboratory settings, IPPs were at first conceived as techniques that could only be administered by professional experts. Concerns of ecological validity (see Figure 7.3b), however, led to increasing interest by researchers in ways of "exporting" the technology to naturally occurring settings in the everyday environment of children. Opportunities for instruction in dressing, for instance, can be built into the routine of getting up in the morning. This theoretical interest meshed with several social and economic concerns of policymakers. Studies of children raised in large institutions in the 1950s and 1960s revealed some dysfunctional consequences of what had been conceived as a philanthropic enterprise, including socio-emotional inadequacy, institutional dependency, and social stigma. The deinstitutionalization movement that gained momentum in industrialised Western nations in the 1970s advocated placing children with special needs in the "least restrictive environment" compatible with those needs. And in Third World countries it became increasingly apparent in the same period that residential special schools established by Western aid agencies, whatever their technical benefits, were inappropriate as a general model for habilitation if only because their unit cost was vastly in excess of the resources available for services to this sector of the population in a nation with scarce economic resources. In short, special education administered by specialist teachers in specialised institutional settings was neither socially acceptable nor economically affordable.

A new policy framework was therefore proposed for delivering the benefits of the IPP technology to children with special needs in Third World countries, under the heading of community-based rehabilitation (CBR) (WHO 1980, 1983). The guiding principle of CBR is that, whenever possible, intervention designed to ameliorate the health, proficiency, and social integration of a person with a disability will be administered by members of their immediate family and community in the context of the client's everyday life in the local neighbourhood (see Figure 7.3c). The principal role of professionals in this type of habilitation is to provide advice as a consultant, rather than direct, "hands-on" treatment, instruction, or care. This has led to an emphasis on "giving away skills" (Mittler and Serpell 1985). The planning of individual programmes used to be seen as an expert function, with family members as mere "implementers" of those plans. With the growth of self-advocacy and parent organisations, greater emphasis has been placed on establishing true partnerships between professionals and the families they advise (Mittler and McConachie 1983).

A fully articulated version of this educational model has been implemented in several rural areas of Zimbabwe under the auspices of ZIMCARE, a national, nongovernmental organisation (Mariga 1989); and comparable, smaller-scale programmes of home-based learning have been described in Kenya (Arnold 1986) and Zambia (Nabuzoka 1986) (see Serpell and Nabuzoka 1991; Serpell, Mariga, and Harvey 1993). Thus, whereas the concept of special education has mainly been applied in highly selective, institutional settings in Africa, it has also given rise to a model of community-based outreach services that combine pedagogical responsiveness to individual needs with ecological validity in the definition of curriculum and a high level of parent–professional collaboration (Serpell 1986).

Health Education for Mothers of Young Children

The concept of school instruction as a condescending process not only interferes with egalitarian discourse; it also disqualifies certain domains from the curriculum. Just as all young children with a particular developmental disability experience certain recurrent challenges for which special education can be designed to prepare them, a mother-to-be can expect with a high degree of reliability to encounter certain quite different challenges. The infant will need to be suckled, comforted, cleaned, and protected against various environmental hazards. Techniques for addressing these needs are well documented and can be effectively taught. But they are typically excluded from the curriculum of IPBS. Instead, they are taught as supplementary services by health workers specialising in the monitoring of maternal and child health (MCH).

With reference to Figure 7.3, this educational activity displays the following important characteristics: (b) a high level of ecological validity; (d) the tasks on which instruction focuses are authentic and thus elicit high levels of intrinsic motivation to learn; (e) technical skills are presented as integrally connected with the educational goals of cultivating social and moral responsibility; (f) the socially distributed nature of cognition is explicitly acknowledged. Characteristics (d) and (e) require little explanation. But it should be noted that they are conspicuously rare in the curriculum of IPBS, where most tasks are artificially concocted for instructional purposes, and technical skills are typically presented as value-free techniques for control over the physical environment.

Regarding (f), the educational outcomes of IPBS are often construed as highly individual proficiencies, analogous to a torch that illuminates directly all that falls within the view of the person who acquires it (Goody 1977; Olson 1976). By contrast, education has sometimes been likened to a hinge that opens doors for the literate individual, which otherwise would remain closed to him or her (Ogbu 1974). An intermediary theoretical perspective centres on the concept of socially distributed cognition: what is imparted by literacy is neither a radical cognitive transformation of *enlightenment*, nor the arbitrary political assignment of *social status*. Becoming literate involves the appropriation of a technology of limited but nonetheless significant utility. The benefits of literacy to a community cannot be gauged by simple aggregation of individual competencies, because the cultural sharing of technology involves socially distributed cognition (Serpell 1994).

Literacy, from this perspective, is a cultural resource at the disposal of participants in various socially organised activities. Its technological characteristics are both constraining and empowering. The cognitive possibilities that it affords are mediated by co-constructive processes. Several studies have drawn attention to the remarkable extent to which the cognitive work of literacy in everyday life is socially distributed (e.g., Reder 1987; Scribner and Cole 1981).

A striking opportunity for socially distributed cognition is afforded by the weight-monitoring growth charts printed on child health record cards throughout Zambia and in many other Third-World countries (see Morley and Woodland 1979). These charts are kept at home by parents, many of whom have received an incomplete primary school education. In my research in Zambia's rural Katete District (Serpell 1993a), I found considerable variations in the level of understanding of these growth charts as displayed by young mothers with an incomplete primary schooling. One mother of two who had completed five years of primary schooling provided us with a clear account of the meaning of the graph, including both the level and the slope. However, her neighbour and close personal friend, with one child and four years of schooling, told us that she did not know what the graph meant. Unable to read at all, she thought the clinic card was only for recording immunisations. None of the women we asked about the growth charts recalled ever learning anything about them at school, and those who understood them affirmed that they had received an explanation at the health centre during an MCH clinic session.

The metaphor of "the road to health" encoded diagrammatically on these charts combines a number of powerful attributes: low-cost user-friendliness (a recurrent theme of Appropriate Technology[4]); semiotic translucency (a valuable resource for cross-cultural communication—see Kiernan 1985); demographic adaptability (guaranteeing transcultural relevance); and statistical calibration (giving it the quantitative sophistication required of a curricular topic in the field of modern science). Yet no attempt is made to explain this ubiquitous document within the school curriculum. This conspicuous omission seems to me to reflect a stereotyped assumption that monitoring the health of an infant is the exclusive responsibility of adult women, whose concerns are defined as remote from the agenda of basic schooling (Serpell 1993a, 270–271).

In reality, however, a great deal of the daily care of infants in Africa is performed by pre-adolescent children (Harkness and Super 1992b; Nsamenang 1992; Serpell 1992). Moreover, from a distributed cognition perspective, the goal of protecting infant health could be (and indeed sometimes is) achieved through collaboration of professional health personnel with mothers who can grasp the essential principles of the "road to health" diagram, without expecting the latter to master the technicalities of calculating statistical norms or plotting graphs. Thus, various types of understanding may inform the ways in which different members of the community "read" the chart, and yet those diverse understandings may converge sufficiently for the chart to serve as an effective shared resource for co-constructive problem solving and action planning.

Apprenticeship in Economically Productive Activities

I will say less about this type of educational endeavour, as there have been numerous experiments and extensive discussion in the literature with respect to agrarian school production units in Africa (e.g., Ball 1983; Van Rensburg 1984). From the perspective of my present analysis the approach to instruction of adults in economically productive activity settings typically displays close attention to ecological validity, focuses on authentic tasks, acknowledges the socially distributed nature of cognition, and also displays the following important characteristics (see Figure 7.3 g-i): (g) use of appropriate technology; (h) integration of learning with economic productivity; and (i) incorporation of the learner as a legitimate (albeit initially "peripheral") participant within a social system (or "community of practice" [Lave and Wenger 1991]) that displays the full range of desirable outcomes of the learning process. As an apprentice, the learner is left in no doubt as to the social and economic significance of what he/she is learning.

Each of the categories of potential student discussed above represents a missed opportunity for IPBS to make a significant impact on a felt need in the local community. If educational reform were to expand the mandated clientele of basic schooling to include adults engaged in economically productive activities, mothers of young children, and children with disabilities, the value of placing greater priority on the linkage of curriculum content with students' ongoing lives in the local community would become immediately apparent. In this sense, I regard the educational imperatives of these types of educational activity as the thin end of a wedge (Serpell 1982) that may serve to open up and reorient the consciousness of educational planners to pay more attention to the pedagogical agenda of basic schooling: the cultivation of children's intellectual and moral development. The pedagogical characteristics of these educational activities are well grounded in contemporary theories of how context interacts with human development, and IPBS excludes them from its scope on grounds extrinsic to education. These forms of education therefore deserve close attention by researchers as models of exemplary practice that could, given some administrative imagination, be emulated within the framework of IPBS.

EXTRACURRICULAR SERVICE FUNCTIONS OF RURAL SCHOOLS

The alternatives to existing practices of IPBS described in the preceding section are not only theoretically plausible, but are actually quite close to certain ongoing activities of many rural African primary schools. The problem is not so much that no one has thought of these options before, but rather that they lack sufficient legitimacy to receive their proper share of attention in the definition of goals and the evaluation of outcomes. These low-profile, peripheral, "extracurricular" activities of existing schools represent for me glimmers of hope—that one day they will receive greater priority in the grand scheme of educational planning.

Many rural primary schools in Africa double as another type of institution when they are not in use for the principal function of classroom instruction they are mandated to perform. Three local service functions deserve special attention in the present context: the library function, the community forum for discussion of public affairs, and the base for continuing education activities.

The Local School as a Community Library

In the period of Zambia's transition to political independence between 1960 and 1965, a network was established of more than 500 small rural-centre libraries, each comprising a collection of between 20 and 100 volumes (Kabamba 1988). Most of these libraries were based in schools. Yet by 1987 this service was effectively moribund. One of the most pressing reasons for advocating the proliferation of this model is that books, magazines, and newspapers are truly scarce commodities in many rural areas of Africa. Governments have tended to leave the production and distribution of printed materials other than textbooks to the private sector. But the extractive recruitment process discussed earlier has seen to it that the market for books or even newspapers in rural areas is too small to attract such businesses. In our follow-up study in Zambia's Eastern Province, the published materials that our rural primary school leavers said they had read in recent weeks were all either religious (distributed by churches at no cost) or books first encountered in the school curriculum.

A library differs as a community resource from a school in interesting ways: elements of the repertoire are organized in an ordered manner in both cases. But in a library, instead of prescribing the sequence of exposure for a client, the full range of materials is open to access by any user at his or her own discretion. This arrangement is more conducive to intrinsic motivation for reading.

One of the more striking findings in our follow-up study was that despite an overwhelming emphasis on English as the medium of school instruction, many of these young adults were more literate in their indigenous language (Chewa / Nyanja) than they were in English. A small but nevertheless substantial published literature has accumulated in Chewa / Nyanja, but scarcely any of it was available at the local school.

Among the significant functions for realisation of the potential of literacy that a local community library could serve are recreation and expansion of the imagination, information retrieval on technical aspects of agriculture, health, law, marketing, and so forth, and focusing discourse among local citizens.

The Local School as a Community Forum

Schools are often perceived in rural areas of Africa as representative of the central government, if only because their personnel are government employees. Thus, when an event of national significance occurs, such as a political election, the celebration of a national holiday, or the observance of a nationally proclaimed thematic activity such as World Health Day, the local school is often chosen as a natural venue for the occasion.

Within the framework of IPBS, many countries prescribe the formation of some type of parent-teacher association (PTA). In our survey of rural schools in Zambia's Eastern Province, we found that the potential of these PTAs for discussion of substantive issues relating to the impact of education on the community was underrealised. But other school systems have experimented successfully with placing more responsibility for decision making in the hands of such organisations (e.g., Comer 1980).

Public primary schools in Africa, as they are presently constituted, tend to specialise in certain rather unique forms of discourse within their walls, characterised by a marked asymmetry of power between the teacher and students. Towards the end of our follow-up study, we attempted to animate community discussions of the significance of schooling in several of the home villages from which our study cohort were drawn (Serpell 1993a). We made an effort to legitimate the opinions of village parents, by focusing the discussion on explicit textual formulations in the indigenous language of strengths and weaknesses of the school's educational programme, identified by parents in individual interviews. However, the authoritarian mode of discourse prevalent in school contexts nevertheless overwhelmed our attempt to promote an egalitarian exchange of views.

Reflecting on this disappointing outcome, we turned to the very different structure of popular participatory theatre, which had been used with some success by health and agricultural development agents in various parts of the continent (Etherton 1982; Mlama 1988). This approach proved to be much more successful in generating opportunities for various constituencies within the community to express their concerns. Although the local school had no previous experience with this ambitious use of drama to address issues of real public concern, the enthusiasm with which several teachers entered into the process was very encouraging. Several African government ministries of education have included drama as one of the peripherally endorsed activities of schools. Thus, an expansion of this type of use of the school as a community forum would appear to be highly compatible with the existing framework of IPBS.

The Local School as a Base for Continuing Education

Many primary schools in Zambia allow the use of their classrooms for evening classes in adult education. Sometimes, especially in rural areas, where teaching personnel tend to be scarce, the teaching of these adult education classes is undertaken by the same teachers who are responsible for teaching the standard primary school curriculum. But in such cases their role as adult educators is strictly segregated from that of primary school teacher (not exactly "moonlighting," but definitely a second job), for which they are accountable to a separate authority with little or no reference to the head of the local school. Yet into these classes will arrive many of the students who were excluded from completion of the basic, primary course for various reasons. Here too, then, is a potential growth point for enhancing the connections between IPBS and the everyday life of the local community.

SCHOOLS AS NODES IN THE PLANNING MODEL: PROMOTING LOCAL ACCOUNTABILITY

In this concluding section I wish to adopt a practical approach. School systems, whatever their ideological and pedagogical flaws, are part of the fabric of most contemporary societies. If a theoretical critique is to make any significant impact on these actual social systems, it must translate its concepts into tangible, administratively feasible proposals for ways of restructuring the existing pattern of IPBS. I will advance three for serious consideration, all of which involve treating the school as a relatively discrete node in the process of aggregating national data.

Parallel Tracks to Various Valued Outcomes

First, at the local level, the school needs to expand its public criteria of what constitutes a successful outcome of several years of enrolment: instead of defining the only index of success as passing an exam to proceed to the next level of the curriculum, schools and the communities they serve need to acknowledge the following types of outcome as highly valued, alternative indices of educational success:

- A student nurses a young child back to health following a spell of serious weight loss

- A team of school pupils builds a new chicken hutch, or grain storage bin for an elderly member of the community, whose previous structure was destroyed
- A group of students mounts a local performance of an entertaining drama with illuminating connotations for a significant social issue
- A young person grows a large crop of cereal or vegetables (perhaps more than anyone else in the village this year, or more than was grown in the same plot last year)
- A young person sews dresses for a young sister, or baby daughter (perhaps in a style that he/she was unable to sew last year; or so well that it earns recognition from the local needlework club)
- A young person with seriously impaired sensory, motor, or cognitive function participates effectively in a public, community activity.

The community and the school would need to consult on how to collate records of such events, and how to evaluate and reward them. But the national ministry of education could catalyse the process by requiring periodic tallies in various categories; for example agricultural achievements, community service, contributions to public health, preschool child welfare, social and vocational habilitation of persons with disabilities, and so forth. The process of acknowledging such outcomes, once initiated, could be further legitimated by the ministry selecting outstanding reports for wider dissemination, and perhaps making awards to schools achieving conspicuous successes in each domain. At the local level, the school could authenticate the significance of such achievements by awarding certificates. In this way, several parallel tracks of valued progress would become visible as alternative, complementary types of outcome of the education offered by the school, rather than a few success stories surrounded by a much larger pool of failures.

Selection Quotas

Second, rather than relying on a single standardised test or exam to recruit unevenly from all the nation's primary schools, a more decentralised selection system could be devised in which some parts of the evaluation are delegated to the local school. The national educational administration might continue to set its overall targets for admission to the restricted higher levels of the school system, but devolve some of the responsibility for identifying which students filled those places. For instance, every school might be assigned a minimum quota of secondary school places per head of school-leaving exam candidates. If the national aggregate were that 15 percent of all grade 7 school leavers nationwide can be accommodated in Grade 8 classes, the minimum quota for each school might be set at 10 percent. Thus a school that registers 40 candidates would be guaranteed at least 4 places in secondary school, and would have a say in the selection of which students qualify, provided they meet certain minimal requirements.

Bonding for Payback

The third strand of this restructuring would involve making secondary students more explicitly accountable to the community that provided their basic schooling. Those students who were selected for a place in secondary school would be bonded to return periodically to their original neighbourhood, perhaps during their school holidays, and to provide some kind of community service, such as tutoring younger children in the basics of reading or participating in an ongoing community service project. This would serve not only to instill an awareness of the sacrifice made by the community on behalf of its outwardly mobile scion, but also to provide tangible evidence to the community of the benefits accruing from its investment.

In short, these three strands, if carefully implemented, hold the potential to replace the current, self-defeating, extractive formulation of educational success with a much more widely distributed set of indices, many of which are inwardly enriching to the community, as well as placing greater emphasis on the social responsibility of education.

CONCLUSION: COSTS AND BENEFITS OF RESTRUCTURING

Ideally, the goals of education should include the cultivation of moral accountability and social responsibility as part of the fruition of intellectual potential. The failure of contemporary schooling to attain this goal for many African communities reflects a prevalent, narrow conceptualisation of the function of school instruction as imparting isolated cognitive skills, cut off from their application to real-world problems, together with a set of institutional arrangements that define success in terms of competitive progression along a rigidly defined staircase. The consequence of this formalisation of education is that small numbers of individuals with great potential to contribute to the life of their local communities of origin are systematically extracted into a separate, and largely alien culture of bureaucratic power, while the majority of those enrolled in school leave it with a sense of frustration and personal inadequacy.

I have suggested that a way forward out of this impasse lies in the integration of the curriculum with the demands of everyday life outside the school, and building local accountability into the overall planning process. My suggestions are offered, not as a "blueprint," but as practical guidelines for a "learning process" (Korten 1980) through which the underrealised potential of public education could be released from the restrictive shackles of a system that was imported from abroad and never fully adapted to the sociocultural conditions of rural African communities.

Some planners will doubtless object to these suggestions on the grounds of a type of cost that was cited frequently in Zambia's national debate on educational reform in the 1970s: the likelihood of "slowing down" the progress of students destined to reach tertiary education. The voices that express this concern tend to be heard exceptionally loudly in the corridors of power. Many of its proponents are university graduates themselves; many of them have children currently enrolled in secondary or tertiary programmes. They know from first-hand experience how distracting it can be to be required to perform community service or national service as part of "the price one has to pay for one's own education." They know how difficult it often is to get through all the requirements of the prescribed curriculum, and how every hour devoted to extracurricular public service activities detracts from the time available for "real studies."

These costs to the elite currently recruited under the extractive model should be set alongside two types of benefit, one to themselves, the other to their contemporaries who do not proceed to secondary or higher education. For the elites, a system that makes them more accountable to their community of origin may serve to reduce some of the feelings of alienation expressed by many formally educated Africans (see Serpell 1993a). For their contemporaries, the shift of emphasis that I propose offers many more ways of deriving practical knowledge and enhanced self-esteem from their experience at school than are currently afforded by IPBS.

At a more systemic level, the benefits to a community of such a restructuring would include opportunities for greater utilisation of local cultural resources such as local languages, multi-age-group peer tutoring, and communal sharing of responsibility. Although social science has correctly identified many points of contrast between the indigenous cultures of Africa on the one hand and the culture of modern science and technology on the other, these ways of relating to the world are not necessarily fundamentally incompatible (Horton 1982). The increasingly interdependent world in which we live demands that culturally contrasting perspectives enter into dialogue and attempt to negotiate a fusion of horizons (Serpell 1994).

> The social relations between . . . the school and the community it purports to serve are integral to the process of education. Education cannot be reduced analytically to microlevel instructional processes on the supposition that these are the "real" or core aspects of education, whereas the rest of the social process is somehow external or incidental. Sociocultural interaction and cultural mediation are an intrinsic part of recruiting the younger generation to a transformative participation in the wider society. (Serpell and Boykin 1994, 402)

NOTES

[1] Much of the argument advanced in this chapter has been developed in more detail in my book, *The Significance of Schooling* (1993a), on which I have drawn extensively in composing the text.

[2] Since this chapter was first drafted, Gertrude Mwape and I have been privileged to observe and document an innovative approach to health education that is incorporated within the mainstream of public primary schooling in Mpika, Zambia. Under the aegis of the national Child-to-Child programme, teachers at Kabale Primary School have successfully applied several of the principles advocated in this chapter, with remarkable results (Mwape and Serpell 1996).

[3] Several other theoretical perspectives in the field of applied developmental psychology concur in advocating that the form and pace of instruction should ideally be adjusted to characteristics of the individual learner (including the behaviour analytic tradition, neo-Piagetian, and information-processing models).

[4] The Appropriate Technology (AT) movement that emerged in the 1960s was motivated initially by considerations of cost-effectivenesss and cultural adaptation. Examples of its application in the fields of health education and habilitation are contained in WHO (1980, 1983) and in Werner and Bower (1982).

REFERENCES

Aries, P. 1962. *Centuries of Childhood.* Translated from the French by R. Baldick. London: Cape.

Arnold, C. 1986. "Family and Parent-Support Programmes: The Community-Based Approach." In *Educating Handicapped Young People in Eastern and Southern Africa in 1981–83*, ed. D.H. Ross. Paris: UNESCO.

Ball, S.J. 1983. "Imperialism, Social Control and the Colonial Curriculum in Africa." *Journal of Curriculum Studies* 15(3): 237–263.

Barnum, H.N., and R.H. Sabot. 1976. "Migration, Education and Urban Surplus Labour: The Case of Tanzania." Paris: OECD, Development Centre Studies, Employment Series No. 13.

Berlin, I. 1956. "Introduction." In *The Age of Enlightenment*, ed. I. Berlin. New York: Mentor.

Bronfenbrenner, J. 1979. *The Ecology of Human Development*. Cambridge: Harvard University Press.

Cherns, A. 1984. "Contribution of Social Psychology to the Nature and Function of Work and Its Relevance to Societies of the Third World." *International Journal of Psychology* 19: 97–111.

Cole, M. 1990. "Cognitive Development and Formal Schooling: The Evidence from Cross-Cultural Research." In *Vygotsky and Education: Instructional Implications and Applications of Sociohistorical Psychology*, ed. L.C. Moll. Cambridge: Cambridge University Press.

Comer, J.P. 1980. *School Power*. New York: Freedom Press.

Court, D. 1985. "Education and Socio-Economic Development in Africa: The Search for the Missing Link." Unpublished manuscript, Nairobi, Kenya.

Court, D., and K. Kinyanjui. 1985. "Education and Development in Sub-Saharan Africa: The Operation and Impact of Education Systems." Nairobi, Kenya: Institute for Development Studies, Working Paper No. 421.

D'Andrade, R.G. 1984. "Cultural Meaning Systems." In *Culture Theory: Essays on Mind, Self and Emotion*, eds. R.A. Shweder and R.A. Levine. Cambridge: Cambridge University Press.

Etherton, M. 1982. *The Development of African Drama*. New York: Holmes and Meier/Africana.

Gallimore, R., T.S. Weisner, S.Z. Kaufman, and L.P. Berneheimer. 1989. "The Social Construction of Ecocultural Niches: Family Accommodation of Developmentally Delayed Children." *American Journal on Mental Retardation* 94(3):216–230.

Goody, J. 1977. *The Domestication of the Savage Mind*. Cambridge: Cambridge University Press.

Harbison, F., and C.A. Myers. 1964. *Education, Manpower and Economic Growth*. New York: McGraw Hill.

Harkness, S., and C.M. Super. 1992a. "Parental Ethnotheories in Action." In *Parental Belief Systems: The Psychological Consequences for Children*, eds. I.E. Sigel, A.V. McGillicuddy-Delisi, and J.J. Goodnow. 2nd ed. Hillsdale, NJ: Erlbaum.

Harkness, S., and C.M. Super. 1992b. "Shared Child Care in East Africa: Sociocultural Origins and Developmental Consequences." In *Child Care In Context*, eds. M.E. Lamb, K.J. Sternberg, C.P. Hwang, and A. Broberg. Hillsdale, NJ: Erlbaum.

Horton, R. 1982. "Tradition and Modernity Revisited." In *Rationality and Relativism*, eds. M. Hollis and S. Lukes. Oxford: Blackwell.

Howard, A., and R.A. Scott. 1981. "The Minority Groups in Complex Societies." In *Handbook of Cross-Cultural Human Development*, eds. R.H. Munroe, R.L. Munroe, and B. Whiting. New York: Garland STPM Press.

Inkeles, A., and D.H. Smith. 1974. *Becoming Modern: Individual Change in Six Developing Countries*. Cambridge, MA: Harvard University Press.

Kabamba, J.M. 1988. "Use Studies of Public Libraries: The Benefits of Community-Based Information Services in Zambia." Preliminary Report of a Pilot Study. Lusaka: University of Zambia, Institute for African Studies.

Kagitcibasi, C. 1996. *Family and Human Development Across Cultures: A View from the Other Side*. New York: UNICEF.

Kiernan, C. 1985. "Communication." In *Mental Deficiency: The Changing Outlook*, eds. A.M. Clarke, A.D.B. Clarke, and J.M. Berg. 4th ed. London: Methuen.

Korten, D. 1980. "Community Organization and Rural Development: A Learning Process Approach." *Public Administration Review* 40(5): 480–511.

Lave, J., and E. Wenger. 1991. *Situated Learning: Legitimate Peripheral Participation*. Cambridge: Cambridge University Press.

Mariga, L. 1989. "Learning Needs of Parents and Lay Helpers in Rural Communities for Home-Based Education of Pre-School Children with Mental Handicaps." In *Early Intervention, Developmental Disability and Mental Handicap in Africa*, eds. R. Serpell, D. Nabuzoka, and F. Lesi. Lusaka: University of Zambia/UNICEF.

McClelland, D. 1961. *The Achieving Society*. Princeton: Van Nostrand.

Mittler, P., and H. McConachie, eds. 1983. *Parents, Professionals and Mentally Handicapped People: Approaches to Partnership*. London: Croom Helm.

Mittler, P., and R. Serpell. 1985. "Services: An International Perspective." In *Mental Deficiency: The Changing Outlook*, eds. A.M. Clarke, A.D.B. Clarke, and J.M. Berg. 4th ed. London: Methuen.

Mlama, P. 1988. "Culture and Development: The Popular Theater Approach in Africa." Paper presented at the Reflections on Development Conference, Rockefeller Foundation, Bellagio, Italy, July 1988.

Moll, L.C., and J.B. Greenberg. 1990. "Creating Zones of Possibilities: Combining Social Contexts for Instruction." In *Vygotsky and Education: Instructional Implications and Applications of Sociohistorical Psychology*, ed. L.C. Moll. Cambridge: Cambridge University Press.

Morley, D., and M. Woodland. 1979. *See How They Grow: Monitoring Child Growth for Appropriate Health Care in Developing Countries*. London: MacMillan.

Mwape, G., and R. Serpell. 1996. "Participatory Appropriation of Health Science by Primary School Students in Rural Zambia." Poster presentation at the 14th Biennial Meeting of the International Society for the Study of Behavioural Development, Quebec, Canada, August 1996.

Nabuzoka, D., ed. 1986. "Reaching Disabled Children in Zambia: Reports and Other Publications on Various Aspects of the Zambia National Campaign to Reach Disabled Children (1980–85)." [mimeo]. Lusaka: University of Zambia, Institute for African Studies.

Nsamenang, A.B. 1992. "Early Childhood Care and Education in Cameroon." In *Child Care in Context*, eds. M.E. Lamb, K.J. Sternberg, C.-P. Hwang, and A. Broberg. Hillsdale, NJ: Erlbaum.

Ogbu, J.U. 1974. *The Next Generation: An Ethnography of Education in an Urban Neighbourhood.* New York: Academic Press.

Olson, D. 1976. "Culture, Technology and Intellect." In *The Nature of Intelligence*, ed. L.B. Resnick. Hillsdale, NJ: Erlbaum.

Reder, S.M. 1987. "Comparative Aspects of Functional Literacy Development: Three Ethnic American Communities." In *The Future of Literacy in a Changing World*, ed. D.A. Wagner. New York: Pergamon.

Rogoff, B. 1990. *Apprenticeship in Thinking: Cognitive Development in Social Context.* New York: Oxford University Press.

Sadler, J. E. 1966. *J. A. Comenius and the Concept of Universal Education.* London: Allen and Unwin.

Scribner, S., and M. Cole. 1981. *The Psychology of Literacy.* Cambridge, MA: Harvard University Press.

Serpell, R. 1982. "Intellectual Handicap in a Cross-Cultural Perspective." Inaugural lecture, University of Zambia, Lusaka, 9th July 1982.

Serpell, R. 1986. "Specialized Centres and the Local Home Community: Children with Disabilities Need Them Both." *International Journal of Special Education* 1(2): 107–127.

Serpell, R. 1992. "African Dimensions of Child Care and Nurturance." In *Child Care in Context*, eds. M.E. Lamb, K.J. Sternberg, C.-P. Hwang, and A. Broberg. Hillsdale, NJ: Erlbaum.

Serpell, R. 1993a. *The Significance of Schooling: Life-Journeys in an African Society.* Cambridge: Cambridge University Press.

Serpell, R.1993b. "Interaction of Context with Development: Theoretical Constructs for the Design of Early Childhood Intervention Programs." In *Early Intervention and Culture*, eds. L. Eldering and P. Leseman. Paris: UNESCO.

Serpell, R. 1994. "Negotiating a Fusion of Horizons: A Process View of Cultural Validation in Developmental Psychology." *Mind Culture and Activity* 1:43–68.

Serpell, R. 1995. "Situated Theory as a Bridge Between Experimental Research and Political Analysis." In *Cultural Psychology and Activity Theory: Essays in Honor of Sylvia Scribner*, eds. L. Martin, K. Nelson, and E. Tobach. New York: Cambridge University Press.

Serpell, R., and A.W. Boykin. 1994. "Cultural Dimensions of Cognition: A Multiplex, Dynamic System of Constraints and Possibilities." Pp. 369–408 in *Handbook of Perception and Cognition, Vol.12: Thinking and Problem-Solving*, ed. R.J. Sternberg. San Diego: Academic Press.

Serpell, R., and G. Hatano. 1997. "Education, Literacy and Schooling in Cross-Cultural Perspective." Pp. 339–376 in *Handbook of Cross-Cultural Psychology, Volume 4,* eds. P.R. Dasen and T.M. Saraswathi. Boston: Allen and Unwin.

Serpell, R., L. Mariga, and K. Harvey. 1993. "Mental Retardation in African Countries: Conceptualization, Services, and Research." *International Review of Research in Mental Retardation* 19: 1–39.

Serpell, R., and D. Nabuzoka. 1991. "Early Intervention in Third World Countries." Pp. 93–126 in *Early Intervention Studies for Young Children With Special Needs,* eds. D.M. Mitchell and R.I. Brown. London: Chapman and Hall.

Shweder, R.A. 1990. "Cultural Psychology—What Is It ?" In *Cultural Psychology*, eds. J. W. Stigler, R. A. Shweder, and G. Herdt. Cambridge, MA: Harvard University Press.

Snelson, P.D. 1974. *Educational Development in Northern Rhodesia: 1883–1945*. Lusaka: National Educational Company of Zambia (NEDCOZ).

Super, C.M., and S. Harkness. 1986. "The Developmental Niche: A Conceptualization at the Interface of Child and Culture," *International Journal of Behavioural Development* 9:545–569.

Tharp, R., and R. Gallimore. 1988. *Rousing Minds to Life: Teaching, Learning, and Schooling in Social Context*. New York: Cambridge University Press.

Van Rensburg, P. 1984. "Looking Forward from Serowe." *Education with Production* (special supplement). Gaborone, Botswana: Foundation for Education with Production.

Vygotsky, L. S. 1978. *Mind in Society: The Development of Higher Psychological Processes*, eds. M. Cole, V. John-Steiner, S. Scribner, and E. Souberman. Cambridge, MA: Harvard University Press.

Werner, D., and Bower B. 1982. *Helping Health Workers Learn*. Palo Alto, CA: Hesperian Foundation.

World Conference on Education for All. 1990. "World Declaration on Education for All." New York: UNICEF (Inter-Agency Commission for the World Conference on Education for All).

World Health Organization. 1980. *Training the Disabled in the Community: An Experimental Manual on Rehabilitation and Disability Prevention for De-*

veloping Countries (prepared by E. Helander, P. Mendis, and G. Nelson). Geneva: World Health Organization.

World Health Organization. 1983. *Training the Disabled in the Community: An Experimental Manual on Rehabilitation and Disability Prevention for Developing Countries* (revised edition) (prepared by E. Helander, P. Mendis, and G. Nelson). Geneva: World Health Organization.

PART III
THE COSTS OF CULTURE AND THE CULTURE OF COSTS

CHAPTER 8

Language Policy in Ethiopian Education

Implications for the Costs of Textbook Production

CHRISTINE McNAB AND PETER STOYE

Common sense and linguistic research suggest that children learn better in the medium of their mother tongue. The problem in multilingual states has been how to facilitate mother-tongue education for all children while meeting the state's need for a language of national unity and international communication. There is no simple resolution of this dilemma and each policy goal carries with it certain costs. If national unity is given priority and one national language is selected for education, then there is the risk of high dropout in the first years of schooling and a possible undermining of the cultures carried by the languages not used in school. If mother tongue is given priority, the arrangements for teacher training and teacher appointment/transfer, educational materials development, and the production of educational materials are likely to be more complex and expensive. However, this might well be offset by increased participation and improved school retention rates.

Ethiopia is now in the process of changing from a monolingual (Amharic) primary education system to a multilingual system. This change in policy is only in part a pedagogical and cultural measure. It is also an expression of the political will of the ruling party to regionalise Ethiopia, reversing the previous long-term trend to centralisation and integration around Amharic culture and language. Implementation of the new policy will necessitate a larger number of textbook titles. The additional cost could be a source of contention, particularly in the short term when the high costs of developing and producing new materials have to be met. This chapter explores the implications for the costs of textbook production and distribution when a multilingual media of instruction policy is put into practice.

THE CONTEXT

Ethiopia in the 1990s

Ethiopia has in the 1990s undergone a series of radical political changes that have reversed a century-long political and cultural centralisation process. One of the first acts of the incoming transitional government, which had its power base in the Tigray People's Liberation Front, was to redraw the political map of Ethiopia, adjusting regional boundaries to coincide more closely with ethnolinguistic areas. At the same time, a change from central government to federal government was initiated. The division of powers and functions between the federal government and the state (or regional) governments is set out in the new constitution of Ethiopia, which was ratified in 1995 (Transitional Government of Ethiopia 1995a).

The change from a centralised to a federal system has not been without personal and social costs. Under both the Imperial and *Dergue* governments, the urban areas of Ethiopia had become increasingly "Amharic" in language and culture. A class of educated people who saw themselves as first and foremost Ethiopians had developed: civil servants and teachers were predominantly Amharic-speaking, even if not in an ethnic sense Amharas. When the regional boundaries were redrawn, and the new state governments and administrations began using the locally dominant regional language as their official language, Amharas were no longer welcome in some regions. Many have had to move away, in some cases from areas where their families had been settled over several generations. There were cases of harassment and even murder. Many officials working in central government ministries and organisations were dismissed, retired, or sent to their "home" regions. Apart from the personal suffering, this process has caused serious capacity problems in central ministries, such as the Ministry of Education, and a skewed distribution of trained teachers between the different states (officially termed "national regional states" in Ethiopia).

The Education System

There have been two major changes in the education system under the new government; first, the language policy for education, and second, the level of government responsible for basic education. The freedom given to the state governments to provide basic education in the regional language is a major break with earlier language policies which had established Amharic, the national language, as the language of instruction for primary school (and English for secondary and higher education). There are three paragraphs on language policy in the Ethiopian Education and Training Policy:

> 3.5.1. Cognizant of the pedagogical advantage of the child in learning in mother tongue and the rights of nationalities to promote the use of their languages, primary education will be given in nationality languages.
>
> 3.5.2. Making the necessary preparation, nations and nationalities can either learn in their own language or can choose from among those selected on the basis of national and countrywide distribution.
>
> 3.5.3. The language of teacher training for kindergarten and primary education will be the nationality language used in the area.
>
> (Transitional Government of Ethiopia 1994)

The intention of the policy is that primary education (at present six grades) will be through the medium of the local language in order to facilitate learning and enhance the local culture. However, the policy also in effect means that there will be a heavy language load in the primary school curriculum, as English will be taught as a subject from grade 1 and, in non-Amhara areas, Amarigna will be taught as a subject from grade 4.

The responsibility for the implementation of these changes lies with the education bureau at state level, as provision of basic education (primary and adult) has passed from the central to the state governments. While overall responsibility for social and economic development is retained at federal (central) level, it is the responsibility of the state governments "to formulate and execute policies, strategies and plans for their economic and social development" (Transitional Government of Ethiopia 1995a). The federal government, however, retains responsibility for setting national standards, and therefore there is still a central Institute of Curriculum Development and Research which, in addition to its main tasks, also writes textbooks.

It is not yet certain how the state governments plan to finance education. Articles 94 and 99 of the new constitution deal with revenue and taxation. Both levels of the government have a right to levy taxes of various kinds, but how this will work in practice, and how federal revenues will be divided between states, is yet to be seen. There is also the question of how foreign development assistance will be divided between central and regional functions. Education development aid to Ethiopia

Table 8.1. Enrolment by Region 1993–1994

Region		Total	%
1	Tigray	293,429	12.8
2	Afar	12,450	0.5
3	Amhara	397,839	17.4
4	Oromia	715,351	31.3
5	Ogaden	0	0.0
6	Benishangul	30,411	1.3
7–11	South Ethiopia	528,617	23.1
12	Gambela	12,717	0.6
13	Harar	11,527	0.5
14	Addis Ababa	263,221	11.5
15	Dire Dawa	18,257	0.8
Total		2,283,819	100.0

includes not only funds for development but also for recurrent expenditures on items such as teacher training and textbooks.

These ambitious changes in language policy and educational administration need to be seen against the background of an education system in crisis. Ethiopia has one of the lowest participation rates in formal education in Africa. In 1993–1994 net enrolment in primary school was only 22 percent (Transitional Government of Ethiopia 1995b). Participation was higher in the 1980s, but the war disrupted the system: parents began to distrust the schools, which were used as recruitment centres by the army, and in the final phase and even after the war, many schools were destroyed. Extreme poverty of the population in many areas makes it difficult for children to attend school. The redeployment of teachers and administrators following the ethnolinguistic federalisation of Ethiopia in the early 1990s has also caused some teacher-supply problems. Enrolment by region in 1993–1994 is shown in Table 8.1.

The Language Situation

The states' ability to implement the new language policy for education is severely inhibited by the highly complex language situation in Ethiopia. There are approximately 170 languages, belonging to four major language groups (Greenberg 1963). Even though the new national regional state boundaries have been drawn up on ethnolinguistic lines, the new states are all more or less multilingual. From an educational administration point of view, some states are in a more fortunate position than others, with clear language majority groups. The latter position is exemplified by the states of Tigray, Amhara, Oromo, Afar, Somali (formerly called Ogaden), and Harar. In Addis Ababa, Amharigna is well established as the language of communication and education. There are, however, far more difficult language situations for the education sector in the west and south of the country: the states of Benishangul, Gambela, and Southern Ethiopia (a union of five regions: Gurage/Hadiya and Kembata, Sidama, Wolayta, Omo, and Kefa).

There are no accurate figures as to how large the different language groups are in each state. A national census in October 1994 asked people for their ethnic identities, but the overall results of the census are not yet published. Therefore, to get some idea of the relative size of the language groups, one must refer to the language survey of Ethiopia that was carried out in 1968 (Bender et al. 1976), which also included Eritrea. The 1968 survey found that three major languages, Amharigna, Oromigna, and Tigrigna, together accounted for the languages used by about 70 percent of the population. The next group of 11 "minor" languages accounted for another 20 percent and "others" totalled 10 percent. Given a total number of languages in Ethiopia of around 170, with the majority in south and west Ethiopia, it can be seen that implementing a mother tongue in education is a long-term project.

Since 1968 there have only been partial surveys, which, because of the border dispute between Ethiopia and Eritrea, have consistently under-reported the languages of Eritrea and Tigray and the languages of the nomadic peoples, the Afars and Somalis (Central Statistical Office 1980, 1985; Government of Ethiopia 1987). A rough estimate of the relative numbers of mother-tongue speakers of the various languages today can be derived by using data from the 1968 survey, the total population from the 1984 census, and the increase in population, which in 1984 was estimated to be 2.9 percent per annum. These figures suggest a total population of about 57 million for Ethiopia and Eritrea together. If the proportions of mother-tongue speakers of the major languages have remained about the same as in 1968, their numbers today, including the area which is now Eritrea, could total as follows:

Amharigna	17.8 million
Oromigna	15.5 million
Tigrigna	8.1 million

The minor languages would be spoken by between 100,000 and two million people each, with some of the "other" languages only being spoken by a few thousand people.

It is even more difficult to estimate which languages are spoken by how many people on a state-by-state basis. From the 1968 survey's language maps, we know approximately which languages were spoken in which regions. But there were large-scale population shifts in the 1980s caused by war, famine, and resettlement programmes, the latter including as many as half a million people (Central Statistical Office 1991). Many of these people have moved back to their original areas. In addition, there are the people who were displaced during the final stages of the war and those who are living outside Ethiopia as refugees. Furthermore there is no available data about the relative rates of population for the different ethnolinguistic groups.

According to verbal information from the Ministry of Education, the states have so far made a variety of choices regarding the medium of instruction for primary education:

1. Amharigna is being used in Amhara, Addis Ababa, Benishangul, and Southern Ethiopia. However, in the latter two cases the intention is for each community to switch to using its own language as soon as possible. Sidamigna is already being taught as a compulsory subject in Awassa, the capital of South Ethiopia. Amharigna is written in the Ethiopian syllabary and Sidamigna in Latin script, although it was previously taught in the Ethiopian syllabary in the literacy campaigns of the late 1970s and 1980s.
2. Oromigna is used in Oromia, but in the towns some of the schools and classes are using Amharigna due to parental and community demand. Oromigna, which was originally written in Latin script but taught using the Ethiopian syllabary during the *Dergue* period, is now once again written in Latin script.
3. Tigrigna is used in Tigray, still using the Ethiopian syllabary.
4. Harari is used in Harar, but it is not certain which script has been selected.
5. Somali is probably being used in Somali, but there is little information on what has happened to education in this state, which has been affected by, among other things, the influx of refugees from neighbouring Somalia.

Providing primary education in regional languages will not be the same as providing mother-tongue education for all children, as is intimated in the education policy. For many children, those who speak the major languages in the "right" regions, the learning environment should be much improved once educational materials are available and the teachers are trained to use them. Yet for some children, changes in the language of instruction from Amharic to a regional majority language will worsen their situation in school. In the worst case, a child will speak a minority language at home, be taught through the medium of the regional language in primary school, learn English from grade 1 as a subject, and Amharic, the federal language of communication, from grade 4. A further complicating factor for the children is that they will need to learn the two scripts.

TEXTBOOK PROVISION IN ETHIOPIA

The System for Textbook Provision

Until recently, Ethiopia has had a single textbook system; that is, for each subject in a grade, the whole country has used the same textbook. The books have been written by staff at the Institute for Curriculum Development and Research (ICDR) and edited, printed, and distributed by the Ethiopian Educational Materials Production and Distribution Agency (EMPDA). The books have been given to the students on loan and the estimated life length of the textbooks in the classroom has been three years. Printing production has taken place mainly at EMPDA, which has been supported by development aid agencies, in particular the Swedish International Development Authority, providing machinery, paper and other consumables, and staff training. The EMPDA printing press has been unable to meet demand, and considerable book quantities have therefore been subcontracted to other printers, mainly to the plants of the Ethiopian Printing Corporation in Addis Ababa.

The decentralisation of educational provision to the states will have considerable consequences for textbook supply, but it will take time to reallocate responsibilities in practice between central and state authorities, especially as the state governments do not yet have a sufficient tax base to finance basic education. The production of textbooks is still carried out at EMPDA, whereas curriculum development is now carried out at both central (ICDR) and state levels, each state education bureau having a small curriculum development unit. The central responsibility is for the national model curriculum, and the state unit is responsible for local adaptation and, where possible, the development of new textbooks.

To handle the production and distribution of the new titles necessary for a multilanguage education system within a very limited time period is a major task. For EMPDA, with its limited resources, the task is staggering. Regional production is being discussed. This is, however, difficult in the short term because of a lack of trained staff and suitable machinery. A further complication is that textbook production is to a large extent financed by foreign donors and donor funds are normally channelled via central government. On a short-term basis there seems to be no alternative to EMPDA continuing as the manufacturer of textbooks, although EMPDA has major difficulties in handling the different languages, even when translations and new titles in the local languages are done collaboratively with writers at regional level. EMPDA's earlier experience, under the *Dergue* government, of publishing literacy materials in 15 languages was not a particularly happy one. The editing had to be carried out by the Department of Adult Education, and EMPDA could not take responsibility for the quality of the materials (McNab 1989). There is no reason to believe that EMPDA's staff can handle the situation any better today than they did in the 1980s.

The short-term demands of the new language policy on the textbook production system can be seen more clearly when the various stages of producing new textbooks are analysed. First, a large number of new titles will have to be developed. In some cases direct translations may be possible, but in many cases titles must be newly written or adapted in order to reflect local cultures as stipulated by the objectives of the decentralised system. With at present about five to six titles per grade in each of the primary school grades, there are 30–35 titles per language; with 11–12 languages, some 300–400 titles have to be translated or newly written.

Normally the development of a new textbook title takes between one and two years. Translation of existing titles requires less time, although often the illustrations will need to be adapted to local cultures. The writing of new titles will be a costly undertaking and because the writing costs are distributed over a smaller number of copies, the cost per copy will be higher. On the other hand, the changes allow the possibility of improving the quality of the textbooks. Many of the books developed for the previous centralised education system are of doubtful pedagogic quality, overly long, and therefore more expensive than is necessary.

Editorial work has until now been done by EMPDA. The new situation will require a substantial increase of editorial resources and it is still an open question whether these will be developed at EMPDA or if each state will create its own editiorial resources, either in the state system or among commercial publishers. The latter alternative could be the more attractive, as competition in the textbook market should increase the quality of the textbooks.

If production remains in Addis Ababa, distribution will, as in the past, take place via regional warehouses, thereby preventing major cost increases that could result from the new institutional framework for textbook provision. However, distribution will become more complex, particularly in the most multilingual regions where "islands" of minority language schools will need to be supplied.

THE COST OF IMPLEMENTING THE MULTILANGUAGE TEXTBOOK POLICY

The textbooks will cost more in the new system with a larger number of titles. The increased number of titles will give shorter print runs, which will increase the unit costs. Instead of 30–40 titles for the primary level, in print runs of between 60,000–400,000 copies each, there will be 300–400 titles in print runs of 1,000–70,000 copies each. The increased production time will incur considerable additional costs. The increased number of titles will not, however, in principle require larger quantities of paper. The total number of copies will be the same. As long as present standards regarding the textbook loan system,[1] book life length, pupil/book ratio, and number of pages per title is not considerably changed, there will be no major increases in paper cost. There will be more need of film and printing plates, but these are small costs compared with the paper cost. However, the cost of writing and editing, and also the fixed costs for printing, will be spread out over much shorter print runs.

In 1994 a report discussed improving the financial aspects of the monitoring of donor support to educational materials; some cost estimates for Ethiopian textbooks were prepared (Graphium Consult 1995) based on EMPDA's own data and calculation models. The reporting system was, however, designed for the reporting of costs and not specifically designed to answer questions of the type: What will the effects on the costs be if we do this or that? Data were not available at EMPDA on other factors which will affect the costs of implementing the new language policy in a decentralised system; for example, information on additional salaries, customs duties, freight costs, and so forth. We have therefore drawn upon publishing experience in order to make the cost estimates. Assumptions are made regarding how the fiscal, administrative, and political systems will develop in Ethiopia.

To make cost calculations accessible to the reader, our example assumes one language in each region, and that Addis Ababa will have books in Amharigna. Therefore, in total we have used 10 languages in our calculations. In reality, most regions will eventually be using more than one language, which is more expensive. But some languages are cross-regional, so some savings could be made by sharing textbook development and production costs across regions. The school data are taken from the Ministry of Education's annual statistics for the academic year 1993–1994.

As we saw earlier in Table 8.1, the total number of children in school is approximately 22 percent of the children between 7 and 12 years of age in Ethiopia. Improved schools, education in the mother tongue, improved books, and decentralized administration will probably lead to increased enrolment. When more children attend school, the unit cost of the textbooks will be lower if book production is increased to cope with a higher number of pupils. Our calculations make no allowance for the projected increase, because it is too early to predict how fast school enrolments will rise and what, if any, the regional variations are likely to be.

Table 8.2 shows the distribution of pupils across the grades in 1993–1994. It indicates the percentage of children who should have received new copies of textbooks that year, according to Ministry of Education guidelines for the provision of textbooks. Table 8.2 shows the printed quantities for the respective grades in the single textbook system. These are estimates which were made in connection with the financial monitor-

Table 8.2. Overall School Enrolment and Books, 1993–1994 (as in a single textbook system)

Grade	Pupils (Thousands)	Books Printed: No of Titles in Grade	Books Printed: Copies per Title (Thousands)	Books Printed: Total Copies (Thousands)	% of Children That Received New Copies per Subject
1	908	5	259	1,296	29%
2	394	5	138	689	35%
3	306	7	78	543	25%
4	252	8	61	491	24%
5	213	7	62	432	29%
6	211	7	58	405	27%
Total	2,284	39		3,856	

ing report mentioned above (Graphium 1995). Twenty-four to 35 percent of pupils received new copies of each title. This corresponds to the targeted life length of the book, which is three years; that is, one-third of the books have to be reprinted every year. The lower percentages mean either that books older than three years have to be reused for a longer time or that two children have to share a book. It seems reasonable that the same relative supply is aimed at also in a multilanguage textbook provision system. These figures have therefore been used in the calculations below.

The costs for the different components of textbook development and production are shown in Table 8.3 for both the old single language system and for the new multilanguage system. It can be seen that the writing cost per copy in the single textbook system was on average 0.21 Birr (approximately 6.5 Birr to $US1 in 1997). The average print run was around 99,000 copies so that the annual author cost for a title would be some 20,763 Birr. This is only a rough estimate, but as an assumed writing time of 18 months, written off over six years, gives a similar result, the figure is at least of the right magnitude.

If lower quantities of a title are produced, as when the total number of textbooks is subdivided into textbooks in different languages, the writing costs per copy become considerably higher, the costs of authoring per copy rising to an average of 1.89 Birr. This could be expected, as the num-

Table 8.3. Cost Components in the Single-Language and the Multilanguage system

Averages	**Single-Language System**			**Multilanguage System**		
Exchange rate	**0.85**			**0.85**		
	ETB	**SEK**	**%**	**ETB**	**SEK**	**%**
Manuscript writing	0.21	0.25	5.0%	1.89	2.22	26.3%
Editorial work	—	—	—	—	—	—
Paper and raw materials	1.99	2.34	46.9%	1.99	2.34	27.7%
Printing production	1.29	1.52	30.4%	2.57	3.02	35.7%
Warehousing of finished books	0.22	0.26	5.2%	0.22	0.26	3.1%
Distribution to districts	0.17	0.20	4.0%	0.17	0.20	2.4%
Distribution within districts	0.36	0.42	8.5%	0.36	0.42	5.0%
Total	4.24	4.99	100.0%	7.20	8.47	100.0%

ber of titles is 10 times higher. The variations between the regions will be large, with costs in the regions with the smallest number of speakers of the dominant language, such as Afar, Gambela, and Harar, being much higher than in majority language regions such as Oromia and Amhara.

We have made some estimations regarding production time, printing speeds, and hourly rates for the EMPDA printing presses. Our calculations of the cost for the copies needed for each grade and each state are based on these assumptions. As the unit cost will be very high for short print runs, we have assumed that if the annual requirement is below 5,000 copies, the books are printed only every two years and that books with an annual requirement of less than 3,333 copies are produced only every three years. The resulting printing cost is some 2.57 Birr per copy, which should be compared with 1.29 Birr in a single textbook system, as is shown in Table 8.3.

The total costs calculated for each region and each grade are shown in Table 8.4 in which the costs for the different components of textbook development and production, as used in Table 8.3, have been included.

Table 8.4. Total Cost of Textbook by Region 1993–1994

		Total			
		No. of titles No. of grades			39 6
Region		**Enrolment**	**Printed Total**	**Cost/Copy Birr**	**Total Cost kBirr**
1	Tigray	293,429	490,156	7.64	3,745
2	Afar	12,450	22,138	53.58	1,186
3	Amhara	397,839	665,218	5.27	3,508
4	Oromia	715,351	1,198,450	5.33	6,389
5	Ogaden	—	—	—	—
6	Benishangul	30,411	48,641	29.61	1,440
7–11	South Ethiopia	528,617	883,990	5.89	5,211
12	Gambela	12,717	21,020	56.02	1,178
13	Harar	11,527	20,159	58.09	1,171
14	Addis Ababa	263,221	474,022	5.61	2,660
15	Dire Dawa	18,257	32,207	39.20	1,262
	Total	2,283,819	3,856,000	7.20	27,750

The average cost per copy is 7.20 Birr in the multilanguage system, compared to only 4.24 Birr in the single textbook system, an increase of 70 percent. The cost of manuscript writing apparently amounts to 26 percent of the total, which is very high compared to commercial writing costs in Europe and Africa. The high costs are the results of including titles that will be needed in so few copies that they would not normally by published by a commercial publisher.

When the estimated costs of implementing the multilanguage textbook policy are broken down by region, it can be seen that in the small population regions such as Afar, Gambela, and Harar, the cost per text book copy will be as high as 53 to 58 Birr. This uneven distribution of costs has serious implications for the allocation of funds for educational materials among the states of Ethiopia. The traditional allocation of national education funds on a per pupil base will no longer give an equitable outcome in terms of the book-to-pupil ratio in the different states.

CONCLUSION

If the ambitions of the Constitution regarding the development of a multi-ethnic society are to be realised, then the provision of primary school textbooks in Ethiopia cannot help but be complex. The large number of languages makes it difficult and costly to develop and produce books in each language, especially considering the limited capacity of the publishing industry and the small number of pupils in some of the minority languages. However, the task should not be impossible, as demonstrated by comparing Ethiopia to other countries. For the major Ethiopian languages and some of the minor ones, the number of pupils is higher, or potentially higher if enrolments increase, than in many small African countries (e.g., Cabo Verde, Guinea Bissau) or in many European countries. For example, Amhara State, with a population of 14 million, has twice as many school-age children than any of the Scandinavian countries. Although Danish, Norwegian, and Swedish are closely related languages, it is not considered an acceptable alternative to import primary school textbooks from each other. The costs of local publishing are accepted as part of the price of sound education practice. Such costs will have to be met in Ethiopia if the language policy is to be implemented.

The provision of education in the mother tongue is likely to improve the quality of education. This should more than compensate for the extra costs of providing educational materials in a number of languages. The reform in itself is educationally sound, and most of the Ethiopian states have sufficiently large populations to make educational publishing in local languages a viable proposition. However, for the new language functions to be realised in education, it is an important condition that the books are provided in sufficient quantities and that they are of reasonable quality, otherwise the expected positive learning and cultural effects of a decentralised education system can instead turn into educational disadvantage for some groups. This is a real problem, as the capacity and the competence to produce textbooks is limited. Many key persons in publishing and printing have during the last few years been transferred or have left their positions, which has aggravated the capacity situation, while commercial educational publishing is very weak after years of state monopoly. It is also doubtful that Ethiopia can finance the transition to multilanguage textbooks on its own. According to a recent report on the economics of publishing in Africa, 70 percent of Ethiopia's educational materials are financed by development aid agencies (DAE 1996). It is crucial for Ethiopia that such support continues so that the printing and publishing industry can build the skills and the capacities required by the new system. The question of where such capacity should be developed, centrally or regionally, will need to be tackled.

If the higher costs are accepted as reasonable in terms of the potential learning and cultural gains, then the method of allocating textbook funds from central government to the state governments will need reviewing. The widely differing costs for materials for different languages means that an allocation of textbook funds with the same amount per pupil in the various regions will no longer be a satisfactory solution to the subsidising of the costs of educational materials. This attempt at predicting the costs of a multilingual textbook system shows very clearly that the regions using minority languages for educational purposes will have very high textbook development and production costs. However, if these costs were to be spread over all the states by means of a subsidy system, then they do not seem unreasonable, particularly if weighed against the savings made in terms of reduced dropout and repetition in primary schools. For many years Ethiopia has had a very high dropout rate in the first year of schooling and it is not unlikely that this has been related to the pupils' language problems.

It should not be forgotten, however, that not all children will benefit from implementing the new system. For some children, the new policy means having to cope with yet another language at school, the state language, if this is not their mother tongue. Nor should it be forgotten that Amharic will still be Ethiopia's language of interregional communication and federal government. For some parents, the purpose of school is primarily the learning of the national language. Some schools, for example in Oromia, have now started offering classes with Amharigna as the medium of instruction because of parental demand.

It is not certain how much support the policy has among teachers, parents, and the children. The history of Ethiopia has been turbulent and it is still too early to see how the new states will develop, and whether the new language policy will be implemented in all the states for all the viable languages.

NOTE

[1]The textbook loan system was established by the former *Dergue* government. For a token fee, children rented their textbooks for an academic year. This money was passed back up the system, but it was not enough to establish a rolling fund for the production of textbooks.

REFERENCES

Bender, M.L., J.D. Bowen, R.L. Cooper, and C.A. Ferguson, eds. 1976. *Language in Ethiopia*, Ford Foundation Language Surveys. London: Oxford University Press.

Central Statistical Office. 1980. *Population, Labour Forces and Housing Characteristics of Seventeen Major Towns: Results of Manpower and Housing Survey 1978*, Statistical Bulletin 27. Addis Ababa: CSO.

Central Statistical Office. 1985. *Report on the Results of the 1981 Demographic Survey*, Statistical Bulletin 46. Addis Ababa: CSO.

Central Statistical Office. 1991. *Report on Census of Population and Housing and on Survey of Demographic Changes in the Resettlement Areas.* Addis Ababa: CSO.

DAE (Association for the Development of Education in Africa). 1996. "Study on the Economics of Publishing Educational Materials in Africa," second draft. (Forthcoming as DAE publication, 1997).

Government of Ethiopia. 1987. *Population and Housing Census of Ethiopia, 1984: Analytical Report on Results for Addis Ababa.* Addis Ababa: Office of the Population and Housing Census Commission.

Graphium Consult. 1995. *Proposed SIDA Textbook Reporting System, Including the Cost of Textbooks.* Stockholm: Graphium Consult. Unpublished report (available from Sida Education Division).

Greenberg, J.H. 1963. *Languages of Africa*, Indiana University Research Centre in Anthropology, Folklore and Linguistics, Publication 25. The Hague:

Mouton & Co. Also published in Part II, *International Journal of American Linguistic* 29 (1).

McNab, C. 1989. *Language Policy and Language Practice: Implementation Dilemmas in Ethiopian Education.* University of Stockholm, Institute of International Education. Stockholm: University of Stockholm.

Transitional Government of Ethiopia. 1994. *Education and Training Policy.* Addis Ababa: Transitional Government of Ethiopia.

Transitional Government of Ethiopia. 1995a. *The Constitution of the Federal Democratic Republic of Ethiopia* (unofficial English translation from the Amharic original). Addis Ababa: Transitional Government of Ethiopia.

Transitional Government of Ethiopia. 1995b. *Education Statistics Annual Abstract 1986 e.c. 1993–1994*. Addis Ababa: Ministry of Education.

CHAPTER 9

The Costs of Culture

Some Dilemmas for Educational Investment in Mauritius

KEITH LEWIN

The debates that surround the meaning and significance of culture have a lengthy history. The spectrum extends from those who regard culture as "the foundation stone of the social sciences" (Chase 1950) that is "all pervasive and has seemed to explain everything" to those who regard the construct with considerable suspicion. Evans-Pritchard (1951) thought the concept of culture was largely irrelevant to the work of social anthropologists. Radcliffe-Brown (1952) argued that culture was a vague abstraction and its use to help explain differences in behaviour and assumptions was "simply a way of avoiding reality." He argued that it was not cultures that interacted but individuals and groups within established social structures that were in themselves in a process of change.

Despite these diametrically opposed views of its importance, the concept of culture continues to be used both descriptively and analytically to explain differences in the process and outcomes of education. Bernstein (1971) and Bourdieu (1977) are both well known for their assertions that education systems and the institutions they contain are arenas in which the power and influence of culture is manifest. Musgrove (1982) notes that many academics have sought to use culture as an explanation for academic failure without being able to empirically validate the causality they assert. For example, he argues that "Lacey (1970) did not bother to show that working-class children were, in fact, failing or that their 'culture' was linked to their performance; Coleman (1961) said that adolescent culture depressed academic performance, but found no evidence that this was generally so."

Some traditions of cultural analysis have no difficulty in adopting hierarchical systems that can be used to categorise levels of culture of different societies according to their sophistication and complexity. These permeate the history of colonialism even among those remembered as social reformers. John Ruskin's inaugural speech at Oxford in 1870 conveys a flavour of this kind of cultural absolutism, which unashamedly values one culture over another.

> There is a destiny now possible for us, the highest ever set before a nation to be accepted or refused. We are still undegenerate in race: a race mingled of the best northern blood. . . . This is what England must do or perish: she must found colonies as fast and as far as she is able, formed of her most energetic and worthiest men; seizing every piece of fruitful waste ground she can set her foot on, and there teaching these her colonists that their chief virtue is fidelity to their country, and their first aim is to advance the power of England by land and sea. (Cited in Thomas 1996, 102)

Cecil Rhodes characteristically managed to concatenate religion and culture in the apparently certain belief of the superiority of his culture over others:

> Whites have clearly come out top . . . in the struggle for existence and achieved the highest standard of human perfection. Within the white race, English-speaking man, whether British, American, Australian or South African, has proved himself to be the most likely instrument of the Divine Plan to spread Justice, Liberty and Peace. . . . I shall devote the rest of my life to God's purpose, and help Him to make the world English. (Thomas 1996, 114)

These culturally absolutist views are in stark contrast to cultural relativists, who reject the notion that one culture is better or worse than another. Their assertions are comfortable in the absence of conflict.

> It was easy to look with equal benevolence upon all sorts of value systems so long as the values were those of unimportant little people remote from our own concerns. But the benevolence is harder to maintain when one is asked to anthropologise the Nazis. (Redfield 1953, quoted in Musgrove 1982)

Cultural relativists appear to deny that progress can occur and hence create a problem for development theorists. If all cultural practices have equal validity, then changes over time within a culture cannot be judged as for the better or for the worse. Thus, we may note that witchcraft may have served particular purposes in the past. Relativists may be reluctant to view its marginalisation in modern societies in Europe as not just a convenient change, but a central characteristic of the development of an age of reason that gave valued benefits to those who embraced new technologies that were empirically grounded and that rejected unprovable superstitions.

For an economist concerned with educational planning, cultural relativism is problematic. Resources are scarce and allocation according to purpose is a central issue. Policies that reflect any given set of priorities arising from the interplay of social, political, psychological, and economic preferences will have costs and consequences that can be compared and are thus capable of being evaluated. The implication is that some choices are more attractive than others in terms of their likely impact on educational development, however this is defined. Educational planning requires evaluation of goals and methods thought likely to result in their achievement.

Similar problems exist for sociologists who espouse cultural relativism when their advice is sought in relation to educational planning. If there is a sociological concern with the reasons why particular groups of students fail to progress through the school system, and if the reasons for this are associated with the characteristics of particular subcultures, then there is an inescapable implication that some subcultures are educationally inferior to others. It follows that, from this perspective, these subcultures need to change if achievement is to improve. The counterproposition, that it is the educational processes that have to change to become more sympathetic and relevant to the values and motivations of marginalised and underachieving subgroups, is a well-rehearsed dialogue with some force. However, at the point where this leads back to cultural relativism—all educational outcomes are equally valuable providing they are valued by those who acquire them—there would seem little basis for a constructive contribution to educational planning.

Culture is widely used in the education and development literature as an explanation for differences in developmental status between countries that cannot be explained in other ways. It sometimes seems that culture is treated as a "residual"—whatever is left to explain after all other factors have been taken into account is assumed to be the result of cultural differences. A possible illustration of this lies in the current debate about the influence of "Asian values" on education and development in East Asia. When the contributions of educational investment to growth are factored out, cultural considerations are often advanced as an externality to explain why economic and educational growth has been greater in these countries than in many other parts of the world. This may be true, but the mechanisms that might result in this are rarely identified explicitly in any way that could lead to testable propositions.

The purpose of this chapter is to analyse some of the ways in which cultural considerations may be reflected in development policy on education and indicate how these may carry a range of opportunity costs that need explicit recognition. In so doing I adopt an admittedly unsatisfactory but convenient definition of culture as it relates to education policy and planning. This definition is simply to say that culture subsumes all the noneconomic reasons that are advanced for pursuing particular policies that would not otherwise be attractive. If choices are made—for example, on the range of subjects to offer, on levels of repetition, on working practices—that do not have an economic justification, then the reasons for them lie in the domain of cultural preferences. These may then lead to tensions between economics and culture—the subject of this book.

It goes without saying that educational decisions cannot and should not be determined on the basis of purely economic considerations. But neither is it likely to be developmentally advantageous to subordinate economic analysis to cultural desiderata if in so doing this obscures the opportunity costs of adopting different policies and the mechanisms through which conflicts of interest are resolved. This chapter tries to explore some of the dilemmas that arise using evidence and experience from a single country—Mauritius.

Three areas are identified below that invite tensions between cultural considerations and the economic realities of planning school systems. Policy in practice is the result of the interaction of what is possible from a resource point of view, and what is promoted by the values and customs that prevail among all those groups involved in the educational enterprise. The first area is concerned with language policy—a dimension which is usually thought central to cultural self-determination and the preservation of values associated with different cultures. The second addresses a common planning dilemma—the extent, nature, and costs of repetition within formal school systems and the extent to which "cultures of repetition" condition investment patterns. The third addresses some management and working practices that create the organisational cultures within which schooling is delivered.

LANGUAGE POLICIES

The dilemmas confronting educational planners in language policy appear to revolve around:

- The choice of medium or media of instruction
- The choice of a second or third taught language and whether this is an "international" language
- The mechanisms through which teachers are trained and deployed in different media of instruction
- The level at which transition into a single national language is made
- The production of learning materials for small language groups
- The provision of language teaching to minority groups

Where monolingualism is prevalent the choice of medium of instruction is generally unproblematic. Where this is not the case the basic dilemma is obvious. The more media of instruction there are, the greater the complications in administering and resourcing schools, training teachers, and channelling students. South Africa now has 11 languages that can be used for instruction in primary schools. Many other countries have more than one. In exceptional cases multilingual schooling continues all the way through to University level (as in Sri Lanka). In most, a transition occurs—sometimes as early as grade 3 (e.g., Zimbabwe), and often at the end of primary school (e.g., Malaysia). In some countries dual media exist in the same schools (e.g., national minority areas in China). Sometimes change of language media is achieved in a transitional year with the attendant cost of an additional year of schooling for some students.

Where two or more media exist in parallel, there are usually additional costs arising from the duplication of administration and facilities. Schools may be smaller with higher overheads than would otherwise be the case. In multilingual systems teacher training may take place in separate institutions, or within dual media colleges. These are also likely to suffer from diseconomies of scale.

All these things may well be worth financing. Politically there may be little choice if social stability is seen to depend on particular accommodations reached in relation to language policy. The problems of the costs and benefits associated with the various options appear little researched. Given that there is usually more than one way of satisfying the various needs created by the adoption of specific language policies, the economic question is: Which options offer the most effective satisfaction of these needs and at what cost?

The language issue in Mauritius that has provoked most tension between economic and cultural perspectives on educational investment arises from the policy of providing Asian language teachers in all schools where parents wish their children to be taught an ancestral language. There are seven ancestral languages—Hindi, Urdu, Marathi, Telegu, Tamil, Arabic, and Chinese. The rationale for this policy is the preservation of the culture and traditions of the different communities, who see their identity as centrally associated with their mother tongues. Asian language teaching is provided for one period every school day and about 60 percent of all students take a language. Those who do not opt for this have the time available to continue other schoolwork and may or may not be taught other subjects during Asian language periods.

To place this policy in a broader context, it needs to be noted that the official medium of instruction in Mauritius is English. However, English is used daily by only a small minority of the Mauritian population. French is widely spoken as is French Creole. Major Indian language groups, notably Bhojpuri, Hindi, and Urdu, are the next most widely spoken languages. Thus, many students are in some sense disadvantaged by the use of English as the medium of instruction and in school examinations. Television and radio provide little exposure to English and most newspapers are in French, as is the majority of written material read by children. Those whose parents use English in the home are at an advantage over those not so fortunate.

Several consequences of this policy impinge differently on different parts of the school system and generate various costs. The widespread prevalence of the teaching of the ancestral language subjects means that Asian language (AL) teachers are provided to primary schools in fairly generous quantities. Overall there are about 1,500 Asian Language teachers out of a total of around 6,000 primary school teachers. These teachers are relatively underqualified when compared to those appointed as general purpose teachers. They are often secondary-school leavers (in some cases primary) who have had some certificate-level training in their language. They are usually restricted to the teaching of Asian languages and associated cultural activities (e.g., music, dance) if they have the skills.

Normal practice in Mauritian primary schools is that class teachers take responsibility for the teaching of all subjects throughout the primary school curriculum. These total about 35 periods per week. The Asian language periods are taken by specialised Asian language teachers. The

Figure 9.1. Pupil-Teacher Ratios with and without Asian Language Teachers

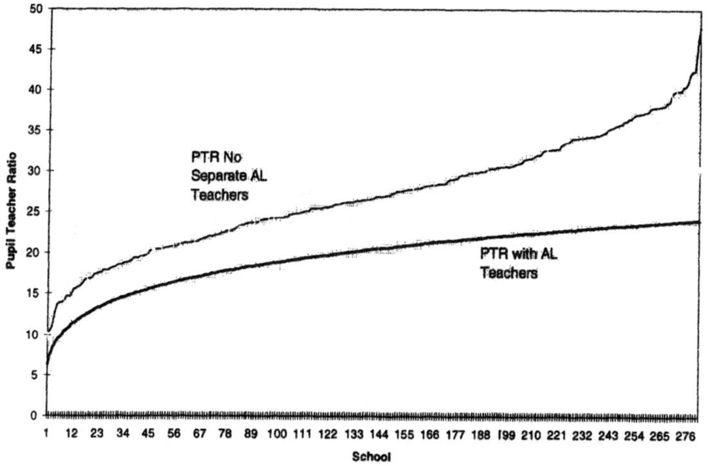

consequence of current policy, which is permissive of very small teaching groups, can be illustrated by some aggregate data and specific examples. First, the ratios of teachers to pupils can be considered with and without including Asian language teachers. Figure 9.1 shows the distribution of pupil-teacher ratios (PTR) in all primary schools when Asian language teachers are included and when they are excluded. The X–axis of Figure 9.1 lists all primary schools.

When Asian language teachers are included, the average PTR decreases from about 25:1 to 19.5:1. Primary school costs in Mauritius are determined largely by the costs of teachers' salaries. The cost per child in the schools is therefore more than 25 percent greater than it would be if Asian languages were taught within the establishment of general purpose teachers at existing pupil-teacher ratios. In some schools the differences in costs would be considerably greater. The last schools listed (from number 200 and above) have relatively large numbers of Asian language teachers teaching very small groups at a high cost per child.

The average unit cost of a primary school place is about Rps 6,000 (1994). The cost per student of Asian language teaching is often many multiples of this. How much more depends on the way in which policy is implemented. A variety of models are possible which all have different

Figure 9.2. Teaching Loads (Pupil Periods per Week) for Different Types of Teachers

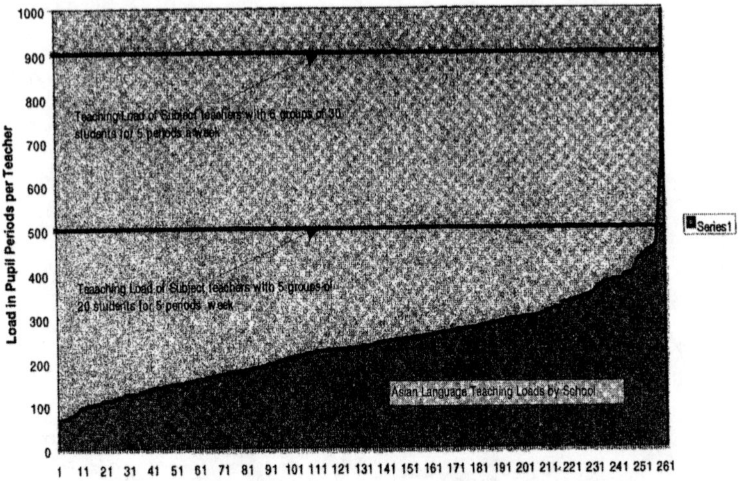

costs. The one which is currently in use is not one of the most parsimonious. There are several reasons. First, Asian language teachers are almost invariably deployed to single schools whether or not the number of pupils electing to take the language is comparable with those studying other subjects. The result is that the typical Asian language teacher has on average about 45 students distributed across six grades, who are taught in class groups of around seven students. The number of pupil periods per week they teach is therefore about 210 (7 pupils × 6 classes × 5 days). In contrast, a normal class teacher would teach about 900 pupil periods per week (30 periods with a group of 30 children). On this basis Asian language teachers' teaching loads are low. Figure 9.2 shows the distribution of teaching loads among Asian language teachers. Some teach as few as 100 pupil periods. The horizontal lines on the figure show the teaching load in pupil periods per week for normal subject teachers with five or six classes of students.

Second, Asian languages are usually taught in grade groups and it is rare for multigrade teaching to be used. This means that small groups of students studying a language are found in each uncombined grade group. There is little enthusiasm for breaking this pattern among Asian language teachers, though it is a source of considerable inefficiency. Thus, there are many small schools where teaching groups of less than five exist for each of the six different grades. Asian languages have been accepted as subjects for assessment in the Certificate of Primary Education. This has made it more difficult to adopt multigrade teaching, since the demands of assessment now constrain the Asian languages curriculum in grades 4 to 6, and there are specified minimum and essential learning competencies for each subject. Teachers claim this necessitates separate grade group teaching.

Third, as noted above, Asian language teachers are rarely employed to teach any other subjects and are often not qualified to do so. Their entry level to teaching has been lower than that for general purpose teachers and many are not thought capable of teaching main subjects to the end of primary school. Even if Asian language teachers were available and competent to teach other subjects, the practice of timetabling whole classes with a class teacher means that there is likely to be little teaching available in the majority of schools, since most have more than a full complement of general purpose teachers.

Fourth, the deployment of Asian language (AL) teachers is uneven. There appears to be no standard ratio of pupils to teachers governing the number of Asian language teachers posted to different schools. The variation is large and inconsistent and is presumably the result of local factors that influence posting. But this has its own costs, since some communities and linguistic groups appear to be more favoured than others. Figure 9.3 shows how the number of AL teachers per student varies between schools. Thus there are schools with around 50 AL students and five full-time AL teachers. Schools with as many as 200 AL students may have as many as eight or nine AL teachers. In both these cases the cost per student of provision is very high.

Fifth, until 1995, Asian language performance was not considered as a component of Certificate of Primary Education (CPE) examination, which determines access to secondary schools and to the "starred" elite schools, for which there is considerable competition. Since 1995 Asian languages have been incorporated as a fifth subject alongside English, French, Mathematics, and Environmental Studies.

There is a cost in introducing an additional examination subject, especially when it is remembered that Asian languages are not one subject but seven. Arrangements have to be made to set and mark papers and moderate marking. Agreement has to be reached on the appropriate method of standardisation and aggregation of marks across the languages and between them and the other subjects. The seven subject

Figure 9.3. Distribution of Asian Language Teachers by Number of AL Students

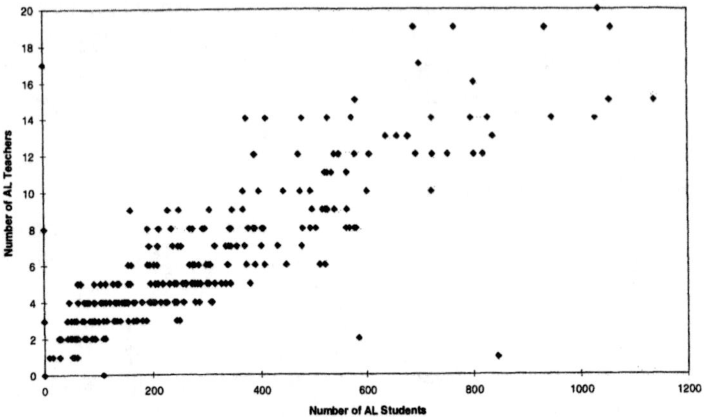

scores will have to be standardised to fall on similar distributions if they are to contribute similar amounts to the variance of overall score. There is the possibility of distortions. Scores in subjects with small numbers of candidates can be influenced by entering more candidates with little chance of success in order to boost the relative performance of the more capable. And there remains the problem of how to reconcile the performance of candidates on five papers with those who do not take an Asian language and thus score on four subjects only.

Asian languages have been accepted as examination subjects to ensure that their teaching is purposeful and focused. At least as important from a political point of view has been the expectation that students otherwise disadvantaged by language might recover some of their competitiveness if allowed to include a mother tongue in their aggregate scores. Whether this is true will depend partly on the statistical moderation applied.

In summary, this analysis indicates that the cost of provision of Asian language teaching in Mauritius is very considerable. It satisfies needs for cultural affirmation among the various interested parties. The adoption of Asian languages as an examination subject at CPE is the result of noneconomic arguments being given precedence over narrower considerations of cost and efficiency. Current teacher deployment policy clearly privileges one group of teachers (in the sense that they enjoy very small teaching groups and relatively light loads). In offering AL subjects on demand, a social principle of universal access is being followed. The cost in terms of provision is very high. There may be ways of reducing this: by making more use of multigrade groups, concentrating the teaching of particular languages at district level in selected schools, or deploying AL teachers across more than one school. However all these options will have to confront the expectations of staff and parents created by the current pattern.

CULTURES OF REPETITION

Repetition is common in many developing country school systems (UNESCO 1991). In some countries in sub-Saharan Africa, repetition is high in grades 1 and 2 and then reduces. In many systems repetition peaks at the end of the primary cycle when there is a school leaving examination. In some there is virtually no repetition, and in others one-third or more students may be repeating.

Repetition carries with it considerable costs. Repeaters occupy places that students not currently enrolled might take up. Where repetition is a precursor to failure and dropout, it may be serving little purpose except to increase the cost of an incomplete and inadequate experience of schooling. Repetition has direct costs in the sense that it adds one or more years to the educational cycle for a repeating child. And teachers have to be provided and space made available for more students than would otherwise be needed.

Policy on repetition would be attractive if it was based on empirically grounded studies that showed there were benefits for individuals and for the society. Such studies are only just beginning to appear (e.g., Eisemon et al. 1993). Policy on repetition seems to arise from combinations of historical practices, beliefs about the benefits of repetition, and pressure from parents and students to have another chance to stay within school systems that provide access to qualification and jobs. There are noticeable differences between countries. Repetition is more common in Francophone African countries than in Anglophone ones.

The reasons for different patterns of repetition (and different costs) seem to have a basis in noneconomic orthodoxies grounded in assumptions specific to particular systems (i.e., culturally grounded). It could hardly be otherwise where data on the actual benefits and costs are lacking. Beliefs about the relative merits of keeping children with their age peers; attitudes towards those who learn at different rates; the acceptability or otherwise of differentiated curricula; and attachment to specific levels of performance for progression (the "standards" debate) combine to create decisions that result in the observed patterns. Language policy is very relevant to these outcomes since much repetition may result from inadequate grasp of a second or third language, rather than any more general learning deficiency.

The case of repetition in Mauritius is illuminating. Unlike most African countries there is virtually no repetition up to grade 6, the end of the primary cycle. At the end of grade 6, average levels of repetition exceed 40 percent. Each year about 35,000 sit for the Certificate of Primary Education. Of these around 45 percent fail. Subsequently about 11,500 retake CPE and in the process occupy a substantial number of classrooms and teachers.

The pattern of repetition in Mauritius is not exactly what it seems. A recent analysis (Lewin 1995) shows that many of those who repeat CPE have actually passed and are seeking to improve their pass grade to obtain access to a better secondary school (listed as pass/pass in Table 9.1). In the CPE the top 2,000 boys and girls are ranked. Places to favoured institutions are allocated on this basis. In practice the competition for the most elite schools is restricted to those who are ranked in the first 500 or so.

Table 9.1 shows that there were about 4,000 pupils (3388 + 200 + 430) who had passed CPE in 1993 and who were repeating in 1994 to improve their scores. About 7,400 who had failed at the first attempt were repeating. Of those who had passed in 1993, 200 failed at the second attempt. Of those who had failed, over 5,000 (68 percent) failed

Table 9.1. Characteristics of CPE Repeaters in 1994

	Pass 1993 Pass 1994	Pass 1993 Fail 1994	Pass 1993 Absent 1994	Fail 1993 Pass 1994	Fail 1993 Fail 1994	Fail 1993 Absent 1994
Total Boys	1,648	129	249	1,107	2,538	346
Form 1	1,027	103	233	19	23	12
Standard 6	621	26	16	1,088	2,515	334
Total Girls	1,740	71	181	1,268	1,880	246
Form 1	922	51	163	24	25	2
Standard 6	818	20	18	1,244	1,855	244
Total	**3,388**	**200**	**430**	**2,375**	**4,418**	**592**

again or did not retake the examination for the second time. For them repetition appears to have had little benefit despite widely held beliefs that repetition is beneficial and worthwhile.

Repeaters of CPE are to be found in Standard 6 and in Form 1 of some secondary schools. If they are in Form 1 they follow the Form 1 curriculum. Of those who passed in 1994, 1,500 pupils were in Standard 6 and 2,500 were in Form 1. Among those who failed and were repeating, 7,300 were in Standard 6 repeating and only 100 were in Form 1.[1]

In principle those repeating CPE from Form 1 are not responsible for any additional direct costs, since they are counted as normal Form 1 students. A cost arises if, as a result of repetition, students succeed in gaining access to a better secondary school and thereby enter Form 1 for a second time. It is difficult to estimate this number, as no reliable data are available. A good estimate is that these pupils number about 500.

Pupils repeating in Standard 6 who have already passed total over 1,400. The majority have poor passes and are trying to improve their grading. A small number will have passed well and are trying for a high rank. They are likely to be concentrated in a few schools. Discouraging this repetition would reduce the number of Standard 6 students by a full 1,400 and remove many of the associated costs.

Thus, there are two motors behind repetition in Mauritius in primary schools—the need to pass CPE to gain access to secondary school at all, and the need to improve scores to be ranked well within the top 2,000. As we have seen, the first motor is not well engineered. Most who fail the first time fail again.

Analysis of the repeaters who have passed and were ranked in the top 2,000 suggests that most who pass and retake in this group fail to improve sufficiently to enter more prestigious secondary schools. Amongst those repeating CPE in 1992 who had passed in 1991 (about 5,400), 18 percent succeeded in being ranked in the top 2,000 boys or girls in 1992. Most repeaters improved their positions but not sufficiently to enter the top 500 ranks. About 13 percent actually received a lower ranking than before. The candidates who improved their ranking were concentrated between ranks 1,000 and 2,000 for both boys and girls, as this group included those previously ranked lower than the 2,000th boy or girl. 15 percent of boys and 11 percent of girls who were repeating were ranked between 1 and 500 at their second attempt, and about twice this proportion were ranked between 500 and 1,000.

Figure 9.4 shows the changes in rank of CPE repeaters when performance in 1993 is compared to 1994 for the top ranked 2000 boys and girls. It indicates that most of this sample of candidates did improve their position in terms of ranking (most candidates have a positive change in rank above the zero change line). Despite this, the numbers with substantial gains (of 1000 or more) are very small. Few not already in the top 500—the level necessary for access to the most elite schools—gained access as a result of repetition. The average improvement in ranking amongst boys in the top 2,000 in 1991 was 194 places while for girls it was 271 places. This may suggest that female repetition was more selective (i.e., girls were less likely to repeat unless they had a good chance of improving their rank). It is also possible that girl repeaters were more motivated to improve and worked harder. The data cannot shed light on which of these two possibilities is true.

Thus we can conclude that the benefits of repetition to improve ranking are marginal for most candidates. Improvement of ranking by 100–200 makes little difference to the school attended. Large numbers are prepared to take the risks and carry the associated costs (e.g., in the form of substantial private tuition payments) (Joynathsingh et al. 1988). There are also additional public costs associated with repetition in state schools. The high level of competition at the end of the primary school system has other costs that are more difficult to measure. The most obvious of these relate to the pressure placed on children to seek any advantage they can obtain from additional tuition, the valuing of competitive rather than cooperative learning, and the narrowing of childhood development towards a focus on the acquisition of the academic knowledge required in the CPE.

Figure 9.4. Changes in Rank of CPE Repeaters

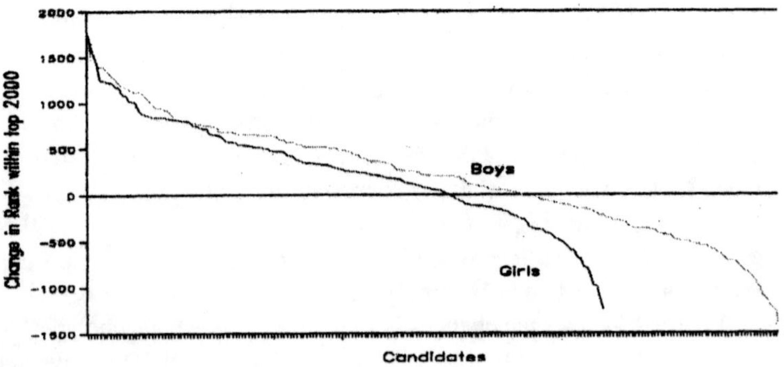

Repetition at secondary level takes on some different qualities and is extensive. Forms 1–3 average 5–10 percent repetition, Form 4 about 30 percent, and over 35 percent is common in Form 5. Repetition rates exceed 50 percent in some secondary schools at Form 4 and 5. Although Form 5 repetition has an obvious explanation—retaking School Certificate (SC) to gain credits in five subjects—it is not immediately obvious why there are so many repeaters in Form 4. Decisions on who repeats are made at school level and seem to involve contradictory assumptions. These allow many children to enter Form 4 with the knowledge that almost certainly they will not succeed in reaching the required standard to be promoted at the end of the year. School administrations may benefit from the extra income and teaching staff they receive as a result of slowing the flow of students and inflating enrolments, but it is not clear how much benefit students derive. The schools with the highest rates of Form 4 repetition are also those with low pass rates at SC.

What is perhaps surprising is that these high levels of repetition appear widely accepted and regarded as almost inevitable. Teachers repeatedly refer to the poor quality of the students as being the underlying reason for repetition, as if everything would be resolved if all students were like the best students and came from well-resourced households that valued education. Few seem to question whether the standards that are being applied, and which are demonstrably unattainable by the majority of children taught under the conditions that currently exist, are inappropriate for the expanded cohort which now has access to secondary schooling. Thus, this "culture of repetition" feeds on itself and has become a normal expectation of many actors in the educational system.

A structural analysis explains these patterns of repetition in terms of a competition for scarce opportunities that is controlled through the "gold standard" of achieving five credits at SC level. The conventional wisdom repeatedly reasserts that this standard, to be achieved at one sitting, represents the only appropriate end point for secondary schooling. The Ministry of Education has placed limits on acceptable levels of repetition—no more than once for each grade up to Form 5 and no school students to be more than 20 years old when admitted to their final school year. But these are not stringent enough to modify practice. There is clearly a tension between concepts of internal efficiency in the school system and common expectations of large-scale repetition. Though curricular expectations of performance are unrealistic for many learners, they remain fixed at a high level most cannot achieve within the existing system. The benefits to the few, which encourage high standards among the academically successful bound for university, have to be balanced by the disbenefits to the majority who fail to gain high levels of academic qualification.

The extent and resilience of repetition suggests that there may be other values and assumptions that are instrumental in sustaining a costly practice that actually excludes many students from secondary school. If so many places were not occupied by repeaters at higher levels in secondary schools, access to Form 1 could be universalised. Arguably in the past noneconomic preferences to allocate opportunities to repeat to those retained in the system have weighed more heavily in decision making than progress towards universalising access to secondary schools. "Cultures of repetition," which seem to regard low probabilities of improved performance as worth a gambler's chance, therefore add another dimension to the debate on tensions between economics and culture.

WORKING PRACTICES AND ORGANISATIONAL CULTURES

A third tension between economics and culture relates to working practices within education systems. The organisational culture that exists in schools will determine the amount of time that is allocated to, and actually spent on, learning and teaching activities in a formal setting. There is a general presumption that there is some relationship between how much is learned and how much time is spent on learning tasks, though of course there is no necessary linear relationship. Costs are likely to be determined by how much time is formally allocated. Educational outcomes reflect the amount of time that is actually provided. There is a considerable amount of evidence indicating that the assumptions that planners often make about the amount of structured learning time available are at variance with that experienced by students. Thus it is possible to isolate a number of different features of organisational culture where custom and practice (i.e., culture) interact with formal requirements and influence effectiveness and costs. These include the number of school days, teacher attendance, private tuition, and the range of subject choices permitted.

The number of formal teaching days in a school year in Mauritius varies between about 180 and 190 days. The number of teaching hours a week is officially between about 22 and 26 at primary level and 26 and 27 at secondary level. The latter translates into about 910 hours of instruction per year. By comparison the average number of school days a year in the countries taking part in the IEA science studies was about 192

(Postlethwaite and Wiley 1992). Hong Kong (207), Japan (210), and Korea (220) all had higher values than Mauritius, and Singapore (180) had about the same. Teaching time per year at secondary level averaged about 985 hours across the countries, with Korea (1083), Singapore (1023), and Hong Kong (1015) apparently having significantly more teaching time than Mauritius.

Actual differences may be more than these figures imply. They depend on the extent to which days officially available for teaching are used. Thus teaching time may be lost to public holidays (and the days immediately surrounding them if absenteeism is high), special events (e.g., sports days, exhibitions) and the time involved in their preparation, and examination schedules, which may disrupt normal teaching for long periods. Table 9–2 below illustrates how many teaching days were available in schools on the island of Rodrigues (part of the Republic of Mauritius) in 1994. This suggests that about 150 normal teaching days were available. It excludes the effects of pupil and teacher absenteeism.

Table 9–2. Maximum Number of Teaching Days Available in Primary Schools in Rodrigues for 1994

Term 1 7/1–8/4	**Days Used**	**Term 2 25/4–22/7**	**Days Used**	**Term 3 16/8–18/11**	**Days Used**
Public Holidays	4.0	Public Holidays	0.0	Public Holidays	2.0
Admissions	1.0	PTA	0.5	PTA	0.5
National Day + Preparation	3.0	Sports Day	1.0	CPE Examinations	3.5
PTA	1.0	Music Day	1.0	Assessment	10.0
Prizes	0.5	Book Festival	1.0	Last Day	1.0
Cyclones	2.0	Outings	1.0		
Assessment	3.0	Cyclones	1.0		
Cross Country	1.0	Assessment	3.0		
		Football Tournament	1.0		
				Days Used (Total)	42
				School Days	190
				Normal Teaching Days (Maximum)	**148**

Teacher absences during normal teaching time are common in many schools. Ministry statistics indicate that officially rates of absenteeism average 10 percent to 11 percent in primary schools in the months of February and March and 9 percent to 10 percent in secondary schools. Teachers are subject to conditions of service that broadly apply to other civil servants. These provide for a variety of types of leave that are classified as casual, vacation, sick, and maternity. In primary schools, about half of all leave taken by teachers is casual leave. The entitlement for casual leave is 11 days a year. Sick leave accounts for about 30 percent of leave taken and is the next largest category with an entitlement of 21 days per year. Vacation leave represents a little less than 20 percent of leave taken. This may be accumulated at a rate between 15 and 30 days a year up to a maximum of between 60 and 145 days, dependent on the grade of the staff member. In secondary schools the most frequent leave taken is sick leave, followed by casual and vacation leave.

The substantive point is that the leave taken by teachers is taken preferentially on school days rather than when schools are not in session. This leave is in addition to the periods when schools are closed, which are enjoyed as holidays by most teachers. It may also be in addition to in-service training time, which may be scheduled during school hours. Teaching time is lost and pupils are not taught unless a floating teacher is available. Quality and continuity therefore suffer, achievement may be impaired, and the likelihood of repetition may be increased. Lower rates of absenteeism would reduce the need for teachers, or alternatively release such teachers to undertake other quality-enhancing tasks.

The organisational culture of many schools appears permissive of high rates of absenteeism amongst staff and students. Justifications for rates of high absenteeism often appear to depend on culturally based arguments—the open-ended demands and obligations created by the extended families to which most teachers belong; the alleged indifference of some staff with respect to their obligations as employees, especially in relation to the State as employer; and the implied cultural poverty of students' homes and the disengagement of parents from concerns with the education of their children, which may condone or encourage truancy.

One problem for planners with these aspects of schools as organisations is that they can generate ambiguous signals to change policy. Teacher absenteeism can result in requests from schools for more teaching staff to ensure that the absences are covered. This invites a possible paradox. Providing more teachers could actually result in higher absenteeism, as more absences can be tolerated without unacceptable levels of disruption. It usually remains untested as to why some schools experience much lower rates of absenteeism among staff and students than others, where external factors appear fairly constant. The school's organisational culture is likely to be partly responsible.

Alongside the problems of the actual amounts of time available for formal instruction, there is another tension with an economic dimension that permeates the school system at all levels. Private tuition is pervasive. Typically this consists of additional class teaching for payment outside normal school hours. It may be offered by students' own class teachers as well as by teachers from other schools and those who run private tuition academies. In the late 1980s over 45 percent of all primary school students and 60 percent of secondary school students took private tuition (Joynathsingh et al. 1988). These proportions have almost certainly increased. Anxiety and stress among pupils are widely reported; parents allocate considerable proportions of income to tuition fees.

Tuition is almost universal in Standard 6 in examination subjects. It is institutionalised in the sense that school premises are used by teachers after school closes at around 2.00 pm for one or two hours. Teachers accept payment from parents on a private basis. The only cost they usually bear is that of additional caretaker time. Students may attend three or more times a week. In schools where teachers are in demand, many Standard 4, 5, and 6 teachers may double their formal salary through this activity. Though officially discouraged, many primary schools also open an hour early to allow preschool tuition classes to take place. Private tuition is often provided by the class teacher of the students.

Predictably there are allegations from parents and from students that many teachers lack commitment to teaching during school time and save their best efforts for tuition time to ensure attendance. Whether this is simply hearsay or has a basis in fact is impossible to judge, but the belief is widespread and attendance high.

At secondary level, tuition in Forms 4 and 5 is also near universal; schools close early in the afternoon and students then move on to tuition classes. At this level classes are held in private premises and are highly organised. No records exist of the number of teachers involved, but it is clearly a substantial proportion of the teacher workforce. There is little difference in tuition take-up rates between students from different regions, but no information is available on the rate of participation by different communities.

The culture of dependence on private tuition reaches exceptional levels in Form 6 (grades 12 and 13). Payment for private tuition is fairly universal both among those taking Higher School Certificate (HSC) for the first time and those repeating. Attendance rates of students among Form 6 repeaters in some schools fall to as low as 10 percent, despite the fact that teachers are provided and classrooms and laboratories are available at public expense. The received wisdom is that students prefer to take private tuition rather than attend school in the belief that this is where effective learning takes place. The waste of resources represented by this is very substantial, as it results in teachers being scheduled for classes that are often attended by few students.

A final dimension of working practices that indicates another kind of tension relates to the patterns of choice available for studying different subjects. Figure 9.5 shows subject entries for HSC examinations and indicates how passes are distributed in different subjects for candidates from the 23 state secondary schools. Maths, accounts, economics, and French account for about 60 percent of all subject entries. Figure 9.6 shows the average number of passes by school. Only the four major subjects are really viable for all schools. In other subjects very small teaching groups must exist (often averaging below 10), investment costs in facilities will be high, and pupil-teacher ratios will be very low with consequently high costs per student (these costs sometimes exceed those for university students). There is suggestive evidence in the data that where there are small numbers of entrants, pass rates are lower.[2] In subjects with large entries, those schools with more students have higher pass rates (Figure 9.7).

Figure 9.5. Passes at High School Certificate Level by Subject

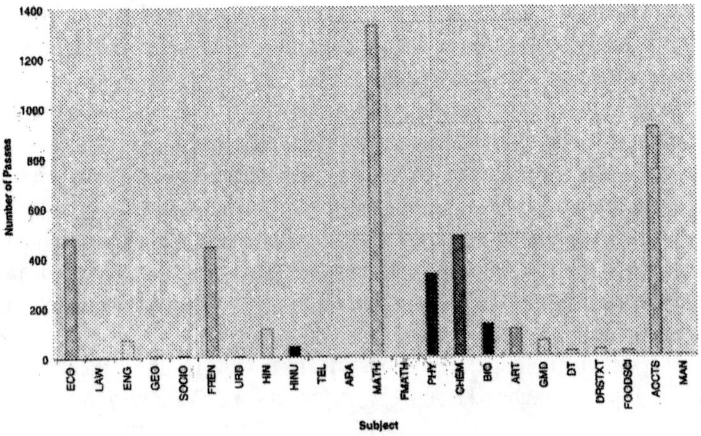

Figure 9.6. Number of Passes at High School Certificate by School and Subject

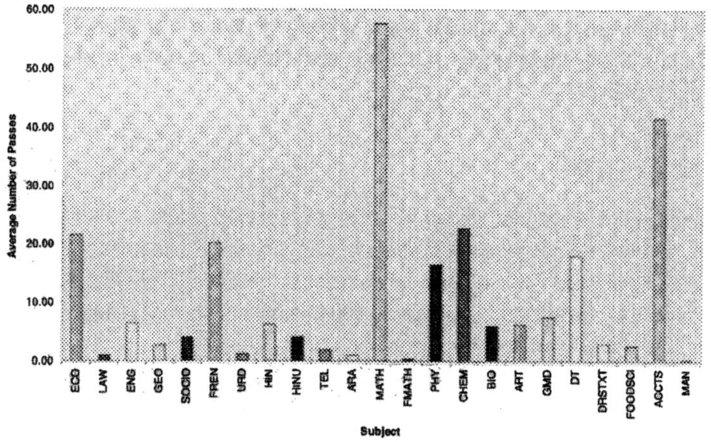

Figure 9.7. Pass Rate by Number of Entrants—Economics

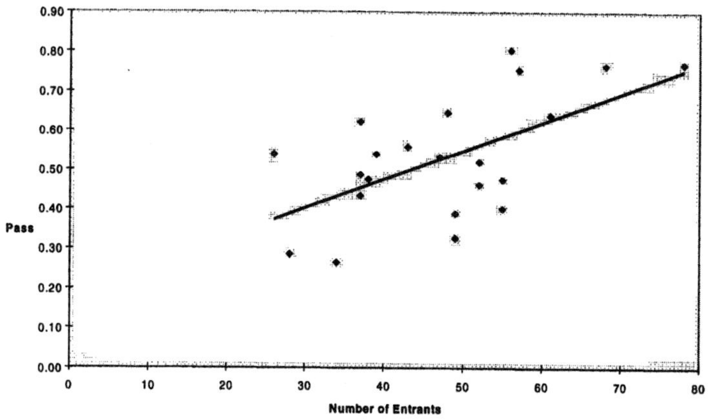

It is not obvious that this pattern of provision is economically rational; it reflects the individual preferences of students, parents, and the decisions made at school level to offer different subjects. But does this imply that any choice that is made is acceptable and should be supported with public money? Or should some criteria be applied to limit choice? And should the opportunity to choose be restricted so as to improve internal efficiency?

CONCLUSION

Educational investment decisions that are economically attractive are often in tension with those that are essentially based on different kinds of priorities that may have a basis in cultural preferences. This chapter has examined some aspects of just three types of dilemma—language provision, repetition, and organisational practices, all of which have cultural dimensions. It implies that arguments about the significance of culture should not be restricted to those that simply address obviously cultural issues (e.g., language policy). "Cultures of repetition" may influence policy in ways that have large opportunity costs; so also may organisational cultures that shape working practices.

In conclusion, several questions are raised by this analysis for planners and economists. First, in which arenas does the dialogue between stakeholders in the educational investment process take place and how are the tensions between economics and culture understood by different interest groups? The answer is often cloudy. Decisions that are made on language policy, repetition, and school organisation frequently appear to be agreed upon at a national level according to the interplay of political forces and practical realities. Bureaucratic systems then attempt to turn these into rules and procedures and apply them systematically. But educational bureaucracies have their own cultures, where often the formal procedures are subordinated to the informal or parallel power structures and relationships that exist between the various individuals and interest groups. Policy often does not translate into practice in a consistent way. Often it is modified, sometimes it is subverted. One response to this insight is to advocate decentralised decision making where those who experience the consequences of decisions are close to those who make them. This carries the promise of greater accountability. But there is no necessary result that local decision making is any more enlightened, resource conscious, or technically competent than that emerging from hierarchical bureaucratic structures.

Second, how are the views and aspirations of different groups (cultures?) to be weighed and taken into account in decision making? The problems are multiple. Means have to be identified of establishing which stakeholders have a legitimate claim to speak and on behalf of whom; which interests are to be placed above or below others; how self-interest is to be reconciled with collective benefit; how effective demand for educational services is to be accommodated even if it appears developmentally regressive; and how, in the competition for resources, are the interests of the marginalised to be promoted?

Third, this chapter ends with an invitation. How can culturally based analyses, as distinct from those grounded in the familiar tools of economics, contribute to the generation of educational investment policy that is both in the interests of the majority and respects the rights and aspirations of individuals? This is a challenge for other contributors to this volume to address.

NOTES

[1] It is not clear how these students can be in Form 1 since they have failed CPE. The statistics indicate they are enrolled!

[2] It may be of course, that this arises from a selection effect—good students enter prestigious schools where teaching groups are larger; marginal students who cannot get admission to these enrol in small schools with no alternative source of HSC students. The question remains as to whether it would be better for these candidates to study in schools with larger subject entry (which are more likely to have better facilities and more highly qualified staff).

REFERENCES

Bernstein, B. 1971. "On the Classification and Framing of Educational Knowledge." In *Knowledge and Control*, ed. M.F.D. Young. London: Collier MacMillan.

Bourdieu, P. 1977. "Cultural Reproduction and Social Reproduction." In *Power and Ideology in Education*, eds. J. Karabel and A. H. Halsey. New York: OUP.

Chase, S. 1950. *The Proper Study of Mankind*. London: Phoenix House.

Coleman, J. S. 1961. *The Adolescent Society*. New York: Free Press.

Eisemon, O., J. Schwill, R. Prouty, F. Ukobizoba, D. Kana, and G. Ganirabona. 1993. "Providing Quality Education Where Resources Are Scarce: Strategies for Increasing Primary School Effectiveness in Burundi." In *Effective Schooling in Developing Countries*, H. Levin and M. Lockheed (eds.), Stanford Series on Education and Public Policy 130. Washington, DC: Falmer Press.

Evans-Pritchard, E. E. 1951. *Social Anthropology.* London: Routledge.

Joynathsingh, M., M. Mansoor, V. Nababsing, M. Pochun, and P. Selwyn. 1988. *The Private Costs of Education in Mauritius*. Port Louis, Mauritius: University of Mauritius.

Lacey, C. 1970. *Hightown Grammar.* Manchester: Manchester University Press.

Lewin, K. M. 1995. "An Evaluation of the Benefits of Repeating CPE and the Effects of Promoting All Who Pass CPE to Form 1." Ministry of Education and Culture, Mauritius.

Musgrove, F. 1982. *Education and Anthropology: Other Cultures and the Teacher*. Chichester: Wiley.

Postlethwaite, N., and T. Wiley, eds. 1992. *Science Achievement in Twenty-Three Countries. The Second International Science Study*. Oxford: Pergamon Press.

Radcliffe-Brown, A. R. 1952. *Structure and Function in Primitive Society*. London: Routledge.

Redfield, R. 1953. *The Primitive World and Its Transformation*. Ithaca, NY: Cornell University Press.

Thomas, A. 1996. *Rhodes: The Race for Africa*. Johannesburg: Jonathan Ball Publishers.

UNESCO. 1991. "Primary Education: Repetition (STE-3) and Secondary General Education (STE-12)." Section of Statistics on Education, Division of Statistics, UNESCO.

CHAPTER 10

Community Financing of Education

Cultural Variations and Policy Dilemmas in Less Developed Countries

MARK BRAY

The economic crisis that has hit many developing countries has severely cut the flow of government funds that can be devoted to education. In many contexts, the search for alternative resources has led to focus on community contributions. In most settings, community resources are only a supplement to government funding. However, they may still be of major significance.

The nature and scale of community financing of education is highly dependent on cultural factors. For example, the Kikuyu and Kamba peoples of Kenya and the Igbo of Nigeria are particularly well known for self-help achievements, both in education and in other sectors. Not all ethnic groups, either in those two countries or elsewhere in Africa, have such strong traditions. This variation has major implications for patterns of development. On the positive side, community projects have generated resources for education and thus for further development of those communities; but on the negative side, self-help has contributed to geographic and social inequalities, and has created policy dilemmas for governments.

This chapter begins by presenting a conceptual framework and definitions of terms. It then comments on the rationales and extent of community financing in a range of settings, before turning to more detailed consideration of patterns in Kenya, Nigeria, and Bhutan. These examples highlight tensions, elaborated upon in the following sections, relating to equality and efficiency. The concluding section summarises points with comments on the implications for government policy.

THE CONCEPTUAL FRAMEWORK

Several terms in the title of this chapter may be ambiguous and therefore require some initial discussion. It is necessary to define the parameters with regard to communities, cultures, financing, and education.

A considerable literature exists on the nature of communities. Hillery's classic paper noted as many as 94 alternative definitions and pointed out (1955, 113) that the list was still not exhaustive. Almost all the definitions that Hillery identified mentioned the need for social interaction. Most also emphasised the importance of geographic area and/or some other common characteristic, such as possession of common ends, norms, or means. Without going too deeply into this topic, for present purposes the type of community under focus is one in which members share important cultural attributes.

The question is, then, what is meant by a cultural attribute. Definitions of culture may be even more numerous than those of community. Camilleri (1986, 8) cites a work by Kroeber and Kluckhohn (1952) who identified no less than 160 definitions, and that was only in the literature up to 1950! The focus in the present chapter is allied to concepts of culture found in the disciplines of sociology and social anthropology. The opening paragraphs of the chapter have already referred to ethnicity and, by implication, to various attributes that may go with it. Aspects of social organisation and behaviour associated with ethnicity will receive particular attention.

Turning to the concept of financing, although in most contexts financing implies direct monetary contributions, much community support for education is in nonmonetary form. Land, labour, and materials have costs associated with their provision, and would have to be purchased if they were not provided directly. Thus the chapter is concerned with both monetary and nonmonetary support for schools.

Finally, the chapter is mainly concerned with formal primary and secondary schools. In many countries, considerable community contributions are made to preprimary and post-secondary institutions, to nonformal education, and to alternative formal systems such as Koranic schools and Roman Catholic seminaries. Discussion of community support in these areas is beyond the scope of the present chapter.

RATIONALES AND EXTENT OF COMMUNITY FINANCING

From the viewpoint of the communities themselves, in most settings the chief reason for undertaking projects is to secure a service that is not provided by the government or any other organisation or individual. In some cases, government schools may be available, but are not of the type or quality desired by particular communities. In other cases government provision is judged inadequate in quantity, and community projects seek to reduce the shortfall. In the latter case, community financing may supplement provision in existing schools, or it may lead to the creation of completely new institutions (Bray 1996a; Bray with Lillis 1988).

The extent of community financing varies widely both within and between countries, and also at different times. It is usually difficult to form precise estimates of the extent, not only because of the paucity of data, but also because of the complexity of assigning monetary values to nonfinancial contributions. Nevertheless, examples from diverse contexts indicate that contributions can be considerable. In Uganda, for example, government provision of education all but collapsed during the 1970s and 1980s. The gap was partly bridged by parents and broader communities, who contributed approximately 80 percent of running costs at the primary level and 60 percent of running costs at secondary level (Opolot 1994, 26). Less dramatic but nevertheless highly significant figures from Chad indicate that community schools comprised 22.4 percent of the total at the primary level in 1991–1992, and catered to 9.3 percent of pupils (Esquieu and Péano 1994, 24); and in Malawi, community-unassisted primary schools in 1992–1993 comprised only 20.5 percent of all primary schools and enrolled 9.5 percent of all primary pupils (Malawi 1993, 8, 30).

Striking examples may also be found in Asia. China had 1.8 million community-employed primary school teachers in 1994, comprising 32.3 percent of the total (Cheng 1995, 1). In Nepal, 18 percent of the secondary schools existing in 1991 were operated by communities with little or no support from the government (World Bank 1994b, 2, 4); in Cambodia, family expenditures on primary education in 1992–1993 were typically between four and nine times the level of government expenditures, with an even wider gap at the secondary level (Bray 1996b, 70–72); and in 1995 Bhutan had 102 lower primary community schools compared with 143 government full primary schools and just 19 government junior high schools (Bhutan 1995, 1).

These are scattered examples from just two continents, and patterns are far from uniform throughout geographic regions (Wolf et al. 1997). However, the examples do indicate that community financing is significant in at least some countries.

PATTERNS AND MECHANISMS OF COMMUNITY FINANCING: THREE EXAMPLES

This section of the chapter presents information on community financing in Kenya, Nigeria, and Bhutan. As mentioned earlier, communities in parts of Kenya and Nigeria have become well known for the scale of their self-help activities. Traditions in Bhutan have a shorter history and are less vigorous, but provide an informative contrast.

Kenya

The self-help movement in Kenya is known as *harambee,* which is commonly translated as "let us all pull together" (Bradshaw 1993, 349; Ngau 1987, 523). At least in rural areas, communities are expected to take responsibility for construction and maintenance of all primary schools, and many communities have established *harambee* secondary schools. Recent policy changes have blurred the distinction between types of institution, but in 1987, *harambee* secondary schools comprised nearly three quarters of the total (Mwiria 1990, 355). Some *harambee* schools, comprising almost 44 percent of all secondary schools, were aided by the government. Others, almost 29 percent of the total number, were unaided.

The first independent self-help schools were opened in western Kenya at the beginning of the century (Abreu 1982, 201; Anderson 1970, 113). These initiatives were soon overtaken by developments in central Kenya, which is the heartland of the Kikuyu peoples. Anderson (1973, 18) records that between 1922 and 1952, nearly 400 self-help schools were established by Kikuyu communities. Other groups, such as the Luo, the Kamba, and the Pokoma also established schools, though not on the same scale, during that period.

Following a 1988 review of the education sector (Kamunge 1988), the government decided to assist all previously unaided secondary schools. However, the government has been unable to meet all needs, and demands on communities remain heavy. Table 10.1 shows official estimates of the value of *harambee* contributions, by sector. Education was by far the largest component, although the volume of contributions fluctuated over the years. In 1992–1993, households were estimated to have met 34 percent of the total costs of primary education (World Bank 1995, 64). Of this, 21 percent, comprising 7 percent of total costs, was raised through *harambee*. At the secondary level, households were estimated to have met 66 percent of total costs. Fees comprised 82 percent of household costs (and 55 percent of total costs), and *harambee* comprised

Table 10.1. Value of Harambee Contribution, by Sector, Kenya (Million Kenya Pounds)

	1986	1987	1988	1989	1990	1991
Education	12.7	33.8	23.2	28.5	24.5	19.5
Nurseries	0.5	1.1	0.7	1.6	0.3	0.4
Health	5.2	0.6	2.9	1.7	0.6	0.5
Social welfare	4.6	3.1	3.9	3.5	15.7	8.9
Domestic	0.2	0.1	0.1	0.1	0.3	0.2
Water	2.9	0.9	1.9	1.4	0.5	0.5
Transport	0.3	0.0	0.1	0.1	0.1	0.1
Agriculture	0.0	0.9	1.1	1.0	0.4	0.3
Other buildings	0.6	0.5	0.5	0.5	0.2	0.3
Other construction	0.3	0.1	0.2	0.1	0.2	0.1
Other projects	0.8	1.1	0.9	1.0	0.5	0.4
Total	28.1	42.2	35.5	39.5	43.3	31.1

Source: Kenya (1994), 250.

5 percent of household costs (and 4 percent of total costs). However, these figures underestimate the true picture, as they were derived from an expenditure survey and omit the value of labour, materials, and land contributed through *harambee*. Moreover, a considerable proportion of the fees could also be considered *harambee* contributions, as they are determined by the school committees at the community level.

Two major studies were made of the *harambee* movement in the 1970s; they presented many insights that are still valid. Mbithi and Rasmusson (1977) combined a large-scale survey with more detailed case studies from almost all parts of Kenya. Hill's work, which was not published in full until 1991, even though the fieldwork was conducted in the mid-1970s, focused more narrowly on a Kamba community in Kitui district. Both Mbithi and Rasmusson (1977, 13) and Hill (1991, 133) point out that the ideology of *harambee* was based on traditions of community cooperation and mutual aid. They referred specifically to the work parties that existed in many Kenyan societies.

Because Hill viewed *harambee* through the lens of a social anthropologist, his study is especially valuable to this chapter and is worth reporting in some detail. Among the Kamba, Hill records various types of work parties that could be called upon to perform tasks such as weeding, harvesting, helping the elderly, and constructing roads, schools, wells, drains, and dispensaries (Hill 1991, 133–162). He documents the systems for organising these work parties, and identifies the rewards for participation and the sanctions for nonparticipation. He also records the strategies through which work was achieved, highlighting the importance of work songs, dancing, and mutual encouragement. Hill distinguishes between three basic types of work party: the neighbourhood *myethya* (singular *mwethya*); the small rotating work team, *mwilaso*; and less formalised help from friends, which had no specific term in Kikamba. All three were *kithio*, customary institutions, although they had evolved in response to broader social change over the decades.

For construction of schools, the most important type of work party was the *mwethya*. This was a long-standing traditional form of organisation that had served various community-identified needs, but that had also been co-opted during the colonial era in order to develop the physical infrastructure. During the late 1950s and early 1960s, *mwethya* activities declined because of nationalist opposition to the use of community labour in this way. However, the rapid revival of many village groups within a year of independence in 1963 reflected the enormous enthusiasm for nation building and local self-help *harambee* development.

This revival was achieved through a combination of popular enthusiasm, encouragement by politicians, and the efforts of the new Africanised district administration. By 1973, 732 village *myethya* had been officially registered by the Community Development Department in Kitui district (Hill 1991, 163). This formal registration reflected the ways in which traditional institutions had been co-opted to serve the purposes of the modern state. Each *mwethya* was in theory represented in the location development committee, a consultative body chaired by the location chief and intended to plan and monitor location development projects. This committee was part of a nationwide structure of development committees that had an input into district development planning.

Hill observes that the numbers and operations of *myethya* had changed significantly over time. He notes that older people "recalled that there were far more *myethya* a generation or two previously, with more participants. . . . There were also stricter sanctions for failing to work" (Hill 1991, 53). The *myethya* had had to face the challenges of labour migration, which had reduced the participation of men. Also, many had incorporated aspects of the market economy, including permitting cash contributions in *lieu* of labour, and providing cash payments to some workers.

In Kitui, as in the country as a whole, education was the principal objective of the self-help movement. Hill observes that in the particular village he studied,

> No one . . . was anything but keen to have their children go to school. . . . [Everyone] had—or potentially had—children who would need to go to school. Those who were initially childless in their first or later marriage would not be so for ever, as supplementary marriage institutions guaranteed the possibility of social paternity or maternity to everyone. (Hill 1991, 170)

All the self-help *myethya* projects involved contributions of unskilled labour and/or money. This was usually done on a per capita basis for villagers, with graduated amounts of money in *lieu* of labour being collected from villagers in outside employment. Some projects involved only the village and were mostly initiated and carried out by the villagers themselves, albeit with some administrative supervision; others were initiated and organised by committees outside the village, requiring only the compliance of the villagers through the *mwethya* structure. The latter projects were coordinated by administration officials, such as location chiefs and subchiefs.

Nigeria

Patterns in parts of Nigeria show some instructive parallels. First, there have been tremendous pressures and successes of self-help initiatives during both the colonial and the post-independence eras. Abernethy (1969, 65) refers to the rivalries among various communities in southern Nigeria. He indicates that the size of the competing groups seemed to expand over time, so that competition, which had at first been confined to small communities, began to occur in the 1920s at the subtribal or higher levels. One expression of this was in the educational activities of tribal or progress unions. He observes (Abernathy 1969, 111) that some tribal unions had a significant effect on expansion of school enrolments during the 1940s.

Igwe (1988) provides a more detailed and more recent account with particular reference to Igbo communities in Imo State. He reports that within these communities the basic social unit is the localised patrilineage known as *umunna*, which consists of individual families whose members are blood relations (Igwe 1988, 105). Families occupy homesteads on defined areas of land, and each lineage group lives together under the moral authority of its oldest male member. Among the Igbo:

> competition between individuals, age groups, compounds, clans and villages is an established and cherished way of life. Every community measures its progress in relation to the achievement of others. For this reason, when the acquisition of academic certificates became identified with personal achievements and salaried employment, the spirit of competition manifested itself in open rivalry for the establishment of schools and the highest enrolment rates. (Igwe 1988, 105)

Documenting the procedures through which schools may be established, Igwe indicates that the first step is for community members to come together under the umbrella of their council of elders and village improvement union to pass a resolution that they want a school. Members then identify a number of possible sites, and make a formal application to the government for approval (Igwe 1988, 110).

To secure the necessary initial finance for schools, it is usual to embark on launching ceremonies. The village improvement union issues a circular letter making it compulsory for all to attend. Special invitations are also issued to in-laws, relations, friends, and well-wishers outside the village. Normally the circular states that heavy fines will be imposed on absent branch unions, age groups, and individuals. Igwe explains:

> In the village, a town crier goes round several times to announce the event and to invite people to decorate the venue before the date of the ceremony. All the village cultural dance, masquerade and other entertainment groups are invited to attend, and the women prepare food for the occasion. . . . The ceremonies are usually held at weekends to enable all public servants to attend and to prevent them from using their jobs as an excuse for absence. (Igwe 1988, 111)

At the ceremony, Igwe continues, people compete to see who will donate the highest amount. There is a similar competition among the age groups. "Everybody in the community endeavours to donate some amount, no matter how big or small, and each donation is announced over the public address system. By the general spirit of the people, it is better to be dead than to be alive and not be able to contribute to the development of one's village or clan" (Igwe 1988, 111).

The launching ceremonies are mainly for initial capital rather than for recurrent income. To meet recurrent needs, Igwe reports, ongoing levies are made of labour and/or cash. Village improvement unions also encourage ostentatious donations of cash from wealthy individuals. Igwe's account shows that, as in Kenya, traditional organisations such as age groups are employed for modern purposes. Another parallel with Kenya is the way in which the monetary economy has been woven into the system, so that people can contribute cash instead of labour. However, the village-level organisations in Nigeria are not incorporated into a national structure in the way that they are in Kenya.

Traditions in other parts of Nigeria, and particularly in the north, are very different from those documented by Igwe. Western-type education developed much more slowly in the north, and regional disparities in educational development have been a major threat to national cohesion (Crowder 1978, 241; Fafunwa 1974, 174). The reasons for slower growth of western-type education were partly geographic, as the schools were originally established by missionaries who arrived by sea in the southern parts of the country. However, they were also religious and cultural. In particular, the fact that Western-type schools were closely associated with Christian missionaries was a major factor in rejection of such schools by Islamic communities. Moreover, to facilitate the British colonial strategy of governing northern Nigeria by indirect rule through the existing emirate structure, the colonial authorities agreed at an early stage that the work of Christian missionaries, and therefore of their schools, would be restricted (Crampton 1979, 54; Ozigi and Ocho 1981, 17). In consequence, the majority of Western-type schools, especially in the Islamic parts of northern Nigeria, were government operated and funded. The general attitude of the population towards these schools was, and remains, very different from that in the south (Junaid 1994).

Bhutan

Traditions of community financing of schools are also relatively undeveloped in Bhutan, though for very different reasons from those in northern Nigeria. Bhutan is a small kingdom in the Himalaya mountains with a strong Buddhist culture. The country was never colonised, and until recently was very isolated. Partly for these reasons, the school system has a short history. Although the Buddhist monasteries have educational traditions stretching back centuries, the first Western-type schools were only established in 1915 (Singh 1978, 185). For the next half century, the number of Western-type schools remained very small. According to one official source (Bhutan 1994, 22), in the late 1950s the country had only 11 schools with 17 teachers and about 440 pupils.

In subsequent decades the system expanded dramatically, so that by 1995 the nation had 281 schools with 2,680 teachers and 75,500 pupils (Bhutan 1995, 1). The bulk of this expansion was achieved through government resources supplemented by external aid, but additional resources had been derived from community and parental contributions. These inputs were especially obvious in the institutions specifically named community schools. As mentioned at the beginning of this chapter, in 1995 Bhutan had 102 community schools, which according to official policy operated only at the lower primary level, compared with 143 full primary schools.

The origin of community schools lies in a policy for extended classrooms (ECRs) launched during the period of the sixth five-year plan (1987–1992). The ECRs provided education up to the first three grades of primary schooling, and were a mechanism to bring schooling physically closer to relatively remote communities. The intention was that each ECR would be attached to a full primary school which would provide an institutional anchor (Harley 1990). However, the linkages to primary schools did not work well, and in 1990 the ECRs were formally separated and renamed community schools. Official guidelines (Bhutan 1992, 12–13) set out the responsibilities of communities in the two types of institution as follows:

Primary Schools
- Construction of all school buildings and teachers' quarters with the exception of roofing materials, wages for skilled workers, items such as cement, nails, door and window bolts, etc.
- Repairs and maintenance
- Transportation of textbooks, stationery, and other supplies from the nearest road heads

Community Schools
- Construction of all school buildings and teachers' quarters
- Repairs and maintenance
- Transportation of textbooks, stationery, and other supplies
- Provision of school furniture as per sample provided by the District Education Officer

A 1994 survey of the ways in which schools were financed found, as in Kenya and Nigeria, a mixture of traditional and modern mechanisms for mobilising community resources (Bray 1995). The monastery schools and the government institutions had almost no interaction. In the words of one senior education officer, they operated independently "like two parallel railway tracks." This feature had some similarity to the separation of Koranic and Western-type schools in northern Nigeria. However, the community and primary schools in Bhutan do benefit from systems of labour taxation that have long traditional roots but have been adapted to modern times.

The two most important labour taxes in this context are called *gungda woola* and *zhapto lemi*. The former requires each household either to provide 15 days' labour each year or to pay a cash substitute. Regulations on how *gungda woola* can be used are laid down by the Ministry of Home Affairs (Bhutan 1993). Under normal circumstances, *gungda woola* is used for national projects rather than local ones for which it is possible to identify the direct beneficiaries, but it has been used on occasion for school construction. Much more common in the education sector is the use of *zhapto lemi*, which is explicitly oriented to village projects from which direct benefits are easily identifiable. *Zhapto lemi* is also used for construction and maintenance of temples, roads, and other public facilities.

Bhutan's population can be roughly divided into three major ethnic groups: Ngalops of Tibetan origin in the west, Sharchops of Indo-Mongoloid origin in the east, and Lhotshams of Nepalese origin in the south. Among the main goals of the present government is the forging of a national identity from diverse ethnicity and culture (Sinha 1993). The southern communities of Bhutan have had stronger traditions of self-help in education than the central and northern parts, in large measure because the southern parts have had greater contact with India, which has a much longer history of schooling. However, the 1994 study of community financing did not identify major variations in other parts of the country (Bray 1995). During the last decade, Bhutan has suffered major tensions between the indigenous Drukpa and southerners who have been identified as recent migrants (Parmanand 1992). However, education has not been an arena for ethnic rivalry comparable to that in Kenya and Nigeria. Rather, the diversity identified by the 1994 study was principally by micro-community, arising particularly from the varying attitudes of specific community leaders and head teachers.

Also worth noting is a contrast with Kenya in the extent to which community members who were not parents were willing to contribute to schools. As noted above, Hill suggested that because of the Kamba system of supplementary marriage institutions, which guaranteed the possibility of social paternity or maternity to everyone, in the Kamba society all members of the community were keen to contribute to educational institutions. Bhutanese societies do not have the same types of supplementary marriage institutions, which is probably one reason why adults without children of their own were less enthusiastic about making contributions to schools.

POLICY DILEMMAS CONCERNING INEQUALITY

The fact that variations exist both by macro- and by micro-region deserves more detailed consideration. Community financing raises obvious issues of inequality because some communities are in a better position to help themselves than are others. When such disparities become excessive, they may threaten broader national stability. For this reason, government planners in Kenya have made periodic efforts to control and even to dampen *harambee* activities (Anderson 1970, 154; Ngau 1987, 530).

In other contexts, self-help activities raise problems not because they are too vigorous but because they are too weak. The question facing governments in such circumstances concerns the amount of help that should be given to communities that do not help themselves. If governments do not aid such communities, regional imbalances are likely to grow; but if governments provide too much assistance, the aid may undermine self-help because the communities see that resources are forthcoming despite the communities' inertia.

Ozigi and Ocho (1981) mention this dilemma in the context of Nigeria's Universal Primary Education campaign during the 1970s. In order to reduce regional gaps, the federal government poured massive resources into areas with low enrolments. The result, however, was that people "tended to fold their arms and leave everything to the government" (Ozigi and Ocho 1981, 123). Subsequently, the federal government funds dried up. When the dynamic communities realised what was happening, they again embarked on self-help initiatives to meet their needs. The less dynamic communities, however, remained relatively inactive, with the result that the disparities were restored or even widened. This pattern was repeated when the national government made a major injection of funds in 1989, but reduced inputs in 1990 and almost totally suspended them in 1991 (World Bank 1994c, 97–98).

Table 10.2 presents figures on regional disparities in *harambee* expenditures for preprimary and primary education in Kenya. In 1992–1993, average household expenditures in rural Nyanza were only Ksh 67 per enrolled child, compared with Ksh 203 in rural Central Province. Accompanying statistics also showed major disparities within provinces. In rural Nyanza the range was from Ksh 49 in Homa Bay to Ksh 108 in Kisii, and in rural Central Province the range was from Ksh 157 in Kirinyanga to Ksh 238 in Nyeri.

Table 10.2 also displays rural-urban disparities. While the figures for Nairobi and Mombasa show unexpected contrasts (Ksh 921 compared with Ksh 88), the average for all urban areas is Ksh 514 compared

Table 10.2. Harambee Expenditures on Pre-primary and Primary Education, Kenya, 1992–1993

	Ksh per Enrolled Student per Year
Coast rural	114
Eastern rural	90
Central rural	203
Rift Valley rural	143
Nyanza rural	67
Western rural	128
Nairobi urban	921
Mombasa urban	88
Other urban	243
All rural (average)	122
All urban (average)	514

Source: Background documents for World Bank (1994a).

with Ksh 122 for rural areas. However, it seems likely that much of this disparity arises from inclusion of pre-primary schools, which are basically nongovernment operations and are much more common in urban than rural areas. Moreover, the figures were derived from an expenditure survey that omitted contributions of labour, materials, and land. Had these inputs been included, the gap would certainly have been narrowed and perhaps even reversed. The types of traditional self-help organisation documented by Hill and Igwe are much stronger in rural than in urban areas. In many urban settings the authorities do demand parental participation in the form of fees and levies, but it is much more difficult to promote broader community contributions. The result in many countries is that governments bridge the gap in urban areas, but expect rural communities to help themselves. This is arguably inequitable, and is an unfortunate side-effect of reliance on community cohesion and traditional methods for raising resources.

Inequalities may also arise within rural self-help projects. Leaders are not always fully representative of the communities they serve, and are not always sensitive to the fact that some families and individuals find it more difficult than others to make contributions. Chung (1989) has reported that in Zimbabwe, communities commonly make decisions by simple majority voting. Sometimes the 51 percent are the wealthy, and the relatively poor 49 percent have little choice. A related observation has been made in Uganda, where executives of Parent-Teacher Associations (PTAs) may not conduct meetings in a free and fair way. Members of PTA executives are often from among the socially and economically advantaged groups, and it is not uncommon for powers to be abused. According to Opolot, decisions on finance may be stage-managed by the organisers:

> Speakers are determined in advance, supporters scattered all over the audience to allay any suspicion and occasionally when some critic is chosen, (s)he is interrupted, booed or the views simply ignored by the chairman. To give the meeting credibility, a motion is put to vote and at times the chairman uses the discretion to force the meeting to endorse minority views. Complaints to challenge the irregularities and undemocratic processes are not tolerated through points of order and/or points of information technicalities. Parents who get tough with figures are accused of not having the school at heart and can be frankly told to withdraw their pupils from the school. Delaying tactics are employed so that financial statements (almost all not audited) are brought in late when the audience is tired and hungry or when others have already left. (Opolot 1994, 112–3)

However, such irregularities have not gone unnoticed by parents. Opolot observed that two categories of parents could be identified: those who advocate PTA increases and always "win," and the generally poorer parents who are against what they perceive to be unfair increases in PTA contributions. Most parents, he indicated, see PTA annual general meetings as a forum for increasing parental contributions. "Most parents go simply to hear what they have to pay, but quite a number simply don't turn up at all" (Opolot 1994, 113).

Not all societies have such severe problems. However, complexities of a different sort that were identified in Bhutan are probably common in many countries. When levies are imposed on households in particular communities, they are usually standardised regardless of the size and composition of the households. This is certainly simple and straightforward, but it causes differential burdens.

The question of labour versus cash can also be problematic. At the extremes in Bhutan are some communities that insist on labour, and others that insist on cash (Bray 1996c, 508). The rationale in communities that insist that all contributions should be in labour seems to be that everyone can contribute labour, while not everyone can easily contribute cash. By contrast, insistence on cash payments may partly be because some parents come from distant places, and are therefore less easily able to contribute labour. However, insistence on cash, paradoxically, can be described as more equitable. In the case of labour, the argument goes, some households may send people who are strong and willing to work hard, while others might send people who are weak or uncommitted. In contrast, it may be suggested, one dollar is equal to another. While this argument might have some face validity, the system discriminates against households that find it more difficult to secure cash.

DILEMMAS CONCERNING INEFFICIENCY, WASTAGE, AND POOR QUALITY

Also underlying the above discussion are tensions concerning potential inefficiency in use of resources. On the positive side, self-help projects may mobilise resources that under other circumstances would not be available for such goals. Mbithi and Rasmusson pointed out that:

> [i]t is a common feature in Harambee meetings to see women and men contributing their personal property such as beads and ear-rings, eggs, foods and artifacts which the income tax collector can never obtain. It is usual for people to work, dance and work day in and day out, hungry, cold, thirsty and uncomplaining on a project they are strongly committed to (Mbithi and Rasmusson 1977, 16)

Mbithi and Rasmusson (1977, 164) added that loyalty among the urban elite to their home areas led to contributions of resources that otherwise would probably have been used for conspicuous consumption of imported goods or for short-run speculative investment of limited national importance. These comments have been echoed by Wilson, who observed that individuals are willing to donate to *harambee* projects because they see their resources as "earmarked" for specific uses, and because they think that the system is organised so that others will also properly cooperate and donate (Wilson 1992, 4).

However, resources may be wasted by projects which are ill-conceived and poorly managed. Many projects both in Kenya and in Nigeria have been based more on a desire to upstage rivals than on more substantial developmental justifications. Sometimes these rivalries are small-scale and local, but they may also have a larger focus. In Kenya, rivalry between the Kikuyu and the Luo had been a major cause of proliferation of projects, to the extent that in the 1970s, Central Province (heartland of the Kikuyu) had a *harambee* project for every 380 persons, and Nyanza Province (heartland of the Luo) had a project for every 430 persons (Mbithi and Rasmusson 1977, 31). These projects were not all necessary and viable.

Olembo makes an allied point by highlighting management problems at the institutional level. "A majority of head teachers and primary school committees," he remarks, "embark on fund-raising and in fact the construction of school facilities without even estimating the cost of the facility" (Olembo 1985, 18). The Bhutan study likewise identified buildings that had been left unfinished because of loss of enthusiasm or divided loyalties. Further, as indicated in the quotation from Uganda, many societies are torn by suspicions of embezzlement and other abuse of community resources. For micro-political reasons, schools may be sited in inappropriate places, and establishment of excessive numbers of small schools overstretches scarce teacher and other resources.

Moreover, self-help projects may subvert planners' goals in quality as well as quantity. Kenya's *harambee* schools have suffered severe problems of quality (Wellings 1983), and have also undermined attempts to link educational output to economic needs through manpower planning. Anderson pointed out that much has been made of the traditional African capacity for communal effort by anthropologists and politicians, and of the role this can play in the process of national development (Anderson 1973, 22). However,

> such effort depends not only on co-operative traditions, but also on individual enterprise and organizational talents. Success or failure depends largely on the initiative and drive of enterprising and energetic individuals. In these circumstances, self-help groups can easily become subject to the influences of particular personalities and parochial interests. There is clear evidence in the past that this has, in a number of cases, prevented effective co-operation on a viable scale, caused duplication of effort, and led to splits and disruptive rivalries between neighbouring communities. (Anderson 1973, 22)

A more recent report from Nepal shows that similar tensions are ongoing in other countries (World Bank 1994b). Commenting on the facilities of secondary schools, the report states that

> [a] few schools in more affluent communities have substantial facilities provided from fees levied on parents over the years. But most schools reflect the poverty of the communities they serve. They lack basic amenities, including electricity, drinking water and sanitation. Maintenance and security are poor and desks and chairs are insufficient (World Bank 1994b, 16)

Given poor-quality inputs in the form of facilities, teachers, and pupils, it is also no surprise that achievements are also poor. In 1992 only 24.2 percent of the 15,000 candidates from community secondary schools who took the school-leaving certificate examination achieved a pass. This contrasted with 29.0 percent among candidates from the government schools, and 81.1 percent among the elite private and boarding schools.

CONCLUSIONS

The extent of community financing of education in different parts of the world varies widely. Only part of this variation arises from differences in need, and cultural factors are also influential. As this chapter has shown, the organisational structure of some societies is more conducive to self-help activities than that of others.

The chapter has taken examples from a range of countries, but has given particular attention to patterns in Kenya, Nigeria, and Bhutan. Kenya has become well known for its *harambee* movement. The chapter has shown ways in which that movement fits indigenous social structures that have been adapted to fit contemporary needs and conditions. A similar observation has been made about communities in southern Nigeria, and the chapter has especially highlighted Igwe's account of social structures and self-help patterns in an Igbo community. In Bhutan, by contrast, the tradition of community financing is less developed. This partly reflects the different cultural context, though it also reflects the fact that the history of Western-type schooling is short, and that it is only in recent times that the government has been unable to meet the full demand for schooling.

In addition to highlighting positive aspects, the chapter has noted some of the problematic features arising from different approaches. Community financing commonly exacerbates regional and social inequalities, and projects are often less than optimal in efficiency and quality. As a result, governments commonly face major policy dilemmas. On the one hand, they are reluctant to dampen the enthusiasm of groups prepared to help themselves, but on the other hand, they see a need to harness forces and avoid excesses. Governments also need to devise appropriate policies towards communities which are less active in self-help projects. It might be undesirable for governments themselves to meet all needs as that would itself vindicate community inertia. However, governments also find that they cannot simply stand by and watch regional and social imbalances become ever more severe.

Finally, the discussion also highlights the importance of taking cultural factors into account when making general recommendations; for example, concerning forms of partnership in educational provision, or the introduction or increase of user charges. Different communities are likely to respond to such initiatives in different ways, and flexibility may be needed in the implementation of general policies.

REFERENCES

Abernethy, D.B. 1969. *The Political Dilemma of Popular Education: An African Case*. Stanford: Stanford University Press.

Abreu, E. 1982. *The Role of Self-Help in the Development of Education in Kenya 1900–1973*. Nairobi: Kenya Literature Bureau.

Anderson, J. 1970. *The Struggle for the School: The Interaction of Missionary, Colonial Government and Nationalist Enterprise in the Development of Formal Education in Kenya*. Nairobi: Longman.

Anderson, J. 1973. *Organization and Financing of Self-Help Education in Kenya*. Paris: International Institute for Educational Planning.

Bhutan, Government of. 1992. *Ninth Quarterly Policy Guidelines and Instructions*. Thimphu: Department of Education, Ministry for Social Services.

Bhutan, Government of. 1993. *Rules and Regulations for Mobilization of Gungda, Zhaptok and Dzongsey Woola*. Thimphu: Ministry of Home Affairs.

Bhutan, Government of. 1994. *Bhutan: Round Table Meeting, 1995*. Vol. 1: *The Progress of the Sixth Plan*. Thimphu: Ministry of Planning.

Bhutan, Government of. 1995. *General Statistics, May 1995*. Thimphu: Division of Education, Ministry of Health and Education.

Bradshaw, Y.W. 1993. "State Limitations, Self-Help Secondary Schooling, and Development in Kenya." *Social Forces* 72: 347–378.

Bray, M. 1995. *The Costs and Financing of Primary Schooling in Bhutan*. Thimphu: UNICEF/Royal Government of Bhutan.

Bray, M. 1996a. *Decentralization of Education: Community Financing*. Washington, DC: World Bank.

Bray, M. 1996b. *Counting the Full Cost: Parental and Community Resourcing of Education in East Asia*. Washington, DC: World Bank, in collaboration with UNICEF.

Bray, M. 1996c. "Equity Issues in Local Resourcing of Education: Community Financing of Primary Schools in Bhutan." *International Review of Education* 42: 495–514.

Bray, M., with K. Lillis, eds. 1988. *Community Financing of Education: Issues and Policy Implications in Less Developed Countries*. Oxford: Pergamon Press.

Camilleri, C. 1986. *Cultural Anthropology and Education*. London: Kogan Page/Paris: UNESCO.

Cheng, K.M. 1995. "*Minban* Teachers in China." Hong Kong: Comparative Education Research Centre, University of Hong Kong.

Chung, F. 1989. Question and answer session on government and community financing of education in Zimbabwe, conference sponsored by the *International Journal of Educational Development*, University of Oxford, UK.

Crampton, E.T. 1979. *Christianity in Northern Nigeria*. London: Geoffrey Chapman.

Crowder, M. 1978. *The Story of Nigeria*. London: Faber and Faber.

Esquieu, P., and S. Péano. 1994. *L'Enseignement Privé et Spontané dans le Système Educatif Tchadien*. Rapport de Recherche No.103. Paris: Institut International de Planification de l'Education.

Fafunwa, A.B. 1974. *History of Education in Nigeria*. London: George Allen and Unwin.

Harley, B. 1990. "Extended Primary Classrooms in Bhutan." Thimphu: UNICEF/ Department of Education, Ministry for Social Services.

Hill, M.J.D. 1991. *The Harambee Movement in Kenya: Self-Help, Development and Education among the Kamba of Kitui District*. LSE Monographs on Social Anthropology 64. London: The Athlone Press.

Hillery, G.A. 1955. "Definitions of Community: Areas of Agreement." *Rural Sociology* 20: 111–23.

Igwe, S.O. 1988. "Community Financing of Schools in Eastern Nigeria." In *Community Financing of Education: Issues and Policy Implications in Less Developed Countries*, eds. M. Bray with K. Lillis. Oxford: Pergamon Press.

Junaid, M.I. 1994. *Basic Education in Nigeria: A Study of Sokoto State*. Sokoto: Department of Education, Usmanu Danfodio University.

Kamunge, J.M., chairman. 1988. *Report of the Presidential Working Party on Education and Manpower Training for the Next Decade and Beyond*. Nairobi: Government Printer.

Kenya, Republic of. 1994. *National Development Plan for the Period 1994 to 1996*. Nairobi: Government Printer.

Kroeber, A.L., and C. Kluckhohn. 1952. *Culture: A Critical Review of Concepts and Definitions*. Cambridge, MA: Peabody Museum of Archaeology and Ethnology.

Malawi, Government of. 1993. *Basic Education Statistics 1993*. Lilongwe: Ministry of Education, Science and Technology.

Mbithi, M., and R. Rasmusson. 1977. *Self-Reliance in Kenya: The Case of Harambee*. Uppsala: Scandinavian Institute of African Studies.

Mwiria, K. 1990. "Kenya's Harambee Secondary School Movement: The Contradictions of Public Policy." *Comparative Education Review* 34: 350–368.

Ngau, M. 1987. "Tensions in Empowerment: The Experience of the *Harambee* (Self-Help) Movement in Kenya." *Economic Development and Cultural Change* 35: 523–538.

Olembo, J.O. 1985. *Financing Primary School Buildings in Kenya*. Nairobi: Transafrica Press.

Opolot, J.A. 1994. "Study on Costs and Cost-Effective Approaches to Primary Education in Uganda." Kampala: UNICEF.

Ozigi, A., and L. Ocho. 1981. *Education in Northern Nigeria*. London: George Allen and Unwin.

Parmanand. 1992. *The Politics of Bhutan: Retrospect and Prospect*. Delhi: Pragati Publications.

Singh, N. 1978. *Bhutan: A Kingdom in the Himalayas*. New Delhi: Thomson Press.

Sinha, A.C. 1993. *Bhutan: Ethnic Identity and National Dilemma*. New Delhi: Reliance Publishing House.

Wellings, A. 1983. "Unaided Education in Kenya: Blessing or Blight?" *Research in Education* 29: 11–28.

Wilson, L.S. 1992. "The *Harambee* Movement and Efficient Public Good Provision in Kenya." *Journal of Public Economics* 48:1–19.

Wolf, J., E. Kane, and B. Strickland. 1997. *Planning for Community Participation in Education*. Washington, DC: United States Agency for International Development.

World Bank. 1994a. *Kenya: Public Expenditure Review*. Washington, DC: World Bank.

World Bank. 1994b. *Nepal: Critical Issues in Secondary Education and Options for Reform*. Washington, DC: World Bank.

World Bank. 1994c. *Nigeria: Social Sectors Strategy Review*. Washington, DC: World Bank.

World Bank. 1995. *Kenya: Poverty Assessment*. Washington, DC: World Bank.

CHAPTER 11

Educational Financing Strategies in Developing Countries

The Case of Cameroon and Uganda

MERCY TEMBON

Educational financing has preoccupied the minds of planners and policy makers at national and international levels over the past three decades. During this period, there has been a serious debate about the role of states and markets in the financing of education between economists from two schools of thought. At one end of a long continuum on state/market involvement are economists who favour active state intervention in the financing of education, in order to achieve greater equity and efficiency. They rest their case on three main pillars. First, the benefits of an individual's education extends to society at large; thus, if individuals were required to pay for their own schooling there would be underinvestment in education. Second, some families are extremely poor and without subsidies they would be denied access to education because of inability to pay. Third, education is a determinant of future incomes; therefore market allocation of education will exacerbate inequalities between the rich who can acquire education and in turn earn high incomes, and the poor who are unable to pay for education and remain poor. In the 1980s an influential second school of economists emerged. They advocated a substantially greater role for the market and price system in the provision and financing of education and have been referred to as "neo-liberal" (Colclough 1993). They argue that public provision results in serious inefficiencies—high costs of production, delays, and misallocation of resources. They hold that prices and markets stimulate competition that leads to greater efficiency in the production of services, greater consumer choice, and increased resources for the sector. The two schools of thought have been extensively discussed in the literature (Klees 1989; Psacharopoulos and Woodhall 1985).

Since the early 1980s, neoliberal economists and education financing policy advisers, notably from the World Bank, have advocated more private financing or increased cost-sharing and a greater role for the market in educational provision in developing countries (Jimenez 1987; Mingat and Tan 1986; World Bank 1986). They argue that the cost of meeting the needs of expanding education systems in developing countries is increasing, but the proportion of national budgets allocated to the education sector has more or less reached a ceiling in most countries. Therefore, more resources need to be mobilised through increased private financing, particularly at secondary and higher levels of education. One prominent strategy for mobilising extra resources for education is the charging of fees, particularly at secondary and higher levels, and the encouragement of private provision.

This chapter argues that there is a case for financing of education through private mechanisms, but that excessive dependence on prices and market allocations, through fees or user charges, may conflict with the economic, social, and cultural circumstances of developing countries. With reference to evidence from two sub-Saharan African countries, Cameroon and Uganda, tensions between economic and cultural imperatives in the financing of education are highlighted. The extent of the educational finance crisis, the coping strategies developed, and the effects of these on vulnerable groups such as girls and the poor are examined in the case of each country.

The next section provides a brief historical overview of the development of a financial crisis in education in sub-Saharan Africa over the past three decades. This is followed by a review of the theoretical framework for educational financing, including neoliberal economic arguments for market allocations and the literature on factors affecting the educational participation of vulnerable groups such as girls and the poor. The two country cases and their comparisons highlight the gap between theory and practice. In the concluding section it is suggested that financing strategies for developing countries must take account of economic, social, and cultural realities.

THE EDUCATIONAL FINANCE CRISIS

In the 1960s many countries in sub-Saharan Africa committed themselves to the attainment of Universal Primary Education (UPE) by 1980. It was hoped that by this date accessible and affordable education for all, particularly at the basic level, would have been established. Until the

1980s, investments in education in developing countries occurred in a climate of optimism. The world economy was growing steadily. Moreover, research evidence on the importance of human capital as the basis for economic growth stimulated unprecedented interest in educational investments by governments and international aid agencies. The agenda for educational development in newly independent countries was based on two main assumptions. The first was that the world economy would continue to grow and the second was that financial provision from external sources would be retained until newly independent countries could attain financial sustainability. Neither of these assumptions has been realised.

In the 1980s the world wide economic recession, characterised by oil crisis, declining terms of trade, increasing levels of debt, and balance of payment crises thwarted the economic growth of many countries, especially those in sub-Saharan Africa. According to World Bank figures (1989), Africa's gross national product per capita (GNP) shrank in the 1980s to the 1967 level in real terms. This obviously had devastating effects on public spending. Public expenditure on education as a proportion of national incomes in developing countries showed either stagnation or slight increases in the 1980s, but the dollar value in real per capita terms declined abysmally, especially in sub-Saharan Africa (Colclough with Lewin 1993). Furthermore, assistance from external sources declined. It is estimated that loans to Africa declined from US $8.6 billion in 1978 to US $5.4 billion in 1985. Within the same period loans to Latin America decreased from US $4.9 billion to US $3.9 billion (Sanyal 1991).

Despite impressive increases in enrolments during the past three decades, many countries have not succeeded in enrolling all children in school. In 1990 it was estimated that there were between 115 and 145 million children aged six to eleven in developing countries out of school, either due to a lack of school places or a lack of money to attend or remain at school. The majority of these children come from disadvantaged groups in society such as the poor, females, and those in rural areas (World Bank 1990; World Bank 1995).

Education budgets have been squeezed to such an extent that quality has been greatly compromised. Heyneman (1989) reports a conspicuous absence of basic materials such as textbooks, chalk, blackboards, and desks in some classrooms. Some schools lack basic facilities such as water and latrines; buildings are hardly maintained and leaking roofs are a common occurrence (Caillods and Postlethwaite 1989). In some countries governments are even unable to pay salaries regularly. In some areas, there are few schools and children travel very long distances in order to attend. It is within this context that concern for the educational crisis in developing countries emerged in the 1980s.

THEORETICAL FRAMEWORK

The allocation of resources for financing and provision of education reflects the importance that both the individual and the society attach to its perceived benefits. Education is considered as an investment, with governments and individuals incurring costs in the present in anticipation of reaping benefits in the future. The balance between costs and benefits is important in influencing both government and individual decisions to finance education. In this section we discuss the costs and benefits of education and provide evidence to show how they affect decisions about educational financing.

ECONOMIC AND MACRO-LEVEL CONSIDERATIONS OF EDUCATIONAL COSTS AND BENEFITS

The provision of education involves both capital and recurrent costs. Capital costs go towards the building and furnishing of schools. Recurrent costs include the payment of staff salaries, the procurement of office supplies such as books and stationery for the day-to-day running of schools, and curriculum materials such as textbooks and equipment to be used by students. Costs are also incurred for other expenses incidental to schooling. These include the cost of uniforms, boarding, food, and transportation from home to school.

Education is considered as an investment that has broad economic, social, and political benefits at macro and micro levels. At the macro level, benefits have been analysed in terms of economic growth. A study of the growth performance of 31 countries in sub-Saharan Africa found that between 1965 and 1983, 30 percent of the growth of gross domestic product (GDP) in these countries resulted from educational investments (World Bank 1986). At the micro level, benefits have been analysed in terms of future and lifetime earnings. Besides economic benefits there are social and political benefits linked to education. It has been noted that in many countries an individual's social mobility, lifestyle, career opportunities, and life chances are linked to his/her level of education (Gould 1993). Literacy enables citizens to participate fully in the political and social development process while maintaining a decent standard of living. Other noneconomic benefits include better health for oneself and for one's offspring, longer life, and the ability of parents to help their children with homework that leads to success and greater likelihood of college attendance (Leslie 1990, 275).

Economists have used estimates of costs and benefits to calculate the rates of return for different levels of education. Rate-of-return studies have been carried out to measure the yield of educational investment in many developed and developing countries. Studies distinguish between returns to individuals, designated as "private returns," and returns to society, designated as "social returns." A comparative survey of the social and private rates of return to education (Psacharopoulos 1993) concludes that private and social rates of returns are highest at the primary level, followed by those at the secondary level; private rates of return to education are higher than social returns; rates of return to investment in education are generally more than 10 percent, which can be read as a rough approximation of the opportunity cost of capital; and the returns to education in developing countries are higher than corresponding returns in developed countries. An earlier review of rates of return to education in developing countries led Psacharopoulos and Woodhall to conclude that for the individual student or family, education is usually a highly profitable personal investment. The expected benefits more than compensate for the burden of costs, including earnings foregone (Psacharopoulos and Woodhall 1985, 119).

Rate-of-return findings have three main implications for the financing of education. First, the evidence that education is socially and privately profitable suggests that the costs of education need to be shared by society and individuals (government and households). Second, the high social rates of return to primary education indicate that top priority for public financing should be given to the primary level. Third, the difference between high private rates of return and low social rates of return for higher education suggests that a greater part of the cost burden for the tertiary level should be borne by private individuals.

Recommendations based on rate-of-return studies have been criticised on several grounds. Critics have referred to inaccuracies in the measurement of costs and benefits, reliance on past conditions which do not necessarily reflect future conditions, the assumption that labour markets are competitive, and the absence of a gender dimension in many rate of return calculations (Bennell 1994; Colclough 1993; Kabeer and Humphrey 1993; Tsang 1988). Despite these criticisms, rates of return are still considered useful in guiding the formulation of policies on education financing for developing countries. Psacharopoulos and Woodhall (1985) accept some of the criticisms but go on to suggest that although rate-of-return studies may not be numerically accurate, they can be useful for ranking investment alternatives. This view is supported by McGavin, who notes that rates of return are not precise. Their policy purpose is to indicate desirable directions of policy change (McGavin 1991, 219).

Recent World Bank policy recommendations for the financing of education in developing countries in general, and sub-Sahara African countries in particular, have been based on these rate-of-return indicators. Public subsidisation of higher education and to some extent secondary education has been perceived as a misallocation of resources because the private returns are greater than social returns. Consequently, neoliberal economists recommend that some of the financial burden at post-primary levels should be shifted to users of the services (World Bank 1986, 1988). Several strategies have been proposed, including fees, loans, and increased reliance on private schools, but the most common and easiest option is the charging of fees for services. Proponents of this strategy believe that private financial contributions will make up for the government's shortfall and also increase equity and efficiency (Jimenez 1987; Thobani 1984).

The emphasis on this strategy has blinded researchers and policy advisers to other factors that are equally important in influencing decisions about educational financing. Given the differences in economic circumstances in each country, there is a danger that policies of cost recovery may backfire and/or conflict with other factors, such as culture and local contexts, that might also have a strong influence on the implementation of the strategy. One problem with the neoliberal economic principles, on which the World Bank and IMF recommendations are based, is the use of money as the basis for distribution or consumption of goods and services. This runs counter to the economic systems of most developing countries, which are agrarian and not monetized. Another important conflict is the gender "blindness" that is inherent within neoliberal economic theories, whereas there are very clear gender biases in parental attitudes towards educational financing.

CULTURAL AND MICRO-LEVEL CONSIDERATIONS

In pre-colonial days in many African countries, payment for goods and services used to be made in kind. Common modes of payment included cattle, food, or even labour, which all people could afford. Now that the modern mode of payment for goods and services is cash, a tension arises when parents can only afford to make payments in kind. As a result, parents who have realised the importance of education and are willing to send their children to school may be unable to do so because of their inability to pay.

The culture of many developing countries, and particularly those of sub-Saharan Africa, revolves around the community rather than the individual. Costs and benefits in such cultures are viewed on a communal basis. There is communal solidarity, as is readily observed in group action. The practice of group cooperation is based on the common saying that "one hand cannot tie a bundle." Mutual support networks of neighbours, friends, and kin are common. It is customary for groups of people to come together and build houses in turn for each member of the group, or to develop farms on a rotatory basis. Rotatory savings groups, known as *Njangi* in Cameroon, are common. Many people in sub-Saharan Africa benefit from these support networks and find them to be convenient means of funding various projects including children's education (Bray and Lillis 1988). Modern economic practices depend on the influence of market forces that concern the consumer and the producer as individuals. Individualism as promoted by market practices undermines communal solidarity inasmuch as using money as the basis for payment for goods and services tends to breed individualism, which is diametrically opposed to communalism.

Some cultures and religious orthodoxies promote a gender bias in education. In many developing countries parents still believe that the returns to investments in female children's education are lower than the returns to male children's education. This belief is reinforced by the assumption that when girls marry they will move to their husband's family and so any gains from their education will accrue to the family of marriage (Kwesiga 1993) (Editors' note: cf. Chapter 14 in this volume by Mikael Palme). Gender discrimination may also be linked to societal gender roles ascribed to women. In many cultural settings it is still believed that "a woman's place is in the home." Women are supposed to be wives and mothers. Schools are often not perceived as the right place for preparing young girls to take up these roles. Consequently, parents decide that girls should stay at home and take care of their younger siblings and help with the cooking and housework, while their brothers, who are expected to work outside of the home in the future, go to school (Odaga and Heneveld 1995). Religious beliefs and practices may also influence parental decisions about schooling. Studies in Côte d'Ivoire (Appleton, Collier, and Horsnell 1990), Cameroon, Sierra Leone (Brock and Cammish 1991), and in the Gambia (Kane and O'Reilly de Brun 1993) have found that Muslims tend to be more reluctant than Christians to send their daughters to school. An analysis of cross-country data reveals that religious beliefs, and in particular Islamic beliefs, are associated with low enrolment ratios for girls (Colclough with Lewin 1993; King and Hill 1993).

From the discussion above we note that there are tensions and conflicts between neoliberal economic prescriptions and contextual circumstances that may hinder implementation or negatively affect some marginal groups. Two areas of tension between economics and culture are (1) methods of payment for education and (2) the role of gender in parental decision making about schooling. With this theoretical background we shall examine how secondary education is financed in two countries, so as to evaluate the validity of the economic prescriptions suggested above.

FROM THEORY TO PRACTICE

Educational financing in most countries is a partnership between the state and household. As already stated, the state finances education for several reasons, including the fact that its investment yields social returns. Families and communities also finance education because of the potential benefits they expect to gain. In this section we discuss the practice of financing secondary education, drawing examples from two countries, Cameroon and Uganda.

CAMEROON

Public Financing

The last decade for Cameroon has been characterised by economic hardship. Prices of the main primary products fell on the world market while levels of international inflation have risen. Oil revenues, which represented 4 percent of the GDP in 1980–1991, soared to 20 percent in 1984–1985, and then plunged to 6 percent in 1986–1987. Estimates suggest that the GDP of Cameroon in the 1980s dropped by an astonishing 19 percent (Blandford and Lynch 1990). These economic setbacks have caused a significant decline in public expenditure for social services in general and education in particular. Although Table 11.1 shows a large

Table 11.1. Public Expenditure on Education in Cameroon

Year	Total Expenditure in Constant Prices	Percentage (%) of GNP	Percentage of National Recurrent Budget
1988	103.7	2.7	16.1
1989	107.3	3.3	18.7
1990	105.2	3.4	20.9
1991	103.8	3.0	21.6

Source: UNESCO Statistical Year Book 1991; Ministry of Finance, Department of Budget: National Budget 1988–1989; 1989–1990; 1991–1992.

increase in the proportion of the national budget allocated for education between 1988 and 1991, there was a declining trend in public expenditure per pupil in real terms during the same period as a result of enrolment increases.

The distribution of public expenditure between 1988 and 1992 for primary, secondary, and higher education is shown in Table 11.2. An increase in expenditure on higher education has been at the expense of primary education. In 1991–1992, higher education, which accounts for less than 1 percent of total enrolments, received almost 35 percent of the resources. Secondary education, with about 18 percent of enrolments, received 26.5 percent and primary education, with about 81 percent of enrolments, received only 44.7 percent.

The decline of public expenditure for education per pupil implies that resources are required from some other source to bridge the gap that

Table 11.2. Proportion of Recurrent Expenditure on Education by Level in Cameroon (%)

Level	1988–1989	1989–1990	1990–1991	1991–1992
Primary	44.2	42.2	42.2	42.1
Secondary	24.5	24.7	24.5	25.0
Higher	31.3	33.1	33.3	32.9
Total	100.0	100.0	100.0	100.0

Source: Ministry of Finance, Department of Budget: National Budget 1988–1989; 1989–1990; 1991–1992.

is created by inadequate public finances. This, in turn, means that the burden of financing education has to be shifted to parents. There are two main types of secondary schools in Cameroon, government and private. Private secondary schools are further categorised into mission schools, which are government-aided, and lay private schools, which receive no financial assistance from the government. Government schools are state funded for their buildings, equipment, and teacher salaries. No tuition fees are charged in government schools. Mission schools are built by the religious organisations that own them. They charge fees and receive financial assistance from the government for teachers' salaries. Private schools, which levy tuition fees, are built and owned by private proprietors.

Results from a recent study revealed that, since 1991, mission schools have received few grants or subsidies from the government (Tembon 1994). To remedy the fiscal crisis, the government authorised the formation of Parent Teacher Associations (PTAs) in government schools to help with buildings, purchase of school equipment, and, in some instances, the employment of auxiliary staff. This move indicates a major shift away from the previous practice of the government as the principal financier of education, towards an increasing dependence on private finance.

Private Financing of Secondary Education

Even in government schools, where tuition is free, parents are expected to make direct cash payments to schools. These payments are sometimes made for registration, building funds, and school activities such as examinations. Parents are also required to pay for school uniforms, which are often compulsory, exercise and textbooks, as well as writing materials. They also have to take care of transportation from home to school, boarding or rents, and food for those who live away from home. In addition, parents are also expected to pay PTA levies that are often used to finance a wide range of projects in the schools.

A survey of secondary schools in the North West Province of Cameroon revealed that annual private direct expenditures incurred by parents ranged from CFAF 122,080 to 242,750 (46 to 51 percent of GNP per capita) (see Table 11.3).[1]

Those whose children are in government schools spent approximately CFAF 10,000 less than those in private secular schools and about CFAF 100,000 less than those in private mission schools. Two main reasons accounted for this difference. First, tuition fees are not charged in government schools. Second, some private schools provide boarding fa-

Table 11.3. Annual Mean Expenditure on Secondary Schooling Reported by Principals (CFAF)

ITEM	Government (n=6)	Private Secular (n=6)	Private Mission (n=4)
Tuition Fees	00	39,750	39,500
Registration	2,333	2,500	2,500
P.T.A Levy	12,916	833	8,125
Other Fees	15,249	43,083	50,125
Books	29,166	27,500	41,250
Uniforms	10,166	10,166	18,625
Stationery	3,333	3,290	5,750
Boarding/Rents	56,833	41,666	115,000
Allowances	7,333	6,666	12,000
Total Expenditure Per Annum	122,080	132,371	242,750

Source: Tembon, M. (1994).

cilities and charge boarding fees, whereas all government schools are day schools. Occasionally government schools are far from students' homes, so they have to rent rooms and prepare their own meals. The cost of this option was found to be less than paying for boarding facilities in a private school. Third, private mission schools provide high-quality education and so charge more for the services they offer. The cost of books, writing materials, and uniforms were similar for government and private schools (Tembon 1994). These expenditures are substantial, especially when one considers that in 1993 (when the study was conducted) the GNP per capita for Cameroon was CFAF 260,000 (US$1000).

Some parents who are anxious for their children to go to secondary school, particularly the poor and those in rural areas, find it extremely difficult to meet the financial demands made on them. Private schools have set up two concession schemes to help parents cope with the high costs of secondary schooling. The first concession is to spread payments over a long period in many instalments. The second is to accept fee payments in kind. Some parents in rural areas, who are unable to raise cash to pay fees for private schools, are given the option of paying with foodstuffs, which can be either used to feed boarding students or sold in the market to recover the cash (Tembon 1994). Such arrangements are not possible in government schools, where, by law, everyone is expected to make payments in cash.

Communities often contribute towards the construction of school buildings either in cash or in materials, such as stones or sand, and labour for those without cash. Community action is very common, not only in education but also in the acquisition of other important facilities such as health centres and pipe-borne water for the village. Young people who have left their village to work in the towns and cities often show community spirit by making contributions towards the building or improvement of educational facilities in their village. Six out of the 15 schools visited in the North West Province had received such contributions.

Parental Attitudes to Girls' Education

Parental attitudes to girls' education varies from one part of Cameroon to another. As in other countries in sub-Saharan Africa, there are more males in schools than females, but the gap is wider in the three northern provinces than in the other seven. The gender gap in education can be attributed to several factors, including parental attitudes to girls' education. A study investigating the causes of girls' underenrolment in schools in the Far North Province of Cameroon revealed that parental education, poverty, and the domestic role of girls in the home were among important explanatory factors (Saidou 1992). Although few studies have investigated parental attitudes to girls' education in other provinces in Cameroon, anecdotal evidence and the general literature on girls' access to schooling reveals that parental attitude to schooling is more negative for girls than boys (Tchombe 1994). The cultural preference for educating male rather than female children has been attributed to the fact that male children carry on the family name, whereas female children are regarded as part of the families of their spouses, in the future after marriage. Daughters are considered transient until they marry (their final destination). Consciously, therefore, families decide to allocate their meagre resources to their male children who are believed to be a source of economic security in the future. The story of Mwansa and Chisha, in Box 11.1, illustrates family bias against the education of female children. It also shows how cultural perceptions of gender roles influence parental behaviour. Such discrimination against female children is exacerbated in harsh economic situations. The poorer the household, the more domestic help is required from daughters, and the greater is the tendency to spend limited family resources for the education of their sons.

BOX 11.1.
WHO SHOULD BE PROMOTED TO THE NEXT CLASS?

Mwansa and Chisha are twins living in a village in Cameroon. They were in the fifth year of a rural primary school. At the end of the academic year they were issued their progress report booklets. Chisha, the girl, had performed brilliantly and was among the top five pupils in the class. She was promoted to primary six. In contrast, Mwansa, the boy, had not done so well. In rank order he featured amongst the last eight pupils. He was asked to repeat primary five. During the long holidays the children's father lost his job. On the first day of the following academic year, the children's mother went to the school and asked to see the class teacher. She told him that they had seen the children's progress reports and read the remarks made by the teacher, but she went on to say that she and her husband had decided that the child to be promoted to primary six should be Mwansa and the one to repeat should be Chisha. The teacher tried to explain the assessment procedures of the school to the mother but she would not understand. Instead she withdrew Chisha from school completely, complaining that the cost of keeping both of them in school was too much for the family.

In the northern provinces of Cameroon, where girls' enrolments at primary and secondary levels are very low compared to other provinces, Islamic religious views about women adversely affect girls' schooling. Girls are not allowed to abandon their traditional value systems. Parents prefer to keep girls at home as a way of protecting them from the proselytising dangers of Western education (Tchombe 1994).

UGANDA

Uganda is a country just recovering from a long period of economic, social, and political instability. While it is true to say that all sectors of the Ugandan economy suffered greatly, it was the education sector, which serves as the base for economic development, which suffered the most. Schools closed down, buildings were destroyed, enrolments declined, educated manpower migrated to other countries, and students stayed away from schools, thus increasing the level of illiteracy.

At the present time, when Uganda is undergoing profound reforms to rebuild the country, finance stands out as the main factor on which any substantial progress depends. Capital is needed to build schools, and money is needed to pay teachers, procure educational materials, and ensure that the many who have been unable to attend school should be able to do so.

In 1995, all secondary schools levied tuition fees and PTA charges. The official annual rate for tuition fees in government-aided schools was statutory and amounted to Ush.13,200.[2] Other fees were collected for a wide range of school activities. There is a wide variation between schools in terms of the fees they charge. A survey of secondary schools revealed that annual secondary school charges range from Ush.49,000 to 405,000 depending on whether the school is government aided or private (MOES, Uganda 1994). Even among government-aided schools there are wide discrepancies, which arise mainly from PTA charges.

In addition to building and providing other school needs, PTA charges are used to supplement staff salaries. The salaries of secondary school teachers are quite low. A graduate teacher earns about Ush.80,000 (US $80) a month while a nongraduate earns about Ush.49,000 (US $49) a month. As a result of low salaries, teachers' morale is low and they tend to engage in several jobs, and thus not concentrate on teaching as well as they might. Salary supplements are used to boost teachers' morale and to keep them in their jobs. They also vary between schools and can range from between Ush. 30,000 ($30) and 170,000 ($170) per month depending on the amount of the PTA charge.

Public Financing

As a percentage of the national budget, spending for education has declined. It is estimated that between 1970–1971 and 1990–1991, both investment and recurrent budgets dropped by 60 percent in real terms. Spending on education in 1988–1989 was only 21 percent of the level achieved in the 1970–1971 financial year. Real expenditure per pupil is estimated to have fallen to 13 percent of the 1970–1971 level (MOES, Uganda 1991). According to the 1994–1995 background to the budget in Uganda, the proportion of total government expenditures allocated to education is about 12.8 percent, quite a low figure when compared to the mean of 15.3 percent for the rest of sub-Saharan Africa (World Bank 1988).

Table 11.4. Percentage of National Budget Spending on Education in Uganda

Year	Recurrent	Development
1988–1989	15.8%	3.7%
1989–1990	14.2%	3.6%
1990–1991	17.2%	4.9%
1991–1992	14.1%	4.9%
1992–1993	14.1%	9.0%
1993–1994	11.2%	7.4%
Average	12.8%	5.6%

Source: Ministry of Education and Sport (1994) School Charges Task Force Report.

Table 11.4 shows the large annual fluctuations in both recurrent and development budgets as a percentage of the total public expenditure budget. Despite the low levels of public allocations for the education sector in general, some levels have benefited more than others. Table 11.5 shows central government recurrent expenditure per student by level between 1989 and 1992. The ratio of government spending per pupil between primary, secondary and university, dropped from 1:6:225 in 1990–1991 to 1:3:157 in 1991–1992.

Within central government recurrent expenditures, a disproportionate portion of resources are spent on food and board and other noninstructional costs, whereas teachers' salaries dropped considerably from 62.9 percent in 1986–1987 to 27.3 percent in 1988–1989 (Levine and

Table 11.5. Central Government Recurrent Expenditure per Student by Level (Ugandan Shillings)

Level	1989–1990	1990–1991	1991–1992
Primary	2,128	2,437	6,153
Secondary	10,873	15,289	16,320
Teacher Education	138,421	142,823	155,471
University	458,269	548,000	967,077

Source: World Bank (1993 Table IV.4, p. 40).

Sentongo 1989). The report of the School Charges Review Task Force revealed that government contributions to the recurrent costs of schools varied from as little as 1 percent to as much as 63 percent (Ministry of Education and Sport, Uganda 1994).

Private Financing

Parents of secondary school students pay a variety of fees. Tuition fees for government-aided schools are statutory and amount to Ush. 4,400, but those for private schools vary and range from 15,000 to 200,100 shillings (University of Surrey 1995). Parents also pay PTA charges, which range from 4,000 to 180,000 annually. Differences in PTA charges may be explained by factors such as the socioeconomic background of the student body (the more affluent the socioeconomic background, the higher the charge), the location and environment of the school (schools in urban locations charge more than rural), and the purpose for which PTA funds are collected (Levine and Sentongo 1989). In addition to tuition costs, parental contributions cover expenses such as incentives or supplementary salary allowances for teachers, development expenditures for school buildings as well as staff houses, boarding, and other expenses such as lunches for day students.

Other sources of income include funds from income-generating projects, fund-raising activities, and private grants and donations from national and international sources. Schools accrue income from sales of farm produce and the hire of school vehicles and school premises. Schools also receive income in kind in the form of books, reams of paper, bags of cement, food, and sometimes manual labour. Income in kind can be quite substantial, but it is often not well accounted for and tends not to feature in school accounts. Consequently, the data on school income often exclude this source.

Parental Attitudes to Girls' Education

Several studies have been carried out in Uganda to investigate parental attitudes to girls' education (Kwesiga 1993). These studies revealed that gender bias and negative parental attitudes to girls' education are linked to several parental concerns: for example, that the family would lose domestic help; that girls' morality would suffer and that they would no longer respect cultural traditions; and that there would be an increase in the number of pregnancies. Parental expectations of the future role of girls as mothers and wives have also been found to deter parents from educating their daughters. These negative attitudes cause parents to invest more in male children. A study to investigate parental attitudes to investments in girls' education in Uganda found that when faced with financial constraints parents would give priority to boys' education (Kwesiga 1993). In another study 130 parents were asked what they regarded as the biggest obstacle to women's education in Uganda. Forty-four percent of the respondents mentioned negative parental attitudes and 25 percent mentioned domestic labour (Kwesiga 1993). Evidence from studies in Uganda support the proposition that parental attitude is an important determinant in parental educational decisions. Even when education is free, girls' enrolments do not necessarily increase in cases where parental attitudes to schooling are extremely negative.

TENSIONS BETWEEN ECONOMICS AND CULTURE

The discussion on the methods of financing education in the two countries above shows that the decline in government spending on education has resulted in the shifting of the burden to parents. In Uganda, the system of financing secondary education is such that the balance between public and private financing tilts more to the private side. It is estimated that parents cover 70 percent of secondary education recurrent costs, whereas government covers about 24 percent, and 6 percent is from other sources (CEC 1995). We also note that this burden consists not only of fees and purchase of school supplies but also the payment of "voluntary" PTA levies. Both cases suggest that the cost of educating a child at the secondary level is very high when compared to family income. This shift may be in line with economic recommendations, but the practicalities leave much to be desired and pose severe problems for some families, particularly those with low incomes. The financial capabilities of many families have been eroded dramatically in recent years. Poverty has been exacerbated by cuts in public sector employment, resulting in job losses, salary cuts, and currency devaluation, which has resulted in sharp rises in prices of basic commodities as well as the cost of education (Graham-Brown 1991). In Cameroon, civil servants lost up to 50 percent of their salaries in the 1993–1994 financial year as a result of salary cuts (Tembon 1994). The situation was exacerbated at the beginning of 1995 when the currency (CFAF) was devalued by 50 percent. In Uganda, where the economy is still "convalescing," the economic situation of many families is still precarious.

The effects of increased parental burden for the financing of education can be observed in the changes in the gender gap in enrolment ratios. Between 1980 and 1993 girls' primary enrolment ratios in Uganda have fallen and the gender gap between male and female pupils has widened from 13 to 16 points (FAWE 1996). Similarly in Cameroon, between 1990 and 1993, gross enrolment ratios have generally declined, with the decline being slightly more for girls than boys (2.1 percent and 1.8 percent respectively) (UNESCO 1993, 1995).

Changes to the traditional kinship structure also contribute to the economic problem. It used to be customary for people to have many children, because the number of children was a measure of family wealth. When the children attained adulthood the older children were expected to take care of their younger siblings. In present times, due to economic difficulties, financial support tends to be nuclear rather than extended. Older siblings tend to concentrate more on their immediate families (husband, wife, and children) than on incurring costs for siblings or other relatives. This, in turn, has caused a severe strain in upholding cultural values and has caused the weakening of close family ties and extended family obligations. Many people are becoming individualistic, a trend which is in conflict with collective or communal tendencies that are traditionally and culturally African.

CONCLUSIONS AND RECOMMENDATIONS

Family incomes have fallen to such an extent that the suggestion of shifting the burden of education financing from government to families as an easy or "quick fix" option creates more problems than it solves. This chapter has demonstrated that the education sector in Cameroon and Uganda is facing severe crisis, but existing initiatives to arrest the situation have proved to be difficult as they tend to create tensions between modern economic practices and culture.

The suggestion to charge fees for education might be a sound economic proposal. Unfortunately the mode of payment, in monetary units, does not take into consideration the economic context in many developing countries where economies are agrarian and not monetized. Similarly, recommendations are made based on economic rates of return that largely overlook the influence of cultural factors and gender bias in parental decisions about financing their children's education.

The poor economic situation has caused many planners to focus on mobilising extra resources while neglecting the equally important aspect of managing resources efficiently. Accountability is still a major problem. Other cost-saving measures, such as the more efficient use of resources, need to be implemented, rather than just shifting the burden onto families. Strategies need to be built on equitable, efficient, and democratic approaches, and to show greater awareness of affordability and sustainability. Financial assistance in the form of scholarships or bursaries could be established for marginalised groups such as the poor and girls. Governments need to increase their contributions to education, especially at the primary and secondary levels. There needs to be a conscious effort by governments to help those who are more likely to drop out of school, either due to inability to pay or as a result of cultural bias. This may require reducing the disproportionate amounts spent on higher education.

Payment strategies for education need to be accommodating of contextual factors. For example, educational financing in rural schools must be diversified and not be strictly limited to cash. In-kind payments would be suitable for boarding schools. Moreover, where income is seasonal, payment of fees should be synchronised to coincide with cash availability.

Government should provide policy guidelines and allow more flexibility at the local level. Insiders or those on the ground are in a better position to suggest strategies that can be implemented. Supervision is, however, necessary to ensure that the guidelines are followed.

The need for more efforts from the public, private, and voluntary sectors is obvious. Rethinking education funding strategies would be a positive step towards achieving education for all. Although the raison d'etre for financing education is based on a cost-benefit framework, other factors such as culture and management support exert a major influence on the success of any funding strategy. Moreover, the present economic hardship that prevails in most developing countries tends to reinforce the influence of these other factors. New thinking, which takes contextual realities into consideration, is required to ensure financial sustainability, equity and efficiency.

NOTES

[1] Exchange rate was US $1 = CFAF 283.2 in 1993 (The Economist Intelligence Unit 1995); GNP per capita in 1993 was about US$820 (United Nations Development Programme 1996).

[2] Exchange rate US $1 = USh. 1003 in 1995 (The Economist Intelligence Unit 1995).

REFERENCES

Appleton, S., P. Collier and P. Horsnell. 1990. *Gender Education and Employment in Côte d'Ivoire*. Washington, DC: World Bank.

Bennell, P. 1994. *Rates of Return to Education: Does the Conventional Pattern Prevail in Sub-Saharan Africa?* Working Paper 10, Institute of Development Studies, Brighton.

Blandford, D., and S. Lynch. 1990. *Structural Adjustment and the Poor in Cameroon.* Washington, DC: World Bank.

Bray, M., and K. Lillis, eds. 1988. *Community Financing of Education: Issues and Policy Implications in Less Developed Countries: Commonwealth Secretariat*. Oxford: Pergamon Press.

Brock, C., and N. Cammish. 1991. *Factors Affecting Female Participation in Education in Six Developing Countries.* London: Overseas Development Administration.

Caillods, F., and T. Postlethwaite. 1989. "Teaching and Learning Conditions in Developing Countries." In *Prospects for Educational Planning*, ed. F. Callods. Paris: International Institute for Educational Planning.

Cambridge Education Consultants (CEC). 1995. *Secondary Education Costs and Finance Study. Final Report*. Cambridge.

Colclough, C. 1993. "Who Should Learn to Pay? An Assessment of Neo-liberal Approaches to Education Policy." In *States or Markets? Neo-Liberalism and the Development Policy Debate*, eds. C. Colcough and J. Manor. Oxford: Clarendon Press.

Colclough, C., with K. Lewin. 1993. *Educating All the Children.* Oxford: Clarendon Press.

The Economist Intelligence Unit. 1995. *Country Profile: Cameroon, Central Africa Republic and Chad, 1994–1995*. New York: EIU Electronic Publishing Services.

The Economist Intelligence Unit. 1995. *Country Profile: Uganda, 1995–1996.* New York: EIU Electronic Publishing Services.

FAWE (Forum for African Women Educationalists). 1996. "Girls' Education in Africa: Translating Policy into Action."

Gould, W.T.S. 1993. *People and Education in the Third World.* London: Longman.

Graham-Brown, S. 1991. *Education in the Developing World: Conflict and Crisis*. London and New York: Longman.

Heyneman, S. 1989. "Economic Crisis and the Quality of Education." Paper presented at the Conference on Development through Education, Oxford.

Jimenez, E. 1987. *Pricing Policy in the Social Sectors: Cost Recovery for Education and Health in Developing Countries*. Baltimore: Johns Hopkins University Press.

Kabeer, N., and J. Humphrey. 1993. "Neo-liberalism, Gender and the Limits of the Market." In *States or Markets? Neo-Liberalism and the Development Policy Debate,* eds. C. Colclough and J. Manor. Oxford: Clarendon Press.

Kane, E., and M. O'Reilly de Brun, M. 1993. *Bitter Seeds: Girls' Participation in Primary Education in the Gambia.* Washington, DC: World Bank.

King, E., and A. Hill, eds. 1993. *Women's Education in Developing Countries: Barriers, Benefits and Policies.* Baltimore: The Johns Hopkins University Press.

Klees, S. 1989. "The Economics of Education: A Slightly More Jaundiced View of Where We Are Now." In *Prospects for Educational Planning*, ed. F. Calliods. Paris: International Institute For Educational Planning.

Kwesiga, J. 1993. "Access of Women to Higher Education in Uganda: An Analysis of Inequalities, Barriers and Determinants." Unpublished Ph.D. Thesis, University of London Institute of Education.

Leslie, L. 1990. "Rates of Return as an Informer of Public Policy." *Higher Education* 20: 271–286.

Levine, V., and C. Sentongo. 1989. *Financing and Efficiency of Education in Uganda: A Pre-Investment Study.* Ministry of Education and Sport, Uganda.

McGavin, P. 1991. "Policy Evaluation of Investment in Education: A Papua New Guinea Study." *Economics of Education Review* 10(3): 213–226.

Mingat, A., and J.P. Tan. 1986. "Expanding Education through User Charges: What Can Be Achieved in Malawi and other LDCs." *Economics of Education Review* 15(8): 273–286.

Mingat, A., and J.P. Tan. 1988. *Analytical Tools for Sector Work in Education.* Baltimore: The Johns Hopkins University Press, for the World Bank.

MINFI (Ministry of Finance), Cameroon. 1989. National Budget.

MINFI (Ministry of Finance), Cameroon. 1990. National Budget.

MINFI (Ministry of Finance), Cameroon. 1991. National Budget.

MOES (Ministry of Education and Sport), Uganda. 1991. Ministry of Education, Planning and Development Report.

MOES (Ministry of Education and Sport), Uganda. 1994. School Charges Review Task Force Report (December).

Odaga, A., and W. Heneveld. 1995. *Girls and Schools in Sub-Saharan Africa: From Analysis to Action.* World Bank Technical Paper Number 298. Washington, DC: World Bank.

Psacharopoulos, G. 1993. *Returns to Investment in Education: A Global Update.* Policy Research Working Paper 1067. Washington, DC: World Bank.

Psacharopoulos, G., and M. Woodhall. 1985. *Education for Development: An Analysis of Investment Choices.* Oxford: Oxford University Press.

Saidou, O. 1992. "Les obstacles à la scolarisation des filles dans la province de l'Extreme Nord du Cameroun." Memoire présenté en vue de l'obtention du diplôme de conseiller d'orientation, Ecole Normale Supérieure, Yaounde.

Sanyal, B. 1991. *Education in a Period of Change and Adjustment: Some International Perspectives*. Contributions No. 9, International Institute of Educational Planning.

Tchombe, T. 1994. "Access of Girls to Basic Education in Cameroon." Dakar: UNESCO Regional Office.

Tembon, M. 1994. "The Financing of Secondary Education in Mezam Division, North West Province Cameroon: An Uneasy Partnership Between Family and State?" Unpublished Ph.D Thesis, University of London Institute of Education.

Thobani, M. 1984. "Charging User Fees for Social Services: Education in Malawi." *Comparative Education Review* 28 3: 402–423.

Tsang, M. 1988. "Cost Analysis for Educational Policy Making: A Review of Cost Studies in Educating Developing Countries." *Review of Educational Research* 58 (2): 181–230.

Tsang, M., and S. Kidchanapanish. 1992. "Private Resources and the Quality of Primary Education in Thailand." *International Journal of Educational Research* 17: 179–198.

UNESCO. 1991. *Statistical Year Book*. Paris: UNESCO.

UNESCO. 1991. *World Education Report, 1993*. Paris: UNESCO.

UNESCO. 1991. *World Education Report, 1995*. Paris: UNESCO.

United Nations Development Programme. 1996. *Human Development Report 1996*. New York: Oxford University Press.

University of Surrey on Behalf of Balfour Williamson and Co., Ltd. For ODA. 1995. Uganda Secondary Education Sub-Sector Studies, Final Report. Surrey.

World Bank. 1986. *Financing Education in Developing Countries: An Exploration of Policy Options*. Washington, DC: World Bank.

World Bank. 1988. *Education in Sub-Saharan Africa: Policies for Adjustment, Revitalisation and Expansion*. Washington DC: World Bank.

World Bank. 1989. *Africa's Adjustment and Growth in the 1980s*. Washington, DC: World Bank.

World Bank. 1990. *Primary Education: The World Bank Policy Paper*. Washington, DC: World Bank.

World Bank. 1993. *Uganda Social Sectors: A World Bank Country Study*. Washington, DC: World Bank.

World Bank. 1995. *Priorities and Strategies for Education: A World Bank Review*. Washington, DC: World Bank.

CHAPTER 12

Educating Girls in Pakistan

Tensions Between Economics and Culture

IFFAT FARAH AND KAZIM BACCHUS

The achievement of universal primary education and 100 percent literacy has been a consistent policy goal of many developing countries. It also appears high on the agenda of international organizations such as the World Bank and other donors who significantly influence and guide policies in developing countries. The expectation that governments and individuals should invest in education is based on the widely accepted proposition that such investment will have high private and social returns (Colclough 1982; Shultz 1993). Based on evidence from several developing countries, Shultz (1993) and others claim that the rate of return for schooling is higher for women than for men both in terms of market earnings as well as nonmarket returns such as low mortality, low fertility, better child health, and children's access to schooling.

Given the claimed benefits of schooling in developing countries, one would expect that girls' participation in schools would be high. However, despite some positive changes in enrollment in many low income countries in Asia and Africa, on the whole girls' enrollment has remained low and the gender differential has remained consistently high (King and Hill 1993). This issue has been addressed by several writers who present economic and sociocultural factors to explain this situation. Some suggest that poverty is the most critical obstacle to schooling. Poor families find it difficult to pay the direct costs including fees, books, and uniforms. Even when these are subsidized by the government, parents cannot afford the indirect or opportunity cost and are unwilling to take the girl away from work to send her to school (Bown 1993; Brock and Cammish 1991; Cammish 1993; Colclough 1993). Moreover, as King and Hill

(1993, 23) propose, the "gender differentials in education endure because those persons (i.e., parents) who bear the private costs of investing in schooling for girls and women fail to receive the full benefits of their investment." Other studies have emphasised the importance of the religious, social, and cultural norms and attitudes in explaining low female participation. For example, Patkar (1995, 401) in discussing female literacy in India points out that "socio-cultural norms are crucial determinants of educational levels among women." She argues that in patriarchal social structures, such as the caste system in India, women have little control over events in their lives, operate within restricted space, and are assigned a lower status. Religious and sociocultural traditions help maintain this lower status. In the context of Muslim countries, King and Hill (1993) point to a dominant perception that there is an inherent bias against women's education (see Finn, Dulberg, and Reis 1979). They suggest that although Islam places no restriction on the education of women, and in fact instructs all Muslims (both men and women) to acquire education, the great concern of Muslim men for women's modesty and its association with men's honour has supported traditions that restrict women's mobility, and consequently their access to schools. Traditions in Muslim societies locate women strictly within the family and discourage the acknowledgment of their independent identity. This view of women's identity is threatened by education that promotes independence of thought and action among women (King and Hill 1993). However, the contribution of Islamic culture in restricting girls' enrollment is challenged by examples of countries such as Bahrain, Libya, and Saudi Arabia where the gender gap in enrollment in schools has narrowed in recent years. Referring to this change in Bahrain and Libya, Chamie (1983) stresses the strong influence of economic development on increased participation of girls.

The above discussion shows that, in their attempt to explain low school participation, most studies identify economic and/or sociocultural factors as significant factors influencing girls' enrollment and retention in school. They also acknowledge that these factors are many and complex and that "gender differential in education cannot be attributed to any one dominant factor" (Patkar 1995, 401). Disentangling these factors is difficult, although attempts have been made to do so (King et al. 1986). Basing the discussion in the context of Pakistan, this chapter will argue that in order to obtain a fuller understanding of the contexts of low female participation in schools, we not only need to identify the various sociocultural and economic factors influencing parents' and girls' own decisions, but also examine the subtle interplay between these factors.

GIRLS' ACCESS TO SCHOOLING IN PAKISTAN

In Pakistan achievement of universal primary education has been an objective of national education policies since the 1950s, with each policy citing a future target date. The latest Education Policy (1992–2002) states the following as one of its objectives: "to ensure 100 percent participation in education at the primary level by the year 2002. . . ." However, this objective appears to be difficult to achieve. According to the Pakistan Economic Survey 1994–1995, the overall school participation rate in primary schools is 71 percent; the participation rates for boys and girls[1] are estimated to be 87 percent and 55 percent, respectively. Although some gains in girls' participation rates have been reported in the past decade,[2] they have consistently remained lower than boys'. What are some of the reasons for this gap? Since sending children to school and keeping them there (through the primary and secondary levels of schooling) is largely a parental decision, in the absence of compulsory primary education,[3] it is necessary to understand the context in which the decision is made. We would like to suggest that decisions about schooling are shaped by a complex interplay of sociocultural and economic factors.

SOCIAL AND CULTURAL NORMS

Commenting on the educational status of women in Pakistan, the National Report presented at the Fourth World Conference on Women states that the socialization process creates gender differences from childhood and inhibits the participation of girls and women in education and training programmes.[4] Women's lives are generally structured by and around those of men. Girls are expected to prepare for and accept this life. In Pakistani society, traditional perceptions of a woman's time and space are limited by her role within the home, as caretakers of men and children, and her status as a symbol of family honour. Thus, on the one hand schooling is often perceived as contributing nothing or very little to preparing the girl for her caregiving role, and on the other it is often regarded as a potential threat to the family's reputation by giving the girl the ability to make her own decisions and even act upon them, thus bringing disgrace upon the family (Farah 1992; Imam 1995). Parents' fears of girls' independent access to the outside world through schooling are reflected in their anxious remarks about the possibility that girls who are allowed to go to school may use their writing skills to write letters to men or take advantage of the opportunity to go out of the house to make contact with men on the way to school (Farah 1992). In addition, parents fear the vulnerability of girls, the possibility of their being abducted, or other such threats. The perceived threats to the honour (of the family, especially father and brothers) and to the girl's safety influence parents' decisions either to not enroll girls in school or to withdraw them at puberty, especially when the school is at a considerable distance from home.

The observance of *purdah* (women's veiling or seclusion) in Muslim societies is seen to place considerable restrictions on women's mobility and their role in public life. According to Klein and Nestvogel (1992, 37) the institution of *purdah* in Pakistan "is bound up with social class and status, particularly in the rural areas." The lower class cannot afford to observe the convention because women are needed as paid and unpaid workers. Among the lower-middle-class and middle-class families, where the observation of *purdah* is most prevalent, it becomes a status symbol to demonstrate that a family does not need its women to contribute to its earnings and to separate them from the lower classes. The upper class, on the other hand, does not need to demonstrate its economic status and is in a strong enough position to challenge and ignore conventions.

Although *purdah* is still a barrier to girl's participation in schools in some parts of Pakistan (e.g., some parts of the North West Frontier Province), its influence has become weak. Just as *purdah* is associated with status, so has education come to be associated with status; those who can afford to have their women observe *purdah* are also expected to be able to afford to send their daughters to school.

ECONOMICS OR CULTURE?

While cultural norms and traditions play an important role in parental decision making about girls' schooling, they may be exaggerated, especially in the context of a Muslim society whose cultural norms are perceived to be restrictive of women. Wrong (1961, 184) makes this point when he draws our attention to the "oversocialized view of man," which suggests that too often the behaviour of men and women is explained mainly in terms of their cultural heritage. We may, as a result, tend to ignore individuals' perceptions of their own interest as a key factor in explaining their behaviour.

An alternative approach would be to view individuals' behaviour as a reflection of rational choices. Taking this approach, we would explain girls' participation in schools as a consequence of rational decisions made by parents based on what they perceive the benefits of schooling to be. In making the decisions, they weigh up, with whatever available evidence, the economic as well as the social benefits they believe are likely to accrue to themselves and their daughters against the costs incurred. However, such reasoning is not readily identifiable as it co-exists with "culture" and "tradition" and is sometimes purposively disguised.

Religio-cultural reasons may camouflage socioeconomic and political reasons. For example, Ali (1994) points out that in the rural areas of Pakistan where agricultural land is the most important asset, landowners, feudal or farmers, do not want to divide the land into small units, especially if it would go to another family through marriage of their daughter as her inherited property. Uneducated daughters, being unaware of their legal rights, or not having access to legal help, are less likely to demand their rights to property.

Even when girls' schooling is not perceived as a threat to the wealth of the male members of the family, it may not be eagerly sought because the economic and social benefits likely to accrue to the parents are perceived to be minimal, doubtful, or nonexistent. In such cases also, parents tend to advance cultural norms and tradition as reasons for denying their daughters an education. For example, data collected from a sample of *pathan*[5] families living in a poor locality in Karachi (Farah, work in progress) shows that "culture" is initially offered as the basis for decisions to stop girls from attending school, especially beyond primary level. "We are *pathans*, our tradition is different, our girls get married very early," "the school is far and our society is such that we can't send our girls out so far" (Farah, work in progress). Further probes reveal that ". . . the main reason is poverty," since it weakens their ability to find funds to cover the real cost of schooling of all children and particularly their daughters. In this example, the excuse of cultural barriers seems to have been used to justify an economic decision to send the son to school.

When resources are limited, decisions are based on what the investment will bring to the family. For example, a mother explained the basis for her decision: "The boys will get jobs, what will they (the girls) do? They will get married." A son's schooling has more potential benefit for the family, because society offers him more job opportunities. A woman recalled her father's reasons for not sending her to school: "My father didn't allow me to go to school. He said 'What will you do with education?' My brother left school after class 8 and joined a workshop, so my father said 'What did he get from school that you will get?' " The father had been referring to the fact that when schooling was unable to ensure an income-generating opportunity to a man, it would bring even less to a woman for whom opportunities for such activities through schooling are even more dismal. This woman is sending her own daughter to a primary school. She was not, however, certain if she would be able to bear the increasing cost of secondary school, or ignore the traditional restrictions.

Tradition and cultural norms can become more flexible when the family has economic security. As a young man comments about his sister continuing her education beyond class 10:

> "It's not nice to go to school now that she is old" and added "I have a cousin in the village (where normally cultural norms are more strictly observed) who is in class eleven. Her father works abroad. He earns seventy thousand rupees per month; he can do it (i.e., send his daughter to school), I can't."

High income enables the father to bear not only the cost of education, but also the psychic cost incurred by disregarding cultural/traditional restrictions on girls' mobility. Changes in economic circumstances are also accompanied by new functions such as corresponding with men who work abroad and interacting with the world outside the home.

> A girl recalled her father's reasoning. "After he went to Dubai . . . he wanted us to be able to read the letters he sent us. . . . my uncles don't speak to us because we go to school but my father says he doesn't care . . . I want to help my father, I work at a clinic now and I earn."

Apparently, this father's economic stability and his awareness of the benefits to the family helped him take an individualistic stance on this issue.

As the above examples demonstrate, in making decisions about which of the children to send to school, an important consideration is what this investment would bring to the *family*. Thus, when girls' schooling is perceived as a family asset, through providing skills needed in the family, reading letters for example, or contributing income, or raising family status, it is acceptable despite cultural challenges.[6]

The cultural norm of marriage at an early age regularly influences parents' attitudes towards girls' schooling. Parents rationalize that the perceived returns of their investment in schooling would accrue not to themselves but to the family into which their daughter is married.

> "What good would it do to me, others would have the fruit of her education," said a poor rural mother who was not sure if she should continue to send her daughter to school. An urban father gave a similar

> argument "No, there is no disadvantage . . . but the girl gets the advantage because she goes to her other home, then does her own work, so she becomes useful to others."

The father's concern that the returns from schooling would go either to the daughter herself, not to the family, or to the family into which she is married creates a resistance to making even a minimal investment in the daughter's schooling.

However, when schooling comes to be perceived as an advantage in the daughter's marriage (which is the parents' responsibility in Pakistani culture), parental views change. Thus the preference of men to marry women who have had some education prompts parents to give higher priority to their daughters' schooling. According to one father interviewed:

> "At first when the girls didn't go to school in the villages, they stayed at home, they got married and then faced problems because their husbands were educated and these girls weren't able to look after the children properly. Now people realize the importance of education."

This realization has helped to dismantle cultural barriers and extend cultural norms. Evidence of similar reasons for parents' willingness to invest in their girls' education is presented in a study dealing with school attendance in Guyana (Bacchus 1994). Bacchus notes that prior to the political developments that ultimately ushered in self-government and independence in 1966, East Indian or Asian girls were poorly represented in education in comparison with the boys and with other ethnic groups in the society. Changes in the political climate were accompanied by a more open labour market. As a result, East Indian boys began to enter the various professional and higher-level white-collar jobs in increasing numbers. As the number of East Indian males in these more prestigious white-collar jobs increased, it began to have a positive impact on the school attendance of East Indian girls. The demand for educated marriage partners for these men and an opportunity for improved social and economic mobility among girls through education became important stimulants for education among East Indian females and was reflected in an increase in the number of East Indian girls attending school.

Similar trends are seen in South Asia (Khan 1993), where increased willingness of parents to give their daughters an education as a means of helping to ensure their economic independence and/or securing a marriage partner of a higher social status and a higher income has begun to break down some of the traditional social taboos against providing educational opportunities for girls.

> Illiterate mothers and grandmothers take a tremendous interest in girls' education these days: they don't make the girls work at home, but rather send them to school. The mothers relate that now with transport available, the girls can later go on to study beyond primary school. There is also a growing demand for educated brides in these communities. The impact of television in changing peoples' ideas has been great, particularly the dramas which often feature educated females as role models. (World Bank 1996a, 15)

The absence of role models in the professions, business, and in formal employment, especially in the rural areas, influence both parents' decisions and girls' interest in schooling and education in general. Where such role models exist, and job opportunities are available, schools attract more girls and parents are willing to relax cultural norms. This is illustrated in the findings of a study of change in rural primary schools in Pakistan (Farah et al. 1996). In the sample of successful girls' schools, enrollment increased when the teachers convinced parents to send their daughters to school and also when a local girl became a teacher, presenting a possibility of employment after completing school. These pioneering women who completed high school and became teachers reported initial difficulties in being accepted by a community dominated by its male members. Evidence of change in parental attitude has also been reported from the North West Frontier province:

> The villagers may be poor but they say that they want to educate their daughters. Later they will be able to find future employment in health fields or in teaching. . . . The men of the village discuss girls' education in the local *hujra* (men's meeting place) . . . they get inspired by seeing educated people succeed. They see many girls going to school. Trends are changing. (World Bank 1996a, 15).[7]

HOW FAR IS THE SCHOOL?

Warwick and Reimers (1995) point out that since independence, successive Pakistani governments have not placed a high priority on educational provision for all children. For example, a policy decision to build two male schools for every female school in rural areas greatly reduced girls' opportunities for schooling. However, in the past few years, the Government, prompted and supported by donor agencies, has paid more attention to providing girls' access to schools (World Bank 1996a). The distance of the school from the place of residence is an important factor in the parents' decision to send their daughters, as well as sons, to school. A census conducted in the province of Balochistan confirmed not only that there were many more schools for boys than for girls, but also that about 21 percent of all girls enrolled in primary schools were going to boys' schools in their home village where no girls' school existed. Evidence from a project to establish girls' schools in rural Balochistan has demonstrated that when girls' schools are available near children's homes and established with the cooperation of the community, parents are willing to send their daughters to school despite cultural restrictions (World Bank 1996a, 1996b). Parents' concern with distance from home is not merely a reflection of their cultural views about girls' space (restricted to the home and the neighbourhood), but a genuine concern for their safety as they walk long distances to school, and about the cost and availability of transport.

HOW GOOD IS THE SCHOOL?

Recent evidence from Pakistan has also begun to indicate that parents' perception of the quality and outcomes of schooling available to their children (both boys and girls) affects their decisions about schooling (Farah et al. 1996; Farah 1997). A comparison of successful and unsuccessful schools in rural Pakistan shows that parents regard the following as important determinants of school quality: presence of a proper building with a boundary wall and toilet and drinking water facilities; an able teacher of good character; a curriculum and teaching practice that give due attention to skill acquisition, the cultivation of virtues, and religious instruction. When a school is perceived to have some or all of these qualities present, parents are more willing to send their daughters even when resources are limited. When these qualities are perceived to be absent, parents often give way to the economic and cultural constraints and either do not send their daughters to school or withdraw them early. A similar conclusion is drawn by Warwick and Reimers (1995, 15):

> Cultural influences, such as the parents' feelings that girls need less education than boys, may also make a difference. But those influences seem to be overcome if suitable schools are built near homes of eligible female students.

CONCLUSION

In this chapter we have suggested that in a context of limited resources, parents are confronted with making choices about sending their sons and/or daughters to school. In making these choices, they have to consider benefits to themselves against the real and opportunity costs they must bear as well as the cultural barriers they must confront. While both cultural norms and socioeconomic benefits support investment in boys' schooling, the interplay between these factors creates a tension with respect to girls' schooling. Traditionally, the son is responsible for supporting parents in their old age, and carrying on the family name. The social and economic gains of the son also traditionally belong to his parents. Male participation in the labour market means that parents place a higher value on the education of boys. Conversely, cultural perceptions of girls' roles and their mobility, reinforced by low expectations of social and economic benefits to the family, strengthen cultural barriers and influence parents in favour of their sons' schooling. Long-term benefits such as lower fertility and better child health are less tangible, and neither the family nor the girl herself can readily relate to them.

Parents' decisions about schooling are not entirely or always representative of emotional submission to cultural norms. They are often based on rational consideration of costs and benefits. An acknowledgment of this fact is instructive for policy. The challenge is to positively affect the attitudes and actions of parents and children regarding girls' schooling. Meeting this challenge will require making inputs into girls' education as well as creating a demand for it.

It will require that schooling at all levels (primary, secondary, tertiary) be available to girls from both urban and rural areas and funds reallocated to ensure improved quality of schooling. Improving quality may involve initiatives to improve school environment, train teachers, and improve syllabi. A key consideration in these initiatives must be to take parents' expectations of school quality into account. Improved quality, when it meets parents' expectations, may not reduce the real cost of schooling for parents, but it will give them a better return on their investment. Parents are more willing to pay both real and opportunity costs for quality and are also more willing to challenge cultural norms when they value the returns. According to Ali (1997), other incentives such as scholarship schemes and free learning materials help change traditional attitudes towards schooling as they reduce real costs. Moreover, they underline the importance of schooling for both parents and girls, as these incentives are seen as rewards for attending school.

School-level initiatives, however, are not in themselves enough to influence parents' perceptions of returns from education. A concurrent strategy is needed to increase opportunities for women by creating more jobs for educated women in both urban and rural areas. This strategy must on the one hand address cultural concerns by creating opportunities for work that are more readily acceptable within the existing culture, and on the other hand attempt to broaden the scope of women's employment. Thus, women should have more opportunities in the education and health professions, which are culturally more acceptable, as well as be encouraged to enter areas not traditionally regarded as women's work, such as business and technical fields.

The benefits of girls' education must become visible. Initiatives are needed to create and advertise role models and to launch campaigns to raise awareness of the social and public benefits, as well as benefits to the family, from girls' education. Cultural norms may be perceived as barriers but they are neither inflexible nor insurmountable.

NOTES

[1] Slightly lower figures are quoted unofficially. The World Bank report (1996) cites overall participation in primary schools to be not more than 60%. The most recent 1997 UN estimates place boys' enrollment at 50% and girls' enrollment at 30%.

[2] According to a World Bank Report (1996a), between 1988 and 1993 the gross enrollment rates in primary school increased by 4.9% (6.1% among girls and 4.3% among boys).

[3] The law for compulsory primary education was recently enacted in two provinces in Pakistan. However, its implementation has not yet become practice.

[4] Fourth World Conference on Women, Bejing, Pakistan National Report, Government of Pakistan, Ministry of Development and Youth Affairs.

[5] People belonging to the areas now within the NWFP province in Pakistan. They identify themselves with strong religious and tribal values and tradition.

[6] King and Hill (1993) define "psychic cost" as the social costs (rejection by friends and neighbours or society in general) of nonconformist behaviour.

[7] Evidence from India and Hong Kong also suggests that when girls do not marry early and contribute to the family income, parents are more willing to educate their daughters (King and Hill 1993).

REFERENCES

Ali, M. A. 1994. "Girls' Schooling in Pakistan and Possible Roles for the Rockefeller Foundation." Unpublished report.

Ali, M. A. 1997. "Incentives for Rural Female Students." Paper presented at the National Conference on New Directions on Research for Women, held at Aga Khan University, Karachi, Pakistan.

Bacchus, M. K. 1994. *Education as and for Legitimacy: Developments in West Indian Education Between 1846 and 1895*. Ontario: Wilfrid Laurie University Press.

Bown, L. 1993. "Preparing the Future by Changing the Present: Women, Literacy and Development." *Oxford Studies in Comparative Education* 3(2): 109–128.

Brock, C., and N.K. Cammish. 1991. *Factors Affecting Female Participation in Education in Six Developing Countries*. London: ODA.

Cammish, N.K. 1993. "Sons and Daughters: Attitudes and Issues Affecting Girls' Education in Developing Countries." *Oxford Studies in Comparative Education* 3(2): 87–107.

Chamie, M. 1983. *National, Institutional and Household Factors Affecting Young Girls' School Attendance in Developing Societies*. Washington, DC: International Center for Research on Women and U.S Agency for International Development.

Colclough, C. 1982. "The Impact of Primary Schooling on Economic Development: A Review of the Evidence." *World Development* 10: 67–186.

Colclough, C. 1993. "Primary Schooling in Developing Countries: The Unfinished Business." *Oxford Studies in Comparative Education* 3(2): 47–57.

Farah, I. 1992. "Literacy Practices in a Rural Community in Pakistan." Unpublished dissertation, University of Pennsylvania, Philadelphia.

Farah, I., with T. Mehmood, A. Shams, R. Jaffar, F. Shams, P. Iqbal, S. Khanam, Z. Shah, and N. Gul-Mastoi. 1996. *Roads to Success: Self-Sustaining Primary School Change in Rural Pakistan*. Oslo, Karachi: IMTEC and Aga Khan University.

Farah, I. 1997. "Roads to Success Phase 2: Stakeholders Consultation on How Primary Schools Change in Rural Pakistan." Report presented to the World Bank.

Finn, J. D., L. Dulberg, and J. Reis. 1979. "Sex Differences in Educational Attainment: A Cross-National Perspective." *Harvard Educational Review* 49 (4): 477–503.

Imam, F. 1995. "Retention of Girls in Schools." Unpublished M. Ed. dissertation, Aga Khan University, Institute for Educational Development.

Khan, S. R. 1993. "South Asia." In *Women's Education in Developing Countries: Barriers, Beliefs and Policies*, eds. E.M. King and M.A. Hill. Baltimore: Johns Hopkins Press.

King, E.M., and M.A.Hill, eds. 1993. *Women's Education in Developing Countries: Barriers, Beliefs and Policies*. Baltimore: Johns Hopkins Press.

King, E. M., J.R. Peterson, S.M. Adioetomo, L.J. Domingo, and S.S. Hassan. 1986. *Change in the Status of Women Across Generations in Asia*. Santa Monica: Rand Corporation.

Klein, G.K., and R. Nestvogel. 1992. *Women in Pakistan*. Lahore, Pakistan: Vanguard Press.

Patkar, A. 1995. "Socio-Economic Status and Female Literacy in India." *International Journal of Educational Development* 15 (4): 401–409.

Shultz, T.P. 1993. "Returns to Women's Education." In *Women's Education in Developing Countries: Barriers, Beliefs and Policies*, eds. E.M. King and M.A. Hill. Baltimore: Johns Hopkins Press.

Smock, A. C. 1981. *Women's Education in the Developing Countries: Opportunities and Outcomes*. New York: Praeger.

Warwick, D., and F. Reimers. 1995. *Hope or Despair? Learning in Pakistan's Primary Schools*. Westport, CT: Praeger Publishers.

World Bank. 1996a. *Improving Basic Education in Pakistan*. Washington, DC: World Bank.

World Bank. 1996b. *Leveling the Playing Field: Giving Girls an Equal Chance for Basic Education—Three Countries' Efforts*. Washington, DC: World Bank.

Wrong, D.H. 1961. "The Oversocialized Conception of Man in Modern Sociology." *American Sociological Review* 26 (2): 183–193.

PART IV

Cultures of Knowledge and Learning

CHAPTER 13

Alternative Cultures of Knowledge in Higher Education in the Australia-Pacific Region

J.I. TEASDALE AND G.R. TEASDALE

For many millennia the peoples of the Australia-Pacific region lived in almost complete isolation from the rest of the world, maintaining intact and coherent cultures. Their systems of knowledge, and their processes of knowledge analysis and transmission, were essentially spiritual and hence relatively stable. The arrival of the Europeans a mere two or three centuries ago brought rapid and profound transformations. The invaders, certain of the superiority of their own wisdom, imposed unquestioningly their languages, political systems, and religious beliefs. The hapless beneficiaries seemed almost powerless to resist, with most eventually being converted, on the surface at least, to Eurocentric ways of thinking and knowing. In particular, many seem to have succumbed to a belief in the superiority of the Western scientific worldview with its emphasis on certainty, objectivity, predictability, and instrumental rationality. Their own antipodean perspectives on knowledge and wisdom were relegated to second place, to be drawn on mainly during times of crisis or ceremony.

In the realm of education the newcomers introduced their own formal processes of knowledge analysis and transmission, and by the final quarter of the 20th century systems of primary, secondary, and higher education were in place throughout the region. While the vernacular sometimes has been retained as the language of literacy and instruction in the early years, the languages of the colonisers are predominant or even exclusive in secondary and higher education settings. The content, processes, and contexts of education at all levels are almost entirely Western. There has been scant if any regard for pre-existing educational provisions. It has been a "top-down" process, based on the newcomers' assumption that their way is correct, regardless of the particular cultural context. The colonisers have had an inherent intellectual ethnocentrism, an intrinsic sense of the superiority of their own ideologies and value systems. This is especially evident in the post-secondary education institutions they have established. Modern scientific ways of thinking are assumed to have a higher order validity, and Western processes of knowledge analysis and transmission have been pursued with almost fundamentalist zeal.

During the final decade of the 20th century these unwitting attempts to colonise the minds of Indigenous peoples are being strengthened by a new wave of economic rationalism that is sweeping through the region. Institutions of higher education are being expected to concentrate almost exclusively on narrow, vocationally oriented goals. The broader sociocultural goals of learning are being subjugated to the short-term demands of the workplace. Technical and skills-based courses are taking priority. At the same time the institutions are being expected to operate within a commercially driven climate, with profit-making taking precedence over human development. The language of the market place has been appropriated by many institutions: college principals and vice-chancellors have become chief executives; students have become clients or customers; knowledge has become a commodity that is bought and sold. In such a climate, decision making is now more centralised, management more hierarchical, and teaching-learning environments more competitive. There appears little or no room for the values and priorities of Indigenous peoples.

Notwithstanding the impact of economic rationalism, however, we have begun to witness the reaffirmation of Indigenous cultures of knowledge and learning in some higher education institutions in the Australia-Pacific region. The movement generally has had a cautious and rather tentative quality, rather like a hermit crab re-emerging from its borrowed shell after a period of prolonged threat. In Australia and Aotearoa[1] New Zealand it has gained some momentum in the higher education sector, thanks largely to government policies that affirm Indigenous rights. Nevertheless, its fragility has been highlighted in Australia during 1996 with the election of a new conservative national government that appears much less supportive of the rights of Indigenous peoples. Elsewhere in the Pacific the movement has been slower and more diffident, although Mel (1995) provides evidence from Papua New Guinea (PNG) of an intensifying search for relevance and meaning in education through a new emphasis on local wisdom and ways of knowing.

Importantly, the reaffirmation of traditional knowledge and wisdom does not represent a retreat to the past, nor an attempt to mummify Indigenous cultures (Teasdale 1994). Rather, it has a dynamic quality, reflecting a search for cultural continuity amidst the constant adaptation and change that occurs whenever two cultures of knowledge interact. Thus, while there are inevitable tensions between economic and cultural goals, Indigenous peoples are not seeking to discard the former in favour of the latter. They seek, instead, to create new bodies of knowledge, and new processes of knowledge analysis and transmission, out of the creative fusion of their own traditions with those they have experienced from the West.

Despite the apparent contradictions between economic and cultural goals, some Indigenous groups have been successful in both conceptualising and accomplishing this fusion in educational settings. Indigenous Australians from Yirrkala, in northeast Arnhem Land, for example, have used the process of *ganma* both as an explanatory device, and as the foundation for an integrated curriculum for lifelong learning. In their vernacular, the term *ganma* refers to the place where fresh water flowing from a river meets salt water in the ocean. There is a constant fusion of the two, yet, on either side of the line of foam that marks this flowing together, each retains its separate identity. In educational terms, *ganma* implies that two bodies of knowledge—the Indigenous and the Western—can fuse together while still maintaining an essential separateness (Teasdale and Teasdale 1994). By taking control of their own education as a lifelong process, the Yirrkala people have been able to put into practice a *ganma* curriculum that successfully blends the goals of Indigenous culture maintenance with the need to live within a Western economic framework.

For the remainder of this chapter four case studies drawn from the Australia-Pacific region will be presented in order to illustrate the re-emergence of Indigenous cultures of knowledge in higher education, and to question the implications of this re-emergence, especially from an economic perspective. All four case studies are based on authentic experiences, although to protect the privacy of participants the names and geographical settings have been varied, and in some cases several episodes have been amalgamated into a single story.

THE COCONUT PALM MODEL

The scene is an institution of higher education in a small developing country in the South Pacific. The participants comprise two groups: the "insiders," who are citizens of the country, all of them professionally qualified teachers; and the "outsiders," a smaller group of highly competent European aid advisers. The action centres around the development of a curriculum for a new course to be offered by the institution.

The outsiders are adamant that the new curriculum needs a "conceptual framework" or a "theoretical model," and one of their number has prepared a couple of examples of what such a model might look like. The response of the insiders has been muted. They view the models as being too cold and clinical, far too removed from reality. And so there is an impasse. Nothing much happens, until early one morning when one of the insiders arrives at work waving a clutch of papers: "I've got it! I've got it! I've discovered a model!" The papers are spread on a desk, and a small group of other early arrivals gathers around.

The model is not immediately apparent. There are certainly no neat boxes carefully interconnected by multidirectional arrows. Instead there is a hastily drawn picture of a coconut palm, firmly embedded in the earth. Looking closer, however, those around the desk can see that each element of the drawing—earth, roots, trunk, fronds, flowers, fruit—is labelled, and that each label refers to a process or product of the curriculum.

As the model is explained the level of interest and excitement around the table rises. Soon everyone is engaged in vigorous analysis, suggesting amendments, extensions, and refinements. The group decides there and then that the "coconut tree model" will become the focal point of a presentation at the next staff meeting. The meeting duly takes place and the presentation is made using a suitably artistic overhead transparency. It is immediately clear that the model has captured the imagination of the insiders. Their response to it is overwhelmingly positive. They obviously feel comfortable with the model: they understand it, they accept it, they seem excited and intellectually challenged by it.

But not so the outsiders. They are decidedly unenthusiastic. Eventually one of their number, grey of beard and supposedly wiser than most, gets reluctantly to his feet: "I'm sorry, but this is *not* a model. A metaphor, perhaps, but definitely not a model. You see it is not completely logical. Some of the categories are not mutually exclusive. It leaves some of the issues open, some questions unanswered. It contains certain conceptual ambiguities. No, it is definitely not a model. And anyway, why choose a coconut palm? They are such untidy and rattly things. Why not a solid, green, substantial mango tree?"

As the outsider sat down there was a sense of deflation right around the room, like a balloon slowly going flat, and the meeting soon drew to a close. Afterwards the original group that had met around the desk for that early morning exchange came together for a kind of post-mortem. Said one: "They just didn't understand the spiritual significance of the coconut tree. Why, I can still go back to my village and identify the coconut palm at whose base my father symbolically buried the placenta and umbilical cord after my birth. That is a profoundly significant and symbolic tree for me."

"No," said another, "Nor do they understand that in our culture we cannot separate out the spiritual, the cultural, and the intellectual. Things don't have to be logically consistent so much as spiritually and culturally consistent. It doesn't matter if there are ambiguities and discontinuities. They are part and parcel of the spiritual dimension, part and parcel of the way we think and live."

"That's right," said a third, "Nor do they understand that we think holistically. Ideas are integrated, not compartmentalised."

Then the first speaker again: "The good thing about our coconut tree model is that it keeps opening up new possibilities, new ideas. It challenges my thinking. The other way closes it up, boxes it in."

End of story. Except to say that the model was accepted within the institution, in a rather unobtrusive way, although the outsiders continued to feel uncomfortable about it, and to refer to it as a metaphor, and not a model.

COMMENT

The outsiders in this story seemed quite unaware of their intellectual ethnocentrism. Like their colonial predecessors, they simply assumed the rightness of their own ways of thinking and knowing. They had come to help ameliorate the economic woes of this small developing country by implementing a new higher education curriculum that would enhance the academic qualifications and potential economic productivity of some of its most able young people. The outsiders were following a carefully documented plan of action prepared by experts from an overseas development assistance agency, a plan based almost entirely on Western curriculum content and methodology, and on principles of economic rationalism. The insiders' proposal to use the coconut palm model did not fit with such a plan, and the proposal therefore became a minor irritant to be swept aside. But the outsiders underestimated the emerging cultural confidence of the insiders.

Interestingly, the insiders were not trying to replace the imposed Eurocentric approach to higher education with their own. They were realistic enough to recognise the strength of the colonial impact on their country's education system, and the extent to which it had transformed their own cultures and lifeways. Rather, they were trying to meld aspects of their Indigenous wisdom and ways of knowing with the introduced system, in order to enhance their own and their students' search for cultural continuity and identity. Unlike the outsiders, they did not see an essential conflict between the instrumentalism and rationality of Western cultures of knowledge and their own more holistic and spiritual ways of perceiving reality. They had a greater tolerance for ambiguity, and therefore were able to reconcile these seemingly disparate perspectives in ways that they found satisfying and meaningful.

WAITING TO BECOME RECOGNISED

Indigenous people in remote Australia are in the process of re-establishing control over their lives and futures. In doing so, they frequently find themselves caught up in a multitude of bureaucratic and seemingly obtuse management tasks required of them by state and national governments. Senior men and women who are fully competent managers in their own cultures can find themselves wanting when trying to manage the affairs that link their people with the wider Australian society.

As part of the self-determination policy of the national government, Indigenous Australians have been encouraged to undertake management training programs offered by Technical and Further Education (TAFE) systems in the various states and territories. In the immediate past, mainstream management courses have been offered to many remote communities. Western educators have received government funding to go into communities to teach an accredited management curriculum. Their success has been negligible, leaving both the educators and the would-be cross-cultural managers with a frustrating sense of failure.

Several waves of research have established that this failure was probably associated with some or all of the following: inappropriate teaching/learning styles, culturally insensitive teachers, insufficient resources, and a "top down" or imposed system of training. Perhaps the most significant finding has related to the unwillingness of nonindigenous educators to let Indigenous people take full control of the decision-making processes about management training in their own communities.

The Pitjantjatjara people, living in homeland clusters across the spectacularly beautiful central Australian desert, made it known through the Aboriginal network that they would like access to cross-cultural management training that took account of their own world view while providing the skills necessary to access mainstream Australian society when the need arose. Those who wished to undertake this management training were already respected managers in their own communities. They spoke both their own languages and English. In Western terms, however, their literacy and numeracy skills were minimal.

"Come and talk with us about it," was their simple request. The non-indigenous person who went was grey haired, possessed the wisdom of age, had the ability to listen and the determination to hear. He spent a year working and talking with the Aboriginal managers. He gathered extensive information about what they felt they needed to know to enable them to manage cross-culturally. It took another year of teamwork, with a predominantly Indigenous Australian course advisory group, to produce a curriculum framework. It looked very different to regular curriculum documents: it used a competency-based teaching/learning technique; it relied on a praxis methodology; it was couched in plain, jargon-free language; and it used visual symbols and illustrations to convey meaning. The framework was, in fact, quite unique. Never before in Australia had a TAFE curriculum been produced to enable people with little or no literacy and numeracy to complete a management course. The course advisory group endorsed the curriculum framework and felt a sense of breakthrough.

The national funding body, which also has responsibility for accreditation, looked long and hard at this unique management curriculum framework. After six months, however, its staff passed on the verdict that substantial changes were needed to make the curriculum conform to the "required standards" before it could be considered for accreditation. In the meantime the Pitjantjatjara managers were waiting for their course to commence. Possessing a great patience, they continue to wait. They wait for the curriculum framework to be nationally accredited. They wait for a management course to be written based on the framework. They wait for that course in turn to be accredited. And finally, they wait for the course to be implemented in their own communities.

This waiting has significant advantages for some. For whom? Well, first there are the many "white" advisers and educators living in Indigenous communities. Some have been there for a long time and know that jobs back in the mainstream are just about impossible to find. If they can stay put, they are assured of a good salary with some very useful remote-area allowances. Then there are the curriculum researchers and writers contracted to work for government. In the current difficult economic times, delays mean more work for them, because the Australian government is embarrassed by its past failures and is trying to "get it right" by the year 2000 Olympiad in Sydney. So it continues to provide funds. The public servants themselves live with delays and constant changes of staff. They meet to discuss the problems related to this small matter in their fast worlds; they search diligently for new strategies for getting this requested management curriculum up and running. They are busy in paid employment.

And where does a resolution lie? There is no simple solution. The discourse is broad. There are many questions that the various players want answered:

> The Government *(in an urgent, somewhat uncertain voice echoing from the wings)*: "How can we enhance the process of reconciliation with our Indigenous peoples before we are exposed to the world's gaze in the year 2000?"
>
> Public Servants *(running hither and thither across the stage, clutching portfolios of documents, stopping to converse briefly in small clusters, with individual voices raised in question)*: "How can we get it right?" "Should we send out consultants?" "What can we really do about it, given our shrinking budget?"
>
> "I'm new to this position, please brief me."
>
> Researcher *(rising from the audience and walking up to the stage to present a question)*: "Shouldn't we listen to the voice of the Indigenous people when they say 'We want to control our own affairs. We can only be empowered if we are in control?' "
>
> Curriculum Writers *(three emerge from left, right, and backstage, each carrying files and speaking in chorus)*: "Don't you realise we are experienced curriculum writers? We've written management curricula before. We get it right. Accrediting bodies endorse our work. We know."
>
> Community Based Educators and Advisers *(file on confidently to form a semi-circle around a group of Indigenous people sitting centre stage, and speak in sotto voce)*: "Can't you see they need us because they're not yet ready to 'go it alone'?"
>
> Indigenous Peoples *(grouped with dignity, centre stage, sitting quietly, averting their gaze from the audience, totally silent, waiting).*

COMMENT

This case study is about the use and misuse of power. There is no question who holds the power over educational processes in this particular situation. Due to a complex set of motives deriving from the political economy of contemporary Australia, an alternative management training program that offers a culturally sensitive two-way teaching/learning process to Indigenous managers is not deemed acceptable. The new program represents a genuine fusion of Indigenous and Western processes of knowledge analysis and transmission. But its acceptance requires the dominant system to "let go," to release its bureaucratic control, to recognise the significance of prior Indigenous cultural learning, and to affirm the rights of Indigenous Australians to create their own curricula. Instead, the nationally recognised TAFE system believes it has a reputation to uphold, a reputation based on its success in providing vocational education and training in mainstream Australia. It therefore asserts that Indigenous Australians can only become recognised as "real" managers if they embark on a long series of preparatory or "catch-up" programs. First, they will have to become literate in the English language. Then they will need to conquer the complexities of Western numeracy. Some may require training in the use of computers and other sophisticated Western technologies. If they succeed in all these courses, they may then be allowed to embark on management training proper. And all of this has to be undertaken in remote and isolated settings many hundreds of kilometres from the nearest town or city.

Within these settings there are a few nonindigenous educators who show extraordinary levels of insight and commitment, and who are working quietly and unobtrusively alongside their Indigenous colleagues to affirm the legitimacy and relevance of local cultures of knowledge and wisdom. But they, too, are trapped in a top-down system that contests any challenges to its power and authority. The hiatus therefore continues. Indigenous managers quietly sit and wait, denied of any empowerment. And those in the system who are denying them the right to make their own decisions are themselves disempowered by their own economically and politically motivated inaction and indecision.

TEACHER EDUCATION FOR CULTURAL IDENTITY

They are the new, enthusiastic cadre: 84 young men and women, selected from over a thousand would-be teacher trainees in this South Pacific nation of Fiji. Academically proven, predominantly from rural areas, highly recommended, and already committed to the teaching profession, they are about to commence their two-year teacher training program. They are the very first intake at this new college. Although they represent a variety of cultures—Indo-Fijian, Indigenous Fijian, Rotuman, and Micronesian—it is sometimes hard to tell to which they belong because they all dress in Western styles, they all speak in English, and they all bring to the college a culture of learning that appears thoroughly Western. Their school years have ensured this.

During the first year when lecturers and trainees are all new, the courses have a tentative quality. Lecturers draw heavily on textbooks, and on the content and style of their own university training. They impart knowledge largely by "chalk and talk". Examinations ask that knowledge be reproduced. Trainees are not dismayed. It is merely an extension of an already familiar system of learning.

As the first year draws to a close, several of the education lecturers responsible for the core courses in the college begin to reflect on alternative cultures of knowledge and learning. Several questions arise: "Why must we teach this way? Why must our trainees learn this way? We have successful styles of traditional learning, why can't they be used?" As the issue is discussed and further explored, the staff become excited about the possibility of enabling trainees to strengthen their own cultural identity, and to learn to understand and respect the cultures of others. As a first step it is decided by consensus that all education courses will emphasise the cultural contextualisation of content. One local lecturer, however, decides to go further by developing a (second) final-year course that focuses specifically on the question of cultural identity. In its planning, she ensures that both the content and the methodology of the course reflect a "Fijian way" yet are inclusive of other South Pacific cultures. Despite some scepticism from Western advisers and others at the college, the course entitled "Education and Society in the South Pacific" is allowed to proceed.

The course model, shown in Figure 13.1, and discussed in more detail by Nabobo and Teasdale (1995), incorporates a traditional Fijian tapa design. It caught the immediate attention and imagination of the trainees. The model itself tells the story of the course. In phase 1 trainees were asked to interview their parents and grandparents in order to document the traditional ways of learning from their own cultures. The next challenge was to impart this knowledge to their peers in a culturally appropriate way. Some hesitated, but led by the dynamic young lecturer who began each week with a motivating, information-packed lecture, and

Figure 13.1. The Course Model

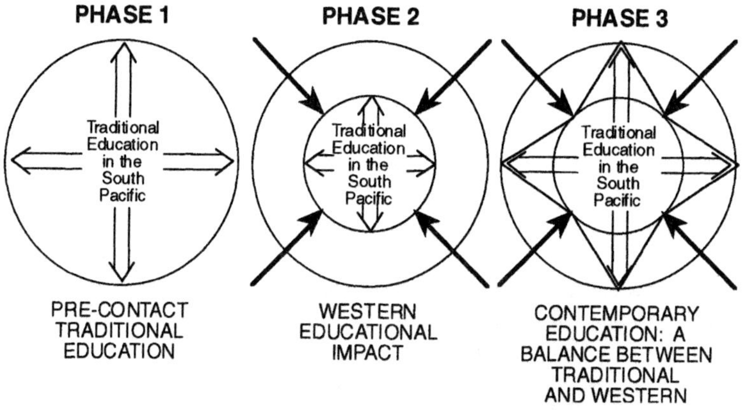

who never hesitated to join in trainee-initiated activities, the trainee-led workshop sessions took flight, with students demonstrating traditional skills through mediums as diverse as dance, art, song and instrument, ceremony, drama, cooking, navigation and boat building, textiles and costume, plant lore, oratory, and much more. Trainees arrived early to classes and left late; they worked collaboratively in groups; they involved everyone in the activities whether they were colleagues, visitors, assessors, or merely onlookers. They were given full control of the workshops, clear guidelines to follow, and strong personal support and encouragement.

Phase 2 of the course looked at the impact of Western education on traditional ways of teaching and learning. Trainees researched the schools from which they had so recently graduated. For the majority, school had been an exceptionally positive experience because they had been among the most academically successful. They returned to their schools with pride and were hailed as role models for current pupils. With careful guidance they built up a personal picture of the coming of Western educators to their villages and through a comparative process began to evaluate the losses and gains of the changes. Again they worked collaboratively and sought creative ways to impart their knowledge in workshops. The major question of cultural identity, until this point covert in the course, was brought into the open with a dramatic presentation by three of the education lecturers. The trainees were silent as they watched an Indigenous Fijian, an Indo-Fijian, and a European act out their interpretation of the colonial coming and its impact on culture and education. Workshops that week were vibrant as trainees reflected on the implications for them as educators influencing future generations of young Fijians.

Cultural identity and contemporary educational issues were examined in phase 3. How can one resolve the tensions that exist between the expectations of one's traditional culture and the impinging Western way? This elusive question initially was tackled visually, with a commissioned picture to encourage trainees to reflect on how they might personally resolve this tension in a constructive, creative, and productive manner (see Teasdale and Little 1995, 585). Lively discussions, debates, role plays, and conversations ensued as trainees examined this question in the context of current educational issues facing the peoples of the small island nations of the South Pacific.

At its conclusion, trainees evaluated the course, unanimously acclaiming it as one of the most intellectually stimulating and inclusive they had ever undertaken. They said that the course had enabled them to take greater pride in their cultural identity and to develop a respect for other cultures. They felt confident to begin teaching, using some of the techniques and methodologies they themselves had used with success in the course. Lecturers were encouraged and began working to improve the course for the following year.

But a few "outsiders" had reservations. One external course evaluator, from a Western university background, carefully praised the course but suggested that its "simplistic" theoretical approach better suited beginning trainees than those in their final year. The relevance of the course to teachers was questioned by some who commented: "Surely trainees are here to learn *how* to teach and *what* to teach. Cultural identity doesn't fit into this framework." This instrumental viewpoint implied that time and money were being wasted with a course of this nature.

Did the course only flourish because it was in the sheltered college environment? Would it have a real impact on trainees once they began teaching in Fiji's secondary schools? These key questions niggled at the back of the minds of staff. A follow-up study conducted after trainees had been teaching for one year revealed that a significant number had been able to translate some of the methodology, knowledge, and values of the course into their teaching, despite the impediment of a dominant Western model of education, driven by a rigorous public examinations system. The issues of culture and cultural identity explored in their teacher training had enabled them to affirm their own identity and the identities of the students in their multicultural classrooms. They believed that the course, in its content and its methodology, had enhanced both their own teaching and their students' performance, and had set their colleagues thinking: a modest but important beginning.

COMMENT

Here is a case study that demonstrates the successful blending of local cultures of knowledge and learning within a teacher education program based largely on Western models and processes. The academic staff who developed the course did not conceptualise the cultural and the economic as antithetical. Indeed, they realised that they were preparing teachers to face the harsh economic realities of a small developing nation. The pursuit of economic goals would be a necessity for most of the pupils their students would teach. Yet staff also were committed to preparing teachers to face cultural realities, and especially the need to reinforce cultural identity through the use of curriculum processes that emphasised a more holistic approach to knowledge and a more interdependent approach to learning. While it was recognised that some tensions can arise between economic and cultural goals, both were seen to be important. In fact, Indigenous students with a clear sense of cultural identity and a deep sense of rootedness in their culture of primary origin are more likely to have the self-confidence and human relationship skills to sustain an economically viable lifestyle.

In spite of criticisms from some employing authorities and doubting colleagues, the spirited determination of the local lecturers and the consistent excellence of their teaching helped pave the way for the success of the new course. The trainee's response to their own achievements transferred positively to other areas of study, thus minimising criticism from the senior management of the institution. Importantly, follow-up research indicated that graduates were viewed as strong and committed teachers producing the results required of them by the employing authorities. However, there was a personal cost for these young people once they began their teaching careers. The examination-oriented and economically driven school system did not support their efforts to explore and affirm cultural identity in teaching/learning situations. As the most junior staff members they were expected by their seniors to maintain the status quo during the school day. Most of them, however, to their credit, were willing to work out of school hours through social, sporting, and religious activities to promote the cultural goals they had so successfully embraced during their own training. Perhaps as time passes they will have other young graduate teachers to support them and possibly a ripple effect will accrue as they themselves attain seniority.

THE DOCTORAL THESIS

The scene is a seminar room in an Australian university. The main actor is Wani, a Ph.D. student who has been enrolled at the university for the past 15 months. Her early years were spent in a small village on a remote northern island of Papua New Guinea. During her childhood she was regularly cared for and educated by her maternal grandparents, neither of whom had had any contact with Western cultures and languages. A particularly bright child, she was selected by her family to go to a secondary boarding school on the mainland, from whence she was chosen for a teacher education program at the University of PNG. After a period as a secondary school teacher she won a higher degree scholarship to Australia, and is now ready to return home to PNG to collect data for her thesis. But first her proposal has to be approved by the usual committee of academics.

Wani is a particularly capable student, and already has completed a first full draft of the theoretical analysis for her thesis, and of the methodology chapter. At her own request, and with the full support of her supervisors, she has decided not to adopt a conventional Western theoretical framework for her writing, but to use her own Indigenous processes of knowledge analysis, fusing these where appropriate with Western elements. Thus her theoretical chapters begin with the telling of a story that provides the context for an overview of key issues. The issues are not separately identified and dealt with sequentially. Instead, Wani seems to approach her research question by "walking around" it in ever decreasing circles, using a holistic or integrated approach. At various stages other stories are told to clarify or explicate. Extensive use is made of literature, both Western and Indigenous, the latter including oral literature acquired from her parents and grandparents.

The research methodology selected by Wani can best be described as "participatory action research". She intends working with village women, training them as researchers and participating alongside them in the processes of data collection and analysis. The ultimate ownership and control of the research will rest with the participants, not with Wani. It is a research technique that nurtures and empowers. The long-term goal is to leave behind a number of small, self-sustaining, self-help projects.

All of Wani's work has been tabled and summarised for the benefit of the review committee. At the end of her presentation there is a long silence. Then the questions begin, quickly revealing two broad reactions. One reaction is of exhilaration and excitement. For a minority of those present, Wani's work opens up previously unforeseen dimensions of intellectual analysis and discourse. The reaction of the majority, however, is one of disbelief and profound scepticism. They simply cannot accept that other systems of knowledge analysis have any validity in Western academe. Nor can they accept that research methods that divest power to the participants (or, as they prefer to describe them, the "subjects") will produce "proper" results. Wani sits bemused as the debate flows around her. In the end, those with "voting rights" do allow her to continue as planned, a credit to the quality and depth of her presentation.

COMMENT

In this situation, Wani's victory was a tiny one. The road she has yet to follow is certain to be fraught with tension and difficulty. So strongly embedded are most Australian academics in the rightness of their own way of looking at the world, that it seems unlikely they will cease their opposition to the processes she wishes to employ to achieve her educational ends. Their own academic successes have been achieved by conforming to the Western way. Indeed, a doctoral thesis has prescribed parameters and deep-seated cultural expectations of its own. To depart from these clearly delineated guidelines is not seen as an option by most Western academics.

Wani also will be enmeshed in the economic provisions of the study leave and funding arrangements she has entered into to study abroad. She will be bound by the economic system that enabled her to undertake her studies and by her own country's need for her expert services as soon as possible upon her return. Curiously, associated with this latter point, is the belief by her compatriots that she will return with a "Western education," a much valued and sought-after commodity. In all probability they will not expect a culture of knowledge and learning that incorporates some of their own traditional ways. In fact, they may well be disillusioned with the end-product of her learning.

DISCUSSION

Until very recently the cultures of knowledge and learning in higher education institutions in the Australia-Pacific region have been totally Eurocentric. The superiority of the Western scientific world view has been unquestioned. Now, however, Indigenous cultures of knowledge and wisdom are starting to claim their place in universities and other post-school institutions, the four case studies in this chapter offering examples of recent initiatives. As we noted earlier, the movement has had a tentative quality, but in the past year or two we have observed a growing sense of confidence, especially in Australia and Aotearoa New Zealand, notwithstanding the increasing stridency of the economic rationalist discourse. There are several reasons for this newly emerging confidence:

1. At an international level Indigenous peoples are gaining increasing support for their rights. The U.N. World Decade for Cultural Development (1988–1997) and the International Year of the World's Indigenous Peoples (1993), for example, have both affirmed in significant ways the rights of Indigenous minorities to maintain and develop their own languages and cultures.
2. In addition to affirmation from without, there is also evidence of a new sense of cultural distinctiveness and autonomy emerging from within. Sahlins (1993) has coined the term "culturalism" to describe this new sense of "cultural self-consciousness" that is developing within many small Indigenous societies. He considers it one of the most remarkable phenomena of the late 20th century. While its manifestations in some parts of the world are overwhelmingly negative, leading to bitter wars and rivalries, in other countries it is finding creative expression in areas such as music, drama, and art, and in a new sense of intellectual and spiritual freedom.
3. In Australia and Aotearoa New Zealand, despite continuing expressions of racism in some settings, there is a newly emerging sense of national pride in the unique contributions of Indigenous peoples to the wider society. Indigenous elements increasingly are being incorporated as an integral part of the national identity of each country.

Within institutions of higher education the intellectual climate also is changing, albeit slowly and rather hesitantly, in ways that support what Alatas (1993) refers to as "the indigenisation of academic discourse". Underlying theoretical shifts are facilitating this process. In the humanities and social sciences, for example, post-modernism is challenging many deeply held assumptions, and undermining the certainties of the scientific approach to the study of humans and their societies. In the physical and natural sciences the changes are even more profound. Quantum mechanics and chaos theory have challenged the very core of scientific thinking. The universe increasingly is perceived as complex and unpredictable. The rational-empirical approach, with its certainty and objectivity, is no longer fully tenable.

Although the impacts of these theoretical shifts are slow and uneven, they are beginning to create a climate of acceptance of alternative cultures of knowledge and wisdom in education, at least in some settings in the Australia-Pacific region. Writing from an Australian perspective, for example, Beare and Slaughter (1993) posit that education is moving beyond scientific materialism and is beginning to accept other categories of knowing. Gale (1995, 610), after extensive research in Northern Australia, has identified the emergence, despite many conflicts, of a distinctively Indigenous and more inclusive higher education curriculum in some institutions in the Northern Territory, a curriculum that challenges the "assimilatory and Eurocentric nature" of mainstream higher education in Australia. From a South Pacific perspective both Helu-Thaman (1994) and Nabobo (1994) allude to a new search for culturally relevant curriculum content and processes at all levels of education, including higher education. Nevertheless, as the case studies so clearly illustrate, there is still strong resistance from those who manage and control education systems and institutions. Many Western educators in the Australia-Pacific region are continuing to contest the rights of Indigenous peoples to draw on their own ways of thinking and knowing in higher education settings.

It is particularly noteworthy that the reaffirmation of Indigenous knowledge and wisdom in higher education is being activated by Indigenous peoples themselves, confirming Sahlins' (1993) thesis that this new sense of cultural autonomy is emerging from within. As illustrated in the case studies, Indigenous academics are starting to take control of their own processes of knowledge analysis and transmission. They are questioning the intellectual ethnocentrism and economic rationalism of contemporary higher education and, notwithstanding the contestation that so often confronts them, are quietly asserting the right to make their own decisions about the content, processes, and management of the curriculum. In so doing they are not reverting to the past by seeking to hold on to former cultural traditions and practices. Nor are they creating a dichotomy between their own cultures of knowledge and those of the West, viewing the two as conflictual or incompatible. It is only outsiders, with their monocultural lenses, who perceive the situation in this way. Rather,

Indigenous people are creating new cultures of knowledge that blend their own processes and practices with those of the West. Thus the economic goals that are so central to contemporary Western higher education are not being discarded, nor seen as irrelevant or irreconcilable.

Wani, for example, in the PNG case study, is using Indigenous processes of knowledge analysis and transmission in training her co-researchers in the villages, but she is also empowering them to function more effectively as interdependent, self-sufficient units within the emerging cash economy of rural PNG. Culture, therefore, is not acting as an obstacle to economic progress, but as a facilitator of it, enabling the development of small self-help projects that generate income for the participants. At the same time, Wani herself, while using Indigenous processes of knowledge analysis in the preparation of her thesis, is openly seeking credentials (i.e., a university higher degree) that will enhance her employability and thus increase her income.

What of the future? We believe that Indigenous cultures of knowledge and learning will become increasingly accepted in higher education. The process will only gain momentum, however, as academics divest control to their Indigenous colleagues. Indigenous scholars must have the freedom to create their own modes of knowledge analysis and transmission out of the interaction between their traditions and those of the West. This is a dynamic process of creation and recreation, reflecting an ongoing search for cultural continuity and identity. It is also a process of adaptation and appropriation as cultures of knowledge and wisdom are constantly reviewed, evaluated, and fused to create an ever-changing *ganma*. In the Australia-Pacific region these processes are starting to lead to more holistic, interdisciplinary, and metaphysical approaches to knowledge analysis, and to modes of knowledge transmission that are more learner-directed, person-oriented, and contextualised.

Finally, we anticipate that Indigenous perspectives eventually will begin to influence our Western ways of thinking about higher education in nonindigenous settings. For example, it seems clear that a much broader economic frame of thinking will need to emerge, reflecting the major transformations that are taking place as we move from industrial to post-industrial societies, even in the developing world. Changing patterns of employment and wealth creation suggest that lifetime paid employment is unlikely to be the norm in the future. Within such an economic context important questions need to be asked: Should higher education focus exclusively on preparation for paid employment? Or should it be preparing people for greater self-sufficiency and self-reliance? If so, how can it foster a greater degree of interdependence, leading to more cooperative lifeways? How can higher education promote the flexibility and adaptability that the post-industrial state will require? Many of the answers to questions such as these may be drawn from the knowledge and wisdom of non-Western societies. Allowing Indigenous cultures of knowledge and learning to play a significant role in contemporary academic discourse may well be the key to our long-term survival.

NOTE

[1] Aotearoa, literally "the land of the long white cloud," is the Maori name for New Zealand.

REFERENCES

Alatas, A. 1993. "On the Indigenization of Academic Discourse." *Alternatives* 18: 307–338.

Beare, H., and R. Slaughter. 1993. *Education for the Twenty-first Century.* London: Routledge.

Gale, P. 1995. "A Fair Chance for All? Indigenous Rights and Tertiary Education in Australia." *Prospects: UNESCO Quarterly Review of Comparative Education* 25(4): 609–621.

Helu-Thaman, K. 1994. "Cultural Democracy for Whom? A View from the Pacific Islands." *Directions: Journal of Education Studies, Institute of Education, The University of the South Pacific* 16(1): 3–19.

Mel, M.A. 1995. "*Mbu*: A Culturally Meaningful Framework for Education in Papua New Guinea." *Prospects: UNESCO Quarterly Review of Comparative Education* 25(4): 683–694.

Nabobo, U. 1994. "Exploring Yalomatua: Fijian Education and the Missing Link." *Directions: Journal of Education Studies, Institute of Education, The University of the South Pacific* 16(1): 41–54.

Nabobo, U., and J.I. Teasdale. 1995. "Education for Cultural Identity: A Fiji Case Study." *Prospects: UNESCO Quarterly Review of Comparative Education* 25(4): 695–706.

Sahlins, M. 1993. "Culture and Modern History." Cited in *The University of the South Pacific Bulletin* 26(6): 1–2.

Teasdale, G.R. 1994. "Education and the Survival of Small Indigenous Cultures." *International Yearbook of Education* 44: 197–224.

Teasdale, G.R., and A.W. Little, eds. 1995. "Open File: Culture and Education." *Prospects: UNESCO Quarterly Review of Comparative Education* 25(4): 585–782.

Teasdale, G.R., and J.I. Teasdale. 1994. "Culture and Schooling in Aboriginal Australia". In *International Perspectives on Culture and Schooling*, ed. E. Thomas. London: University of London Institute of Education.

CHAPTER 14

Cultural Ambiguity and the Primary School Teacher

Lessons from Rural Mozambique

MIKAEL PALME

In most developing countries, a qualitative and sociologically reflective approach is an urgent requirement in basic education; it is an imperative for improving the quality of teaching. This means that educational planners and policy makers, education officers at national and regional levels, instructors engaged in teachers' pre- and in-service training, primary school teachers, and not least educational researchers themselves must learn to address cultural aspects of teaching and schooling. There should be a strong call for the kind of insights that linguistics, anthropology, and sociology can provide. However, current trends in donor support tend to emphasize the importation of management-oriented and cost-effectiveness models, both in research and in strategies for quality improvement. Instead of becoming a complementary approach, this importation is often to the detriment of genuinely qualitative approaches.

This chapter addresses the question of quality and culture in primary teaching on the basis of a discussion of research findings from various studies recently made in Mozambique. First, the nature of classroom interaction—in school effectiveness research, normally reduced almost to invisibility in a poorly developed category labelled "process"—will be briefly described and some cultural factors determining this interaction identified. Next, an attempt will be made to picture the so-called "context" of schooling in the matrilineal, rural areas of the northern province of Nampula. Further, the question of the position of the rural primary school teacher as a cultural mediator between modernity and what is commonly referred to as "traditional" society will be addressed. Finally, the conditions and priorities for a quality improvement strategy in a country such as Mozambique will be briefly discussed.

The argument presented here will come close to what Fuller and Clarke (1994) recently have named a "classroom culturalist" approach and indirectly be critical of what they termed the "policy mechanics" perspective. Education development programmes based primarily on organizational or economic models tend to neglect most of the social, cultural, and linguistic factors that determine education as a process of cultural transmission. As a consequence, such models tend to perpetuate the existing state of ignorance of what actually goes on in schools and to be followed blindly. Not surprisingly, they also become insensitive to the potentialities of change.

CLASSROOM INTERACTION: RITUALS AND HIEROGLYPHS

Classroom practices, learning outcomes, and their relation to the teaching materials in use in Mozambican primary schools were closely studied in a national evaluation of primary education textbooks undertaken by a joint national and international research team between 1990 and 1992.[1] The study comprised observations of more than 150 lessons in grades 1 to 5 in eight schools in two regions of the country. Further, more elaborate observation of 22 lessons in four schools focused on qualitative aspects of language use. In addition, assessment tests in the key subjects were conducted, as well as a large number of pupil and teacher interviews.

Results show that teaching in Mozambican primary schools is characterized by remarkably little pupil participation in verbal exchanges or other classroom activities. On average, the teacher occupies as much as 93 percent of all speaking time. In lessons in grades 1 and 2, the probability is that a pupil will speak individually once every third or fourth day. It should be noted that such speaking normally consists either of simple confirmations ("Yes!" or "No!") or of repeating short sentences from the teacher or textbook. As regards reading, the probability is that an individual pupil will read aloud in the classroom (on average for less than one minute) once every three weeks.

If listening to the teacher is the dominant pupil activity, then the next one in importance is waiting. Pupils spend approximately not less than one-third of their time in the classroom waiting. They wait for the teacher to begin the lesson, to write the name of the school, the title of the lesson, or various other texts on the blackboard. They wait for their peers to finish exercises they themselves have finished a long time ago or, at least as often, for others to finish an exercise they themselves had not been able to understand. They also wait for others to be corrected, so that their turn will come.

The third activity in importance is copying. Perhaps the major part of all time used for written exercises is consumed by copying the exercises as such (most often sentences) from the blackboard. Little time is left for actually doing the exercise. In fact, observations confirm that many pupils never reach the phase of executing the exercise itself. When they have managed to copy it to their exercise books, the teacher and the best pupils have already come to the phase of correction.

The study suggests that the dominant pattern of classroom interaction is characterized by a very high level of pupil passivity. Activities are almost entirely reproductive in character. The more qualitatively oriented part of the classroom study confirmed the routine character of teaching. Questions asked by the teacher are predominately closed in character (there is only one correct answer and it can be taken directly from the pupil's textbook or from what the teacher has previously said). Teachers rarely ask questions that refer to experiences outside the school context or the context of the textbook. Verbal interaction consists almost entirely of monologues from the teacher or of exchanges between teacher and pupils of the well-known question/answer/evaluation type. There are few or no verbal initiatives from the pupils' side, nor any verbal exchanges between pupils. The explanations given by the teacher rarely go beyond what is said in the pupil's textbook, with teachers tending to use the exact words or formulations found in the textbook or in the teacher's manual. Further, pupils' exercises seldom make reference to their own experience or go beyond the context of the textbook.

Finally, there is little or no individualization. Teachers normally address themselves to the entire class. Even corrections, which occupy a considerable time in teaching (on average about 13 percent), rarely give individual help to the pupils (for example, by explaining mistakes), since teachers normally only check if answers are correct or not.

It is not surprising, then, that perhaps the most striking feature of teaching in Mozambican primary schools is its strong ritualization. The teacher asks questions and organizes exercises, and pupils listen to the teacher, answer the questions, and do the exercises. But in doing all this they focus not so much upon the content of what is being said or done but on formal aspects of the interaction. There are a number of rules for classroom behaviour that work independently of any content. Pupils learn early, for example, that one basic rule is that one should not expect that what the teacher says is necessarily understandable. Teachers learn the corresponding rule that pupils are often unlikely to understand and rarely seek clarification. Further, unintelligibility is not a justified reason for the teaching to pause or for the pupils to interrupt the teacher with questions. Classroom ritual, then, has it that even if a considerable part of the teacher's discourse is likely not to be understood by the pupils, either because the language is too difficult or because the subject matter is, or both, teaching goes on *as if* everything was all right.[2]

Even if it is obvious that these rituals are pedagogically counter-productive, it is important to understand their functional value. Above all, they permit teaching to proceed, even when conditions for real learning do not exist. This is vital, since taking these problems seriously would often mean going back to the syllabus in the very early grades of primary education. There is, for example, evidence that many pupils up to grade 4 still use counting on their fingers and toes as a dominant method in mathematics.

Ritualistic teaching, then, can partly be seen as a rational response of teachers to the impossible mission they have been given by national curricula, textbooks, and teachers' manuals. Two equally important factors are teachers' poor mastery of their subjects and their lack of teaching skills. Studies on teachers' conceptions in relation to subject matter taught in Grade 4 and 5 indicate clearly that primary school teachers often face problems very similar to those of their pupils in understanding key notions in, for example, science education. (See, for example, Januário, Jasso, and Popov 1998). Therefore primary school teachers normally rely on the explanatory texts of teachers' manuals or textbooks and have great difficulty in finding their own ways of explaining new concepts. Further, as classroom interaction rituals so clearly demonstrate, primary school teachers possess an extremely limited repertoire of teaching methods. As a result, even repetition of subject matter tends to be pedagogically meaningless.

A result of the teaching practices described above and of the survival strategies pupils develop is a growing discrepancy, from Grade 1 upwards, between the level of pedagogical transmission and the level of reception, i.e. understanding and assimilation by the pupils. Since so much of what is supposed to be taught, and learned, in early grades is in fact not learned at all, teaching constantly demands skills and knowledge of pupils that the majority do not have. One effect is repetition and dropout. But even with the extremely high rates of repetition and dropout found in the Mozambican primary school (on average, one-third of all pupils in

Grades 1 to 5 fail to pass at the end of the year, and a mere 23 percent of all school beginners graduate from Grade 5; see Palme 1993), it is probable that the majority of pupils in the last grades of lower primary school are far from possessing the skills and knowledge required of them.

SOME FACTORS DETERMINING LEARNING[3]

Perhaps the most striking aspect of classroom interaction is the constraint on communication due to the pupils' lack of language proficiency in Portuguese. Outside properly urban schools, pupils even in Grades 3, 4 and 5 have difficulty in understanding most of the explanations given by the teacher. When interviewed after lessons, pupils often cannot relate the essentials of what the teacher has said. Moreover, texts in the teaching materials normally surpass the reading proficiency of the pupils, making the assimilation of concepts particularly problematic. Likewise, pupils' difficulties in writing mean that writing exercises takes excessive time and often does not achieve desired outcomes.

But that is not all. The low proficiency in the language of instruction places major constraints on verbal exchange within the classroom. Textbooks and teachers' manuals place little emphasis on "dialoguing" as a pedagogical method, which is aimed at creating links between the pupils' previous experiences and conceptions and the new subject matter. The little room there is for verbal exchange is normally reduced to a bare minimum because of the ritualization of classroom interaction. The constraints placed on classroom interaction are particularly important, as the distance between pupils' experiences and previous conceptions, on the one hand, and the subject matter and new concepts, on the other, is probably far greater than for school children in the industrialized world. Language is an indispensable means of creating the necessary links, that is, for creating conditions for a reasonable dialectic between assimilation and accommodation, to put it in Piagetan terms, and in this case mastery is inadequate.

The evaluation project focused on very different linguistic situations in three social settings. In rural areas in the northern Nampula province, Portuguese tends to be spoken only in school. Children are linguistically socialized in their mother tongue, which they learn to master as any other member of the local community. In the few properly urban schools, most pupils have Portuguese as their mother tongue and will use a few words or expressions from Mozambican languages only occasionally. In suburban shanty towns, however, the linguistic situation is complex. Tests and interviews with pupils testify that children are brought up in a linguistic context in which neither their original mother tongue nor Portuguese is dominant. As a result, a specific suburban language seems to develop, which takes most of its characteristics from traditional regionally dominant languages (in the capital of Maputo these are Ronga and/or Changana), but which at the same time does not include all the vocabulary and linguistic subtlety of the language of origin. An example of this specific linguistic competence produced by urbanization is that a majority of suburban pupils in Grades 4 and 5 used the word *rio*—river—for describing any assembly of water, being ignorant of the various words available in their mother tongue and also of the specific Portuguese word for such things as "river," "canal," "beach," "lake," and so forth. It should be noted that the suburban language is not necessarily unsophisticated, only different in vocabulary and syntax.

In addition, interviews made in relation to the textbooks in science and geography highlight the pedagogical problems arising from the simple fact that pupils' experiences are shaped, and restrained, by their social and geographical surroundings. For example, the thermometer is an unknown phenomenon among the majority of Mozambican children, and a considerable proportion of pupils in the suburbs of Maputo, which is situated on the coast, have difficulties in grasping the notion of "sea," as they have never been to the beach. More interesting, a small exploratory interview study on the northern Ihla de Mozambique showed that children in fishing families often had specific difficulties in understanding the teaching of the cardinal points, since the local conceptual and linguistic system for designating geographical directions, adapted to the necessities of navigation and based mainly on names given to winds coming from various points of the compass, was considerably more elaborate than what was taught in the syllabus (Peacock 1995).

Since teachers' explanations are given in a second (or, more accurately, foreign) language, pupils are all the more dependent on their factual experiences for understanding new concepts. Makua-speaking children in rural Nampula schools, grasping very little of the teacher's explanations about the water cycle, tried to give meaning to a word such as "vaporization" by applying the semantic connotation of the mother-tongue expression for describing the disappearance of water (*owelela*), which normally is that it disappears *into* the ground (as water in rivers might appear to do). The application of the semantic field of the mother-tongue expression was confirmed by the natural tendency of children not to believe things that they cannot see, such as invisible vapour. As a result, Makua-speaking school children appeared to have greater difficulties than, for example, Changana- and Ronga-speaking children in the south—who would normally think in terms of the established mother-tongue concept of "smoke" (*musi*)—to grasp the notion of vaporization.

The evaluation concluded that existing curricula and textbooks are badly adapted to Mozambican school children's conceptions of the world, in the first place, and that this poor adjustment is further strengthened by the predominantly passive role given to pupils by the instructions in the teachers' manuals. Since actual teaching practices with few exceptions affirm student passivity, and since the use of Portuguese as the sole language of instruction imposes severe constraints on conceptual understanding and verbal exchange, virtually no negotiating (Hewson 1988) takes place between pupils' previous conceptions and experiences on the one hand, and new experiences and information handed to them in the classroom or by the textbook on the other. It is no wonder, then, that the few students who manage to survive throughout the years are profoundly transformed by the education process and, because of the general amnesia produced by the nature of this transformation, normally conceive of the modern, educated world into which they have managed to enter as being totally different from, and superior to, the backward world from which they came.

The simple point to be made in relation to this discussion of classroom interaction and learning in the Mozambican primary school is that there seems to be no shortcut to more "effective" teaching. In order to address cultural obstacles to learning, curriculum developers, writers of teaching materials, instructors on pre-service and in-service training courses, and, most of all, the primary teachers themselves, must be equipped with at least some instruments enabling them to identify and understand the cultural and linguistic mechanisms that shape the teaching process, in order to promote a minimum of fruitful "negotiation" between existing cultural and linguistic identities and the particular versions of modernity for which the school is a carrier. Perhaps the only asset the primary school teachers possess, along with the pride some of them still may have in their profession, is their familiarity with local, social, linguistic, and cultural traditions. Of the many factors that block the use of this resource at least one is mutable, namely the priorities and constraints set by national educational planners and decision makers in their strategies for quality improvement. The national elites, while striving for modernity and legitimizing their positions by claims to modernity, have little understanding and interest in what they tend to see as "particularistic" and generally backward local or regional traditions.

THE "CONTEXT": SCHOOLING IN A MATRILINEAL RURAL SOCIETY

As Robert Serpell convincingly argues in his contribution to this volume, the weak impact of basic education in Africa should be seen in relation to the "extractive" nature of schooling and its lack of relevance to the local community.

The problem of the significance of schooling was the focus of a sociological analysis of families' educational strategies in the general context of social reproduction in a rural, matrilineal community in Nampula (Palme 1993), which generally supports Serpell's analysis. The study comprised interviews with 30 Makua peasant families, including local traditional chiefs and religious leaders, on their understanding of schooling, as well as interviews with primary school teachers, school children, and local administrators. The findings indicate that peasant families were largely unable to ascribe any particular meaning to curricular content. Subject matter—concepts, factual information, and even skills such as measuring—in subjects like geography, science, or history were not merely poorly understood; they were seen as belonging to a closed universe to which ordinary people had no access and which, further, had no significance whatsoever for normal life. Instead, schooling was basically ascribed a purely functional value, that of opening the door to modern society and its alleged well-being. But even in this respect, the relationship to schooling was ambiguous.

On the one hand, getting educated meant the possibility of abandoning the peasant condition, of obtaining employment and a salary, and eventually of being able to live in the city where signs of wealth such as electricity, running water, cars, and even television sets, at least according to rumour, were abundant. The education of a son or a daughter would not only be an honour for the family, but secure its well-being in future. Education was one of the few available means for individual social mobility.

On the other hand, the peasant families knew from experience that the road to success was long, costly, and insecure. It would not suffice to send the children to the neighbouring school, at walking distance, where grade 6 was taught; it would be necessary to arrange for continued studies in the suburbs of the city. This implied finding accommodation through the extended family network of solidarity ties. The educational ambitions of most peasant families had to stop here. They had no contacts whatsoever in the cities, and boarding schools became increasingly rare when state expenditure for education was reduced. Those few with the good fortune of having close relatives in town would be well off. More often, children had to stay with distant relatives and in households where they might be treated as servants, as was confirmed by interviews with young men who had returned to the village after a year of humiliation and starvation in the city. No one included in the study had been able to complete Grade 7.

Sending one's daughter to town in order to continue her studies could turn out to be a most dangerous strategy. Separated from the extended family, which in normal circumstances would function as a moral safeguard, the young woman might be unable to confront the radically different social environment that town life offers. It should not be forgotten that when a peasant family sends a child to town it will, in a sense, lose the child to an unfamiliar society within which they do not feel at ease. The picture of the humble peasant father waiting for hours outside a suburban school to get a word with the teacher about his child being expelled for alleged truancy or some other problem is an illustrative one. Finally, sending children to town in order to continue school meant economic sacrifices that could be substantial. The family not only lost a productive member, but had to send food (and money) to town, which was a time-consuming and often expensive undertaking.

However, the educational project was not only costly and hazardous. It was also contradictory. Those who managed to "succeed" usually changed. From the point of view of the village, a city dweller, an educated or a rich person, was named a *mkunya*, a "white person,"[4] regardless of his or her colour of skin. This expression was often used both ironically and critically, but basically expressed both superiority and difference, "not one of us." Getting one's daughter married to a *mkunya* was an honour because it meant being connected to another, probably superior, world where wealth was available. But the undertone of irony or criticism in the use of the notion of *akunya* (plural form) was equally important. In traditional peasant society there is little room for individuality: the individual cannot exist alone outside the pattern of family relations to which he or she belongs and where his or her position to a great extent is defined from birth. The transformation brought about to the individual by education did not necessarily threaten solidarity ties to the group of origin—at least not according to harmonious ideals set up by some peasant families—but it was far from unproblematic, as witnessed by numerous stories of ungrateful relatives whose behaviour, once they had disappeared to the city, showed little respect for their group of origin and its needs. The "secrets" of school and of formal education, into which the educated young man (or woman) were considered to be initiated, also represented a potential danger to the moral values which guaranteed the unity of the group.

This transformation might be accepted for boys, but represented a considerable risk for girls. An educated girl would not be able to marry a man with less education than herself. Uneducated men would not dare to approach her and in any case such a marriage was generally seen as unhappy and unstable, since the woman would know secrets that her husband did not know. This would severely limit the range of potential suitors and put the family in a situation where it became dependent on unknown suitors whose intentions and behaviour were equally unknown. According to matrilineal tradition, the married woman should remain in the area of her family of origin. This was seen as a guarantee for stability and future reproduction, since children were to be brought up in proximity to the extended family to which they belonged, that is, that of the mother. The educated woman, then, might either continue as unmarried (and be a burden and a shame for her family) or marry a man who was unlikely to respect tradition, but without representing any other visible advantage such as wealth or high social position. In either case, the whole basis upon which family reproduction rested was put at risk. It was also generally thought that the educated girl would change her attitudes, become less respectful to her parents and to traditions and rituals, and lose her taste for manual labour in the fields. The education of girls thus threatened social reproduction and since any real advantage of schooling was so uncertain, families were less inclined to pursue it.

In order to understand this culture, we must consider the structure of the Makua matrilineal society (Geffray 1990). Traditionally, the family economy is based upon the labour force provided by the young men who marry into the family, the products of this labour being the rightful property of their mothers-in-law, who "feed" the family and see to its well-being, that is, redistribute the products of labour to family members. The senior mother—the "mother of mothers"—is the central figure in the family network, even if the real chief of the family conglomerate would be one of her brothers or maternal uncles. As her own children grow up and her daughters get married, the young woman passes from being junior—which implies subordination to her own mother (and her mother's brothers or uncles)—to the group of senior women who, benefiting from the labour of their sons-in-law, can guarantee the well-being of their family network. It is particularly important for her to give birth to daughters at an early stage of her social career, since she, later on in life, as Geffray shows, can rightfully "adopt" one or several of her granddaughters, thus reproducing a situation in which she, by marrying off these adopted daughters, can benefit from the suitors' labour force, without which she would survive with difficulty. Becoming a respected and influential senior woman is the accomplishment of the social career of a young woman.

It is crucial, then, that a family conglomerate (comprising several generations) produces girls and that these girls stay closely attached to the family of origin in order to guarantee the inflow of new suitors or husbands and their labour force. The status of the woman, then, makes her immobile. If she were to leave with her husband, she would not fulfil this function; neither would she later on in life benefit from her position as a senior woman. School, then, does not fit well with the conditions for social promotion of women in Makua society.

For boys, education is a less contradictory project. The main responsibilities of husbands are to secure the reproduction of their wife's lineage, constructing a house for the family and securing its material well-being. Within their own lineage, for example, as brothers (to their sisters) and uncles (to their sisters' children) or as nephews (to their maternal uncle), they assume wider responsibilities. They will supervise the education of children (including their initiation through rituals and ceremonies) and protect the interests of the family in questions of marriage or land disputes. Belonging to "the same stomach," the same lineage group (*nloko*), means considering nephews and nieces as one's own children, thus assuming full moral and material responsibility for their well-being and future. Being both husband and brother (nephew, uncle, etc), the man must procure the means for the survival of the group. This, of course, is normally accomplished through agriculture, but might very well include such things as selling his labour, travelling, or getting educated and entering into modern society. In doing this, the man should, traditionally, act as a representative of the group, rather than an individual fortune seeker, and act on its behalf and for its benefit. Individual achievement, either in education or in a professional career, is ideally an accomplishment of the group itself. Educating sons, male nephews, or male grandchildren, is to educate an organic member of the group and is a means for the group to secure its future well-being.

This is, roughly, the ideal representation of things. However, peasant families were aware that reality was often different. The transforming force of education was tangibly felt. School leavers from higher grades who had returned to the village because of lack of opportunities in the town wanted nothing else other than to get away again. They had lost much of their faith in the values that build up traditional peasant life. They questioned or ridiculed the secrets of the elders, which were transmitted through initiation and other rituals. New categories of thinking had entered their minds and they would typically express themselves, at least in the interview situation, using oppositions such as "old-fashioned"/"modern," "superstition"/"science," "local"/"universal," "eventless"/"eventful," and so forth. The uneasiness they felt embraced all aspects of daily life, such as the lack of taste and variety of traditional food, the poor houses, the hard and never-ending work in the field, the unattractiveness of local women, the dullness of entertainment activities, the obsolescent rituals, and so forth. They were, to use Pierre Bourdieu's expression, people whom school had consigned to a warped position in history (*une position en porte-à-faux*). They belonged neither to the peasant society they came from, nor to the modern world to which they aspired. Facing the sociologist, as the personification of modern society, they had to conceal the extent of their participation in traditional beliefs and practices. In their home village, they had to conceal some of the beliefs and attitudes acquired in the city because of their blasphemous or irreverent character. Their doubting the values of traditional peasant society, in particular the belief in the cult of the ancestors, put into question its very base, the unity of the group, by challenging the way of understanding solidarity ties between its members. Hence, education, as the vehicle for this transformation, tended to threaten the whole base upon which traditional society rested, and to give way to an individualism which was its antithesis.

Thus, peasant families were aware of the changing force of education. The contradictions of the educational project were perhaps most openly visible in this ambiguous attitude towards education: desiring it as an instrument for social improvement and rejecting it as a threat to the solidarity of the group.

THE RURAL PRIMARY SCHOOL TEACHER: A STRUCTURALLY AMBIGUOUS POSITION

The sociological study of the relationship to education among rural families in northern Mozambique points to the crucial importance of redefining the predominantly "extractive" function of schooling, as described by Robert Serpell. However, Serpell's proposed redefinition in terms of "accountability" of the local school and of formal education to the local community is problematic, as he himself recognises in his recent book on the significance of schooling in Africa (Serpell 1993). I will point to one constraint, that of the position of the rural teacher as a cultural mediator. The discussion is based on a recent study of primary school teachers in Mozambique, in which 35 teachers in three provinces of the country were interviewed (Baloi and Palme 1996), and on a number of exploratory interviews with rural teachers, peasant families, and representatives of the traditional power structure in a matrilineal community in the Nampula province (a more remote community than the one referred to previously).

The social image of the Mozambican primary school teacher is typically dualistic. On the one hand, he (almost all rural primary teachers are, for social reasons, male) is often presented as a hero in the development process, fulfilling his modernising mission under harsh and unfavourable conditions. On the other hand, he is perceived as a poor and badly educated representative of modern society and given most of the blame for the shortcomings of primary education. Probably this dualistic perception in itself expresses a social-class-related contempt on the part of the urban middle class and national elite.

The study showed that almost all male primary teachers are of peasant origin. With their relatively high educational level, currently grade 6 or more, they often represent an exception in the family of origin and hold a position of responsibility in the family network, taking care of the younger family members.

Because of his ascending social trajectory, the group of origin often invests a collective expectancy in the teacher, hoping that he will improve its living conditions through his connection to the modern world, the world of the *akunya*. In view of the present unfavourable economic situation of teachers, such hopes are very rarely satisfied. However, even if the rural teacher does not have the economic means to meet such demands, this is partly compensated for by the social and symbolic capital he possesses, being regarded as an educated man who deserves respect. The rural teacher continues to be the most important mediator between the rural world and its inhabitants and the modern world, functioning both as interpreter and messenger.

But if the primary teacher is respected in the rural community for his educational and cultural level, modern society tends to accord him disrespect for the same reason. Being of modest social origin, holding a modest educational diploma, and receiving a low salary, the primary teacher does not meet the criteria for social distinction in modern society. This ambiguous position may explain the social frustration from which so many teachers suffer. The educational and cultural capital that grants him his respected position in rural society represents a relatively weak asset in the modern world that confers this same capital. In other words, the rural primary school teacher is expected to exert a social power or influence that he does not possess.

The frustration experienced by so many primary teachers also stems from the gradual degradation of their material conditions during the last 15 years. Current salaries are so low that additional income sources are necessary in order to survive. The dramatic poverty imposed on rural areas by the recent civil war has also destroyed the old system of local community support to teachers. As a result, the primary teacher, with his reduced salary and without support from the local community, sees the whole social definition of his identity at stake when he is obliged to face his pupils wearing ragged trousers and badly worn shoes.

In fact, the question of clothes crystallizes much of the typically intermediary position of the rural teacher. Teachers who were interviewed stressed the importance of dressing in a civilised manner even under harsh conditions. Wearing a clean shirt and ironed trousers was one means of maintaining social distance from the surrounding peasant society, as was the civilised use of Portuguese that teachers aspired to. This corporal relationship to the world clearly expresses one fundamental aspect of the position of the rural teacher, namely that of being the farthest outpost of modern society and its legitimate culture, language, and values. Defending the correct use of Portuguese, a language that they themselves badly mastered, and insisting on performing classroom rituals in the local school in a basically unsympathetic environment, these teachers in a sense fought barbarism on behalf of a modern civilisation, in which they themselves ironically are to be found at the bottom of the hierarchy.[5]

However, their role as defender of civilisation is only one aspect of the position of the rural primary school teacher. Being themselves of peasant origin and living in an almost entirely rural environment, all teachers were at the same time firmly integrated into the rural community. Marrying locally, they were obliged to respect the rules of behaviour in the matrilineal society. Most teachers had, for example, not been authorized by the *humu*, the head, of their wives' family to move their spouses and children out of their family's area of influence. The family's incompatibility with the modern education system, in which teachers are regularly transferred from one school and area to another, and the organisation of matrilineal society thus often imposed on the teachers a form of bachelorhood and isolation. In their own extended families, on the side of their mother, they would also have to submit to the authority of the elected *humu*. Teachers who had accumulated respect in their families of origin would also after retirement be likely candidates for becoming *wahumu* (plural form). As already indicated, they also continued to share most of the religious and so-called animistic beliefs of their community.

The structurally ambiguous position of the primary teacher sheds light on the question of how school knowledge relates to local systems of knowledge. It was obvious that the teachers experienced the conceptual universe of school and modern society as totally separate from that of the traditional society. They also recognized that the modern "scientific" explanations of natural phenomena that they themselves tried to teach in school and that were to be found in teachers' manuals and textbooks probably were incompatible with the explanatory systems used in daily life. Their practical solution to this contradiction was to claim that one conceptual system was valid in school and another in the community, and that, in practice, these systems rarely or never met as antagonistic or competing explanatory systems. They thus resolved the contradiction by operating with a categorisation of "in-school knowledge" and "out-of-school knowledge," which, in fact, also corresponded well to the marginal role of school in the daily life of the local community.

The teachers normally had few reasons to challenge this state of affairs. Since what was taught in school was largely incomprehensible in the local community or else reduced to the surface value of tangible skills such as reading, writing, or counting, no one would dare to question the content of teaching. In fact, the local school—as a physical representation of modern society and its secrets—was regarded almost as foreign territory by peasant parents, who normally feel insecure in these unfamiliar surroundings.

The point to be made here is that serious attempts to culturally adapt teaching to local needs and to culturally and linguistically determined conceptual systems would demand a new definition of the role and position of the primary school teacher in relation to the local community and its social structures and practices. In one particular area, school teaching could involve important local beliefs and practices, namely in sex education. Being well aware of the social turbulence that would follow, teachers confessed that they deliberately avoided teaching such subject matter and strongly advised that it should not be part of the curriculum. Family heads (*mahumu*) and local kings (*mamwene*) also confirmed that most leading representatives of the traditional rural community would react violently to the introduction of sex education in school.

Peasants declared that they would welcome the school dealing with basic aspects of community life, such as sanitary and health problems. So striving for cultural adaptation of school teaching to local culture and needs does not necessarily involve conflict with the local community. The question is rather to what extent and by which means the role of the local primary school teacher and principal can be redefined so as to promote a fruitful new relationship with the local community. It seems obvious that in such a process, the rural primary school teacher himself represents an irreplaceable asset insofar as he normally possesses a profound and indispensable knowledge of the local community, that is, of language, conceptual systems, and social organisation.

On the other hand many obstacles and challenges remain. First, the primary school teacher himself must be assisted in redefining his conception of school knowledge and its relationship to other conceptual systems. Liberating teachers' cultural competence and turning it into a resource in school development would imply that the hierarchically structured education system itself—from the donor agencies and national education officers to regional education directorates and teacher training colleges—is able to recognise and respect both the complexity and the importance of regionally differing cultural systems, so as to promote such aspects in curriculum development, the writing of teaching and learning materials, and the design of pre- and in-service training. Second, the cross-cultural communicability between supposedly "modern" knowledge systems and "traditional" or local ones would need to be explored in practice. If we, with Robin Horton (Horton 1993), regard traditional beliefs and conceptualisations not as pure products of fantasy, but as explanatory systems that are quite functional in their context and in this sense not different in nature from those of modern science, modern concepts would have to be negotiated in relation to these alternative explanations. The difficult social aspect of such a negotiation is that different groups in the local community would tend to differ substantially in what they would accept, and consequently the process of negotiating would tend to create new social tensions. The authority to possess knowledge in specific areas is socially conferred and normally strictly regulated, as is the specific authority that knowledge confers to its holder. The cautious rural primary school teacher would never dream of interfering in religious affairs or even pronouncing on beliefs or practices with which only the properly initiated members of the local community could possibly deal. Third, any attempt to adapt the content of teaching to local needs and local conceptual systems would have to face the problem of convincingly showing that school knowledge really does have value in the local community. For example, primary school teachers may not be able to offer any school-based knowledge that is worthwhile in, for example, improving agriculture. Fourth, a pedagogy based on a new definition of the role of the learner, for example by expecting pupils to actively seek information from parents or other adults or to form their own opinion on various topics, is likely to come into conflict with the socially accepted view of children. In many rural settings, school-aged children are not expected to address adults or elders on their own at all, and certainly not to scrutinize or question their conceptual beliefs. Finally, a new definition of school knowledge and teaching would obviously have to address expectations of what should happen in school at all. Rural families' understanding of teaching tends to be conservative; school should teach their children to read and write in the official language, not to spend time on vernaculars or on subject matter that is better dealt with outside school.

CONCLUSION: "CULTURE" AND EDUCATIONAL IMPROVEMENT

What is needed, above all, at the various levels of the education system, is a greater awareness of cultural aspects of teaching and learning. Without such an awareness, it is highly unlikely that national curricula will ever be more fruitfully adapted to the conditions of teaching, that teaching and learning materials will be developed that are operational in the classroom, or that pre- and in-service training programmes will be able to address the key problems of education.

At the national level, the urban upper middle class that dominates state administration would have to be manoeuvred into a position in which the defence of its privileged position does not necessarily imply a suppression of a cultural competence that goes beyond the cultural capital currently held by—and unifying—the national elite itself. This applies perhaps above all to the question of language policies in education. One of the main obstacles to the promotion of bilingual education programmes is probably that they tend to be perceived as a potential threat to the position of Portuguese as an absolute criterion for social selection.

The recognition of Mozambican languages as a legitimate source of cultural capital would create some uncertainty as regards the definition of social hierarchies.

The current strong trend of inculcating the national elites in the education sector, including the small research community, with the models celebrated by the donor community—survey techniques, statistical analyses at macro level, internationally produced and imported instruments such as the IEA assessment programme (Vedder 1994)—must be balanced by a donor input recognising and encouraging other kinds of investments more specifically oriented towards elucidating the national cultural complexity that is influencing primary teaching (Serpell 1993). At one level, this simply means spending more money on exploring linguistic and cultural conditions for successful teaching[6] and on experimental pilot projects linked to curriculum development and pre- and in-service training. In assessment, this means developing a national assessment competence designed to identify weaknesses in curricula, teaching materials, and teaching, against the specific cultural and linguistic realities of the country.

When the quality of education and teaching is discussed, one fundamental question is normally omitted, namely, what is the role of social agents who define not only how educational policy is developed, but also what constitutes legitimate ways of thinking about and discussing educational matters? For an extremely poor country like Mozambique, chances may be small for the poorly developed national elite to create a national competence that goes beyond the need to satisfy today's definitions of what are the legitimate problems of education. The tendency is for the national elite—if this sociologically vague terminology can be accepted—to orient itself primarily to the small modern sector and the international donor community, given that the world of the donors is the most visible landscape. It is very unlikely that a large academic field, as in Western countries, will exist in the near future in which various traditions can exist and develop and within which young researchers and future education officers can be trained and develop an identity. Even if, today, quality is on the agenda, it is unlikely that the selection mechanisms of those who will deal with educational questions in future will support the kind of investments that are needed for the development of a real national competence in this respect. Such a competence would imply profound knowledge of the particularities of regionally different national languages and cultures, as well as interest in and respect for low-status primary school teachers and their problems. This kind of knowledge is not likely to become a criterion for the selection of elites. Indeed, the acculturation effects that are so obvious and visible in the national education system—the experience of becoming different by and through education and the entrance into modern, "civilized" society (the *akunya* effect)—combined with the requirement to adapt to the world of the donor-ruled elite, favour other basic qualities. After all, forgetting or suppressing one's cultural origin and opening oneself to the language, the values, and the ways of thinking and being of the really dominating culture—that of management, statistics, English, planning—produces an African copy of the organisational culture of the dominating donor agencies so necessary for their management of education in Africa.

NOTES

[1] The textbook evaluation was undertaken at the initiative of the Mozambican Ministry of Education and funded by the Swedish Authority for International Development (SIDA). The research team involved researchers from the Mozambican National Institute for Education Development (INDE), the Stockholm Institute of Education, the Center for Research on Bilingualism at Stockholm University, and the Department for Teacher Training and Didactics at Gothenburg University. The main results are summarized in Palme (1997), Hyltenstam and Stroud (1997), and Kilborn (1997). These reports are also available in Portuguese versions in the INDE research reports series *Cadernos de pesquisa* (INDE, Maputo, Mozambique).

[2] A strikingly open form of classroom ritual is the often criticised, but much used, chorus answers. In normal Mozambican primary school classrooms, pupils repeatedly confirm that they are present, that they are listening, and that they understand by saying "sim!" ("yes!") or "não!" ("no!") in response to the teacher's explanations, often encouraged to do so by a rhetorical question from the teacher (for example "Estão a perceber?" "Do you understand?"). Another common form of ritual confirmation that everything is going well is when teachers pause before uttering the last word of a sentence, so that pupils can fill in the missing word (or missing end of a word). In this case the missing word is normally evident from the context, so that pupils do not have to listen carefully to the meaning of what is being said to be able to produce it. When, as sometimes happens, the correct answer is not known or evident from the context, at least one or two of the best pupils or of the repeaters will know what kind of answer is required. When the teacher repeats the question, everybody, just through listening to these pupils, will know the expected answer. Yet another form is a purely rhetorical question which requires either a confirmative chorus answer ("Sim!") or a nonconfirma-

tive one ("Não!"). In such cases, the pure intonation used by the teacher indicates whether the answer should be confirmative or nonconfirmative. Thus, pupils can participate in the ritual without understanding much or anything of the content of what is being said.

[3] More profound cultural factors determining school learning, such as the culturally framed conceptualisations of education and learning among specific ethnic groups discussed, for example, by Serpell (1993) or Riesmann (1990), are not discussed here. The Mozambican studies referred to were more limited in scope and did not directly address such questions.

[4] Literally, "a Portuguese speaking person."

[5] A similar structural position is held by the teacher training colleges in a way that threatens to turn them into obstacles for any development programme aimed at improving primary education. The colleges primarily recruit students and instructors who have been excluded from secondary school and higher education, and who have high social ambitions—becoming a teacher candidate or an instructor also keeps the door open to future studies. Hence, they tend to develop a contempt for low-prestige primary teaching. Interviewed instructors usually understood their present condition as temporary, and further emphasized that their role was to give the necessary "theoretical" foundations for sound teaching, not to inform the candidates on how practical teaching could be done. Thus, reproducing the division between "theory" and "practice," they also managed to free the social image of their own profession and position from the suspicion of being in any sense close to that of primary school teachers.

[6] Even though some of the trends in school effectiveness research lately have come to acknowledge the fundamental importance of context-related social and cultural differences between schools (Proudford and Baker 1994), the statistical means and simplistic categories to which educational realities tend to be reduced in this kind of approach makes it rather useless for qualitative improvement, for example through pre- and in-service training of teachers. However, since macro-level research of this kind perfectly corresponds to the worldview of many educational planners and decision makers and since school effectiveness traders are not absent from the market, school effectiveness research obviously has become a growing business in developing countries. Since the field of educational research in low-income countries is so limited, this new importation is often not balanced or tempered by other research traditions.

REFERENCES

Baloi, O., and M. Palme. 1996. *Vocação ou exclusão. Um estudo sobre o professor primário recém-formado* (Vocation or Exclusion? A Study of the Recently Trained Primary School Teacher). *Cadernos de pesquisa* 11. Maputo: INDE.

Chiau, S. 1994. *O ensino da Geografia na 5a classe: influência do vivido na representação e aprendizagem de alguns conceitos.* (Geography Teaching in Grade 5: The Influence of the Living-Experience on the Understanding and Learning of Some Concepts). *Cadernos de pesquisa* 6. Maputo: INDE.

Dinerman, A. 1994. "In Search of Mozambique: The Imaginings of Christian Geffray in La cause des armes au Mozambique. Anthropologie d'une guerre civile." *Journal of Southern African Studies*, 20(4): 569–586.

Fuller, B. 1991. *Growing Up Modern. The Western State Builds Third-World Schools.* New York: Routledge.

Fuller, B., and P. Clarke. 1994. "Raising School Effects While Ignoring Culture? Local Conditions and the Influence of Classroom Tools, Rules and Pedagogy." *Review of Educational Research* 64(1): 119–157.

Geffray, C. 1990. *Ni père, ni mère. Critique de la parenté: le cas makhuwa.* Paris: Seuil.

Geffray, C. 1991. *La cause des armes au Mozambique. Anthropologie d'une guerre civile.* Paris: Karthala.

Hewson, P., and M. Hewson. 1984. "The Role of Conceptual Conflict in Conceptual Change and the Design of Science Instruction." *Instructional Science* 13: 1–13.

Hewson, M. 1988. "The Ecological Context of Knowledge: Implications for Learning Science in Developing Countries," *Curriculum Studies* 20: 317–326.

Horton, R. 1993. *Patterns of Thought in Africa and the West. Essays on Magic, Religion and Science.* Cambridge: Cambridge University Press.

Hyltenstam, K., and C. Stroud. 1998. *Final Report and Recommendations from the Evaluation of Teaching Materials for Lower Primary Education in Mozambique. II. Language Issues.* Research Report Series, Sociology of Education and Culture. Uppsala: Uppsala University.

Januário, F., M. Jasso, and O. Popov. 1998. *Contextual and Conceptual Framework for Understanding Primary Science Curriculum in Mozambique.* Research Report Series, Sociology of Education and Culture. Uppsala: Uppsala University.

Kilborn, W. 1998. *Final Report and Recommendations from the Evaluation of Teaching Materials for Lower Primary Education in Mozambique. III.*

Mathematics. Research Report Series, Sociology of Education and Culture. Uppsala: Uppsala University.

Linha, C., M. Palme, and C. Xerinda. 1997. *As concepções das crianças e o ensino de Ciências Naturais* (Children's Conceptions and the Teaching of Science). *Cadernos de pesquisa* 21. Maputo: INDE.

Palme, M. 1993. *The Meaning of School. Repetition and Drop Out in the Mozambican Primary School*. Education Division Documents, 60. Stockholm: Sida.

Palme, M. 1998. *Final Report and Recommendations from the Evaluation of Teaching Materials for Lower Primary Education in Mozambique. I. General Issues*. Research Report Series, Sociology of Education and Culture. Uppsala: Uppsala University.

Peacock, A. 1995. "Access to Science Learning for Children in Rural Africa." *International Journal for Science Education* 17(2): 149–166.

Proudford, C., and R. Baker. 1994. "Looking at School Improvement from a Contextual Perspective." *School Organisation* 14(1): 21–35.

Riesmann, P. 1990. "The Formation of Personality in Fulani Ethnopsychology." In *Personhood and Agency. The Experience of Self and Other in African Society*, eds. M. Jackson and I. Karp. Uppsala Studies in Cultural Anthropology 14. Uppsala: Almqist & Wiksell International.

Serpell, R. 1993. *The Significance of Schooling. Life-Journeys in an African Society*. Cambridge: Cambridge University Press.

Stroud, C. 1996. "The Development of Metropolitan Languages in Post-Colonial Contexts: Language Contact and Language Change and the Case of Portuguese in Maputo." *Nordic Journal of Linguistics* 19: 183–214.

Vedder, P. 1994. "Global Measurement of the Quality of Education: A Help to Developing Countries?" *International Review of Education* 40(1) 5–17.

CHAPTER 15

Economic Imperatives and Cultural Discontinuities in Science Education

A View from the Solomon Islands

JOHN LOWE

Coming from a Third World country, how can I not appreciate how applied science has helped to curtail malaria, eradicate smallpox, reduce infant mortality, enable double cropping and the green revolution? But neither can I at the same time be unaware of or insensitive to the fact that these same benefits have taken their toll of cultural and social costs and unanticipated dislocating effects.

(TAMBIAH 1990, 154)

SCIENCE, DEVELOPMENT, AND SCIENCE EDUCATION

Science and technology are almost invariably afforded a central place in the development plans and policies of developing countries. This in turn leads to the identification of science as a central concern in education policy (World Bank 1995, 80). The emphasis on science and technology in the development process arose, at least initially, from an interpretation of development in terms of economic growth that would depend largely on industrialisation and the "modernisation" of agriculture. Both of these strategies for economic growth were seen to be dependent on science-based technology which would require a cadre of highly trained specialists for its introduction, adaptation, and, later, its development. Within education systems, these concerns translated into what Ware (1992) describes as the "first wave" of science curriculum development. This emphasised science as a body of theory and facts and was primarily intended to meet the needs of those who would go on to a scientific or technological career.

At the time of this first wave, some 30 to 40 years ago, the dominant paradigm in development thinking was that of modernisation. While the introduction of "modern" economic practices and structures is a key part of this paradigm, it also stresses the need for "modern" value systems and attitudes among the population at large—or at least among that part which is to be in the vanguard of development (Webster 1995). Derived largely from Weber's characterisation of modernity as increased rationality, modernisation theory sees the development of both institutional and personal rationality as an essential part of the development process (Moore 1977). Science (together with mathematics) is commonly perceived as the epitome of rationality in the cognitive domain and thus it made sense to extend the teaching of science to all—certainly all who reached secondary school and, increasingly, those who received any formal schooling at all. This, it was claimed, would help to establish the broad base of "rational" attitudes and ways of thinking about and interacting with the world seen as essential for modernisation.

This trend was further reinforced by a recognition that the successful expansion of an economy based on increased utilisation of science-based technology requires a supportive environment among the population as a whole; that some degree of scientific literacy is essential among the consumers of this technology as well as its producers, if it is to take root (APEID 1975; Chisman 1984; Medvitz 1985; UNESCO 1974). The term "scientific literacy" became commonly used to signify some level of scientific understanding and knowledge that it was felt desirable for all to have, although its precise meaning was rarely defined (Miller 1983). There was a move within science education to emphasise processes and skills rather than knowledge. These, it was felt, would be transferable to the learners' daily lives and be more relevant than a knowledge of scientific facts and theories alone. The aims of science education began increasingly to be seen in terms of changing attitudes, developing "scientific" ways of thinking, and promoting a "scientific worldview." By the late 1980s this, together with other influences, was to encourage a "second wave" of science curriculum development that emphasised science for all, science in society, and processes rather than knowledge (Ware 1992).

But the modernisation paradigm within which science had established its central role in development had become increasingly challenged and rejected during the 1970s: among other reasons, as being an attempt to impose a Western model of development, with associated cultural norms, on the rest of the world (Hettne 1995). To a large extent, however, science escaped this "cultural imperialism" criticism. Even among those alternatives that challenged modernisation, notably the dependency critiques, science retained its prestigious, central role. This is probably in part attributable to its being perceived (and "sold') as a-cultural, as being a body of "objective" facts discovered by culture-free, rational methods of investigation; but it also reflects the fact that both modernisers and their critics still thought of development almost exclusively in economic terms, and the economic transformative power of science and its technological products could not be ignored. And so it was convenient to see science not as a Western cultural artefact, but as part of a global human heritage (Bajah 1987; Odhiambo 1993).

Increasingly, however, the interpretation of "development" was broadening and to some extent detaching itself from economic growth (Corbridge 1995, 10). An expanding economy was accepted as essential for development but also as being less than the whole picture. Concerns over economic and social justice, gender issues, cultural continuity and integrity, environmental degradation, sustainability, individual and community empowerment all became part of the development debate and development policies. It is interesting to note how science education has been enlisted in support of many of these wider interpretations of development; it has retained the central role claimed earlier on the grounds of its contribution to economic growth, but now with a range of new justifications too. Perhaps much of this stems from the notion that "knowledge is power" and scientific knowledge represents one of the most potent sources of power (Host 1995). Reflecting the Weberian roots of the modernisation paradigm, Apter (1987, 23) has suggested that a "scientific attitude" is now seen as "the functional equivalent of the Protestant ethic" that was credited with being the driving force of European capitalist development. Thus, for example, it is argued that scientific knowledge is essential for effective participation by individuals and communities in controlling the processes of change that are enveloping them and that frequently derive from the introduction of new technology. It is also argued that a knowledge of science better enables these communities and individuals to manage and protect their own natural environments (UNESCO 1983). This wider view of the nature of development, with its various claims on the usefulness of science, provided another moving force behind Ware's second wave of science curriculum projects.

Given these increased expectations of science education, it is not really surprising that during the 1980s it began to be recognised as a cultural process, as a means of producing significant cultural change (Aikenhead 1996; Maddock 1981). The only surprise is that this recognition was so long in coming. Although a key purpose of science education had been to encourage changes in attitudes and ways of viewing the world that could only be interpreted as cultural changes, it was convenient to preserve the a-cultural myth of science, to see it as somehow belonging "outside" culture because of its "value-free," "objective" rationality. And this remains the "weak" form of the recognition of the cultural nature of science education: to see it as the promotion of part of a general human heritage rather than a product of a particular, Western European, culture.

But there is a "strong" form, too, which rejects the divorcing of modern science from the particular cultural context in which it has developed. Though the contributions of the Muslim and possibly the Chinese world may be recognised, this version of the cultural nature of modern science emphasises its occidental roots, notably the contributions of ancient Greece and renaissance Europe (Graham 1973; Lindberg 1992; Sarton 1948). White (1968), for example, argued that there is a direct line from medieval Western Christian natural theology to modern science and that although science and religion diverged in Western Europe some two centuries ago, an underlying Judaeo-Christian heritage remains a defining driving force in modern science, though rarely recognised by practitioners simply because it has become so embedded and taken for granted. A central element of this heritage is a dichotomy between human beings and nature, with the latter seen as existing purely for exploitation by the former. Modern science and technology have become the means and manifestation of control by human beings over a nature of which they are not a part. The existence and nature of this occidental cultural influence remains disputed and my own position is that it is unlikely that the specific content—the "facts" and theories—of science is significantly influenced, let alone determined, by culture. The cultural influence appears at the deeper levels of attitudes and purposes, which influence the definition of domains of legitimate interest. But as far as the majority of those learning science in school is concerned, it is these broad issues that may ultimately prove more important than the detailed scientific knowledge—a situation which is commonly recognised in the defence of "science for all" courses. Many of the facts and theories taught in science lessons will be forgotten or superseded; but an understanding of the limitations and possibilities of science, of its underlying value orientations and purposes, is of central importance to nonspecialists if they are to feel comfortable with science, to feel empowered by it, and to be able to contribute to development which increasingly relies on the use of science.

We are left with a wide range of expectations of science education, especially at primary and secondary school levels. Its anticipated contribution to economic growth probably accounts for most of the emphasis it receives. This will occur through the development of knowledge and skills in those who will eventually be scientific or technological specialists. For the nonspecialist masses, science education is expected to support economic development through a less clearly defined mechanism of widespread "scientific literacy" and the inculcation of positive attitudes toward science and technology that will promote their acceptance and consumption. There are noneconomic (or less directly economic) goals for science education too. It is seen as a key element in the cultural preparation for modernity through the development of a range of mental traits supposedly characteristic of science: increased rationality of thought, the rejection of superstition, an attitude of critical scepticism, curiosity, empirical investigation, and others. It is also important that these transfer to the learners' everyday lives outside the school setting. Science should be seen as relevant both at the personal and at the community or national level. Science education is further expected to promote a greater awareness and understanding of the natural environment while instilling a sense of empowerment, an acceptance of the possibility of effecting change, and a desire to bring about change.

That these diverse expectations of and claims for science education are commonly made can be confirmed from an examination of educational policy documents produced by countries themselves and by international donor agencies. (See, for example, Schirmer 1987 for a review of science education aims in African countries.) What unfortunately seems to be missing is a solid body of evidence to support them, to indicate that the expectations are realistic and are borne out in practice.

The next part of this chapter is a summary of some research findings relating to these claims about the impact of science education. It was not, and was not intended to be, a detailed study, but rather a preliminary investigation to map out ground for later more detailed study. The account of the findings presented here is necessarily brief. The subjects of the study were students in a secondary school in Honiara, the capital city of Solomon Islands—students between about 12 and 19 years of age and including both those who had already begun to or were intending to specialise in science subjects and those who were or would be nonspecialists. Information on the impact of science education on these students was obtained in a variety of ways: interviews, discussions, questionnaires and other written instruments, and observation. Full details of the data collection methods are given elsewhere (Lowe 1994). Although some observation and discussions were carried out outside the school, the majority of data were collected within the school context. The limitation of this is recognised and discussed later.

SOME IMPACTS OF SCIENCE ON SOLOMON ISLAND STUDENTS

It was not within the scope of the investigation to determine whether science education was meeting the country's economic needs in terms of the supply of trained manpower for science-based occupations. It was known that almost all of those who specialised in science subjects in their last year of the secondary school in question went on to further and higher education in courses intended to prepare them for such occupations, and several others who left school a year earlier did start vocational courses that were technology-related. Furthermore, scholarships for science-based higher education courses, provided by the government to meet its own manpower needs predictions, were all taken up by suitably qualified students. The later progress of these students who began these science- and technology-based career paths, however, is less well known. Anecdotal evidence and limited personal contact with students in later years suggests that there was considerable dropout from science and technology courses, or transfer to nonscience courses, among those who entered various universities, but the full extent of this was unknown. Serious shortages of qualified personnel for scientific and technological posts were obvious in many occupational spheres, perhaps none more so than science teaching, which stubbornly remained dominated by expatriates.

The students' own perceptions of the economic importance of science education, both in national and personal terms, were investigated. There was almost unanimous support for the idea that science could contribute significantly to national development, but most students interviewed were not very clear about the nature of this contribution. Development was generally interpreted as an improvement in living conditions, most notably through the provision of better medical care; and medicine was the most commonly given example of the useful application of scientific knowledge. A few of the older students, especially those who were specialising in science, seemed to have an image of a more technological society but, beyond the mention of computers and communications, the specifications of this society were vague. Some students did refer to the importance of science to agriculture through improved crops and pesticides.

Almost all interviewed students were able to suggest modern-sector occupations that required a knowledge of science, and a list of some 30 such occupations was generated. At the personal level, about one-third of over 400 students completing a written questionnaire aspired to jobs that they felt required some knowledge of science, these being predominantly as engineers or mechanics (boys) and in medicine (boys and girls). (It should be noted that another third had no specific job aspirations.) It was clear, however, that the perceived personal importance—and popularity—of school science was only rarely derived from its future occupational relevance: only about 10 percent of students interviewed suggested that their interest in science stemmed from its potential usefulness to future employment.

A point which quickly emerged in interviews was that there was a third level at which economic relevance should be considered, that of the local community. Several students indicated in interviews that their occupational aspirations were strongly influenced by parents, relatives, and the broader home community. Three occupations appeared to have particularly high community value: doctor, lawyer, and engineer. Any individual who attains one of these posts would be expected to use his (usually) or her position and skills for the benefit of the home community. This was quite acceptable to the students who felt a strong sense of community identity and obligation. Thus a science education could have particular importance if there were a locally perceived need for a doctor or engineer (although "engineer" often meant "mechanic," and vice versa). A strong impression was gained in interviews, discussions, and through observations in and out of school that the community—one's *wantoks*, in Pidjin—was a much more important unit than the nation when it came to questions of development.

To look only at future waged occupational aspirations, however, misses aspects of the economic significance of science education that were stressed by the girls in particular. Just about all of the girls anticipated that they would become mothers and would be responsible for the health and nutrition of the family. The boys too, in general, accepted that these would be the girls' responsibility. The usefulness of science as a preparation for this role (which is, after all, an economic as well as a social role) was recognised much more widely than for waged employment. This applied, of course, almost exclusively to biology rather than the physical sciences. Girls who aspired to be nurses (a more common aspiration than a doctor for girls) sometimes commented that an additional advantage to this option was that their training would also be useful in caring for their families' health. Several girls further anticipated that at some stage in their future life they would be involved in agriculture, even if only in looking after an urban vegetable garden, and felt that biology once again provided useful knowledge to assist them in this. For some girls, and for an occasional boy too, agriculture remained a safety net in case they failed to find modern sector employment, and a scientific knowledge of plant growth was highlighted as a particularly useful legacy of their science education. Boys were more likely than girls to see future involvement in agriculture in terms of waged employment, such as an agricultural extension worker, but even this was rare.

In a more general sense of "useful," rather than the strictly economic, most students responded positively when asked if the science they had learned at school had been or would be useful in their everyday lives, but few were able to give examples of this usefulness. The examples that they did give were mostly drawn from biology and the term "personally relevant" is probably a better label for these than "useful." A knowledge of the workings of their own bodies, together with nutrition and the causes and prevention of disease, were the science topics that students most frequently claimed to be personally relevant.

For the great majority of students, the attraction of science lay in its products rather than its processes, in scientific knowledge and the practical use to which it could be put, rather than the methods by which it was obtained. When asked how scientists carry out their work, almost all students thought that they spend their time performing experiments or making observations. These activities were known to be the source of "theories" and new knowledge (but only rarely of concrete products), although the nature of the link between theory and experiment was in general only vaguely articulated. The usefulness of scientific knowledge was more important to the majority than its origins, but the "proof" of this knowledge through practical demonstration and application was of great significance, and resonated with the pragmatism of traditional Melanesian epistemology. As one student put it: "Well, it's practical. We use it. We test it. If we learn about it and we don't test it . . . it's not really . . . real, true to me." Although scientific knowledge was recognised as powerful and useful, the students felt this utility was more likely to be fulfilled in the hands of others, not the scientists themselves. Almost no students expressed an interest in a career in pure science; it was the engineering and medical applications of scientific knowledge that attracted them, even the most senior and successful of the science specialists.

It was suggested in the previous section that a further economic role expected of science education is the establishment of widespread scientific literacy and positive attitudes towards science among those who are not directly involved in science- or technology-related occupations. The modernisation paradigm sees these as essential support for the development of a modern economy, and goes further to claim that the widespread adoption of a scientific worldview is essential for thorough modernisation. As the above account indicates, the students in this study were generally very positive about the value and usefulness of scientific knowledge, at national, community and personal levels. They could also certainly claim at least a minimal level of scientific literacy, if this be judged by their performance in national examinations (and international examinations for the older science specialists). Although those who obtained the best results tended to go on to specialise in science, the standard among future nonspecialists was also high, and positive attitudes to science were common to almost all. Science lessons were commonly ranked as among the most enjoyable and few interviewed students felt school science in general was particularly difficult.

On further investigation, however, it was clear that there was a danger of reading too much into this widespread positive response to science. It is important to distinguish school science lessons from science itself. The former were enjoyed, but at least some of this enjoyment arose from the practical emphasis in science lessons that provided a contrast with most other subjects. This practical emphasis also did much to promote the validity of scientific knowledge in the students' eyes, but it seems that ultimately a large proportion of the students are left in awe of science and those who practise it. It was very common for students, when asked about their images of scientists, to refer to them as being exceptionally clever, as being geniuses, even as omniscient: "He will know everything that . . . will happen in the future." Although among older students this attitude was more prevalent among the nonspecialists in science, it was also noted among specialists. This is perhaps easier to understand when one remembers that few of these specialists regarded themselves as "scientists" as such, but rather as future technologists keen to learn useful scientific knowledge.

There were some students who were clearly excited by the opportunities for understanding that science opened up. For a few it was not just the "facts" of science that were important but a possibility of explanation that science offered:

> Especially when I am small I just thought, "Oh, these things are coming from this and this." But when . . . say for example acids and things like that . . . how tides move. Especially those things, say, for example, the rainbow. I may have thought about it as the Bible said, "God created this and that." And when I came to form 1, we learn about the . . . evaporate and how the water rises and caused by the wind blowing, caused the rain. Therefore I know and understand.

But such students, who seemed to feel personally empowered by their contact with science, were few, and it would be wrong to assume that there was unequivocal acceptance of the worldview of science and the exclusive validity of the knowledge it generated. In a written questionnaire on various aspects of attitudes to science, it was in items dealing with its epistemological validity that science received by far the weakest support: items such as, "Science tells us the truth about the world around us," and "Custom ideas and explanations can often be trusted more than science." The students were clearly accepting the usefulness of science and the economic importance of science-based development, but they were much less sure about science at a more fundamental level, at the level that can usefully be seen as one of worldview.

This apparent inability of science to penetrate to the level of the students' worldview—despite their apparent "scientific literacy"—was further supported by a variety of written and oral investigations of their belief in magic and the worldview that underpins it. This is presented elsewhere in some detail that will not be repeated here (Lowe 1995). It is sufficient to state that a belief in the existence and efficacy of a broad range of magic was widespread among the students, and that they accepted the traditional world of spirits (most significantly, ancestral spirits) that were commonly seen to be a source of much of this magic. The involvement of these spirits in daily activities and occurrences was widely accepted and several students gave accounts of personal experiences with them. This acceptance of magic and associated traditional interpretations of natural events did not seem to be influenced by achievement in school science or recognition of the transformative power of scientific knowledge. The most effective challenge to magic came from Christianity, not science. In the most commonly noted form of this challenge, Christianity is observed to triumph over magic and its associated traditional practices through its greater power, but it supports rather than denies the worldview of traditional belief systems: namely, one in which the ultimate source of power in the physical world is spiritual. Thus, acceptance of Christianity allows the believer to be "modern" without abandoning basic principles of the traditional worldview. Perhaps surprisingly, the adoption of Christianity allows considerable cultural continuity at the level of worldview: "Hence the conflict between the traditional religions and the so-called 'world religions' is not so much a conflict between radically different world-views as a conflict over what to worship and what to eschew within a single pantheon" (Horton 1982, 213).

Acceptance of the validity of the scientific worldview, on the other hand, entails the rejection of the very basis of traditional culture. Christianity forbids the eating of the fruit of the tree of magic, and may try to lop off major branches, but it leaves intact the roots that are the roots of traditional culture. Acceptance of the mechanical, materialistic worldview of modern, Western science, on the other hand, demands that the whole tree be uprooted. Furthermore, science suffers from a form of incompleteness that troubles neither Christianity nor traditional religions. Ultimately, it cannot guarantee the truth of its own statements but only argue for the superiority of its methods. It promises unsettling, perpetual change and an impersonal vision of the world that offers no exception to the individual. As such, it is difficult to embrace. Rather, it is treated with the respect due to its power, used when needs be, but ignored when possible.

MODERNISATION REVISITED: "US" AND "THEM"

The children who were the subject of the above study would appear to present a paradox. They enjoy school science and feel they largely understand it. They do well in the subject and could, within the common usage of the term, be described as scientifically literate, for their age at least. They recognise the material and economic power of scientific knowledge and they see its application as key to the future development of their society. And yet, they also commonly endorse a view of the world which can be considered fundamentally antithetical to science.

The first point to be made is that the majority of students with whom this situation was discussed had no great sense of any tension, any contradiction in their holding apparently conflicting sets of ideas about the world. It would be easy to say that this was because they simply had not thought about it, but this does not do them justice. Though rarely able to point to specific areas of conflict, they were aware that science and religion and science and magical explanations were often in disagreement. The absence of any awareness of tension within themselves suggests that they had, without conscious effort, devised mechanisms for defusing it. There was very little evidence that students attempted to fuse science and magic/religion into a unified worldview, and almost none that they totally rejected one or the other. The commonest strategy seemed to involve a division of the world into domains of applicability of each of the potentially conflicting worldviews. In some cases, these domains are identifiable as particular phenomena or aspects of the physical world. Thus, electricity is in the domain of science only. Illness is carved into separate domains, of which the largest is now claimed by scientific medicine but with custom magic seen as the only possible source and cure of certain afflictions. For many students, questions of the origins of the universe and of mankind in particular are the domain of religion, not science.

But the "domainisation" to which I refer is more complex than a division of the physical world. The domains of applicability are related to the social and physical environment of actions or events, and to their purposes. When students talked to me of experiences with ancestral spirits, for example, these were much more likely to have taken place "back home," rather than in the urban setting of the school. Spirits could visit one in dreams in Honiara, but one was much less, if at all, likely to have direct dealings with them there. Although students did occasionally resort to "custom" medicine when at school, they claimed that the chances of being the victims of magic were greater at home. When out in rural areas with the students, I noticed how even those brought up in town appeared to be more sensitive to "custom" ideas and explanations, how they were much more wary of bringing misfortune upon themselves through incorrect observance of taboos than they were within the school. Despite minor incursions of Western technology, the rural areas of Solomon Islands remain largely traditional-with-Christianity in their social organisation. And this social organisation is both rooted in and supportive of traditional ontology and epistemology. Several students talked of the changes in behaviour that they were obliged to make when they went back to their home villages. For most of them, these changes were made automatically; they slipped between the two sets of behavioural expectations quite naturally. As already indicated, they appeared to slip comfortably between worldviews. Just as they have two repertoires of behaviour easily available, they also have two sets of understandings about the nature of the world, between which they can change when the social circumstances demand.

These observations pose some important questions about the relationship between science education and development as proposed by modernisation theory and largely supported by national development policies. Perhaps we need first to ask whether science education can bring about the sort of fundamental changes in attitudes and worldview that are deemed necessary for social and economic modernisation. The limited evidence presented here suggests that the process is not as clean-cut as may be hoped. Science education may certainly expose children to alternative ways of seeing the world, and they may become quite fluent in the use of these alternatives, but we must be wary of reading too much into such fluency. If the cultural context in which science is learned remains distinct from that of the wider society, then it will be a matter of social survival for the children who learn science to be able to switch between alternative worldviews depending on their social and cultural context.

But we must also question whether such fundamental changes in worldview are indeed necessary for development. I suspect that the belief that they are stems from a tendency to dichotomise the world into the modern and the traditional, into "us" and "them." Are the children whose beliefs and understandings have been outlined here really so unique? Certainly there may be remarkable similarities between these Solomon Islanders and children in other developing countries, but there is evidence that these similarities are more widespread than that. Phelan, Davidson, and Cao (1991), for example, have investigated the "multiple worlds" of children in a United States school. In the industrialised countries, the last 15 years or so of science education research have been dominated by investigations into children's understandings of the world that have revealed a vast body of shared conceptions and "alternative frameworks" that are the currency of much out-of-school interaction with the physical world, and which resist attempts to change them through school science teaching. Since these children are from the "modern" world their ideas are not treated as "traditional beliefs," but rather as "common sense" or "life-world knowledge": labels that suggest not only a down-to-earth practicality that merits our respect, but also deny any cultural origins for such knowledge (see Geertz 1983 on the cultural nature of "common sense"). This distinction between a culturally based "traditional knowledge" and an a-cultural "common sense" is part of the process by which we dichotomise the world into the "modern" and the "traditional" (or even, still, the "modern" and the "primitive'). This, in turn, is part of our identity formation, in which "we" are in part defined by the contrast we make between ourselves and an "other."

Much of this research into children's ideas has been driven by educational concerns: how alternative conceptions developed outside the classroom interfere with our attempts to teach the equivalent conceptions within the framework of modern science. The purpose is most frequently to understand how we can better replace "wrong," socially reinforced ideas with the "correct" ideas of science. As a consequence, the research tends to be carried out from within an educational setting: either non-naturistically in written tests, clinical interviews, or contrived practical situations, or through "naturalistic" science class observations. If our concern is with the effectiveness of science education in achieving the economic and cultural goals that are expected of it, I suggest it is just as important to investigate the interaction between school science ideas and the life-world of the students in the everyday situations of their out-of-school lives. For we appear to have remarkably little evidence in support of the grand claims that are made for the impact of science on the individual's interactions with the world. If we wish to observe the impact of school science on students' everyday activities and on the way they view the world in their life outside the classroom, then that is where we must observe and question them.

This perspective is more visible in some of the research into the "public understanding of science" that has attracted interest in the United Kingdom and the United States in recent years, although most of this falls short of the ethnographic approach that I would advocate (Layton et al. 1993). This appears to have been primarily concerned with the understanding of science among adults and as such may be more difficult to relate directly to the impact of science education, but its broad findings are very significant for any consideration of the role of scientific awareness in modernisation. To the great concern of many it has revealed widespread ignorance of science, both content and process, among populations that are supposed to be "modern." For example, Miller summarised his review of survey evidence about Americans and "the scientific approach" by stating that only about 10 percent understood what such an approach entailed, "but a substantially larger proportion did have a higher level of confidence—or faith—in what they perceived to be scientific studies" (Miller 1983, 38). This suggests that a "modern," economically developed society is characterised not by a widespread level of scientific understanding, but rather by a faith in the power of science. To some extent this was what appeared to be happening in the Solomon Island students who saw the scientist as a new shaman, but these students also retained elements of an alternative source of interpretations of the world. Modernisation theory, and its associated lines of thought, maintain that these alternatives must be eradicated in the name of development. It would appear, however, that the models set up by modernisation theory for the developing countries to emulate are but myths and shadows; and if this is the case, the cultural demands of modernisation must be re-examined.

Almost 30 years ago, Lynn White, discussing the ecological damage wrought by a science and technology based on "orthodox Christian arrogance toward nature," suggested that since "the roots of our trouble are so largely religious, the remedy must also be essentially religious, whether we call it that or not" (White 1968, 93). What he had in mind was not a radical revision of the content of science, of its theories and facts (for that will happen anyway), nor of the basic methodology of science, but of its purpose, direction, and rationale; of aspects of the worldview currently associated with science. What science needs is an input from another culture with a radically different way of perceiving the world and mankind's position in it. The hybridisation that lends vigour in plants is urgently needed in a science that has grown so expansively on the roots of one culture but which remains deeply flawed. Perhaps this will come from the Solomon Island students and others like them. I confess to be somewhat wary of the deliberate "harmonisation" approach to the disjunction between scientific and traditional worldviews advocated by, for example, Ogunniyi (1988), believing that a persistence of tension may, in the long term, be beneficial to both non-Western science students and the whole enterprise of science itself. If this is to happen, then we must certainly continue to teach science to all. But we must also be aware of the cultural nature of the exercise, be sensitive to the possibility of committing cultural damage that is both unnecessary and detrimental to the healthy growth of a science that can make meaningful contact with the full range of human cultures, rather than demand their demise.

REFERENCES

Aikenhead, G. S. 1996. "Science Education: Border Crossing into the Subculture of Science." *Studies in Science Education* 27: 1–52.

APEID. 1975. *Science in Basic Functional Education: Philosophy, Approaches, Methods and Materials*. Bangkok: UNESCO, Asian Programme of Educational Innovation for Development.

Apter, D. E. 1987. *Rethinking Development: Modernization, Dependency, and Postmodern Politics*. Newbury Park, CA: Sage.

Bajah, S. T. 1987. "Science for Welfare, Peace and Development: Focus on Africa." *Educafrica* 13: 275–285.

Chisman, D. G. 1984. "Science Education and National Development." *Science Education* 68(5): 563–569.

Corbridge, S. 1995. *Development Studies: A Reader*. London: Edward Arnold.

Geertz, C. 1983. *Local Knowledge*. New York: Basic Books.

Graham, A. C. 1973. "China, Europe and the Origins of Modern Science: Needham's The Grand Titration." In *Chinese Science: Explorations from an Ancient Tradition*, eds. S. Nakayama and N. Sivin. Cambridge, MA: MIT Press.

Hettne, B. 1995. *Development Theory and the Three Worlds*. 2nd ed. Harlow: Longman Scientific and Technical.

Horton, R. 1982. "Tradition and Modernity Revisited." In *Rationality and Relativism*, eds. M. Hollis and S. Lukes. Oxford: Basil Blackwell.

Host, V. 1995. "The Aims of Science Education in the Coming Decades." *Prospects* 25(1): 41–48.

Layton, D., E. Jenkins, S. Macgill, and A. Davey. 1993. *Inarticulate Science? Perspectives on the Public Understanding of Science and Some Implications for Science Education*. Nafferton: Studies in Education Ltd.

Lindberg, D. C. 1992. *The Beginnings of Western Science: The European Scientific Tradition in Philosophical, Religious and Institutional Context, 600 BC to AD 1450*. Chicago and London: University of Chicago Press.

Lowe, J. A. 1994. "Social and Cultural Influences on Students' Responses to Science in a Solomon Islands Secondary School." Unpublished Ph.D. thesis., University of London.

Lowe, J. A. 1995. "The Impact of School Science on the Worldview of Solomon Island Students." *Prospects* 25(4): 653–667.

Maddock, M. N. 1981. "Science Education: An Anthropological Viewpoint," *Studies in Science Education* 8: 1–26.

Medvitz, A.G. 1985. *Problems in the Application of Science Education to National Development*. Nairobi: Institute of Development Studies, University of Nairobi.

Miller, J. D. 1983. "Scientific Literacy: A Conceptual and Empirical Review." *Daedalus* 112(2): 29–48.

Moore, W. E. 1977. "Modernization as Rationalization: Process and Restraints." In *Essays on Economic Development and Cultural Change in Honor of Bert F. Hoselitz*, ed. N. Manning. Chicago: Chicago University Press.

Odhiambo, T. 1993. Address to the International Forum on Scientific and Technological Literacy for All, Paris, 8 July, 1993. Paris: UNESCO.

Ogunniyi, M. 1988. "Adapting Western Science to Traditional African Culture." *International Journal of Science Education* 10(1): 1–9.

Phelan, P., A.L. Davidson, and H.T. Cao. 1991. "Students' Multiple Worlds: Negotiating the Boundaries of Family, Peer, and School Cultures." *Anthropology and Education Quarterly* 22: 224–250.

Sarton, G. 1948. *The Life of Science: Essays in the History of Civilization*. New York: Henry Schuman.

Schirmer, A. 1987. *Science Education: Philosophy, Media Assessment, Teaching and Learning: The Case of African Countries*. Bonn: DSE German Foundation for International Development.

Tambiah, S. J. 1990. *Magic, Science, Religion, and the Scope of Rationality*. Cambridge: Cambridge University Press.

UNESCO. 1974. "Science and Technology in African Development." Conference of Ministers of African States Responsible for the Application of Science and Technology to Development, Dakar, 1974. Paris: UNESCO.

UNESCO. 1983. *Science and Technology and National Development*. Paris: UNESCO.

Ware, S. A. 1992. *Secondary School Science in Developing Countries: Status and Issues*. Washington, DC: World Bank.

Webster, A. 1995. "Modernisation Theory." In *Development Studies: an Introduction Through Selected Readings*, ed. R. Ayres. Dartford, Kent: Greenwich University Press.

White, L. 1968. *Machina ex Deo: Essays in the Dynamism of Western Culture*. Cambridge, MA: Massachusetts Institute of Technology Press.

World Bank. 1995. *Priorities and Strategies for Education: A World Bank Review*. Washington, DC: World Bank.

CHAPTER 16

Cultural Perceptions of the Role of Mathematics and Mathematics Education in Economic Development

Examples from Kenya

FLORENCE KIRAGU NYAMU

Most countries invest heavily in education with the assumption that education is the path to social, political, and economic development. In Kenya, approximately 40 percent of the national budget is spent on education, although there are indications that the government wants to reduce the figure to 30 percent. Many countries are faced with severe economic hardships and hard decisions have to be taken about which type of education is most desirable and who pays for it.

Usually these decisions are made outside the local community, by people who are not the direct users or stakeholders of the system, that is, by the central government, or even by donors as part of their aid agenda. This situation presents difficulties because cultural and societal considerations in the design and delivery of formal education are likely to be less important than economic considerations. Also, if stakeholders are not fully involved in the policy-making process, sustainability may well be a problem. A good example of this situation is the launching of the 8–4–4 (eight years of primary schooling, four years of secondary schooling, and four years of university education) system of education in Kenya in 1985, which was implemented nationally without pilot testing, national debate, or a feasibility study.[1] The policy to implement the system was based on a recommendation made by a presidential working party. The new system promoted a more relevant and vocational curriculum, which caught parents, communities, teachers, and practitioners unawares as they found that they had to raise funds to build and equip workshops and laboratories. Ten years on, there have been numerous complaints from parents, students, teachers, and educationalists that the curriculum is overloaded, children are stressed, and the system has not improved employment opportunities as originally anticipated. Parents are disillusioned, arguing that the 8–4–4 system is expensive and fails to prepare children well for life within Kenyan society.

According to Serpell (1993), the education process, whether formal, nonformal, or informal, is intended to fulfil three purposes, namely to: (a) promote economic progress; (b) transmit culture from one generation to the next; and (c) cultivate children's intellectual and moral development. Ideally, the education process should address these three purposes simultaneously. In practice, however, cultural considerations lack congruence with the economic. One of the reasons for this lack of congruency, particularly in the poorer developing nations, is the fact that these societies have traditional ways of initiating their children into adulthood, the aims of which do not necessarily conform with those of formal schooling. For example, in some parts of Kenya, particularly in the arid and semi-arid areas commonly inhabited by pastoral communities, some parents prefer not to send their children to school, arguing that education will alienate them from their culture. This is particularly true among the Pokot and Marakwet of the northern part of the Rift Valley Province.

Before the onset of formal schooling, "traditional" communities, such as those found throughout Africa, perceived their culture as a way of life that comprised shared meanings, shared norms of behaviour, and common religions and language. For example, among the Kikuyu, the largest ethnic group in Kenya, both girls and boys underwent an initiation ceremony at about age 13 or 14, during which they were educated in all the ways of the society and prepared for their future role as adults. Despite the advent of formal schooling, the home and the community continue to play a role in socializing the young. Before the child enters formal schooling, the aunts, uncles, relatives, and other members of the community share with the young the beliefs and cultural practices of the clan or ethnic group.

If the schooling process does not reinforce the cultural practices and belief systems that the child has already acquired informally, the discrepancy could have lasting implications. For example, it is common these days to hear young men and women treat older people with disrespect by shouting at them or refusing to be reprimanded or corrected, where traditionally older people were treated with respect, acknowledged as more experienced, and therefore in a position to correct the young. In modern society, economic power has become more powerful than sociocultural tradition. Serpell (1993, 2) observes that "economic power attracts prestige, with the result that the cultural practices of economically powerful groups often become a target of emulation by less powerful groups." In post-independence Africa, many African elites have denounced traditional African values and adopted values that have a heavy Western influence. One of the implications of this rejection is that the values imparted through schooling, which is associated with economic empowerment as a result of the link between qualifications and white-collar jobs, have become more important than the socialisation in the home and family environment. Unfortunately, Serpell's suggestion that the schooling process, in addition to promoting economic progress, should be a medium for transmitting culture from one generation to the next and should cultivate children's intellectual and moral development, does not appear to hold in the African context.

In this chapter I propose to take the example of mathematics education to explore how different perceptions of the role of mathematics in economic development reflect these tensions between cultural and economic considerations within the school setting, taking some examples from Kenya. In exploring these perceptions I address four basic questions: What is mathematics and mathematics education? What are the cultural perceptions of the role of mathematics and mathematics education in economic development? What kind of mathematical knowledge is appropriate for whom? And, who should shoulder the costs?

WHAT IS MATHEMATICS AND MATHEMATICS EDUCATION?

Mathematics is considered an important subject in both developed and developing countries. In many countries it is compulsory for all students in primary and secondary school. At higher levels, students studying subjects such as architecture and engineering are usually required to take mathematics as a service subject. In practice, mathematics serves as a "critical filter that successfully inhibits participation in many occupations and in career advancement and change" (Fennema 1990, 2).

> Mathematics is a science, a language, an art, a way of thinking and as Galileo said: The universe stands continually in our gaze, but it cannot be understood unless one first learns to comprehend the language and interpret the characters in which it is written. It is written in the language of mathematics, and its characters are triangles, circles, and other geometric figures, without which it is humanly impossible to understand a single word of it.
>
> (Theoni, cited in Pappas 1989)

Derived from the Greek word *Mathematikos*, from *Mantheim*, meaning "to learn," for the Greeks mathematics represented learning, all of knowledge (Fass and Newman 1975). Fennema (1990, 2) refers to mathematics as a "unique product of human culture" and states that the understanding of this culture enables students to enjoy the beauty of mathematics and hence transmit the culture to future generations. According to Davis and Hersh (1981), there is hardly any society, however primitive, which does not exhibit some rudimentary kind of mathematics. So if, then, mathematics is the language of the universe, an integral part of humanity, and a human activity that is of benefit not only to the individual but to the society as a whole, why does it remain a misunderstood and unappreciated subject? For it is very common to hear adults remember mathematics during their school days with antipathy. Many remember unpleasant experiences and comments like "mathematics is only for the gifted."

In addition to transmitting culture from one generation to another, mathematics education should, if we continue with Serpell's other two purposes of education (1993), cultivate children's intellectual and moral growth and promote economic development. There is no doubt that education makes its greatest contribution to development not when it is reserved for a privileged few, but when it is widely and equitably distributed. The same can be said of mathematics education, for it would make a better contribution to economic development if it were made more available and accessible to all students. The role of mathematics and mathematics education in promoting economic development can be understood in terms of its application in daily life, buying and selling of goods, banking, the calculation of income tax, and so on, as well as the transfer of knowledge acquired through problem solving to other aspects of life such as decision making and a general form of intellectual discipline that emphasizes processes as well as products. This will be examined in the next section.

WHAT ARE THE CULTURAL PERCEPTIONS OF THE ROLE OF MATHEMATICS AND MATHEMATICS EDUCATION IN ECONOMIC DEVELOPMENT?

Each culture has its unique characteristics and expects its youth to study all aspects that enable them to propagate the culture to future generations. One would expect, therefore, that the mathematics taught in schools would reinforce the cultural mathematical knowledge that the students may have acquired during their early childhood socialisation. However, as already explained, this is not the case in African countries.

There is no doubt that cultural factors influence the way students perceive mathematics. For example, there is evidence that differences in cultural practices between the Japanese, Chinese, and American cultures are at the root of differences in academic achievement in East Asia and the United States of America. In a comparative study of learning patterns in mathematics, Stevenson and Stigler (1992, 106) found cultural differences in perception such that the East Asian children perceived themselves as members of a group, saw school as a central part of their lives, and placed emphasis on effort rather than ability as a prerequisite for learning. The American children, however, were socialised to see themselves as individuals, did not consider school as a central part of their lives, and placed emphasis on ability rather than effort. From this research on mathematics learning, they found that Japanese children refused to give up and persisted in solving a problem that had no solution. The cultural perception of the Japanese is, therefore, persistence and the motto seemed to be "work hard and persist." The emphasis on problem solving in Japanese and Chinese mathematics classrooms explains, in part, the observation that East Asian children perform better in mathematics compared to their American counterparts.

The tests given by Stevenson and Stigler (1992, 43) were claimed to be culturally appropriate. In mathematics they tested understanding of basic concepts such as counting, place value, addition, and subtraction. Their results showed that "Japanese children showed consistently superior performance from kindergarten through fifth grade."

One of the cultural aspects that differentiates one culture from another is language. If it is the case that cultural perceptions influence learning in mathematics, it is important to consider the medium of instruction used in teaching mathematics. In numerous developing countries, particularly in Africa, mathematics is mainly taught in a child's second language. This may be one of the reasons why they fail to understand the basic concepts. Students then tend to make a distinction between the mathematics they learn in school and the mathematics they learn in their home and community. For example, in the society I grew up in, six is referred to as "twice three" and eight as "twice four." A child coming from my society would have learned to count that way. However, in school, mathematics is taught according to European traditions of calculation, and in English.[2] Yet, it would appear sensible if mathematics were used in school to reinforce language and taught in a language that would help children understand its basic concepts.

If a society's youth were schooled in the way of life of that society, one would expect that, in an agricultural setting, students would learn enough mathematics to participate fully in agricultural practices. Similarly in areas where business practice is common, it would be expected that students learn the kind of mathematics that enables them to fit into the world of business, that is, to acquire practical mathematical skills. The same reasoning goes for other occupations such as tailoring and carpentry.

However, it is not surprising that the mathematics taught in school does not teach practical, occupationally relevant skills. As already indicated, economic power attracts prestige. School mathematics is associated with elitism for those who succeed and fear for those who do not. The mathematics that is taught in schools tends to be the mathematics of the elite, of those who will continue to study it to an advanced level, and will probably obtain salaried employment and economic prosperity. It is generally abstract, with no concrete real life examples. A student who is good at mathematics is expected to enrol in higher education courses such as engineering, architecture, and more recently, computer science, and attract very highly paid jobs later in life. In contrast, the mathematics encountered in real life is usually given little time and little consideration, because it is considered not to be intellectually stimulating and therefore not worthy of much attention.

Any discussion of the cultural perceptions on the role of mathematics and mathematics education in economic development needs to consider differences in perception that relate to gender. Mathematics and science are generally perceived as masculine inasmuch as the scientist and the mathematician are perceived as male. In many societies, women and girls are not expected to achieve as well as men and boys, particularly in mathematics (as Mary Harris' chapter in this volume clearly shows). The reasons underlying these expectations are, however, complex and difficult to specify.

In some societies, the cultural expectations are that the men are the economic providers, who will occupy high positions in society and become the leaders. Thus, they are considered more in need of the elite kind of mathematics that is taught in schools. In my own interviews with secondary school girls in Kenya, some indicated that their teachers told them in class that they do not need to do well in mathematics because their husbands will do it for them. The women are expected to get married and the men will take care of them. In such societies, then, when a family is faced by economic hardships, the decision made as to who goes on to the highest level of education or who studies mathematics, favours the male children. This situation means that many girls are excluded from high-level mathematics and science-related careers. It also influences girls' decisions whether or not to study mathematics beyond the minimum required levels. Girls' low participation in mathematics and science-related careers is, according to Fennema (1990, 2), "partially the cause of the economic problems faced by many women." Denying them access to mathematics education will make it more difficult for them to lift themselves out of poverty.

It is interesting that in most ethnic groups, the propagators of the culture are older women who teach oral history and cultural norms to the young. The assertion by Fennema (1990) that those who are now students need to transmit the culture to the next generation suggests that it is necessary for women to be exposed to mathematical experiences that are enriching and stimulate intellectual growth, which they can then pass on to the young through folklore and traditional songs.

WHAT KIND OF MATHEMATICAL KNOWLEDGE IS APPROPRIATE FOR WHOM?

From my earlier discussion it is clear that mathematics should not be considered as culture-free. The degree to which it is meaningful is in part influenced by the context in which it is located. When I worked as the officer in charge of mathematics at the Kenya National Examinations Council, I remember one occasion when we were looking at a question that related to a game with billiard balls. I asked for an explanation from the setter (a British national), who explained in the best way he could. I insisted that if I could not understand it, it should not be expected that students would and the question was duly thrown out. Fortunately, there has been a lot of indigenisation in the questions, and almost all questions at the secondary school level examination refer to contexts that are familiar to the students. If students have to appreciate the beauty of mathematics and transmit the culture from one generation to another, the mathematics must not only be relevant to them, but also be meaningful to them given their cultural orientations.

According to Lesh and Landau (1983, 4), the concern of mathematics educators should be "not what a student will do on a given problem when unaided, but what she or he is optimally capable of doing on a class of problems, or what she or he could do when accompanied by minimal guidance or when following theory-based instruction." The concern for teaching mathematics should thus be to "broaden and strengthen deficient conceptual systems." This calls for adequate explanations about mathematical concepts, relationships among them, and their relationship to real-life experiences wherever possible. That is, conscious efforts must be made to concretise mathematics and make it less abstract.

Mathematics culture should be seen as sets of broad ideas rather than sets of isolated facts. Pappas (1989, ii) asserts that "to experience the joy of mathematics is to realize mathematics is not some isolated subject that has little relationship to the things around us other than to frustrate us with unbalanced cheque books and complicated computations. Few grasp the true nature of mathematics, so intertwined in our environment and in our lives. So many things around us can be described by mathematics. Mathematical concepts are even inherent in the structure of living cells."

It is in enjoying mathematics that students will desire to learn more. The kind of mathematics, then, that is taught to different cultural groups must be one that reinforces their culture and one that they enjoy so as to desire to learn more. This calls for different types of mathematics for different groups even within a country. For example, the pastoral groups who live in the arid and semi-arid areas of Kenya may require different basic mathematics from the groups that live in the central part of the country, which is mainly agricultural. Those people in business communities require business mathematics and those who are aiming at pursuing mathematics at higher levels should be exposed to mathematics that requires more abstract reasoning.

The dilemma, though, is illustrated in a point made about the teaching of arithmetic as related by Wilson (1961, 3). He asserts that "purposeful teaching is directed by clearly perceived aims. Without the guidance of aims, teaching is apt to be routine and formal; frequently such teaching means time is practically wasted; often it leads to results that are definitely detrimental, for example confusion and unfavourable attitudes." He continues to cite the history of teaching arithmetic in America where the original purpose was to introduce arithmetic into the schools "because of its practical value as a tool in business." Several problems arose. First, the teaching of arithmetic was the responsibility of mathematics teachers, who had limited knowledge of the business world. Second, the content to be taught was designed by mathematicians, based on the "science of number" as conceived by the Greeks, who saw it as independent of practical utility.

The argument here, then, is that there is a need to appreciate that not all mathematics is appropriate for all students at all levels and in all societies. This raises questions such as: Should a society have different mathematics objectives for different groups of students? To what extent should the utility value of mathematics be the primary function of mathematics education? My answer to these questions is that the utility value of the mathematics taught will determine the levels of enjoyment and acquisition. It is no use teaching the binomial expression to a child in the northeastern province of Kenya, where it is unlikely to be of use to the majority of children. This calls for a different perspective in curriculum development whereby the people in the world of work within each community are called upon to decide what kind of mathematics is appropriate for each society. This is an expensive process but will reap benefits in the long term.

The introduction of new mathematics in Kenya in the early 1970s illustrates the point. Prior to 1968, mathematics in Kenyan schools was taught using traditional approaches with emphasis on computation, proof of theorems in geometry, and solution of algebraic equations of different kinds. At about the same time in the United States and Britain, and with the onset of computers, there was a move towards teaching "new" concepts including number bases, transformational geometry, and vectors. Foreign education advisers talked about the "new" mathematics to the Director of Education in Kenya and argued that it was necessary to introduce it into Kenyan schools if the students were to benefit from the new advances in technology, particularly the use of computers. On the basis of this advice, a decision was made to implement the new mathematics in schools. There was no consultation with parents or the business community. The secondary school syllabus was changed to reflect the new topics and approaches, and a set of books, the *School Mathematics of East Africa (SMEA),* was produced as an adaptation of the *School Mathematics Project (SMP)* in Britain. Later, the primary school syllabus was revised in line with the changes. However, the teachers were not adequately trained to teach the new topics such as set theory and there were numerous complaints from parents and the business community that the students could not count or make accurate transactions. It was clear that the new mathematics was not preparing the students to fit into and participate in society, as promised. After many complaints the President decreed that the new mathematics be abolished in 1981.

"As long as society is changing, the aims of teaching must change" (Schipp and Adams 1965, 9). The majority of the students who terminate schooling at the end of primary school can only benefit from mathematics that is of practical value to them and relevant to their way of life. For example, in Kenya, only about one-third of primary school leavers proceed to secondary school and only approximately 8 percent of secondary school leavers enter university. The majority in each case are relegated to activities dominated by simple crafts and trades such as carpentry, tailoring, retailing, and subsistence agriculture. The kind of mathematics relevant to these activities would include simple arithmetic and geometry with an emphasis on topics such as simple accounting, simple banking, concepts of profit and loss, measurement, and estimation. For the students who pursue mathematics up to higher levels there should be adequate motivation that challenges them to desire to learn more once they enrol in institutions of their choice. Currently, much high-level abstract mathematics is taught at both primary and secondary school, which neither prepares students for higher mathematics nor, should their formal education terminate at those levels, for life.

WHO SHOULDERS THE COSTS?

If communities are to benefit directly from the education provided to young people, particularly at the lower levels, some would argue that they should shoulder some of the costs. When people feel that they own a programme and that the programme is relevant to their way of life and will contribute to their economic progress, they will work towards its sustainability and improvement. It will also mean that as the society changes, they are more likely to re-examine the contents, methodologies, and the utility value of the programmes. In order to develop ownership, communities must have a voice in the formulation of curriculum and education policy. As indicated at the start of this chapter, this is not the case in Kenya.

This raises two questions: First, if pupils acquire an education that does not equip them for their future lives, that does not provide them with skills to enable them, for example, to farm, which is the mainstay of the people in rural areas, because schooling has concentrated more on the acquisition of academic skills, should parents still shoulder the costs? Second, if communities are to contribute, is there a case for creating education programmes, particularly in developing countries, in which students study the kind of mathematics that will enable them to become self-employed and economically productive? If such an approach is adopted, ministries of education should only develop syllabi after thorough consideration of, and consultation with, parents, the business community, and the wider community.

CONCLUSION

In this chapter, several issues that pertain to the role of mathematics and mathematics education in economic development have been raised. I have suggested that mathematics is a product of human culture and that it is important that all students study some mathematics. A major dilemma concerns the kind of mathematical knowledge appropriate for students at different levels, which will allow them to extract economic benefits.

I have made a case for parents, communities, business people, and other "users" of education to participate in the development of the content of mathematics to be taught and the methods of its instruction. While it would be very expensive to have education subsystems that provide relevant education for different categories of people, it may prevent parents and communities from withdrawing their children from formal schooling when they think the school is alienating the children from their culture, as occurs among some pastoral communities in Kenya. What appears to be a compromise is to get policy makers to work closely with the communities at the grassroots level with a view toward identifying community needs and considering the implications for educational policies and practice.

The other issue that is pertinent and worthy of mention is the teaching of mathematics in a foreign language, particularly at the primary school. The majority of children in the lower primary school classes find it difficult to understand mathematical concepts when they are presented in a foreign language, and this provides a shaky base for the understanding of mathematics. A practical suggestion in this regard is that young children be introduced to mathematical concepts in their mother tongue whenever possible and that teachers be trained to use concrete objects to explain concepts, particularly at the primary school level.

I wish to suggest that the curriculum development process include ideas and identification of mathematical needs by the "users" of mathematics. The panels for developing the syllabi must have some members from the business community, and the research and evaluation section of the Ministry of Education must carry out surveys that document parents' and communities' aspirations for education. In Kenya, students continue to fail mathematics in large numbers. At the secondary school level, only an average of 25 percent of the students pass with a grade C and above, which makes it difficult for them to pursue careers requiring higher level mathematics or science-related courses. The major question is, "What kind of mathematics have they failed?" If they were exposed to the mathematics that is relevant to the way of life in their societies, would they fail in the same way? These are issues that need to be examined for each society if all students are to benefit from the mathematics they learn. I submit that it would be of greater benefit to students if the views of the users of mathematics are sought, and examinations oriented towards more concrete rather than abstract mathematics.

NOTES

[1] This replaced seven years of primary schooling, four years of secondary schooling, two years of advanced-level schooling, and three years of university education.

[2] The official language policy in Kenya is that the medium of instruction in Standards 1–3 is the vernacular and English the medium of instruction from Standard 4 onwards. However, the stiff competition of the Standard 8 school-leaving examination means that teachers start teaching in English as early as nursery school, even in rural areas.

REFERENCES

Davis, P.J., and R. Hersh. 1981. *The Mathematical Experience*. Boston: Houghton Mifflin.

Fass, A.L., and C.M. Newman. 1975. *Unified Mathematics: Content, Methods, Materials for Elementary School Teachers*. Lexington, MA: D.C. Heath and Company.

Fennema, E. 1990. "Justice, Equity, and Mathematics." In *Mathematics and Gender,* eds. E. Fennema and G. Leder. New York and London: Columbia University, Teachers' College Press.

Lesh, R., and M. Landau, eds. 1983. *Acquisition of Mathematical Concepts and Processes*. Orlando: Academic Press.

Pappas, T. 1989. *The Joy of Mathematics: Discovering Mathematics All Around You.* San Carlos: Wide World Publishing/Tetra.

Serpell, R. 1993. *The Significance of Schooling: Life-Journeys in an African Society*. Cambridge: Cambridge University Press.

Schipp, D.E., and S. Adams. 1965. *Developing Arithmetic Concepts and Skills*. Englewood Cliffs, NJ: Prentice Hall.

School Mathematics of East Africa (SMEA). 1973. Nairobi: East African Publishing House, Cambridge Press.

Stevenson, H.W., and J.W. Stigler. 1992. *The Learning Gap: Why Our Schools Are Failing and What We Can Learn from Japanese and Chinese Education.* New York: Simon and Schuster.

Wilson, G. M. 1961. "Aims and Purposes of Arithmetic." In *Improving Mathematics Programs: Trends and Issues in Elementary School*, ed. M.V. Devault. Columbus, OH: Charles E. Merrill Books.

CHAPTER 17

Women and Mathematics

Ignoring a Majority?

MARY HARRIS

THE SPECIAL POSITION OF MATHEMATICS

Mathematics holds a unique position in economics, education, and society generally. It is the tool that handles how costings are made, resources are priced, personnel are paid, results are monitored, and the means through which planners and bankers with no spoken language in common can communicate. In manufacturing industry, scientific research, and technology, mathematics is the life blood, the "handmaid of science," the provider of models, the arbiter of progress, the measure of success. Within education, mathematics enjoys enormous prestige. It is the subject more than any other that is used to mark differences in student abilities. In daily life mathematics also has high status. It is the yardstick that measures intelligence, that separates the "brainy" from the not so gifted. It is a gateway to jobs and to further and higher education. It is the language of wages, allowances, and pensions. So exalted does it stand in these processes of control that in most societies, the sort of mental activity that is done by labourers, artisans, and homemakers as they estimate and measure, count and calculate, plan and design in the course of their daily round, is not called mathematics at all but "common sense" or "practical numeracy." Mathematics is something that only clever people do.

Whether in the hierarchies of government or aid programmes, of industry and daily labour, or of education, mathematics has power—power to support, control, and communicate; to grade, label, and classify; to summarise, calculate, and condemn. Its abstract and infallible nature gives it authority above mere human endeavour. Its figures, symbols, and processes are widely seen as cold, hard, and unemotional, reassuring of rationality, unaffected by the culture of its user, dependably neutral. Yet, people decide which mathematical model or process to use, and which particular aspect from the whole spectrum of mathematics should be taught at school and, within school, which items are taught to whom, how, and in what order.

Childhood memories of inexplicable instructions to "turn upside down and multiply" or of ridiculous problems about filling baths with no plugs, are personal experiences of the agonies of learning it. How can so neutral, so abstract, so revered a subject be the very instrument of politicians or bankers in bending the truth, and the cause of such misery, indeed panic (Buxton 1981) among those who have to study it?

What has happened to mathematics? What has happened to that cerebral activity of the glorious Greek civilization that elevated it above the affairs of men? Why does the mathematical thinking of those who work with their hands not "count" as mathematics? Why is so much mathematical advance so closely related to instruments of war and death? How do we account for the mathematics of those who were mathematicians before the arrival of the Greeks? Why do we assume that there is only one mathematics (Joseph 1991)?

The number of those who still believe that mathematics was discovered by a few pure, white, male, and godlike inhabitants of some Mediterranean shores of congenial climate, within a certain historical period of time, are dwindling rapidly. The Greeks themselves acknowledged their debt to the mathematicians of Africa and the Levant on whose intellects they drew. It was not they that invented the myth of Aryan superiority (Bernal 1987).

Just what does go on behind the facade of the world's most esteemed subject? Why is there such a universal problem in learning it?

MATHEMATICS AND SCHOOLS

Howson and Wilson (1986, 7) have observed that there is "an astonishing uniformity of school mathematics curricula worldwide. . . . It is still true that, faced with a standard school mathematics textbook from an unspecified country, even internationally experienced mathematics educators find it almost impossible to say what part of the world it comes from." By way of example, school mathematics education in England and Wales began formally in the years of the developing British Empire and was a product of its time, place, and history. In the liberal education ideal espoused by the Victorians, mathematics inherited a status second only to direct revelation from God (Harris 1997). Victorian society was rigidly based on a hierarchy of social classes and gender, with women's place confirmed by social Darwinistic philosophies of the day (Dyhouse 1976). The fact that the children of manual workers received any mathematics education at all was only due to a grudging recognition in days of electoral reform that the working classes must be at least minimally educated. Literacy was necessary as the skill for Bible reading, but numeracy could provide skills to question their place in society (Williams 1961). Strictly limited arithmetic for the workers' children became a curriculum subject in conformity with the ethos of social control.

Working-class, elementary education was an entirely separate system from the education of the new middle classes and the traditional classical education of the very small minority of the upper classes, in those private schools oddly still called "public" from which the country's rulers were drawn. Mathematics education for them was the classical works of Euclid, studied for their argument, not their usefulness. "Usefulness" was a matter for the middle classes, whose own mathematical education was spelled out by the Taunton Commission in 1862, in its review of middle-class education outside the "public" schools. Like Gaul, this education was divided into three parts. The upper grade was for the sons of "men with considerable incomes independent of their exertions," or of businessmen "whose profits put them on the same level," together with professional men, particularly clergy, doctors, and lawyers and all who, having had a classical education themselves,wanted the same for their sons but with more mathematics. The second grade was for children of the "mercantile classes" where a less classical, more practical curriculum was seen as needing "arithmetic, [and] the rudiments of mathematics beyond arithmetic." The third grade, the sons of the smaller tenant farmers, small tradesmen, and superior artisans "needed only very good arithmetic" as part of a curriculum based on the 3Rs (Cooper 1985, 36).

Thus at all levels of society, social class and school mathematics defined each other, and the social gradings of colonial England translated without much difficulty into racial grading in the British colonies. The gradings are visible to this day in the social inferiority of the terms "basic skills" and "numeracy" and the felt need for hierarchical progress in the relentless pursuit of qualifications up the ladder of internationally imposed approval through mathematics. They are maintained through the hegemonic forces of government funding, aid programmes, and European-based textbook publishers and examination boards. Mathematics education is not culture free.

MATHEMATICS AND WOMEN

A characteristic of the mathematical hierarchy of the Taunton Report is that it addressed males. Though women have always worked in jobs that have expected them to be numerate (Harris, 1997), mathematics was always assumed to be a masculine activity. Indeed the assumption still holds in many circumstances today. In the foundations of English education, the same history and the same philosophies that established mathematics as the acme of human intellect, established women as the lowest form of human life. If women are inferior to men, and working-class men inferior to middle and upper-class men, then working-class women are doubly at the bottom. The education of girls in the new state systems was seen as different from that of boys, as was made clear in constant references to "education" and "girls' education." Working-class girls may have been permitted a basic 3Rs curriculum, but the overall aim was domestic femininity. The paradigm domestic task was needlework, plain for the working classes, and intricate for the middle and upper classes. While girls spent considerable school time in needlework lessons, boys very often had the opportunity to study more arithmetic, and so to the assumption that girls neither needed nor had the ability to be mathematical was added the inevitable low attainment compared to boys. The same historical prescriptions that made needlework the symbol of domestic femininity confirmed mathematical activity as male, and the polarity of both stereotypes was built into the curriculum.

Serious challenge to the belief that girls and women cannot do mathematics is a mere 30 years old. It is impossible to begin to summarise here what is now a very large international literature (Leder 1992), but a recent succinct review from Australia (Willis 1989) demonstrates how the research questions have changed from assumptions of female disability to attempts to understand the social conditions that seem to imply it. Differences between mathematical performance of boys and girls lie not in biological differences between the sexes, but within the extreme complexity of the gendering of roles in society. The stereotypically male image of mathematics is widespread in Western countries and the countries they influence, and the perception that femininity is antithetical to mathematics is still prevalent. What is needed, argues Ernest (1995, 2), is a reconceptualisation of mathematics.

MATHEMATICS IN WORK

The mathematics assumed to be needed by people in manual work, as incorporated into the 19th-century working-class curriculum, has changed little since the 17th century. While logarithms and slide rules have been replaced by computers, skill lists are remarkably similar to those of today. The equation of low-level work with low ability and low-level arithmetic remains widely unquestioned, as governments worldwide trumpet for "basic skills."

In the 1970s in England and Wales the flurry of research into the mathematics of workplaces could have enlightened the field, but succeeded chiefly in maintaining the status quo, for research questions were taken from the old paradigms of mathematics in work, and questions about the four rules, fractions, and percentages produced responses about the four rules, fractions, and percentages (Harris 1991). Arithmetic is relatively easy to identify. What are less easy to identify in a work situation (and much less easy to assess in a training programme) are the visual, spatial, and problem-solving activities of workers that generate the need for arithmetic. By looking at the contexts of work, of "situated cognition," rather different pictures emerge of what people actually do. A well-known early paper of Scribner (1984) describes the problem-solving strategies of workers that could not have been detected in research that assumed that working mathematics is only arithmetic.

School mathematics is the individual pursuit of abstract and symbolic procedures in artificial situations. Workplace mathematics is more often performed in a cooperative, social context where to ask advice is not cheating but common sense, where significant variables are not presented on a page but have to be identified from insignificant ones in practice, where numbers are not the cleaned up whole ones of textbooks, and where there is often no right answer to be rewarded by the red ticks of social approval. Workplace mathematics is everything school mathematics is not.

GENDER IN WORK

Most work is gendered; most women do work which is mainly done by women. The everyday phrase "women's work" refers both to that done in the home, where most work is seen as women's, and in the labour market, where most work is seen as men's; the range of paid jobs in which women work is limited. The content of work varies historically, and within and across cultures, but the crucial constant is gender hierarchy

(Holland 1991). Throughout the world, and in the shifting job markets that are accompanied by the lowest wages, the textiles industry is the largest employer of female labour. This does not mean that men do not work in either domestic or industrial textiles, but that when they do, the work acquires masculine status. In Senegambia for example, where weaving is a male preserve, it is regarded as an intellectual activity, unsuitable for women (Harris 1987). The exploitative working conditions of women in the textiles industry worldwide are well described by, for example, Chapkis and Enloe (1983), Joekes (1985), and the ongoing work of SOMO, the Centre of Research on Multinational Corporations, based in Amsterdam.

WHO DOES MATHEMATICS?

If the mathematics of workplaces is everything that mathematics in school is not, and if it does not consist of the four rules, ratio, and percentages, of what does it consist? Bishop (1991) notes that six fundamental mathematical activities are undertaken by every culture that has been studied: counting, locating, measuring, designing, playing, and explaining. But in vocational mathematics, counting and measuring predominate: the visual, spatial, and philosophical items of Bishop's list do not feature, for they are made invisible by a dominant Eurpoean culture's 19th-century criteria of what is appropriate for workers.

Contrary to the projected public image of mathematics as objective and neutral, mathematics is a social construct. It is not a body of absolute knowledge, a collection of the objective and infallible truths of a classical liberal education, filtered through the texts and examinations of higher authority. Challenge to the absolutist idea comes also from within mathematics itself, in contradictions derived from within its own theories: other philosophies must now account for the nature of mathematical knowledge. Once mathematics is recognised as a social construct (and therefore subject to human fallibility), it becomes a process of inquiry, a continually expanding field of human creation and invention, not a finished product. No longer can mathematics be seen as irrelevant to some sectors of the population, such as women, or to its relationship to human affairs, such as the transmission of social and political values and its role in the distribution of wealth and power (Ernest 1991, xi). Such a dynamic view of mathematics has powerful educational consequences.

The aims of teaching it need to include the empowerment of learners to create their own mathematical knowledge, and mathematics can be reshaped, at least in school, to give all groups more access to its concepts. The social context of the uses and practices of mathematics can no longer be legitimately pushed aside; the implicit values of mathematics need to be squarely faced. When mathematics is seen in this way, it needs to be studied in living contexts that are meaningful and relevant to the learners (Ernest 1991, xii).

COMMON THREADS: WOMEN, MATHEMATICS, AND WORK

In the 1980s, while working in England at the interface between school and work mathematics, I set out to challenge both the accepted masculinity of mathematics and the accepted femininity of needlework as its intellectual opposite, in an exhibition that demonstrated the range and depth of the former within the latter. All exhibits were cloth and all captions were mathematical descriptions of it. I thus took the high-status language of mathematics and the low-status results of women's work, in both domestic and industrial spheres, and wove them together so that one had no coherence without the other. I called the exhibition "Common Threads" in a deliberate play on words that encompassed both the ordinary and universal nature of cloth and the seamless robe of mathematics.

Common Threads carried different messages to different people, but its appeal was so widespread that it was taken over by the British Council and redesigned in two copies to fill the demand for it from 23 countries. Its world tour extended its main message, that traditional women's work has always incorporated mathematics, beyond the school sector, into the arena of women's development, where many women are taught textiles work, either in small groups or on large projects aimed at their economic independence.

If needlework involves mathematical activity, then it should be possible, while teaching it, to reveal, teach, develop, and accredit its inherent mathematics at the same time. Such an idea would be a natural extension to work already underway in several countries relating to the changing paradigms of mathematics and mathematics education. In South America, for example, there is an increasing body of knowledge of differences between mathematics as practised in "unskilled" work and the mathematics of schools (Carraher 1991), and of the mathematics that landless peasants themselves demand (Knijnik 1993). In Mozambique, mathematics education programmes increasingly give attention to the results of ethnomathematics research into Mozambican weaving, notably the geometric work of women (Gerdes 1986, 1995).

Translating such radical ideas into practice in the field of women's development is a rather different matter. Many women's groups struggle against enormous financial and physical odds, certainly without the support of international academe. Those that are aid-funded tend to be staffed by skilled volunteers from a craft background. Even if they teach numeracy as well as textiles crafts, that teaching tends to be traditional and unsupported by the experience of better resourced and researched mathematics education. In institutional settings, many women's vocational courses are located in buildings near higher-status science and technology centres, a physical siting that can serve to emphasise their relatively low importance: there are obvious status differences between a room full of women working at sewing machines and one full of men using milling machines. Even when there is a clear intention to make improvements, too much seems stacked against women for any real possibility of change: for traditions, habits, and perceptions of them and their work can be just too strong.

KNOTTED THREADS: MAINTAINING THE STATUS QUO

Intended social change often succeeds in changing very little, for all the theories and most of the perceptions are gendered (Porter 1991). Writing from within the Third World, Fasheh (1990) argues that intellectual development in a colonial hegemonic context is designed to provide ideology without a basis in power. It is the ideology, says Fasheh, that marks the boundaries of permissible discourse, that discourages the clarification of social alternatives, and makes it difficult for the dispossessed to locate the source of their uneasiness, let alone remedy it. It allows intellectuals to participate vicariously in the moral, intellectual, humanitarian, and technical aspects of Western culture, as well as in educational, scholarly, and research activities, but produces people who have lost their power base in their own culture and society. They are being provided with a foreign culture and ideology, but without a power base. And it is this lack of power that causes them to overvalue the symbols of hegemonic power, the degrees, and the status symbols of the dominant culture. Fasheh (1990, 25) writes, "The power of Western hegemony rests on the claims of superiority, universality and ethical neutrality of Western mathematics, positivistic science, technology and education. These claims of Western superiority extend into social, cultural, moral, political and intellectual spheres."

But education can do one of two things; it can either introduce hegemony into the community, or it can reclaim and develop what has been made invisible by hegemony, for within the concept of hegemony lies counter-hegemony. Counter-hegemony in mathematics education can only occur through conscious cultural change. It was through his observations both of the mathematics of his mother and of himself, a Western-trained mathematician on the losing side of a war, that Fasheh came to realise that his work as a mathematics educator was merely symbolic, its power that of the Western hegemonic culture that had engendered it, and without whose official ideological support system it had no worth. His mother, an illiterate dressmaker, routinely took rectangles of fabric and, with few measurements and no templates, cut them into small parts and constructed them into new wholes, each with their own style, shape, size, and form for a unique, three-dimensional body. This sort of mathematics was beyond his comprehension. For him, mathematics was subject matter he taught; for her it was "basic to the operation of her understanding" (Fasheh 1990, 22). For him, mistakes were a matter of more symbolic marks on paper; for her they entailed practical consequences. His mathematics had no connection to power in the community or the practical world of making things. Hers had no symbols of power, but had its value in concrete and immediate needs and actions. The hegemonic power of Fasheh's mathematics limited his mother's "empowerment by minimizing the value of her experience, discrediting her as a woman and an uneducated person" (Fasheh 1990, 22). Hegemony does not simply provide knowledge; it substitutes one kind of knowledge for another in the context of a power relationship. "Power, in this sense, is almost defined by what is excluded" (Fasheh 1990, 24). The real world is what formal education marginalizes and excludes.

SEAMLESS ROBES AND OTHER DREAMS

Counter-hegemony can begin with individuals or groups. In England and Wales, the National Federation of Women's Institutes (NFWI), a women's organisation of some 250,000 members, used its needlework courses as a training arena for mathematics instruction. Research by this author (Harris, 1994) found that the courses involved the use of many mathematical skills—skills which in the stereotypical women's work of sewing are taken for granted and invisible, not least to the women themselves. One of NFWI's current aims is to gain accreditation for these skills. A further aim is to provide courses on the social, historical, and cultural place of mathematics.

The nonaccreditation of mathematical skills acquired through needlework is also common in developing countries. Typically, needlework courses (for young women) run parallel to courses in such subjects as carpentry and motor mechanics (for young men). In the latter, mathematics is usually explicit and sometimes accredited. Accreditation of needlework courses tends to be through a foreign and traditional form of assessment that does not yet recognise their potential for teaching mathematics. Categories of aid funding do not generally encourage the crossing of traditional boundaries: reform is required to allow the accreditation of projects that embrace gender development, textiles skills, and mathematics.

CONCLUSION

Projects in women's development and in mathematics education are initiated and supported through quite different, noncommunicating categories, and both enforce the boundaries and hierarchies that maintain the lower educational and economic status of women. The potential for cooperation is immense. Much rhetoric on women's development remains—and will remain—until the processes of analysis, planning, and provision are widened to allow for the consideration of possible alternatives. A stronger partnership between mathematics education and women's development could launch some fresh and very positive initiatives for both economic and educational development, starting from within traditional female culture.

REFERENCES

Bernal, Martin. 1987. *Black Athena: The Afro-Asiatic Roots of Classical Civilization. Volume I. The Fabrication of Ancient Greece 1785–1985.* London: Free Association Books.

Bishop Alan. 1991."Mathematics Education in its Cultural Context." In *Schools, Mathematics and Work*, ed. Mary Harris. London: Falmer Press.

Buxton, Laurie. 1981. *Do You Panic about Maths? Coping with Maths Anxiety.* London: Heinemann Educational Books.

Carraher, David. 1991."Mathematics In and Out of School: A Selective Review of Studies from Brazil." In *Schools, Mathematics and Work*, ed. Mary Harris. London: Falmer Press.

Chapkis, Wendy, and Cynthia Enloe. 1983. *Of Common Cloth: Women in the Global Textiles Industry.* Amsterdam: Transnational Institute.

Cooper, Barry. 1985. *Renegotiating Secondary School Mathematics. A Study of Curriculum Change and Stability. Studies in Curriculum History 3.* London and Philadelphia: The Falmer Press.

Dyhouse, Carol. 1976. "Social Darwinistic Ideas and the Development of Women's Education in England, 1880–1920." *History of Education* 5(1): 41–58.

Ernest, Paul. 1991. *The Philosophy of Mathematics Education.* Basingstoke: Falmer Press.

Ernest, Paul. 1995. "The Political Dimensions of Mathematics Education." *Science Education Newsletter* 118. Manchester: The British Council.

Fasheh, Munir. 1990. "Community Education: To Reclaim and Transform What Has Been Made Invisible." *Harvard Educational Review* 60(1): 19–35.

Gerdes, Paulus, 1986. "How to Recognise Hidden Geometrical Thinking:A Contribution to the Development of Anthropological Mathematics." *For the Learning of Mathematics* 6(2):10–17.

Gerdes, Paulus. 1995. *Women and Geometry in Southern Africa: Some Suggestions for Further Research.* Mozambique: Universidade Pedagógica.

Harris, Mary. 1987. "Mathematics and Fabrics." *Mathematics Teaching* 120: 43–55.

Harris, Mary. 1991, ed. *Schools, Mathematics and Work.* London: Falmer Press.

Harris, Mary. 1994. Report on needlework courses at Denman College. Unpublished.

Harris, Mary. 1997. *Common Threads: Women, Mathematics and Work.* London: Trentham Books.

Holland, Janet. 1991. "The Gendering of Work." In *Schools, Mathematics and Work*, ed. Mary Harris. London: Falmer Press.

Howson, Geoffrey, and Bryan Wilson. 1986. "School Mathematics in the 1990s." *ICMI Study Series*, eds. A.G. Howson and J-P Kahane. Cambridge: Cambridge University Press.

Joekes, Susan. 1985. "Working for Lipstick? Male and Female Labour in the Clothing Industry in Morocco." In *Women, Work and Ideology in the Third World*, ed. Afshar Haleh. London: Tavistock Publications.

Joseph, George Gheverghese. 1991. *The Crest of the Peacock. Non-European Roots of Mathematics.* London and New York: I.B Taurus & Co Ltd.

Knijnik, Gelsa. 1993. "Culture, Mathematics, Education and the Landless of Southern Brazil." In *Political Dimensions of Mathematics Education 2. Curriculum Reconstruction for Society in Transition*, eds. C. Julie, D. Angelis, and Z. Davies. Cape Town: Maskew Miller Longman.

Leder, Gilah. 1992. "Mathematics and Gender: Changing Perspectives." In *Handbook of Research on Mathematics Teaching and Learning*, ed. D.A. Grouws. New York: Macmillan.

Mosse, Julia Cleves. 1993. *Half the World, Half a Chance. An Introduction to Gender and Development*. Oxford: Oxfam.

Porter, Paige. 1991. "The State-Family-Workplace Intersection: Hegemony, Contradictions and Counter Hegemony in Education." In *Power and Politics in Education*, ed. David Dawkins. London: Falmer Press.

Scribner, Sylvia. 1984. "Studying Working Intelligence." In *Everyday Cognition. Its Development in Social Context*, eds. Barbara Rogoff and Jean Lave. Cambridge, MA, and London: Harvard University Press.

Williams, Raymond. 1961. *The Long Revolution*. Harmondsworth: Penguin.

Willis, Sue. 1989."Real Girls Don't do Mathematics." *Gender and the Construction of Privilege.* Geelong: Deakin University Press.

CHAPTER 18

Education, Social Identity, and Occupational Aspirations in Brazil

Reasons for (Not) Learning

TEREZINHA NUNES AND ANTONIO ROAZZI

> *The difficult thing to explain about how middle class kids get middle class jobs is why others let them. The difficult thing to explain about how working class kids get working class jobs is why they let themselves.*
>
> (WILLIS 1977, 1)

The analysis of the intergenerational transmission of social status and its relationship to education has seen waves of research and theory with markedly different orientations. The early evidence of an association between performance in intelligence tests and social class (Terman and Merril 1937), coupled with a view of society as a meritocracy (Herrnstein 1971), made this intergenerational transmission unproblematic in the past. Schools could be treated as a black box (French 1990), where children learned according to their abilities and their motivation; once they left school, society placed them in jobs that were adequate for their educational achievement. Theory and research were then geared to determining how much of the observed differences in intelligence tests were a consequence of heredity and how much resulted from the environment. With the increased investments in compensatory education in the 1960s and the allegedly small return in changing the intergenerational transmission of social status and its educational component ("Compensatory education has been tried and it has failed"; Jensen 1969, 2), some researchers became aware of the need for a paradigm shift. The role of schools in the intergenerational transmission of educational failure

(Bourdieu and Passeron 1977) was then recognized and documented through sociological analyses of who succeeds and who fails. However, these analyses do not tell the whole story because there is no strict determinism in social and educational status across generations in democratic societies (Bourdieu 1974), and researchers turned once again to closer analyses of individuals, their backgrounds and their trajectories through school.

Barros and Lam (1996), working in Brazil, investigated whether the intergenerational transmission of educational status could be explained simply by economic factors. Because educational level and economic status are highly correlated, it was possible that this transmission of educational status across generations was a result of economic conditions such as poorer families' need for youngsters to become economically active at earlier ages, thus leaving school or showing inconsistent attendance patterns and consequently having to repeat the school year. Using census data for two urban regions of the country that differ in industrialization, average income, and educational levels, they analysed the simple correlations between parents' and grandparents' education as predictors and the number of years of schooling completed by 14-year-olds. In both regions, a high correlation was observed between parents' and grandparents' education and the children's (of the order of .7 for parents' and children's education). In a series of regression analyses, Barros and Lam explored the possibility that it was income rather than parental education that explained these correlations by controlling for income before entering the parents' education in the regression equation. Although the correlation between income and the children's education was significant, the relationship between parents' and children's education remained significant even after income had been controlled for. They summarized the findings of the prediction equations in a very concrete manner:

> It would require about a 50 percent increase in parental income in order to have the same impact on schooling of 14-year-olds as a one-year increase in the mean education of fathers. It would take roughly a 100 percent increase in mean parental income in order to have the same impact on child schooling as a one-year increase in the mean schooling of the mothers. (Barros and Lam, 360)

Barros and Lam concluded that there are persistent household characteristics that affect schooling across generations—such as "taste for schooling" or other nonobservable parental characteristics. These results indicate that, in order to understand the intergenerational transmission of educational status, we must examine sociocultural aspects of children's background.

In this chapter we explore three specific and interrelated hypotheses that focus on aspects of children's sociocultural background, which we believe contribute to our understanding of the intergenerational transmission of educational status. We suggest that this phenomenon results from a process of socialization that is simultaneously cognitive and social. Youngsters from lower and higher socioeconomic backgrounds build different consensual worlds that give middle-class children reasons for learning and working-class children reasons for not learning in school. Although youngsters from diverse socioeconomic backgrounds hold the same cultural myths about the value of education and its role in relation to social and economic status, we hypothesise that they differ in: (1) their specific representations of social and educational stratification, (2) their identity in this represented social world, and (3) the types of knowledge which they consider "worth learning," given their own identity and position in society. Our own work to support these propositions was carried out in Brazil and with urban children. We refer in this chapter, even if briefly, to relevant results from other countries, because we do not believe that the processes examined here are specific to the Brazilian context. Although definitions of socioeconomic status (SES) and level of mobility vary across countries, the relationship between SES and educational success remains strong when country boundaries are crossed. It is possible that this socialization process also takes place in other societies where educational status is transmitted across generations and where the relationship exists above and beyond what would be expected on the basis of economic factors alone.

The chapter is divided into four sections. In the first section we will examine how youngsters from different social backgrounds represent social and educational achievement. In the second section we will examine how they apply these categories to themselves. In the third section we analyse briefly the existence of alternative forms of knowledge (in this case, arithmetic practices in Brazil) and how the social marking of knowledge influences learning: knowledge which is considered "practical" is seen as worth learning by those who intend to leave school, whereas knowledge which is viewed as "theoretical" is only seen as worth learning by those who intend to remain in school after the basics of reading and arithmetic have been mastered. We conclude with a fourth section that contains a discussion of the relationship between education and the development of identity as a major aspect of the intergenerational transmission of educational success.

SOCIAL REPRESENTATIONS OF STRATIFICATION: INCOME AND EDUCATIONAL LEVELS

Our first hypothesis is that youngsters from different social backgrounds represent social stratification differently. Research on youngsters' understanding of social stratification in England and Scotland (Dickinson 1986; Emler and Dickinson 1985; Himmelweit, Halsey, and Oppenhein 1952; Jahoda 1959, 1984), and the United States (Leahy 1983; Simmons and Rosemberg 1971), shows that, independent of socioeconomic background, youngsters are aware of differences in wages and social status across professions. In these studies, the children were interviewed about wage differences between professions presented through pictures or drawings and the reasons for these differences. The youngsters explained these differences by attributing greater significance to the work carried out by people in higher paying professions (e.g., doctors have more responsibility, they save people's lives, and bus drivers just drive buses). They also attribute higher levels of competence to the better paid professionals, recognizing that they attended school for much longer. Thus youngsters from higher and lower socio-economic levels share the cultural myth that greater levels of education result in a higher social status and better pay.

However, this similarity in the common-sense view of educational consequences for social stratification does not preclude the existence of differences that might result in different motivation to achieve in school. Social background affects how much the youngsters differentiate between professions in the higher and the lower clusters of social stratification. Whereas working class youngsters perceive clear distinctions across the lower paid professions and make fewer distinctions across the higher paid professions, exactly the opposite is observed amongst middle- and upper-class youngsters. Carraher and Carraher (1982) first documented in Brazil the high level of discrimination shown by poor adolescents of low-status occupations by asking them what they would ideally like to become in occupational terms (their "phantasy occupation," to use Himmelweit, Halsey, and Oppenheim's term [1952]) when they left school and why. The adolescents were students attending evening classes at the primary level to catch up after having fallen behind in their school progression (either because they had repeated several grades or because they had dropped out and then returned when too old to attend the same classes as school children). They surprised us by showing a highly differentiated representation of lower status professions and using in their classification of desirable and undesirable professions criteria which middle-class adolescents typically do not consider. For example, occupations which seemed similar (and equally undesirable) to middle-class adolescents were distinguished in terms of desirability by the adolescents from poorer backgrounds on the basis of criteria such as whether work is done in the shade or in the sun, whether it is done sitting down or standing up, whether it is a clean or a messy job, and whether there are pressures to perform or not. Occupations such as teller in a supermarket and telephone operator were considered highly desirable by the low SES adolescents, because the work is done in the shade, sitting down, it is a clean job, and pressure to improve performance is perceived as absent. We suggested that these distinctions in the perception of social structure and job desirability could be related to the students' relatively low educational aspirations; their motivation to progress in school would be to achieve educational levels compatible with the occupations to which they aspire, rather than a general motivation to achieve the highest educational levels in society. Similar trends in the level of differentiation between jobs with diverse social status had been observed by Himmelweit, Halsey, and Oppenheim (1952) in England through interviews with working- and middle-class boys in Greater London. Alongside a difference in the perception of social structure, they also documented an overestimation of the prestige of the father's occupation by the working-class boys and an underestimation in the prestige of the father's occupation in the middle-class boys.

Besides differing in their perception of social structure and job desirability, youngsters from different backgrounds also differ in their representation of the wage rewards associated with occupations of different social status. For example, Dickinson (1986) and Emler and Dickinson (1985) presented a list of professions (represented through pictures) to youngsters from different social backgrounds in Scotland and asked them to estimate the wage values for each of the professions. To indicate the wage levels, the youngsters distributed a fixed number of chips between the occupations: the larger the number of chips, the larger the wage estimated for the occupation. Youngsters from working-class backgrounds estimated the gap between the least and the most paid occupations to be significantly smaller than the wage gap estimated by middle-class and upper-middle-class youngsters.

Recently we (Roazzi, Sales, Carvalho, and Nunes 1997) replicated these results in Brazil and related them to the youngsters' representations of level of schooling required by the different occupations. Youngsters (n=180, age range 7 to 12 years) from different social backgrounds (attending private schools, state supported schools, and school dropouts) were asked to estimate the wages (through the distribution of 80 tokens) and the educational level of 24 occupations. The occupations included some which depend on a university degree (e.g., medical doctor), high-status occupations for which no degree is required but where education is in fact necessary (e.g., bank manager, politician), lower status white-collar occupations where educational requirements are undefined (e.g., policeman), vocational qualification (e.g. bus driver), and no qualification required (e.g., road sweeper).

Figure 18.1 shows the mean wages in number of chips attributed to a sample of occupations by youngsters from low and middle SES. The occupations appear in the figure in their order according to the mean number of chips attributed by the total sample: representations of youngsters from poor families attending and not attending school are merged because there were no differences between the two groups. The figure shows that the wage estimates offered by youngsters from poorer backgrounds for professions lower in the scale were higher than the estimates offered by the middle-class youngsters, whereas the converse is true for professions higher in the scale.

To test whether these differences are statistically significant, the wage estimates were analysed in a 2 (SES levels) by 3 (age levels) by 8

Figure 18.1. Estimation of the Relative Pay-Off of Different Occupations by Adolescents of Low and Middle SES

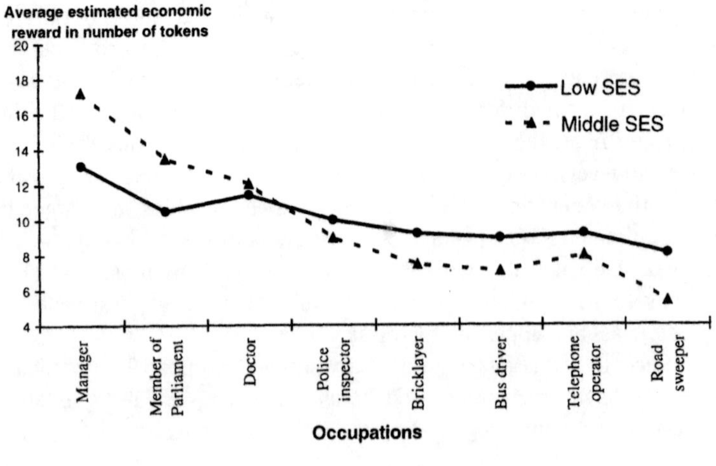

(professions) analysis of variance. In this analysis, a significant effect of profession indicates that the participants realize that the different jobs receive different levels of wage; a significant effect of age indicates that older adolescents perceive the differences in wage level more clearly than younger children; a significant interaction indicates that the wages attributed to the professions vary depending on the group's social background. Thus if youngsters from different social backgrounds do, in fact, perceive the social structure differently, we should observe a significant interaction between social background and the youngsters' wage estimates. The analysis produced a significant interaction between the youngsters' socioeconomic status and the type of profession as expected ($F = 6.76$ $p<.001$) and significant main effects of age ($F = 2.08$ $p<.012$) and of profession ($F = 33.78$ $p<.001$). We concluded that social background does affect the youngsters' perception of the socioeconomic structure of their society.

The participants were also asked to indicate how much education they thought people in these occupations would need to be qualified for their jobs. Answers could be given in general terms (e.g., "a university degree") or specific terms (e.g., "finish up to grade 8"). Figure 18.2 shows the mean levels of education estimated as necessary for the different occupational categories; youngsters in and out of school are considered separately in this analysis because of differences between their representations. Educational levels are measured in years and the structure of the Brazilian school system is outlined at the axis.

Young people from poorer backgrounds underestimated the level of education necessary for some of the more prestigious occupations, although they were quite realistic in understanding that the least prestigious occupations require little schooling. The educational requirements for all occupations were estimated at higher levels by middle SES youngsters.

To test whether these differences in perception are significant, we carried out a similar analysis of variance where group membership (3 levels: high SES, low SES attending school, and low SES not attending school) and type of occupation (5 levels defined by the actual qualifications required) were the factors (between and within subjects respectively), and the judgment of level of education was the dependent variable. If the youngsters from the different groups perceive the levels of education required for the professions differently, we should observe a significant interaction between the youngsters' background and their representation of the relationship between educational success and occupa-

Figure 18.2. Estimation of Educational Levels Required for Different Occupations by Adolescents from Low and Middle SES Groups

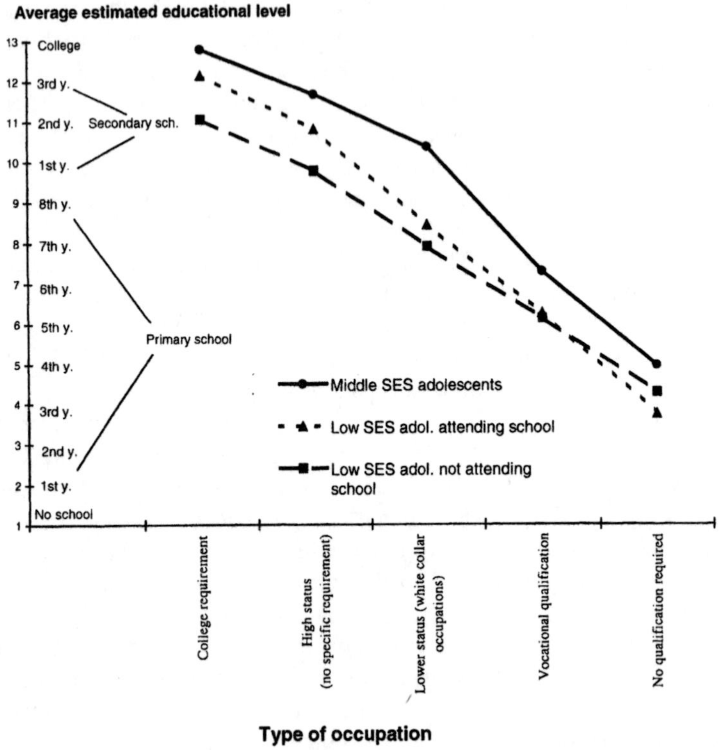

tion. A significant effect of profession indicates that they differentiate amongst the professions. This analysis produced significant main effects for group ($F = 21.58$ $p<.001$) and type of occupation ($F = 710.66$ $p<.001$) and a significant interaction ($F = 4.85$ $p<.001$). Tukey post-hoc comparisons[1] showed that middle SES adolescents gave higher estimates for the levels of education necessary for the different occupations in comparison to both groups of adolescents from low SES backgrounds; the only exception was the education estimated for occupations with the lowest status, where all three groups recognized that no qualification was required. Comparisons between the low SES adolescents attending school and those who had left school showed that those still in school gave higher estimates for the levels of education necessary for the two most prestigious occupations. Other differences in estimated education were not significant when these two groups were compared. For all three groups of adolescents, perceived educational differences were significant across levels in social stratification.

In short, these studies in Brazil confirm and expand the studies revealing different representations of social structure across SES groups in other countries. Our results show similarities and differences between the representations of social and educational stratification of youngsters from low and middle SES. Both groups recognize that educational qualifications are associated with socioeconomic status. However, low SES youngsters tend to underestimate the educational requirements of higher status occupations and their pay-off, by comparison with the youngsters from middle SES backgrounds. These discrepancies are very likely to result in differences in their motivation to learn in school, particularly in a society where education is portrayed as a means to social and economic success.

LEARNING AND BECOMING: PROJECTED OCCUPATIONAL IDENTITY AND DEVELOPMENT IN SCHOOL

Our second hypothesis is that pupils' representations of what they are likely to become within a stratified society plays a role in their view of what education can do for them. Although poor youngsters might aspire to vertical mobility, they may also realize that what they are likely to become is limited by their circumstances. They do not view education as a secure means of mobility.

We remarked earlier on the study by Carraher and Carraher (1982) indicating that poor adolescents attending night school expressed the desire to achieve what could be viewed as rather low levels of occupational aspirations. In a subsequent study, we (Roazzi, Sales, Carvalho, and Nunes 1997) attempted to replicate and expand on these results by asking a sample of 180 adolescents from different SES backgrounds what occupation they would ideally like to have (ideal aspirations) and what occupation they saw themselves as likely to have when adults (realistic aspirations).

The pattern of results is illustrated in Figure 18.3, where two lines are included in each graph, one representing the type of profession which the adolescents would ideally like to have and the second representing

Figure 18.3 (a) (b) (c).
Ideal and Realistic Projections of Occupational Aspirations by Low and Middle SES Adolescents

(a)

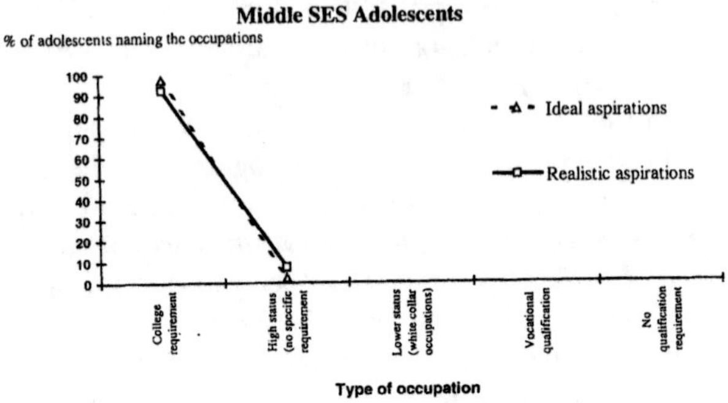

(b)

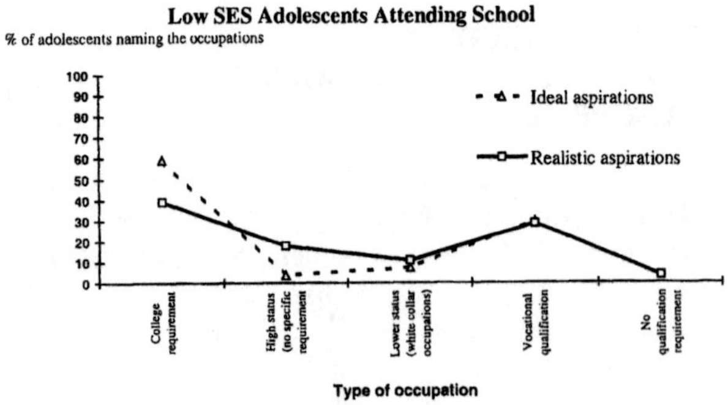

(c)

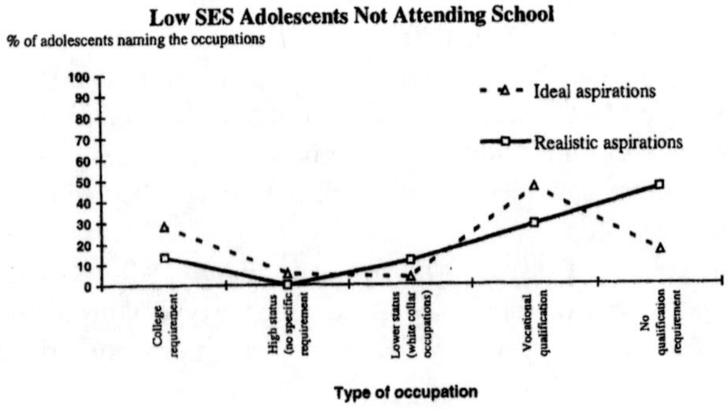

what job they realistically expected to have in the future. A separate graph is presented for adolescents from each group.

For the adolescents from middle SES backgrounds (top graph), there was little difference between what they would ideally like to be and what they thought themselves likely to be in the future: their answers invariably indicated the more prestigious occupations. When asked to indicate the degree of certainty of their answers (that is, to say whether it was very likely, likely, unlikely, or very unlikely that they might hold an occupation), these adolescents from middle SES backgrounds made no distinctions among the occupations of low SES: they were all very unlikely.

In contrast, the adolescents from low SES backgrounds realized that there was a large gap between what they would ideally like to be and what they realistically saw themselves doing in the future. They also placed their ideal aspirations at a lower level in the social stratification scale than the aspirations of middle SES adolescents. When speaking about what they actually saw themselves doing, there was greater discrimination between the occupations of lower socioeconomic levels: for example, bus driver and road sweeper were not just treated equally as "highly unlikely," because bus driver was seen as desirable, whereas road sweeper was an occupation to be avoided as much as possible.

The questions on ideal aspiration and realistic aspiration were analysed separately to test the significance of these differences. For both analyses, the five occupational levels described in Figure 18.3 were used as measures of levels of aspiration, and two factors were entered in the analysis: group membership (middle SES versus low SES attending school; middle SES versus low SES not attending school; low SES attending school versus not attending school) and type of occupation. The statistical significance of the differences was tested through a series of loglinear analyses for two-way contingency tables (Aitkin, Anderson, Francis, and Hinde 1989; Baker and Nelder 1978; Healy 1988). These analyses indicate whether it is possible to predict to which group the adolescents belong if we know what their occupational aspiration is. A significant effect of "group" would indicate that it is in fact possible to make this prediction.

For the ideal aspiration, the comparison between the three groups indicated a significant difference between middle and low SES adolescents attending school (scaled deviance [s.d.] = 42.49, d.f. 4, $p<.01$), and not attending school (s.d.= 91.78, d.f. 4, $p<.01$), and also a significant difference between those adolescents from low SES attending versus not attending school (s.d. = 21.16, d.f. 4, $p<.01$). Parallel trends were observed with respect to realistic aspirations: significant differences were observed between middle and low SES adolescents attending school (s.d. = 59.76, d.f. 4, $p<.01$), and not attending school (s.d. = 129.30, d.f. 4, $p<.01$), and between low SES adolescents attending versus not attending school (s.d. = 43.84, d.f. 4, $p<.01$).

A comparison across the two types of question—ideal versus realistic aspiration—can also be carried out. This comparison indicates whether the discrepancy between the ideal and the realistic occupational aspirations varies across groups; significant differences here indicate that the gap between ideal and realistic aspirations is larger in one group than in the other. To test the significance of the differences between ideal and realistic occupational aspirations, we used a loglinear model for two-way contingency tables. This analysis indicated a significant difference for the low SES adolescents attending school (s.d. = 10.82, d.f. 4, $p<.05$) and for those not attending school (s.d. 13.78, d.f. 4, $p<.01$). There was no difference between ideal and realistic aspirations of the middle SES adolescents (s.d. 2.19, d.f. 1, p = n.s.).

Thus, adolescents from different social backgrounds not only perceive the social stratification differently but also apply this stratification to themselves in terms of ideal and realistic aspirations in different ways. Whereas the middle SES adolescents see themselves as attaining what they ideally aspire to and make little distinction between lower-ranking occupations, the low SES adolescents understand that attaining what they ideally want is unlikely, and therefore realize the importance of understanding well the differences between lower-ranking occupations.

In the next section we will look at evidence that shows that these differences in their consensual world affect what they define as useful knowledge to be acquired.

THE SOCIAL MARKING OF KNOWLEDGE STRUCTURES

Our third hypothesis is that knowledge is socially marked and that the knowledge that adolescents aspire to acquire is related to their identity. The first indication of social marking of knowledge which we observed in Brazil was related to the use of the terms "literate" and "illiterate": for example, the same university lecturer in Brazil might say that her cook, who left school after second grade, is "literate" but that her university students are "illiterate" (Carraher 1986, 1987). What is implicit in these assumptions is that the cook is literate for her purposes, whereas the university students are not meeting their required level of literacy. Literacy, therefore, is not a neutral cognitive competence but a socially marked form of knowledge.

The social marking of knowledge in Brazil was also documented in the domain of numeracy. Nunes, Schliemann, and Carraher (1993) observed that young street vendors were quite capable of solving arithmetic problems when selling produce in street markets (an average of 98 percent success). However, when asked to solve sums in a test-like situation, instead of using the oral calculation methods which they used so successfully when calculating in the street market, most of the time the youngsters chose to use written algorithms, which they did not master and which often led to error (an average of only 37 percent success). A similar discrepancy between oral and written competence in problem solving was later observed by Nunes (1993) in the domain of negative numbers: youngsters attending evening school (Grades 4 through 6) were much more likely to succeed in solving problems with negative numbers if they used oral rather than written calculation, and were also conscious of their higher ability in oral calculation. This discrepancy in performance by low SES youngsters in oral versus written arithmetic posed a puzzle: Why did the youngsters choose to solve the test items using written arithmetic when they were better at oral arithmetic and recognized this difference in their ability? A possible explanation is that these two forms of knowledge are socially marked—they are viewed as appropriate for different situations and suited for use by different people.

De Abreu, Bishop, and Pompeu (1997) pursued this question in a later study and hypothesized that the explanation would be in the social marking of knowledge: teachers and pupils in primary school attribute different values to these two forms of numeracy practice and this difference in perceived value affects both pupils' choices of what form of knowledge to use in different situations and what form of knowledge they aspire to learn. De Abreu et al. tested this hypothesis in a study of a poor rural community in the northeast of Brazil, where the majority of unschooled agricultural workers would have been exposed to oral arithmetic practices. They interviewed schoolchildren (from Grades 3 and 5), their teachers, and their parents about their awareness of the existence of different arithmetic practices and their valorization of these practices. They found that teachers and pupils alike considered the oral arithmetic used outside school as "practical" and school arithmetic as "theoretical." They often recognized that both forms of numeracy can lead to correct results; however, they valued the practices differently. In the study, the teachers involved realised that street mathematics could be efficacious and even impressive (one teacher acknowledged that her unschooled father could calculate better using oral arithmetic than she could with her school methods). But in school they aimed at teaching only the written algorithms, which were perceived as the way to success in the educational system. The pupils' attitudes varied: some pupils considered that oral arithmetic leads to correct results but did not think it was "the right way" of doing sums, whereas others valued it as highly effective. The same diversity was observed with respect to school methods: some pupils considered school methods less effective than oral arithmetic, whereas others considered them important alongside oral methods.

In the study by De Abreu et al. (1997), particularly amongst the older pupils (Grade 5), success in learning school methods was associated with a positive attitude towards them, with or without a devaluation of oral arithmetic. Their performance in oral arithmetic, however, was clearly independent of their performance in school mathematics: pupils who were successful in the school methods were no more likely to know than not to know the oral arithmetic practices used outside school. De Abreu et al. note that as pupils grow older, some become more involved in productive activities outside school. For these pupils, the identification with school as a learning place declines. They value the work that they do outside school and the numeracy that they learn in practice and come to devalue school mathematics as "too theoretical" and not practical for solving problems in everyday life. These pupils are much more likely than others to show a marked discrepancy between their knowledge of oral and written school practices.

In short, De Abreu et al. did not find relationships between the two types of knowledge at the cognitive level, but found that pupils who valued school mathematics were more likely to succeed in learning this form of numeracy.

Studies in other countries have also highlighted the conflicts between the identity one could have by becoming a schooled person and the existing identity of adolescents from minority or low SES groups. Willis (1977) documented this conflict in working-class boys in England, Ahai and Faraclas (1993) among the "rascals" in Papua New Guinea, and Ogbu (1983) among United States blacks. In all of these examples, the connections between who the pupils are, how they perceive school knowledge, what kind of knowledge they value, and who they aspire to become are closely related to pupils' reasons for learning or not learning in school.

CONCLUSION

The evidence considered here supports the theory that, although youngsters from different social backgrounds value education and recognize its role in socioeconomic stratification, they represent the social stratification differently. For youngsters from higher SES backgrounds, higher status occupations are differentiated according to their preferences: they may want to be medical doctors, engineers, or lawyers as a matter of personal ambition. But there is no discrepancy between what they ideally would like to become and what they believe they are likely to become in terms of the level of educational qualification that they expect to reach. Lower ranking occupations are all highly undesirable and need not be distinguished. Educational requirements for all occupations are estimated at higher values than the estimates of lower SES youngsters; the pay-off of higher levels of education is also estimated at a higher value. This view of social structures in their society is likely to motivate them to learn what is offered by schools and not aim at learning knowledge that is socially marked as useful for jobs lower down in the social scale.

In contrast, low SES youngsters comparatively underestimate the levels of education required for occupations as well as the pay-off of higher levels of schooling. They realistically foresee a significant difference between what they ideally would like to become and what they are likely to become. In consequence, they make finer distinctions between the lower ranking occupations and express the intention to avoid the undesirable ones as much as possible. They also regard some of the knowledge that they are taught in school as distant from their practical knowledge needs: they learn to value knowledge which is not taught in school, but is useful for the sorts of activities which they will actually engage in. Their realistic view of their occupational chances, their devaluation of the need for, and of the wage benefits from, higher levels of education, along with the marking of practical knowledge as of significance for their future, amounts to a consensual world where the "taste for schooling" is unlikely to be a high priority.

Teachers also realise that knowledge is socially marked and prefer to focus in school on those forms of knowledge marked as "academic" and exclude "practical" knowledge. The interaction between students' representations of stratification and their experience of schooling probably makes them see schooling as irrelevant to their lives and economic survival once they have acquired the most basic literacy skills.

To conclude, we stress that more research is needed on this theme, in particular to analyse the interactions between school performance and possible changes or strengthening of specific identities over time. However, it is worth considering, even if briefly, the challenges stemming from this analysis for educational practice: Is it possible to change the social marking of knowledge by conferring to everyday and practical knowledge official recognition in the school curriculum? Would this official recognition of practical knowledge facilitate the process of identification of low SES youngsters with the goals of school? Can schools be more open to learners from all backgrounds in order to make learning compatible with a variety of identities?

NOTE

[1] Tukey post-hoc comparison is a particular type of post-hoc comparison between means.

REFERENCES

Ahai, N., and N. Faraclas. 1993. "Rights and Expectations in an Age of Debt Crisis: Literacy and Integral Human Development in Papua New Guinea." Pp. 82–101 in *Knowledge, Culture, and Power: International Perspectives on Literacy as Policy and Practice,* eds. P. Freebody and A.R. Welch. London: Falmer Press.

Aitkin, M., D. Anderson, B. Francis, and J. Hinde. 1989. *Statistical Modelling in GLIM*. Oxford: Clarendon Press.

Baker, R.J., and J.A. Nelder. 1978. *The Glim System Release 3 Manual*. Oxford: Numerical Algorithms Group and Royal Statistical Society.

Barros, R., and D. Lam. 1996. "Income and Educational Inequality and Children's Schooling Attainment." Pp. 337–366 in *Opportunity Foregone. Education in Brazil,* eds. N. Birdsall and R. H. Sabot. Washington, DC: Inter-American Development Bank.

Bourdieu, P. 1974. "The School as a Conservative Force; Scholastic and Cultural Inequalities." Pp. 32–46 in *Contemporary Research in the Sociology of Education,* ed. J. Eggleston. London: Methuen.

Bourdieu, P., and J.C. Passeron. 1977. *Reproduction in Education, Society and Culture*. London: Sage.

Carraher, D.W., and T.N. Carraher. 1982. *"O que eu mais gostaria de ser e caixa num supermercado. O dilema das aspiracoes ideais deprimidas."* Sociedade Brasileira para o Progresso da Ciencia, Reuniao Anual, Rio de Janeiro, Brazil.

Carraher, T.N. 1986. "Alfabetizacao e pobreza: tres faces do problema." Pp. 47–98 im *Alfabetizacao. Dilemas da pratica*, ed. S. Kramer. Rio de Janeiro: Dois Pontos.

Carraher, T.N. 1987. "Illiteracy in a Literate Society." Pp. 95–110 in *The Future of Literacy in a Changing World*, ed. D. Wagner. Oxford: Pergamon Press.

De Abreu, G., A. Bishop, and G. Pompeu.1997. "What Children and Teachers Count as Mathematics." Pp. 223–264 in *Teaching and Learning Mathemat-*

ics. An International Perspective, eds. T. Nunes and P. E. Bryant. Hove: Psychology Press.

Dickinson, J. 1986. "The Development of Representations of Social Inequality." Unpublished Ph.D. dissertation, Dundee University, Scotland.

Emler, N., and J. Dickinson. 1985. "Children's Representations of Economic Inequality." *British Journal of Developmental Psychology* 3: 191–198.

French, J. 1990. "Social Interaction in the Classroom." Pp. 31–48 in *The Social Psychology of the Primary School*, eds. C. Rogers and P. Kutnick. London: Routledge.

Healy, M.J.R. 1988. *Glim: An Introduction*. Oxford: Clarendon Press.

Herrnstein, R. 1971. "IQ." *The Atlantic* (September): 43–64.

Himmelweit, H., A.H. Halsey, and Oppenheim. 1952. "The Views of Adolescents on Some Aspects of the Social Class Structure." *British Journal of Sociology* 3: 148–172.

Jahoda, G. 1959. "Development of the Perception of Social Differences in Children from Six to Ten." *British Journal of Psychology* 50: 158–196.

Jahoda, G. 1984. "The Development of Thinking about Socio-Economic Systems." In *The Social Dimension: European Developments in Social Psychology*, ed. H. Tajfel. Cambridge: Cambridge University Press.

Jensen, A. 1969. "How Much Can We Boost IQ and Scholastic Achievement?" *Harvard Educational Review* 39: 1–123.

Leahy, R. L. 1983. *The Child's Construction of Social Inequality*. New York: Academic Press.

Nunes, T. 1993. "Learning Mathematics: Perspectives from Everyday Life." Pp. 61–78 in *Schools, Mathematics, and the Worlds of Reality*, eds. R. B. Davis and C. A. Maher. Boston: Allyn and Bacon.

Nunes, T., A.D. Schliemann, and D.W. Carraher. 1993. *Street Mathematics, School Mathematics*. New York: Cambridge University Press.

Ogbu, J. 1983. "Literacy and Schooling in Subordinate Cultures: The Case of Black Americans." Pp. 117–138 in *Literacy in Historical Perspective*, ed. D.P. Resnick. Washington, DC: Library of Congress.

Roazzi, A., L.C. Sales, M.R. Carvalho, and T. Nunes. 1997. "A Representacao de Estatus Social Entre Adolescentes de Diversos Meios Sociais." Recife (PE): Universidade Federal de Pernambuco.

Simmons, R.G., and M. Rosemberg. 1971. "Function of Children's Perceptions of the Stratification System." *American Sociological Review* 36: 235–249.

Terman, L.M., and M.A. Merril 1937. *Measuring Intelligence*. Boston: Houghton Mifflin.

Willis, P. 1977. *Learning to Labour. How Working Class Kids Get Working Class Jobs*. London: Saxon House.

PART V

DILEMMAS FOR EDUCATIONAL AID

CHAPTER 19

Whose Rules Apply?

Educational Project Management in Less Developed Countries: Cultural Considerations

MICHAEL DELENS

There is growing interest in the link between culture and many fields of human activity. The demise of political ideology as a source of conflict after the Cold War has prompted the cultural analysis of conflict (e.g., Huntington 1996). There is interest in culture and economics (e.g., Harrison 1992), as well as in culture and political systems (e.g., Fukuyama 1995), and many other areas. Thus it is no surprise to find the same debate in the field of education, and in particular in English language teaching (ELT), at all levels. This debate shifts from the role of English in national education systems (Phillipson 1992, 1996), to the appropriateness of mainstream language teaching methodologies in non-European contexts (Ellis 1996), to debates about the utility of teaching culture explicitly as a vehicle for the teaching of language (Porto 1996), to more guarded views of the benefits of teaching cultural conventions to learners whose motivation in learning the language is purely instrumental (Richards 1996).

This latter debate focuses on the interaction between grammar and pragmatics, or the rules governing language use. The way language is used is part of behaviour and derives from cultural conventions. The debate raises important questions: Does learning a language necessarily involve absorbing the culture associated with that language? Should culture be explicitly taught in order to train learners in "correct" language behaviour? For example, White (1993) examines the use of "please" by Japanese speakers of English, who, while quite capable of producing grammatically well-formed sentences, are led by the Japanese cultural insistence on politeness to inappropriate use of the politeness marker "please." In English "please" is generally restricted to the speech act of request, in which an action of the hearer will benefit the speaker. The use of "please" in utterances which are intended as acts of agreement, promise, or statement, for example, tends to make these different speech acts look like requests when they are not: there is a mismatch between the grammatical form of an utterance and its intended communicative function. This mismatch stems not from lack of knowledge of the foreign grammatical code, but from attempts by non-native speakers "to transfer their native [cultural] conventions to the target language" (White 1993, 193, my parenthesis). White points out that each instance of this "pragmalinguistic failure" (White 1993, 194) may be unimportant in itself, given a reasonably flexible native-speaker hearer, but that "repeated instances can lead . . . to a ruffling of the smooth waters of interpersonal relationships" (White 1993, 200).

These observations lead White to ask the question which is the title of this chapter—whose rules apply? Those of native, or non-native, speakers? The question also encapsulates a major dilemma in cooperation between diverse groups in all fields, not only on ELT projects but on educational development projects more generally, which represent a cross-cultural communication situation par excellence. In such circumstances

> successful communication involves inter-cultural understanding, which, among other things, means avoiding making wrong attributions. Erroneous attributions occur when either or both sides in an inter-cultural exchange violate not just the surface features of language, but the conditions which give meaning to speakers' and hearers' intentions and interpretations. (White 1993, 201)

Most non-native speakers of English in the world today have an instrumental, not an integrative, motivation (Gardner and Lambert 1972) in learning that language. The language is a tool providing access to information; most learners are not interested in acquiring the cultural baggage of native speakers in order to be accepted into native-speaker communities. Therefore native speakers, communicating with non-native speakers in what is to the former a non-native environment, have to deal with non-native cultural conventions in the use of language. It is argued here that, in the same way, people from "less developed" societies who want technical skills and knowledge from the developed world do not necessarily also want to accept the cultural baggage that usually accompanies efforts to transfer technical skills. Successful projects are usually those in which it is recognised that the cultural rules of the majority, the "beneficiaries," will play a significant role. If projects are to succeed in bringing about changes in values and attitudes for the purpose of development, there can be no outright imposition of the values of the donor. It is further argued here that project managers can only achieve sustainable transfer of skills and knowledge if they build on indigenous values and attitudes, and bridge the cultural gaps between donors and recipients.

These propositions will be illustrated in two ways: first, with reference to the author's experience of project management on an ELT project in Côte d'Ivoire at the National University from 1989 to 1995. There were two halves to the project: one involved advising teachers of English for specific purposes (ESP) in the different faculties of the University, while the other was to set up and run a postgraduate programme in applied linguistics. Second, reference will be made to various analyses of culture, in particular that of Hofstede (1980, 1983, 1986). He identified dimensions of culture along which every culture could be analysed: power distance—a measure of human social inequality; uncertainty avoidance—a measure of the societal norm for tolerance of ambiguity or uncertainty about the future; individualism—a measure of the way the individual relates to the collectivity; and masculinity—a measure of the extent to which the biological differences between males and females condition their roles in society. To these he later added (Hofstede 1994) long-term orientation—a representation of Asian, Confucian values that measure the extent to which societies provide for the future or live for the present.

PROJECT PLANNING

The importance of culture has been recognised in the area of curriculum design, particularly in relation to indigenous and immigrant minorities, but seldom acted upon in broader contexts. Recently, however, culture has been explicitly or implicitly invoked in areas such as financial planning for education, accountability, monitoring, school management, and decentralisation and privatisation of education (Caillods 1989; Klees 1989; Riddell 1996; Verspoor 1992).

Planners are becoming increasingly aware of the importance of culture, but have not yet developed systematic means for incorporating cultural factors into their plans. A recent proposal for educational policy analysis purports to have developed a planning methodology that takes account of the specifics of planning for education, and explicitly names cultural development as one of the background factors in identifying educational problems (Cheng and Cheung 1995, 11). However, the only example given of a traditional belief is that of English being considered the language of choice for education in the Hong Kong context. Hofstede (1994) would probably have classified this as an instance of long-term orientation, adopting foreign cultural elements for local advantage, rather than as a traditional belief. However this may be, the planning literature still offers little guidance on how to incorporate cultural information, or what such information might entail, and there are still complaints about cultural inappropriateness, even in the Hong Kong context. For example, Han-Siu Chow (1995) criticises management-education textbooks and methodology in Hong Kong for their culturally incompatible assumptions.

In addition, the increasing emphasis on accountability in donor nations means that resources devoted to development assistance must be accounted for in ways that satisfy politicians and voters (Hofstede 1994). Hence, development projects are more likely to embody explicit donor nation values, a trend reinforced by the process of globalisation of the world economy, which may mean Europeanisation or Westernisation: MacLaughlin (1994) and Baumgratz (1995) both trace the roots of globalisation back to European expansion from the 15th century. Senior officials in less developed countries (LDCs) who are involved in project negotiation are themselves likely to share donor values, belonging to an "indigenous technocracy" whose role is to create a national policy environment that is compatible with the ideological framework of donor organisations (Carr-Hill 1994,86).

Finally, project planning is carried out in bureaucracies, in both donor and recipient nations, whose organisational culture would be, according to Handy's (1981) taxonomy, a role culture (Leach 1991). Concerns include the definition of objectives, identification of implementation strategies, smooth transfer of resources, and arrangements for monitoring. This is done in a role culture mind-set that seeks to ensure that the necessary roles exist on both sides of the partnership. There will thus be little consideration of the cultural values pertaining on the ground and affecting those who will fill the roles, such as the project managers. At the planning stage, project managers are themselves considered merely as an input on the project framework document, along with whatever budgets and equipment are required. The fact that they are also people who must interact with others of a different cultural background is not taken into account. Thus project managers, on arrival at the project site, must reconcile the donor values implicit in the project plan with the reality on the ground.

CULTURAL INTERFACES

Handy (1981) was writing primarily about business and industry in a Western context, but if, following Leach (1991), we apply his analysis to development projects, it becomes apparent that project managers are likely to find themselves operating at the interface of several different cultural configurations:

1. A task culture generated by the project itself, characterised by collegial relationships between managers, counterparts, and staff, where the structure is horizontal and communication is through meetings and daily contact (Handy 1981)
2. The bureaucratic role culture of the host institution, probably a ministry or ministry division, in which decision making is from the top downwards and communication is vertical (Handy 1981)
3. The role culture of the donor institution (not the same as the role culture of the host institution; it will be similar in overall character, but influenced by differences in national culture—see 4 and 5 below)
4. The national culture of the recipient society, which will be strongly reflected in the organisational culture of the host institution (Hofstede 1980)
5. The national culture of the donor society, which itself will be reflected in the donor institution culture and the project culture

Hofstede (1980) has shown that although organisations have their own subcultures, which may even transcend national boundaries in the case of multinational organisations, organisational culture is highly conditioned by the national culture of the society in which the organisation is located. Figure 19.1 on page 342 illustrates the conflicting cultural forces.

The symmetry of the diagram may give the false impression that projects are balanced equally between two national and two organisational cultures; in practice, it may be that donor values are most apparent to the casual observer, while local values prevail in reality. Further, the project culture itself may develop characteristics that are quite independent of the other cultural configurations noted above.

Figure 19.1. Cultural Interfaces: Forces Operating on a Project

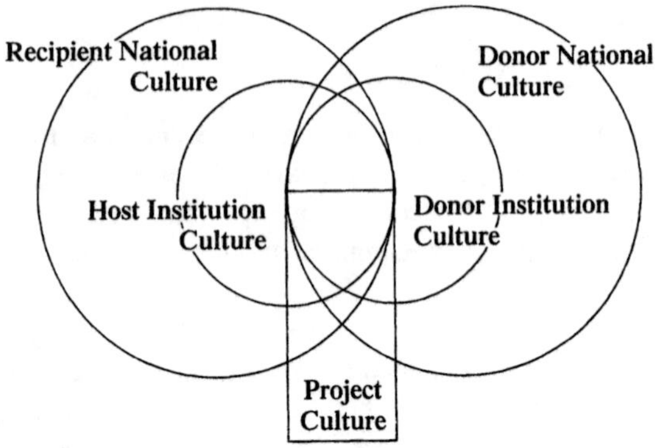

Cultural Conflicts

This combination of factors may produce conflicts which are cultural in nature and which need to be recognised as such if project managers are to resolve them. There are many examples; one is provided by Leach (1994), who, in describing relationships between Western expatriate experts and their counterparts in a technical education institute in the Sudan, observes that counterparts were unwilling to participate in organisational changes dictated by project objectives because these would have involved them in clerical or manual duties. Such duties would not have been "appropriate to the individual's status" (Leach 1994, 223). This observation is characteristic of Hofstede's (1980) high power distance cultures. Sudan is a predominantly Arab society in northeast Africa. While there is no information specifically on Sudan in Hofstede's work, both the East African and Arab groups of countries score highly on Hofstede's power distance index, a measure of the extent to which societies are organised hierarchically into status/wealth levels (Hofstede 1986), and manifest structures where status differences are explicitly recognised. The expatriate experts cited by Leach ended up doing the organisational work required by the project themselves, thus spending less time transferring technical skills.

The Côte d'Ivoire applied linguistics programme mentioned in the introduction was aimed at qualified, practising English language teachers in secondary schools, the university, and other institutions. It faced, initially, much opposition within the department of English, where it was based. First, it was seen as a teacher training programme, and therefore should have been based at the national Teacher Training Institute; in addition, it was felt that it was not possible to do "respectable" research in ELT. Students had to submit a dissertation as part of their Master's degree, and they were encouraged, since they were based in schools, to do small pieces of action research, following mainstream ELT principles (cf. Nunan 1992) that are quite normal in Anglophone countries for this kind of programme. Often this research involved observation of classroom interactions, application of different methodological treatments with a pre-test and a post-test, and so on. In other words, it was empirical research, and it was often criticised for lacking theory (even though, in reality, all empirical activity had a theoretical base). These objections to the programme may have been cultural in nature: Côte d'Ivoire's education system is modelled on that of France. France is high on Hofstede's uncertainty avoidance index, and one characteristic of high uncertainty avoidance is faith in absolute truth (as against relativism), and a consequent high value placed on theoretical rather than practical contributions to knowledge (Hofstede 1980). There is no direct information on Côte d'Ivoire's position on the index: we may infer that it would match Hofstede's West African cluster of countries (Hofstede 1983). If so, it is at the middle of the scale, lower than France, which is near the top. The fact that the applied linguistics programme is still running may be evidence of this lower uncertainty avoidance score, or it may mean that whatever people's attitudes are at the outset, they can change through exposure to alternative ideas. What is certain is that, if the project management had been aware of the cultural basis of this conflict at the outset, it would have been much easier to manage.

False Impressions

Furthermore, in this complex cultural interface, the project-generated task culture may create false impressions about the attainment of project objectives. Counterparts, released from "normal" work, may conform to the project culture, participating in meetings, working enthusiastically as team members, acquiring technical skills, and so on. However, in Gilbreath's (1986) terminology, projects are "non-operational"; that is, innovations developed by projects are unsustainable until they are incorporated into the wider cultural context of the host institution, or "institutionalised" (Verspoor 1989). This will not happen if counterparts are unable to maintain the "new" behaviour acquired in the project culture when back in the wider context.

An example is the perceived dichotomy between teacher training and subsequent classroom practice in the Côte d'Ivoire project. A major part of project activity was devoted to methodology training through workshops and seminars, and sometimes U.K. training courses. This training was always "communicatively" oriented. Communicative language teaching (CLT) views language not as something to learn about, but as something to learn to use (e.g., Brumfit 1984). It therefore involves learners in activities that can only be completed through using language purposefully, either in groups or pairs. The important point is that learners communicate with each other and their teacher in order to get information necessary for the completion of the task. A whole-class grouping with the teacher as fount of knowledge is of limited usefulness in this approach. Instead, teachers are facilitators, fellow participants, fostering cooperation and group activity in which learners are responsible for their own learning and that of others. In ESP especially, where teachers are unfamiliar with the specialism of their students, there may be cooperation between teacher and students in which teachers admit they have little knowledge and exploit the opportunities this provides. For example, learners can impart knowledge of their specialist subject to the teacher as a means of practice.

In the Côte d'Ivoire project, teachers demonstrated understanding of the underlying principles, and performed well in peer-teaching situations. However, transfer of this understood and acquired skill to the classroom was problematic. The reason is patently not inability to use the techniques; moreover, in a collectivist society such as Côte d'Ivoire, group-based cooperative approaches should be second nature. The reason may lie in the notion of high power distance, in which effectiveness of learning is related to the excellence of the teacher (Hofstede 1986). Moreover, where uncertainty avoidance is high, it is unacceptable for teachers to admit to knowing less than their students: they "are expected to have all the answers" (Hofstede 1986, 314). In addition, according to Hofstede (1986), adults in a collectivist society cannot usually accept student roles or participate in the same activities.

These phenomena were observed by project managers but not understood at the time they occurred. An awareness that they could be explained by culturally determined differences in values and attitudes might have avoided, in White's (1993, 201) terms, "erroneous attributions" on the part of the project management when trying to tackle the problems.

MANAGERS "BY DEFAULT" AND THEIR LIKELY APPROACHES TO MANAGEMENT

Of the many approaches to management, two broad trends seem particularly relevant to educational project management in developing countries. These are related to systems theory and strategic management, both of which are manifestations of Western, particularly American, culture, and are therefore "natural" to Western expatriate project managers.

Systems Theory

In systems theory, organisations are viewed as collections of interdependent elements that together form a system. All parts of the system (subsystems) must function properly in order for the system as a whole to function. An example would be the ignition subsystem in a car engine: if the capacitor in the distributor does not work, then the whole power distribution subsystem will not work, even if its other parts are in perfect condition. Moreover, the malfunctioning of one subsystem will prevent the proper functioning of other subsystems so that the whole system (the car) is immobilised. Organisations are viewed in a similar way, but they are "open" systems that need to interact with their environment, needing inputs, throughputs, and outputs, and feedback about their effect on the environment to determine whether they are functioning effectively. In education systems, inputs include pupils, teachers, and resources. Pupils/students are throughputs as they move through the institution, and become outputs when they leave as qualified persons. Ongoing assessment while in the system and information about their subsequent life in the wider world both provide feedback which helps to monitor performance of the system. Another tenet of the theory is that systems strive for completeness and tend to become more complex in that new subsystems evolve (Havelock and Huberman 1977). Education systems in developing countries are largely ineffective because they are incomplete, lacking, for example, trained personnel, resources, or equipment: the consequent malfunctioning of one or more subsystems prevents the proper functioning of the system as a whole.

The role of managers is to ensure that all parts of the system are working properly, to monitor input, throughput, output and feedback, and to identify where the system is incomplete. Managers are controllers rather than leaders, and are interested in maintaining the equilibrium of the system. In such an approach, individuals and their attitudes do not figure at all. It is an approach consistent with bureaucracies and role cultures (Handy 1981), in which it is the organisation that has aims, rather than the individuals in it, and in which all members are assumed to agree with the aims.

This technical view of society has formed the basis for planning and managing educational reforms in developing countries (e.g., Havelock and Huberman 1977). Project managers are frequently appointed for technical expertise rather than for management skills. Projects are seen as opportunities for skill transfer in which the technical "expert" will train counterparts on the job. Nevertheless, this operation has to be managed, and "experts," as sources of technical knowledge, are expected to perform this task as well. These de facto managers are often inexperienced in management, and even if they are experienced, may bring with them culturally inappropriate expectations of the operations of organisations, so that their management experience is less valid. Westerners, who come from predominantly individualist cultures, are used to perceiving society in terms of systems (such as health, education, and social security). They commonly see themselves, not only subjectively as part of these systems, but also objectively as users of them. Expatriate project managers, whose role is temporary, are unlikely to feel membership of developing country systems, working practices, and products in a way that they would in their own community. They are likely to take a dispassionate, objective, and technical view of the organisation in which they are to work. Even if they are unaware of systems theory, they are likely to subscribe to its principles.

Efforts to reform ELT management at the National University of Côte d'Ivoire provide a good example. A fresh phase of project activity was devised in 1994 with the aim of centralising the management of ELT throughout the University (Delens 1994). Hitherto, each faculty had had its own, separate, ELT operation. This arrangement had led to inefficiencies, as there would be periods of the year in which English teachers from one faculty were underemployed, while counterparts in other faculties were overworked. It was impossible to redeploy those underemployed teachers to help their overworked colleagues without paying them overtime, even though they were working in the same institution. There was also a lack of effectiveness: teachers were only experienced in specific-purpose English in one faculty, whereas wider experience would have made them more consummate professionals, able to operate as language teachers in more subject areas. The proposal was to create a language unit within the University that would provide a service to all faculties. Part of the reasoning behind this, in addition to improving efficiency and effectiveness, was to create a higher profile for the teachers concerned, who were all secondary teachers "lent" to the University by the Ministry, and therefore had little status.

This proposed innovation can be seen as a response to a subsystem malfunction. Not all students were getting the amount of English to which they were entitled: there was more pressure on some teachers than on others; the subsystem was unable to spread the load. This information came from feedback, such as observation of outputs in terms of standards of English, and satisfaction of students and teachers. The objective of the innovation was to restore equilibrium to the system by spreading the load more equally and at the same time to broaden teachers' experience and professionalism by exposing them to different kinds of ESP. It was a top-down innovation, following a report commissioned by the Vice-Chancellor and subsequent recommendations. The report quantified inputs in terms of contact hours and use of equipment and classrooms. It evaluated the quality of instruction and the learning accumulated by throughputs/students as they progressed through the system, and measured outputs in terms of numbers receiving adequate training. The innovation was, in Havelock and Huberman's (1977) terms, an example of the fusion of subsystems (faculties) designed to create more openness: easier deployment of teachers where needed, and less isolation of individual teachers and groups. Nevertheless, there was opposition to this scheme by the teachers themselves. They did not, however, produce many convincing reasons for their opposition, other than point out practical difficulties such as having to travel between two campuses on a single day and incurring extra travelling expenses, all of which could easily have been resolved. In a collectivist society, a more compelling reason for their opposition may be that employment in separate faculties constituted membership of an in-group, a condition more valued than the prospect of other perceived benefits such as higher status and greater professional satisfaction, which entailed leaving the in-group for another structure where the group constitution was untried (Triandis 1990). Hui's (1990) findings point to a further consideration: institutional loyalty in collectivist societies may be more for departments of an organisation than for the organisation as a whole—in this case, for faculties rather than the wider University.

It would appear that expatriate project managers, influenced by their cultural orientations, are likely to try to effect changes by manipulating subsystems, feeling that a change in one part may bring about desired consequences in other parts. In contrast, individuals in developing societies may not see things in these terms at all: they are likely to be more collectivist, and to see society in terms of in-groups and out-groups, and relationships between groups. Project managers, if they perceive this kind of cultural orientation at all, are likely to think of it as an obstacle of the kind that can be overcome through strategic management techniques.

Strategic Management

Strategic management (e.g., Hickman and Silva 1984; Peters and Waterman 1988) is an approach to both planning and management that seeks to define organisational roles in relation to the external environment. It admits that planning cannot account for every eventuality, and hence seeks to be flexible, ready to respond to the unexpected. It explicitly takes account of cultural as well as other factors in the environment, and sees mistakes as an opportunity for learning. It underlies what educators such as Fullan (1993) and Whitaker (1993) describe as "learning organisations," one feature of which is that the culture of the organisation precedes and defines the structure, since it is consciously and deliberately receptive to its environment and open to change. In fact culture is seen as a manipulable tool, and the reason for analysing culture would be to identify "areas of activity which may be open to influence in order to promote desired organisational values" (O'Neill 1994, 106). In Fullan's words, "focussing on restructuring prior to working on reculturing puts the cart before the horse" (Fullan 1993, 67). This link between organisational culture and structure can be seen in the global factories now being created by enterprises (Todaro 1994), where instead of hierarchical, bureaucratic structures based in one country with branches elsewhere, units of production are located wherever is convenient, are more independent, and part of a flatter, less hierarchical overall structure. This "restructuring" could not have come about without a change in attitudes, a cultural change, at least on the part of the management. The extent to which "reculturing" precedes "restructuring," or vice versa, at lower levels within the workforce is less clear.

What is clear is that today, strategic management has enormous influence on approaches to school management, in Britain and elsewhere (e.g., Davies 1996). It is also seen as an appropriate tool for project management in developing countries (Caillods 1989; Verspoor 1992). According to Rondinelli et al. (1990, 23), management strategy and structures should be determined by the project's level of innovation (project objectives), the nature of the environment, and the value orientation of the implementers. However it is clear that for them local cultural values may be regarded as potential barriers to change, rather than as foundations on which change can be built, and they explicitly enjoin project managers to neutralise social or cultural traditions and practices that might conflict. In this way, the imposition of Western values continues, and strategic management techniques are routinely exported for application in schools in developing countries (cf. Commonwealth Secretariat 1993). Yet because of strategic management's explicit orientation towards coping with uncertainty in the environment, it may not be appropriate in cultures where certainty is highly valued (Hofstede's uncertainty avoidance), whether or not that certainty is real. Similarly, in societies where power distance (Hofstede 1980) is high and structures are vertical, as in many societies in the developing world, the flatter, horizontal organisational structures produced by strategic management may simply not function.

Project managers, faced with culturally based problems of implementation, are also likely to attempt to "reculture," although they may not view their activities in such terms. Such an effort preceded the attempted centralisation of the management of ELT at the National University of Côte d'Ivoire. In 1993 it was agreed by the donor that the ESP project should have a publications budget to enable publication of project-generated learning materials for sale to students. An investment was made to purchase paper and other materials for a print run of 1,000 copies of first-year ELT textbooks for the faculty of economics. The success of the publication could not be predicted with ease; since it was course material, in principle, every student should buy a copy. Therefore it should be priced lower than the cost of making photocopies, but with, initially, a small margin to cover costs through a relatively small sale. Thus, the price was cost plus a small profit. These materials turned out to be extremely popular, and sold out quickly, necessitating a new print run. Because of the volume of sales, even with a small margin, the total profits amounted to a sizeable sum, and it was the intention of the project managers not only to reinvest in further publications for other faculties, but also to help towards the purchase of project equipment, such as tape recorders and computer equipment. Here was another conflict: teachers in the faculty, who had worked hard to produce the materials, wanted to reward themselves for the work they had done, and thought that any equipment purchased should be for their faculty only, rather than for the project as a whole and for the nascent university-wide language unit. Triandis (1990) gives an account of how the distribution of resources is viewed in individualist and collectivist cultures. The project managers, being individualists, wanted to apply the principle of equity, and distribute any benefit evenly throughout the project. The teachers, collectivists, wanted the in-group, their faculty group, to benefit.

With hindsight, it is clear that the introduction of this publications operation as part of the project can be regarded as an attempt to "reculture," prior to introducing the new management structure. Project managers wanted to create a cross-faculty activity involving all English language teachers in the organisation, whose work would be "owned" by all of them. This would be a first step on the way to creating a feeling of professional solidarity and identity. Unfortunately, it was undertaken without sufficient cultural insight.

MORE APPROPRIATE APPROACHES TO MANAGEMENT

What, then, could be an approach to project management in developing countries that takes account of local cultural factors, that recognises that these are going to be the rules that apply, and that does not treat local values and attitudes as obstacles to be overcome? In short, how can cultural factors be turned into building blocks rather than stumbling blocks, and how can bridges be built between prevailing local attitudes and the foreign attitudes that development assistance inevitably brings with it? It seems that a great deal can be usefully learned from the work of educators with indigenous minorities, and with immigrant minorities, particularly in Europe.

Indigenous Minority Education

Stairs (1988) describes two models of curriculum development that have been used with indigenous minorities. The first of these, the cultural inclusion model, is criticised by Stairs because it involves external experts gathering information about the indigenous culture and language, developing a curriculum and materials in a sort of "tacking on" process in which indigenous cultural elements are simply added to dominant cultural elements. Subsequently, in training programmes for indigenous teachers, "selected people are retaught information as it has been selected and structured by the external culture" (Stairs 1988, 310). Indigenous people are used only as informants, and do not participate, while supposedly universal principles of pedagogy, literature, and child development, which already exist in the dominant culture, are used to incorporate the indigenous cultural knowledge into school programmes. This risks presenting the cultural specifics of the experts as universals, and it is a methodology which has much in common with the cultural manipulation proposed by strategic management approaches. Such cultural manipulation may be acceptable and practicable within national cultures where the values of individuals, the values of the organisation in which they work, and the proposed new values of the "reculturing" process are more likely to be compatible, but where distinct cultures meet across national boundaries for the purposes of development, the gaps may be too wide to bridge in this way. Stairs's own model, the cultural base model, presupposes that universals exist in all cultures, and that universals of human perception, thought, and language can be "learned through the specific knowledge and transmission style of any indigenous culture" (Stairs 1988, 309). Thus an indigenous child can learn non-indigenous mathematics concepts, for example, in an indigenous way.

Stairs illustrates the kind of information that is needed to develop indigenous culture-specific curricula according to this model: indigenous culture-specific information about childhood development stages and adult culture is added to culture-universal information on the same topic (Stairs 1988). It will be noted that there is no input from the dominant culture in which minority cultures find themselves. More recently, however, Stairs (1994) has come to consider dominant culture inputs: she suggests that the technological and communications revolution has made it impossible for dominant cultures to pretend that they are absolute, and thus "the negotiation of indigenous education is a two-way process: both insiders [indigenous peoples] and outsiders [dominant peoples] are changed" (Stairs 1994, 73, my brackets). In other words, there is the development of what she calls a "third culture" in indigenous schools, which is a linking of dominant and minority cultures. This goes beyond the practice of "culture domain separation," which some indigenous peoples have felt necessary to protect their fragile cultures (Aikman 1994; Teasdale and Teasdale 1994), because it permits access to other cultures while protecting the minority culture. Culture domain separation involves a decision by members of a minority culture to reject the influence of the dominant culture in the educational process. The decision may be conscious and explicit, as in the case of certain Australian aboriginal groups, who decided to adopt wholly aboriginal curricula (Teasdale and Teasdale 1994); or it may be a less conscious reaction, as with the Peruvian minority group discussed by Aikman (1994), who simply did not take part in any aspect of the organisation of the schools serving their community. In a world increasingly characterised by globalisation, "third cultures" are essential if globalisation is not, in reality, to mean a stark choice between Westernisation and marginalisation.

Intercultural Education

Other initiatives that seek to preserve the integrity of minority cultures while enabling them to interact on equal terms with dominant cultures are those of the Council of Europe to promote intercultural education. The context of these initiatives is that of immigrant minorities in Europe, in contrast to the indigenous minority context of Stairs's "third culture" concept. The aim, however, is similar. The intercultural movement grew as a result of the increasingly multicultural nature of European society, and the need to cater for an increasing number of minority groups. It is a reaction to the cultural inclusion model. The "tacking-on" process of this model gave rise to a number of problems in the European context: Which elements of the "culture of origin" should be tacked on? Even the mother tongue of many immigrant children is not necessarily the same as the national language of the country of origin, and learning it may be as much of a barrier as learning the host country language. What are the basic constituents of a culture, and how should they be taught? The cultural inclusion model risks both losing a structured approach to the culture of the country of origin, and presenting objects of that culture out of context. It also risks seeing cultural identity as something static rather than dynamic (Perotti 1994, 27–28). Further, it does not help minorities to deal with other (perhaps dominant) cultures on equal terms.

In the intercultural approach, individuals are seen as structured by their ethnic, cultural, and linguistic origins, but should also be capable of transcending ethnocentrism and integrating into the wider (and more diverse) networks of society on equal terms (Perotti 1994, 18). Surely this is, at least in part, how the newly industrialised countries (NICs) of East Asia have become a part of the global economy. Approaches to educational development projects that seek to achieve similar integration on equal terms fit well with Stairs's cultural base model, but they need, in addition to information about minority/indigenous cultures, inputs from dominant cultures so that commonalities can be established. Such approaches go beyond culture domain separation because they preserve the indigenous cultural base while enabling participation in a wider context. They are more analogous to Stairs's "third culture" concept.

The intercultural approach to education is thus a function of a policy of integration. Integration is contrary to assimilation (Perotti 1994). It refers to ". . . the accommodation that comes about when different groups maintain their respective core cultural identities, while at the same time merging into a superordinate group in other, equally important respects" (Furnham and Bochner 1986, 28). It involves, fundamentally, the capacity to compare and exchange values, norms, and behavioural models from a "position of equality" (Perotti 1994, 88). In this context, tradition is valued, but seen as something dynamic. According to Gokalp (1982), tradition is not something static, but is a process of reconstruction, in which people reinterpret, in the light of experience, their knowledge, behavioural models, self-images, and community identity as products of previous generations. They then select and reject from this reinterpreted data in a learning process.

IMPLICATIONS FOR PROJECT PLANNERS AND MANAGERS

Attempts to achieve acculturation towards Western values, whether conscious or unconscious, through development projects may lead to failure of those same initiatives if no account is taken of pre-existing local values. It often looks as if the new Asian economies have become more Western: this may only be part of a long-term orientation, in which elements are borrowed for their utility. Dia (1991, 12) cites Japan, Korea, and Taiwan as "examples of economies that have achieved high levels of modern production and advanced technology while maintaining their unique national traits."

If these "unique traits" are to become building blocks for change, project managers need to take on a "mediation function" (Caillods 1989, 33; Ellis 1996, 217; Furnham and Bochner 1986, 239). By mediation is meant "acting as a link between (cultures), representing each to the other" (Furnham and Bochner 1986, 239). It is what Stairs (1994) calls "negotiation." Project managers need an ability to bridge cultural gaps, if they are to mould the task culture of their projects in such a way that it can be integrated into the dominant culture of the host institution, while at the same time bringing about change. They need to understand what motivates their counterparts if they are to achieve project objectives, and may need to modify objectives in ways that make them acceptable and achievable. Ellis (1996) reports on an attempt by an ELT teacher trainer to make a methodology course acceptable in China: it had to be reframed in keeping with Chinese values, in such a way that the new knowledge could be incorporated into existing sets of beliefs and values. This is a familiar pedagogical concept: new knowledge can only be made sense of if it can be related to old knowledge. It is also an example of building a "third culture" in which something new is created, while the values of both teacher and learner remain intact. Furthermore, the distinction between teacher and learner, expert and counterpart, becomes blurred in a process of cooperation.

But what insights and skills do project managers need to be able to undertake this process of mediation? Of course, there is no substitute for experience, but education and training can also contribute. Project managers need to understand the cultural basis of their own attitudes and beliefs before they can understand those of others. It is encouraging that donor and development organisations now increasingly seek to recruit personnel designated as "project managers," people with management skills in addition to technical knowledge, rather than "technical experts" who are also expected to function as managers. It should be recognised, however, that Western management skills are based on Western cultural values, and may not always be appropriate in non-Western cultural contexts. Project management in alien cultural contexts is a different skill from management at home, especially as it usually involves skills transfer and institution building, and particular training is required.

Cultural training and self-training programmes based on cultural analyses such as that of Hofstede are known as culture-general assimilators. A good example is that of Brislin et al. (1986), in which participants attempt to analyse the (unexpected) outcome of intercultural interactions in cultural terms. Donor agencies need to make use of and develop this kind of instrument for project managers.

In addition, those with educational project management experience in different cultural contexts should be brought together to exchange their insights. This would produce a considerable amount of information that could form input for training and training materials such as those described above. Indeed "this body of knowledge should be called upon by project agencies in the planning stage" (Bradley 1994, 8). Logical framework analysis, for example, which is widely used in project planning, rests upon assumptions that certain activities will produce certain results under certain conditions (Eade and Williams 1995). However, these assumptions are often rooted in the donor culture and it is advisable to verify their viability in the target context at the planning stage. Project evaluations, too, rarely have a cultural focus and are often done inadequately if at all, since they increase the cost of projects. Yet assessment of successes and failures in cultural terms would provide useful feedback for planners. However, evaluation also limits the funds available for further projects, which are more of a priority for official, national, and international donor agencies, as it is politically expedient for them to be seen to be involved in more rather than less activity. Indeed, all of the suggestions made above involve expense; the question is whether additional expense can be justified by additional benefits and greater sustainability. This observation applies equally to small NGO projects and to larger, official donor projects (Riddell and Robinson 1992).

CONCLUSION

None of the above will come to be until there is a recognition that cooperation for development involves the meeting of cultures for the creation of "third cultures," and both donors and recipients move "from an ethnocentric perception to a non-dualistic, 'metacultural' perception" (Ellis 1996, 217). The fundamental question is whether the objectives of development projects are to be analogous to the concept of cultural assimilation or to that of integration as defined by Furnham and Bochner (1986): that is, whether they seek, consciously or unconsciously, to replace the values and attitudes of the beneficiary community with those of the donor, or whether they seek, consciously, to maintain positive aspects of both cultures and thereby create a common vision. Educational development projects are intended to improve the quality, quantity, efficiency, and effectiveness of education, but if such improvements are conceived solely in the terms of the donor, the power relation between donor and beneficiary is analogous to that between dominant and minority cultures, whether indigenous or immigrant. There may be, of course, many reasons for failure to achieve project objectives; but where failure can be attributed to cultural factors, a parallel may be drawn with the phenomenon of culture domain separation, in which there is rejection of the values of the dominant culture. Project planning must therefore include a negotiation, much like that discussed by Stairs (1994), that aims to discover cultural commonalities and differences, and to evaluate the worth of aspects of one culture to the other in the partnership. This is the basic tenet of intercultural education, and there is no reason why project planners and managers should not apply similar principles. Planners need to do more than determine the necessary roles in the project structure; they need also to consider how individuals in those roles will interact with one another and react to the changes implicit in the project plan. Project managers need an ability to interpret the behaviour of counterparts and the resources to communicate effectively with project staff.

The work of Hofstede (1980, 1983, 1986, 1994) provides a useful cultural analysis for both planners and managers. Hofstede's dimensions are not perhaps the only ones, nor indeed can they always explain behaviour in different societies. However, they do provide useful parameters for analysing the directions in which cultures and values might differ. Handy's (1981) description of the types of culture that may characterise organisations is also useful. Familiarity with these and other cultural analyses might have predicted, for example, the reactions of the Sudanese counterparts discussed by Leach (1991, 1994). It might predict where strategic management techniques may be of less value than they are in Western societies. Such awareness, coupled with a willingness to negotiate projects on a cultural level, could lead to an agreed reculturing and then to a successful restructuring to achieve project objectives. Those involved with educational development at any level should be in the forefront of such initiatives.

REFERENCES

Alaluf, M. 1982. "The Education and Cultural Development of Migrants." *Migrant Culture and Culture of Origin,* Project No. 7. Strasbourg: Council of Europe, Council for Cultural Cooperation.

Aikman, S. 1994. "School Curriculum as a Forum for Articulating Intercultural Relations with Particular Reference to the Peruvian Amazon." In *International Perspectives on Culture and Schooling: A Symposium Proceedings,* ed. E. Thomas. London: Institute of Education, University of London.

Baumgratz, G. 1995. "Language, Culture, and Global Competence: An Essay on Ambiguity." *European Journal of Education* 30 (4): 437–447.

Bradley, S. 1994. "A Framework for Identifying the Elements of Change in Overseas ELT Projects." *ELT Management* 14: 6–8.

Brislin, R., ed. 1990. *Applied Cross-Cultural Psychology.* Newbury Park, CA: Sage.

Brislin, R., K. Cushner, C. Cherrie, and M. Yong. 1986. *Intercultural Interactions.* London: Sage.

Brumfit, C. 1984. *Communicative Methodology in Language Teaching,* Cambridge: Cambridge University Press.

Bush, T., and J. West-Burnham, eds. 1994. *Principles of Educational Management.* Harlow: Longman.

Caillods, F., ed. 1989. *The Prospects for Educational Planning.* Paris: IIEP.

Carr-Hill, R. 1994. "Cultural Conditionality on Aid to Basic Education." In *International Perspectives on Culture and Schooling: A Symposium Proceedings,* ed. E. Thomas. London: Institute of Education, University of London.

Cheng, Y.C., and W.M. Cheung. 1995. "A Framework for the Analysis of Educational Policies." *International Journal of Educational Management* 9 (6): 10–21.

Commonwealth Secretariat. 1993. *Better Schools: Resource Materials for School Heads.* London: Commonwealth Secretariat.

Davies, B. 1996. "Re-Engineering School Leadership." *International Journal of Educational Management* 10 (2): 11–16.

Delens, M. 1994. "Effective Management Structures in Service English at Tertiary Level." *ELT Management* 15: 11–12.

Deregowski, J., S. Dziurawiec, and R. Annis, eds. 1983. *Expiscations in Cross-Cultural Psychology.* Lisse, Netherlands: Swets and Zeitlinger.

Dia, M. 1991. "Development and Cultural Values in Sub-Saharan Africa." *Finance and Development* (December): 10–13.

Eade, D., and S. Williams. 1995. *The Oxfam Handbook of Development and Relief.* Oxford: Oxfam.

Ellis, G. 1996. "How Culturally Appropriate Is the Communicative Approach?" *ELT Journal* 50 (3): 213–218.

Fukuyama, F. 1995. *Trust: The Social Virtues and the Creation of Prosperity.* London: Hamish Hamilton.

Fullan, M. 1993. *Change Forces.* London: Falmer.

Furnham, A., and S. Bochner. 1986. *Culture Shock: Psychological Reactions to Unfamiliar Environments.* London: Methuen.

Gardner, R, and W. Lambert. 1972. *Attitudes and Motivation in Second Language Learning.* Rowley, MA: Newbury House.

Gilbreath, R. 1986. *Winning at Project Management.* New York: John Wiley and Sons.

Gokalp, A. 1982. "Methodical Approach to the Problem of the Cultural Identity of the Children of Migrants." Appendix to *Migrant Culture and Culture of Origin,* Project No. 7. Strasbourg: Council of Europe, Council for Cultural Cooperation.

Handy, C. 1981. *Understanding Organisations,* 2nd ed. Harmondsworth: Penguin.

Han-Siu Chow, I. 1995. "Management Education in Hong Kong: Needs and Challenges." *International Journal of Educational Management* 9 (5): 10–15.

Harrison, L. 1992. *Who Prospers? How Cultural Values Shape Economic and Political Success.* New York: Basic Books.

Havelock, R., and A. Huberman. 1977. *Solving Educational Problems.* Paris: UNESCO.

Hickman, C., and M. Silva. 1984. *Creating Excellence.* London: Unwin.

Hofstede, G. 1980. *Culture's Consequences.* Beverly Hills: Sage.

Hofstede, G. 1983. "Dimensions of National Cultures in Fifty Countries and Three Regions." In *Expiscations in Cross-Cultural Psychology,* eds. J. Deregowski, S. Dziurawiec, and R. Annis. Lisse, Netherlands: Swets and Zeitlinger.

Hofstede, G. 1986. "Cultural Differences in Teaching and Learning." *International Journal of Intercultural Relations* 10: 301–320.

Hofstede, G. 1994. *Cultures and Organisations: Software of the Mind.* London: Harper Collins.

Hui, C. 1990. "Work Attitudes, Leadership Styles, and Managerial Behaviours in Different Cultures." In *Applied Cross-Cultural Psychology*, ed. R. Brislin. Newbury Park, CA: Sage.

Huntington, S. 1996. *The Clash of Civilisations and the Remaking of World Order.* New York: Simon and Schuster.

Klees, S. 1989. "The Economics of Education: A More Than Slightly Jaundiced View of Where We Are Now." In *The Prospects for Educational Planning*, ed. F. Caillods. Paris: IIEP.

Leach, F. 1991. "Counterpart Relationships on Technical Cooperation Projects: A Sudanese Study." Unpublished D.Phil. thesis, University of Sussex.

Leach, F. 1994. "Expatriates as Agents of Cross-Cultural Transmission." *Compare* 24 (3): 217–231.

MacLaughlin, J. 1994. "Globalisation and Territorial Identities: A Review of Recent Literature on the Politics of Place and Cultural Resistance." *Journal of Multilingual and Multicultural Development* 15 (5): 431–443.

Nunan, D. 1992. *Research Methods in Language Learning.* Cambridge: Cambridge University Press.

O'Neill, J. 1994. "Organisational Structure and Culture." In *Principles of Educational Management*, eds. T. Bush and J. West-Burnham. Harlow: Longman.

Perotti, A. 1994. *The Case for Intercultural Education.* Strasbourg: Council of Europe Press.

Peters, T., and R. Waterman. 1988. *In Search of Excellence: Lessons from America's Best-Run Companies.* New York: Harper and Row.

Phillipson, R. 1992. *Linguistic Imperialism.* Oxford: Oxford University Press.

Phillipson, R. 1996. "Linguistic Imperialism: African Perspectives." *ELT Journal* 50(2): 160–167.

Porto, M. 1996. "Integrating the Teaching of Language and Culture." *IATEFL Newsletter* 132: 14–15.

Richards, L. 1996. "Bursting the Culture Bubble." *IATEFL Newsletter* 132: 16.

Riddell, A. 1996. "Globalization: Emasculation or Opportunity for Educational Planning?" *World Development* 24 (8): 1357–1372.

Riddell, R. and M. Robinson. 1992. *The Impact of NGO Poverty Alleviation Projects: Results of the Case-Study Evaluations,* Working Paper 68. London: Overseas Development Institute.

Rondinelli, D., J. Middleton, and A. Verspoor. 1990. *Planning Educational Reforms in Developing Countries: The Contingency Approach.* Durham, NC: Duke University Press.

Stairs, A. 1988. "Beyond Cultural Inclusion: An Inuit Example of Indigenous Educational Development." In *Minority Education: From Shame to Shame*, eds. T. Skutnabb Kangas and J. Cummins. Clevedon, England: Multilingual Matters.

Stairs, A. 1994. "Indigenous Ways to Go to School: Exploring Many Visions." *Journal of Multilingual and Multicultural Development* 15 (1): 63–76.

Teasdale, J.I., and G.R. Teasdale. 1994. "Culture and Schooling in Aboriginal Australia." In *International Perspectives on Culture and Schooling: A Symposium Proceedings*, ed. E. Thomas. London: Institute of Education, University of London.

Thomas, E., ed. 1994. *International Perspectives on Culture and Schooling: A Symposium Proceedings.* London: Institute of Education, University of London.

Todaro, M. 1994. *Economic Development.* 5th ed. Harlow: Longman.

Triandis, H. 1990. "Theoretical Concepts That Are Applicable to the Analysis of Ethnocentrism." In *Applied Cross-Cultural Psychology*, ed. R. Brislin. Newbury Park, CA: Sage.

Verspoor, A. 1989. *Pathways to Change: Improving the Quality of Education in Developing Countries.* Washington, DC: World Bank.

Verspoor, A. 1992. "Planning of Education: Where Do We Go?" *International Journal of Educational Development* 12 (3): 233–244.

Whitaker, P. 1993. *Managing Change in Schools.* Buckingham: Open University Press.

White, R. 1993. "Saying Please: Pragmalinguistic Failure in English Interaction." *ELT Journal* 47(3): 193–202.

CHAPTER 20

Dilemmas Between Economics and Culture in Educational Aid

Lessons for Donors

FIONA LEACH

The chapters in this book have highlighted the interplay of economic and cultural considerations in educational decision making among a variety of stakeholders, including policy makers, planners, local officials, community groups, teachers, parents, and students. This rich panorama has ranged from the Pacific Islands through Asia, Africa, and the Middle East, to Latin America.

Within this collection there is a cluster of chapters that seek to highlight the dominance of economic paradigms in educational planning and policy making to the neglect and even the exclusion of cultural considerations. Some authors see formal education as having killed cultural diversity through the devaluation of local or nonschool knowledge. Konai Helu-Thaman on Tonga, Robert Serpell on Zambia, Munir Fasheh on Palestine, Bob and Jennie Teasdale on the Pacific Islands, Mikael Palme on Mozambique, and Mary Harris on the subject of women and working mathematics all write from this perspective. To them the "real" learning that takes place outside the school is at best devalued, at worst totally ignored, by the imposition of standardised curricula emanating from distant ministries of education. At the same time, ironically, schooling itself has all too often become meaningless, with no useful learning taking place; Michael Palme's chapter on Mozambique is particularly evocative of a process which has been reduced to empty rituals. A number of authors point the finger of blame at European colonialism which, along with early missionary activity, served to introduce and to perpetuate a Western model of education that in its new contexts was no longer able to serve the goal of cultural continuity and renewal for which it had been originally created. Rather it has led to cultural dislocation, to what Ali Mazrui (1980, 51), speaking in the context of Africa, calls the "western onslaught on the African mind."

To those holding such views, colonialism with its negative influences is far from dead. It lives on in its new guise of multinational and global corporations; in northern hegemony over global political, economic, and technological developments; and in the international development agenda whereby aid agencies in the north hold a monopoly not only over accepted definitions of development, but also over the options and choices made available to resource-poor governments and individuals in the south. These agencies determine not only how development should be viewed but also how it should be shaped. To Munir Fasheh, writing in this volume about Palestinian aspirations for self-determination, this includes the control of people's minds and the limitation of their dreams.

These chapters lay out a rich carpet of cultural complexity and multiple realities alongside what would appear to be starker and simpler economic imperatives. Brian Street's chapter offers a good example of this. He points to the simplistic definitions of literacy which prevail in international development thinking. These are based on outsiders' misreadings of people's daily interactions that may include informal modes of written as well as oral communication. This written communication may be largely hidden to the outsider and hence remain unrecognised because it does not form part of the formal schooling process and does not utilise school literacy. People are branded illiterate because they are not versed in this official school literacy, despite using alternative literacies in real situations with real purposes (commercial literacy and koranic literacy, in Brian Street's example). As he points out here and in previous writings, illiteracy is associated with ignorance and inferior social status; it is even seen as a disease which has to be eradicated through campaigns (Street 1990). By not acknowledging these alternative literacy skills, large numbers of people are condemned as somehow inadequate members of society.

While Brian Street's concern is with literacy, other writers view formal education in a similar way. The definition and content of (formal) education is determined by politicians and bureaucrats who, through their own educational experiences and access to international fora of debate, feel relatively at ease with the alien concepts, norms, and values imported into their societies from Western cultures through, among other things, the medium of schooling. In this respect, schooling has been a divisive force: just as prevailing definitions of literacy classify people as either literate or illiterate, so does formal education divide them into those who are educated and those who are not. In some instances, this may be little more than a distinction between those who have adopted Western lifestyles and those who have not. Reading Mikael Palme's vivid description of Mozambican classrooms as providing a sterile and stultifying learning environment, one wonders what type of knowledge is being taught, especially when it is contrasted with the richness of local culture and indigenous learning. It is not difficult to see that in such circumstances formal education has become divorced from learning.

The reality is that in many contexts the actual content of education has become less important than the status bestowed on the individual through the acquisition of paper qualifications. It is the traditional link between education and salaried employment, and hence with economic wealth and social status, that allowed Western-style schooling to take hold in every corner of the globe, and in so doing to have inadvertently played a major role in creating a class structure in countries where it barely existed previously. The close link between education and jobs has now been severed in the poorest countries, which have suffered economic recession and chronic unemployment, resulting in some cases in reduced demand for schooling; it is nevertheless largely tolerated by parents because they still perceive it to be the only possible route to economic success for their children. In contrast, they do not see it as having any intrinsic value in enhancing daily life in the community or providing a vehicle for cultural renewal. Quite the opposite: the school's high walls symbolise its separation from the community and, as Mikael Palme's chapter shows, schooling can even be seen as a threat to community stability and harmony.

While not denying the importance of economic development and the role of education in promoting economic growth and prosperity (for some), the authors in this cluster of chapters make a powerful plea for more culturally sensitive and meaningful learning environments for young people and for a more sophisticated approach in which the school and the economy are not separated from indigenous learning and local culture. The need for cultural sensitivity even extends to the financing of education: Mercy Tembon, in Chapter 11, argues that current patterns of private financing, which rely exclusively on cash payments made by individuals, conflict with traditions of communal solidarity, communal perceptions of costs and benefits, and payments in kind (e.g., livestock, farm produce).

A contrasting perspective, persuasively argued, is offered by two contributions to this volume: Chapter 8 by Christine McNab and Peter Stoye on Ethiopia, and Chapter 9 by Keith Lewin on Mauritius. While acknowledging the importance of culturally appropriate curricula and flexible forms of schooling, they point forcefully to the significant costs that policies based on a respect for cultural values and diversity in the provision of education may incur. This may be in terms of teaching in national or regional languages, or tolerating a wasteful system of high repetition rates or high teacher absenteeism. To these writers, the validity of decisions influenced by cultural considerations needs to be justified in economic terms; in other words, there need to be clear benefits to educational quality in terms of improved achievement or cost-effectiveness. These authors are also much more conscious not only of the "costs of culture" but also of the problematic nature of the term "culture." Whose culture? Defined and endorsed by whom? As Keith Lewin points out:

> Culture is widely used in the education and development literature as an explanation for differences in developmental status between countries that cannot be explained in other ways. It sometimes seems that culture is treated as a "residual"—whatever is left to explain after all other factors have been taken into account is assumed to be the result of cultural differences (155).

At the same time, the belief that students in school absorb Western "culture" as an all-embracing body of knowledge, ideas, values, and practices like sponges is clearly simplistic. As John Lowe points out in his chapter, Solomon Island students were quite capable of subscribing to two parallel conceptual frameworks and moving with relative ease between them. They accepted the usefulness of science in everyday life and the economic importance of science education without adopting a corresponding science-based world view, preferring instead to maintain their cultural integrity and faith in familiar traditional beliefs, including magic.

ECONOMICS, CULTURE, AND THE DONOR AGENDA

Beyond the immediate contexts presented in this volume, there is no doubt, as Angela Little pointed out in her introductory chapter, that the economic paradigm has dominated in the minds of both educational policy makers and planners in developing countries and international donor officials over the past half century. The discourse surrounding the relationship between education and development has been indisputedly an economic one: the language of economics, of human capital, rates of return, investment in human resources, budgetary allocations to education, and labour market linkages predominates. At the same time, as Brian Street points out, "culture" as a fixed concept has been seen as an obstacle to progress and modernity, a "problem" and a negative influence; it has not been viewed as a resource, an ally, and a strength to be harnessed to the cause of social, economic, and individual advancement. In the field of education, taking cultural factors into account is seen as detrimental to increased efficiency. As a result, those alternative perspectives which argue that greater equity in education (e.g., for minority groups, for women) or greater responsiveness to the needs of self-development and cultural regeneration will of themselves help deliver a more effective system and ultimately national prosperity have not been heard as loudly on the international development arena as have economic viewpoints; hence, they have not been reflected in educational policy, planning, or implementation. The importance of this volume, therefore, is that it has given its contributors the opportunity to bring together and to contrast perspectives which reflect more forcefully either the economic or the cultural dimension of education. It also provides a long overdue forum to those who wish to espouse the cause of greater cultural sensitivity in education.

However, a debate which poses economic progress against cultural tradition in the postmodernist era of the 1990's would be simplistic and ill-founded. Earlier decades produced plenty of examples of the naive belief in a single linear path to development along which some societies had progressed further than others (Inkeles and Smith 1974; Lerner 1958; McClelland 1961; Rogers and Svenning 1969). The current trend towards globalisation and interconnectness, with the growth of global corporations, integrated markets, mobile sites of production, and migrant labour, alongside the emergence of the "Asian tiger" economies, has fundamentally shaken the old world order and the old way of thinking. Jock Stirrat, speaking from an anthropologist's viewpoint, makes the point forcefully in Chapter 2 that it is no longer acceptable to believe that economic theory (which was at the heart of the model of linear progress) is based on a scientific rationality which exists independent of culture and offers universal models and frameworks. Jock Stirrat views economics as a cultural construct, as much a part of human activity as for example religion, art, or music. As he points out, neoclassical economics originated in the practices of the 18th-century marketplace of Europe. He cites other writers to support him in this refutation of economics as an objective, neutral discipline, with methods of analysis and interpretation which can be applied to all types of economic systems, whether "developed" or "developing." Yet economics has proved to be very powerful, retaining its legitimacy as the foremost analytical and predictive tool available to nation states, despite numerous empirical failures. Economists have been particularly effective at claiming it to be above questioning and, like religion, incapable of disproof (Stirrat, 38).

In the domain of education, economics also dominates, with its own subdiscipline in the economics of education and its own theory on the link between education and development, namely human capital theory. Since the 1960s, this theory has dominated international development thinking on education, arguing that governments need to view education as investment, not consumption, the product of which is an educated and disciplined workforce, which will in turn generate economic growth. However, if economic theory is culture bound, as Jock Stirrat suggests, then so must human capital theory be; in other words, it is a product of Western intellectual perspectives and socioeconomic circumstances. A sad consequence of the failure to grasp the problematic nature of these claims to universal validity is that donors have ignored the possibility that other cultures may have their own valid economic paradigms and development discourses, what Jock Stirrat calls "alternative rationalities."[1] As Sheila Aikman shows in Chapter 6, peoples living in close geographical proximity can have very different perspectives of what constitutes development for themselves and for the region and hence different views of the purpose of education. In ignoring the existence of multiple perspectives and paradigms, donors are attempting, as Angela Little suggests in Chapter 1, to transfer concepts of education's role in development across cultures "blind."

In this final chapter, I seek to examine briefly the role that donor agencies, bilateral as well as multilateral, have played in determining and promoting these universalistic economic views of education, and will argue that donors' own attempts at promoting economic and social development in the poorer countries of the world have largely failed because they have not recognised that their proposed solutions and strategies were themselves culture bound and may therefore be inappropriate to the contexts into which they were introduced. I will suggest that donors need to move away from looking at educational provision in exclusively quantitative and economic terms and relying on universal models, towards a more varied and complex portfolio of forms of support, which will assist governments and groups to produce their own customised solutions.

Some of the chapters in this volume make specific reference to donor activity in education and development, in particular Chapter 19 by Michael Delens, but also those written by Munir Fasheh (Chapter 5), Jennie and Bob Teasdale (Chapter 13), and Konai Helu-Thaman (Chapter 4). Most have negative views of this intervention; some (e.g., Robert Serpell in Chapter 7 and Mikael Palme in Chapter 14) go beyond criticism to offer suggestions as to how donors and governments can develop culture-sensitive and innovative strategies for dealing with issues of nonenrolment, inequity, and poor quality that will reap benefits in the long term.

DONORS AND THE ECONOMIC IMPERATIVE

I will start by suggesting that aid, whether in education or other sectors, is an industry and as such it is driven by a largely economic agenda. Indeed, aid is a truly global industry. In 1995, for example, the major bilateral and mulilateral donors, together with the development banks, disbursed over $60 billion to 163 developing countries and territories (OECD 1996), much of it on a loan basis, with repayment conditions and interest rates as in any other commercial venture. (Grants are only given to the poorest countries and not by the World Bank, which nevertheless offers them highly preferential lending rates.)

The aid industry is made up of a relatively small "club" of international development banks,[2] multilateral, and bilateral donor agencies (supplemented by NGOs and religious or charitable organisations, whose contribution in monetary terms is a negligable percentage of the total). However, it employs a vast army of personnel, from directors, divisional heads, and regional desk officers down to office drivers and cleaners in a powerful bureaucratic network which straddles the globe, from headquarters in the rich donor cities of the north to regional and national offices in the poor recipient countries of the south.[3] Because international agencies offer employment opportunities to people from the south as well as the north, tens of thousands of people have a vested interest in seeing the aid industry grow and prosper. Like all business ventures, aid agencies have short-, medium- and long-term plans, budgets with complex accounting procedures, annual audits, and certain recognised procedures of accountability and quality control. Not surprisingly, they also have to produce results—results that can be reported to the presidents of the World Bank and the IMF, to the administrators of U.N. agencies, to government ministers, to directors and executive boards, to trustees, and to the general public whose taxes fill the aid coffers in the first place. This requirement to produce results which can be quantified, evaluated in the short term, and translated into tangible benefits means that donor personnel need to operate comfortably with economic models and formulae. It is therefore not a coincidence that economists continue to predominate in the development banks and donor agencies, although in recent years increasing numbers of sociologists and anthropologists have been recruited in the face of public attacks on donor proposals to fund projects which are considered to threaten people's livelihoods and to increase social inequalities.

As already indicated, the belief that there is a single path to development that all nations can follow, and that states can control its course in a rational and orderly fashion, while holding back the trend towards fragmentation and disintegration, has been discredited. Nevertheless, most development agencies continue to live in a modernist era and to subscribe to human capital theory, although, as Angela Little points out, a greater awareness in recent years that economic growth is not an end in itself has led to a less rigid and unquestioning faith in its power and to a broader view of the benefits of education. These now include improved health and nutrition, reduced fertility, enhanced citizenship, and increased equity. This theory has provided a rationale to both governments and donors to put often scarce resources into educational development, and, more recently, to engage in educational reform and rationalisation. The exact nature of the benefits that aid has brought to education, let alone to other sectors, has never been truly assessed and certainly cannot be addressed here. However, it is probably not inaccurate to generalise that aid has, at least over the past two decades, most benefited those countries which had already developed the rudiments of an industrial base, some sound infrastructure, and a consistent policy commitment to human resource development, in particular at the basic education level (i.e., most countries in East and South East Asia, some South and Central American countries). A stable political system, and—the World Bank (1995) would argue—sound governance, have no doubt also helped. In other words, aid has benefited those countries which least needed it. For the poorest countries, which are mainly to be found in sub-Saharan Africa and South Asia, where almost all economic activity is around agriculture or natural resources, where the pool of trained workers is smaller, and where political instability and mismanagement are all too common, aid is most needed but ironically has had the least effect, some would argue even a negative effect, on development.

Over the past decade sub-Saharan Africa has received in the region of $16–19 billion annually in official development assistance (1994 values), representing between 30 and 39 percent of the total aid budget (derived from OECD figures, 1996). Previous decades would have seen slightly lower figures. In total, this represents a massive amount of aid for sub-Saharan African countries in the post-independence era. Part of this development assistance was used to help governments throughout the 1960s and 1970s to fund a phenomenal expansion of state-provided education which in the end has proved unsustainable. For, despite the aid, their educational systems, like their economies, are crumbling. It is not insignificant that donor interventions during this period specifically supported expansion: building more colleges and faculties to absorb the graduates of the mushrooming primary and secondary schools, helping to train more teachers and, in the case of the poorest countries, contributing to recurrent education costs through balance of payments support. Later, in the 1980s, donors became concerned with the consequences of this unbridled expansion, seeking to advise and support the elimination of inefficiencies such as high dropout and repetition rates, the reduction of excessive bureaucracy, and improved planning and rationalisation of procedures. These have been largely quantitative concerns. Qualitative inputs, such as reforms to improve the relevance and quality of the school curriculum, asssessment practice, or teacher education, were far less common. Even where there were attempts by donors to encourage governments to address local needs through curriculum reform, as in the failed diversification of secondary schooling, the incentive for this was provided by economic needs (to provide young people with skills to make a living in their local community), not cultural needs.[4]

This focus on expansion is not surprising given the predominance of the economic model of development, and human capital theory in particular (more schools to produce more workers). Qualitative modifications to a well-tried and tested model that had worked well in the half century or so of compulsory state-funded schooling in Western Europe and the United States appeared unnecessary.

It is not easy to assess the extent to which this heavy emphasis on quantitative aspects of educational development at the expense of the qualitative, combined with donor imperatives which have demanded quick and easily interpretable results, have contributed to the poor performance of sub-Saharan Africa's educational systems. Perhaps greater attention to the curriculum and greater sensitivity to the need for cultural relevance, including the medium of instruction, might have reaped benefits in the long run. Looking for new, alternative approaches, doing things in a qualitatively different way, adapting and thinking creatively and flexibly might have been better than seeking to do the same things more efficiently. It is also true that the educational record of the first wave of so-called Asian tiger economies (Hong Kong, South Korea, Singapore, Taiwan) and the until recently expanding economies of the second wave in South East Asia (e.g., Malaysia, Indonesia, and Thailand) has been much better than that of sub-Saharan Africa, although their systems have also not been noticeable for embracing innovation and seeking to modify the imported model of schooling. However, their governments would appear to have been better positioned through their relatively greater economic strength to resist the vagaries of donor policies and to use aid to education more discriminatingly. This has allowed them to develop their own priorities without interference (e.g., good basic education for all, before expanding at higher levels) in a way which has served the economy more effectively than those determined under the tutelage of donors in resource-starved, relatively powerless, sub-Saharan Africa.

I now wish to look at one specific feature of aid, the project, and in so doing to continue the theme of the previous chapter. Drawing on research carried out in the Sudan in the late 1980s, I suggest that the project may well be presented as an appropriate means of delivering development assistance in all situations, but that, like economic theory and the notion of literacy, it is culturally constructed. The failure to recognise this has meant that the project has been more of a handicap than an asset in the development struggle.

THE PROJECT AS CULTURAL ARTEFACT

For decades, the project has been a favourite vehicle for disbursing aid money to the poorer countries of the south, with the aim of helping them to develop their own social and economic infrastructure. It has been the mainstay of most technical cooperation agreements between developed and developing countries. Although somewhat out of favour now as a freestanding intervention, projects have become part of broad programmes of support to a whole sector (e.g., education) or sub-sector (e.g., basic education, vocational education). It is more common now to find large multifacted programmes of external assistance given by a cluster of donors and comprising a number of projects or other interventions. One example would be the District Primary Education Project (DPEP) in

India, which by 1995 covered 12 states (Varghese 1996) and involved a large number of multi- and bilateral donors in a broad programme linking a variety of interventions.

The origins of the project lie in Western and more specifically American industry, where research and development (R&D) projects were first set up to develop innovations, to advance technology, and to enhance productive capacity and profits. Governments also fund research projects, for example, to search for new cures to cancer, or to examine the links between ill health and poverty. In such projects the emphasis is on planning, on purposeful execution and completion, and on positive outcomes. Some of the essential characteristics of a project might therefore be considered as follows: a project has a specific goal or set of goals; it is short-term and transient (it is dismantled when the task is complete); it is staffed by people who possess the requisite expertise and/or qualities for the task in hand; it is relatively well resourced; it is divorced from the routine work of the organisation in which it is based, so that it generates its own dynamics and work patterns; and its effectiveness is judged in terms of tangible outcomes, for example, a new design, a new product, or a new set of data.

The original project was therefore the product of a particular cultural context. It was developed in a setting where certain principles of planning and rationality prevailed and where the aim was to fulfil a predetermined economic or social need. The development project of the type supported by donors has evolved in a different context, this time a cross-cultural one. Nevertheless, it still has many of the formal characteristics of a R&D project, in particular in that its brief is very specific, with clearly laid down goals and procedures, clear funding criteria, and a short timescale (typically 3–5 years). It is still very much the product of "Western" thinking in that it is designed largely by donor officials and advisers (who are overwhelmingly from Western countries), albeit with varying degrees of consultation of officials on the recipient side. It is thus still embedded in Western ways of perceiving reality, Western forms of social and institutional behaviour, and Western views of the individual and society (Sachs 1992). The process of implementation is usually supervised by expatriate personnel working with national counterparts identified by the host institution, whether this be a ministry, a university/college, a research centre, or some other type of government-supported agency. It is usually well resourced, in particular in relation to the national institution, and is not expected to contribute to the routine work of the latter; rather it is responsible for developing and introducing some kind of institutional change (new course materials, new technologies, or new work practices).

The success rate of projects in terms of generating *sustainable* development in the poorest countries has been very disappointing (despite some protestations to the contrary, e.g., Cassen 1994). I would suggest that this is in large part due to the donors' irresistible desire to run the development project as if it were an R&D project, in other words to develop a new product as quickly and as cheaply as possible. Yet, the development project is a radically different concept to the R&D project, in that the *product* ought to be less important than the *process*. In the context of an education project, "product" might refer to numbers of teachers trained, students enrolled, new schools built, or textbooks written. "Process" would refer to what is called "institution-building" or "capacity-building." This would include generating and institutionalising new knowledge, skills, and practices which would lead to increased institutional effectiveness and efficiency, and a greater ability to respond to new challenges and changing environments. This is the long-term goal of most development projects, and technical cooperation in general. However, the reality is that donor priorities to see the project completed within its original timescale usually prevail over those of the recipients' need for open-ended, sustainable, and self-reliant development. In other words, the donors' economics-driven agenda, which demands that the project achieve tangible results (which address, of necessity, short-term goals) as a reasonable return on their initial investment, dominates over the more elusive, less tangible, and more complex needs of institution-building. These are likely to be time-consuming, involving, for example, the sharing of ideas and experiences, trying out a range of alternatives, and allowing people to learn from their mistakes. The imbalance in power between donor and recipient, between product (results) and process (institution-building), parallels that between economics and culture. Donor views of development and donors' choices of available options prevail because it is the donor who holds the purse strings (and is at the same time anxious to spend money). Yet, the benefits of project interventions are only sustainable if there is internalisation of new ways of thinking and doing and improved practice, and this cannot take place in the short term.

As a result of the "rational" economic considerations underlying the project dynamics, expatriate personnel are obliged to supervise the project in such a way that logical frameworks are adhered to, deadlines met, quarterly reports produced, and other donor requirements attended to which will indicate that the project is progressing satisfactorily. However, on the recipient side, the low motivation, lack of professional support, and poor pay which appear to characterise public-sector employment in the poorer countries of the world and which usually makes moonlighting a necessity, means that national counterparts are often unwilling to devote themselves with the same level of commitment and energy as the expatriates to meeting the project's goals. At the same time they are accustomed to working in a cumbersome and hierarchical bureaucracy (what Handy 1985 would characterise as a role culture) and are ill-prepared for the pressurised hothouse atmosphere of the project (Handy's task culture). This creates an incompatability of work styles, differing perceptions of how the project should be run and what its purpose is, and different time horizons. The end result is that the expatriates do the bulk of the work on the project, acting as both managers and implementers, and converting what may have started as a collaborative working relationship (essential for genuine institution-building) into a superior-subordinate relationship. This is one in which the expatriate wields most of the power because he/she controls the project budget, takes most of the decisions, and becomes increasingly dismissive of the opinions and actions of other people (Leach 1997).

On the Sudanese projects researched, such a heavy-handed approach created indifference and resentment, and in some cases even led to blocking or delaying tactics by national staff. The resulting scenario is far from encouraging for the development of interdependent structures and processes within the host institution, and means that the project operates in isolation, developing no sense of ownership of the change process among national staff. Its presence may even weaken the already underdeveloped local capacity, if, for example, project management spills over into routine institutional management and donor personnel end up making all important policy decisions. In this way it is actually hindering rather than promoting institution-building; it is *counter*-developmental. For development to take place, the expatriate needs to act as a guide and a facilitator, and *not* as an authoritarian leader or a project implementer who takes on routine operational tasks in order to meet short-term objectives.

Hence cultural forces on the ground, pertaining to both the organisational culture of the host institution (cf. Michael Delens' chapter) and the wider national/local culture, mean that the project takes on a life of its own; just as the school in rural Mozambique (and elsewhere) has become a meaningless parody of its original model and has ceased to be a forum for real learning, so does the project lose all resemblance to its original design and ceases to be an effective tool for development. Like the school in rural Mozambique, it has been mediated and altered by "culture"[5] and has not been adapted significantly enough to allow it to meet its goals in a radically different context.

CROSS-CULTURAL TRANSFER

There is another dimension to the argument that the development project is a cultural artefact. Central to the concept of technical cooperation is the notion that the knowledge and skills which are judged (it is not always clear by whom) as lacking in the host institution will be passed on to national counterparts by expatriate personnel during the process of working together within the project environment. This is the apprenticeship model of informal "on-the-job" training. There has been a tendency among donor-based policy makers and planners to see such transfer as fairly straightforward and unproblematic; this is largely because it is assumed that the new types of knowledge and skills being introduced have universal relevance and applicability, and that the benefits of acquiring such knowledge and skills will be immediately apparent to national staff. Neither assumption is correct. It is naive to assume that knowledge is in some way neutral or culture-free and will be accorded equal value by all parties, for the way in which it is defined, interpreted, and selected for transfer, the uses to which skills are put, and the manner in which they are used, are all mediated by cultural context. While there is general acknowledgement that the transfer process is problematic, there has been little effort to understand why this is so.

The success of the transfer process, and of the project as a whole, is dependent on the internalisation of the new knowledge and skills, which in turn would normally result in new (and improved) practices. And it is the introduction of new *practices*, not the knowledge and skills per se, which is highly problematic. This is clearly shown in Michael Delens's chapter in the context of attempts to reform the management of English language teaching at the National University of Cote d'Ivoire. For the practices being suggested through the medium of the project reflect Western ways of thinking, doing, and behaving which may not suit the norms and values embedded in the receiving culture. They are clearly culture-specific and have no objective or neutral value. Just as Brian Street has argued that we cannot talk of one model of literacy or a fixed notion of culture (Chapter 3), Jock Stirrat that economic theory is a cultural construct (Chapter 2), and Mary Harris that school mathematics is only one form of mathematics (street mathematics and women's working mathematics being of equal worth) (Chapter 17), so also is the project a cultural product. Hence, what is being offered for transfer as an essential part of institution-building, whether it be knowledge, skills, or new forms of institutional behaviour, does not necessarily carry the same value and meaning for counterparts as it does for their expatriate colleagues.

One particularly salient example of this relates to the changing nature of professional work, not least in the field of teaching. In Northern European countries over the past two decades, there has developed a strong tradition of student-centred, problem-solving teaching methods which often involve students carrying out practical tasks and engaging in project work. This usually takes place within the school, but it may at times involve going out into the community (e.g., to carry out a survey, or investigate some natural phenomenon). However, in societies where there is strong social conformity and a rigid social hierarchy, such changes in classroom practice can be perceived as threatening both in terms of status and customary work patterns. Student-centred teaching can be seen as undermining the conventional authoritarian teacher-student relationship, while practical work can be seen as threatening the status of an academic, who regards his/her work as being mainly in the theoretical domain (with theoretical knowledge considered superior to practical).

At the same time, in the countries of the north there have been dramatic changes in work practices over the past decade or so, as both public and private organisations have been required to implement economy measures and improve efficiency by cutting back on office support staff and introducing more flexible roles and practices. This, together with the growth of information technology, has meant that professionals have had to become accustomed to carrying out certain tasks which were in the past seen as belonging to the domain of administrators and secretaries, such as word-processing, managing a budget, and photocopying. This has so far not been the case among most professionals in the south, at least not among those in government service. They would consider their status as professionals severely compromised if they were to take on administrative tasks (Leach 1995). Yet most projects contain implicit assumptions about the need for democratic management styles, clear division of responsibilities, high levels of accountability, flexible work practices, and in the context of education, more practical components to both academic and vocational courses. A commitment to meeting such goals would be likely to be seen as threatening the existing power structures and informal networks of the host institution (Reilly 1987).

The perceived superiority of theoretical/academic knowledge over practical/vocational knowledge means that even the mode of transfer of knowledge and skills within the project may well be questioned. On-the-job training, being a form of apprenticeship often associated with artisan work, may not be recognised as a valid form of knowledge and skills upgrading for a professional, whereas an academic qualification would be. Where national counterparts hold comparable academic qualifications to the expatriate "expert" (and in some cases higher) as is increasingly the case, there is likely to be resentment at the suggestion that the expatriate is training the counterpart. Indeed, my research into a number of aid projects in the Sudan revealed that on the whole the national staff did not see the benefits of the project at all in terms of acquiring new knowledge or skills, or engaging in institutional change; rather they saw it purely in terms of the project providing badly needed resources, the lack of which was the main reason for the institution's underperformance (Leach 1991).

Ultimately, within the project setting, the readiness of local counterparts to change their attitudes and behaviour and to adopt new work practices, for example different teaching methods or a new management style, may depend on whether they see these as appropriate to their specific work situation, as benefiting them personally or the institution as a whole, and as having a positive rather than a negative impact on their occupational and social status. Fullan (1991) teaches us that change is stressful and it consumes much time, energy, and commitment. *All* development projects involve change, often quite radical change, for counterparts, a fact which expatriates preoccupied with meeting project targets all too often forget. Rarely do they or the project's planners ask themselves whether national counterparts and others affected by the project do indeed see the benefits of the changes being asked of them. Unfortunately, the reverse is all too often the case, with the project seen as a *threat* and not as a benefit.

I would suggest, therefore, that many projects fail totally to reach their development objectives because the transfer of knowledge, skills, and practices across cultures is highly problematic. While individuals may acquire new knowledge and skills appropriate to their discipline or profession, they may choose not to put them into practice if they see them as incompatible with their own working environment or of no particular benefit to themselves.

THE CONSULTANT AS ECONOMIC AGENT OR CULTURAL MEDIATOR?

In this final section, I examine the role of the consultant within the project context. As Michael Delens has shown in the previous chapter (Figure 19.1), the expatriate operates at the cultural interface between the donor organisational culture and the host organisational culture (which themselves are embedded in their own broader national culture) in a potential position of coordinator or mediator. Hence he/she is at the heart of any tensions that may exist between economic and cultural considerations surrounding the project. In this section, I shall offer a contrast between the role of the long-term expatriate consultant (more frequently termed "adviser" or "expert" in the literature) and the short-term consultant,[6] whose presence on the development scene for a range of reasons is becoming much more prevalent, and to consider whether the trend towards short-term consultancy is beneficial or detrimental to the development process, at least in education.

The advantage of the long-term expatriate presence on a project was that, if the person was "culture-sensitive," he/she could get to know the national and local context thoroughly, acting as an intermediary between the donor agency employing him/her and the ministry or host institution in which the project is based. Such a person would supposedly know how to get things done without treading on toes, while circumventing troublesome bureaucracy. More importantly, he/she could establish a strong collaborative relationship with counterparts and allow the project an element of stability and continuity (in the past, it was not unknown for expatriates to stay 8–10 years on a contract basis in any one post).

The disadvantage, and in most instances the reality, was that the presence of resident expatriates created a situation of dependence on the expatriates to get things done and to move the project forward, as has already been shown, to a point where often the daily running of the project was carried out almost exclusively by the expatriate(s), in some cases overlapping with management of the host institution. This then created resentment and led to non-cooperation (Leach 1995). Not surprisingly, over time some developing country governments became extremely sensitive to the proliferation of expatriates and the escalating costs associated with their employment, and questioned the continuing need to rely on outsiders, in particular for routine project management and implementation.

Hence the attractiveness of the short-term consultant: local staff are actually left to implement the project themselves, while receiving regular assistance from one or more consultants who act as facilitators, sources of information, and specialist advisers rather than as trainers and project managers. In this way, dependence on outsiders is reduced and capacity-building is much more likely to take place. National staff are able to make their own decisions, act independently, and manage the project themselves. This should make for a less patronising and more equal relationship. However, the reality is that, whereas the long-term expatriate could in fortuitous circumstances act as a mediator and a filter between the two cultures, in the case of the short-term consultant, there is not the time and the space to develop strong relationships, for he/she is even more constrained by financial and time pressures than the resident expatriate. As Arthur and Preston (1996, 8) state in their study of overseas consultancy, "the dynamics of the market are paramount." For the growth of private consultancy firms, the introduction of competitive tendering by donor agencies (reflecting the national political and economic orthodoxies of donor countries), the increase in freelance consultancy as jobs in the north become less permanent, and the expectation by cash-strapped universities that academics will/can raise money through consultancy work, has radically changed the conditions under which consultancy work takes place. It has become a commercial activity, the dynamics of which do not encourage genuine development work any more than did the long-term consultancy model.

Skills transfer and training are probably the least effective part of consultancy work (Arthur and Preston 1996, 20–21). The transient nature of the project, the fact that few consultants are trained trainers, the lack of time available in a tight schedule, the uncertainty of the outcomes of any time spent in training, and the difficulty of evaluating its effectiveness, mean that it is not given a high priority. My research in Sudan in the late 1980s in fact showed that the institutions needed not so much training or skills transfer in *technical* areas (as is usually indicated in the project aims), but rather training in *management*, in other words a change in working practices which, as has already been suggested, is highly problematic (Leach 1991).

Despite this shift from long- to short-term consultancy, it could be argued that little has changed in reality in the donors' approach to technical cooperation. As Jock Stirrat points out elsewhere (1997), consultants continue to work within a modernist paradigm, a world in which rationality, certainty, predictability, and "objective" knowledge prevail. They see their work as technical and rational, and therefore in some way universally valid; in no way would they see it as a form of cultural activity.

Yet, as with the project, the school, and the bureaucracy, consultancy reflects certain views and norms of behaviour which emanate from a particular cultural context. The conventions of consultancy work, of how to carry out the work, how to write a report (and how to ensure the donor gives you more work), all come from a shared culture, the "culture" of aid. This is one in which the donors' terms of reference, priorities, and report guidelines determine the nature, content, and even to a certain extent the outcomes of consultancy work.

Whether long or short term, the same model prevails. Even attempts to counteract accusations of a continuing neocolonial relationship by employing more local consultants has been problematic: local consultants have found it difficult to meet the deadlines set by donors (they are likely to have other commitments such as teaching), they are less familiar with the conventions of consultancy report writing, and when part of an evaluation team, their function is seen by external consultants as being to provide local knowledge of the country but not to be involved in intellectual analysis, or in making recommendations (Arthur and Preston 1996). Moreover, as Buchert and King (1996, 14) suggest, the growth in consultancy work resulting from the donors' obsession with accountability and value for money has resulted in a brain drain of competent professionals from the public sector in the poorest countries (e.g., universities, research centres) to jobs with official donor agencies and NGOs, both in their country offices and overseas headquarters. In turn, the consequent reduced capacity for in-country research and evaluation has had a negative impact on development efforts, in particular institution-building, which ironically has fuelled the need for more consultants. In addition, the increasing amount of time that government officials have to spend on generating statistics, reports, and other documentation to satisfy the donors' insatiable demand for information (King 1991) has further undermined national capacity, even for rountine management. Donors are thus ironically perpetuating dependence on outside support through their own short-termism (Buchert and King 1996) and so the proliferation of consultants in development work is counter-developmental.

LESSONS TO BE LEARNED

In this chapter I have attempted to show that the dominance of economic considerations renders the aid industry an ineffectual means of generating sustainable development in developing countries. In particular the rational planning model that underpins the concept of the development project, with its claims to objective analysis, standardised solutions, and universal applicability, and its insistence on tangible outcomes and short timescales, does not allow for development in the sense of genuine capacity-building to take place. While the aid agenda is driven by economic considerations, the agenda itself in respect of priorities set, plans produced, and activities engaged in, is culture-bound. For the project, whether in terms of its design, implementation strategies, or evaluation, reflects the ways of seeing, thinking, and doing of those who exercise the most control over it, in particular its resources. Aid projects, whether bilateral or multilateral, are on the whole the product of Western minds, either of nationals of Western countries or individuals accustomed to living and working in accordance to recognisably Western organisational norms and practices.[7] So the solutions proposed are likely to be ones that would work for people with similar outlook but not necessarily for those who see the issues from a radically different perspective. Hence, the failure to take cultural considerations into account when designing interventions, and to recognise that what is considered of value and relevance to one party may not be seen as such by other parties, has meant that the project has been unable to fuse with existing structures and processes in the host institution in such a way that it could act as a catalyst for change.

So what lessons should donors learn from the mistakes of the past? Four of the most important are listed below.

The first lesson to be learned is that there are no ready-made solutions to the problems of poverty, inequality, and injustice in the world, hence there are no models of development and no "standard" development projects. There is also no possibility that genuine development can occur through exogenous interventions, however well designed and resourced they may be, without the full participation of the target group(s).

The second lesson, a sobering one for donors, is that despite the huge sums of money and unlimited "expertise" at their disposal, the best known and most successful projects have tended to be "home grown"; in other words, they have been initiated by individuals or groups working directly with communities in the countries concerned, with few resources and little influence. Projects such as the Bangladesh Rural Advancement Committee (BRAC), the Grameen Bank, also in Bangladesh, and the Self-Employed Women's Association (SEWA) in India, each of which has since its creation helped at least a million individuals to significantly improve their lives, were established from within the country and without donor support. They only later looked for, or were offered, external funding.

The third lesson is that donors need to exercise a little humility and to recognise that others, albeit poor and powerless, have valuable knowledge and skills to contribute to the development process. People's culture and heritage, from which they draw strength, should be built on, not ignored. Development initiatives have largely ignored or undervalued local knowledge, while still paying lip service to its importance, and in so doing have failed to take on board the "multiple realities" (Fullan 1991) of people's lives. All too often individuals like Elizabeth, cited in Brian Street's chapter, have become disempowered and marginalised by the development process (in her case, the arrival of the literacy class and a new set of community-state relations) where once they had been a central part of that process.

The fourth lesson is that to ignore culture is to be economically irresponsible. Culture must cease to be seen as a barrier and become part of the solution, a strength to build on. Culturally sensitive approaches may be initially costly, but will prove to be cost-effective in the long run if greater levels of success can be assured. As Christine McNab and Peter Soye in Chapter 8 suggest in the context of teaching multiple nationality languages in Ethiopia, where additional costs lead to an improved learning environment (higher levels of achievement, lower levels of dropout and repetition), then cultural considerations can have an economic pay-off.

THE WAY FORWARD

So what is the way forward? Despite the poor track record of donors, there are some optimistic signs of improved practice, for example, through the greater use of sociologists and anthropologists in project design and monitoring, increased involvement of NGOs in the delivery of development assistance, especially in supporting community-based schooling and healthcare, and a willingness to support community-led innovative schemes and alternative forms of schooling that are more appropriate to local circumstances.

If we start to view economic theory as a cultural construct and as the product of a certain world view, perhaps then we can get rid of the dichotomy between economics and culture and argue for greater determination of educational needs and appropriate practices by those on the ground so that education will both address local markets and economies, and recognise the need to respond to global economic forces. The hegemony of economic theory over the development process will then be reduced and a discourse of equal value between economics and culture can occur, in which we no longer talk of the one as a force for progress and the other as a barrier. Some of the alternatives to formal schooling put forward by Robert Serpell in Chapter 7, will then appear more attractive, in particular developing the school as a community resource; for example, by maximising its facilities for extra-curricular development work and adult continuing education, broadening the range of validated outcomes considered appropriate for a school, and creating greater accountability of students to the community (by bonding them to regular community service).

However, for their interventions to be more effective, I would suggest that donors will have to move away from monolithic models of development and be ready to fund smaller, more complex, and more open-ended projects which allow groups (institutions, communities, etc.) to generate their own solutions. Donors might offer a portfolio of options for support, out of which recipients can choose and assemble according to their needs and circumstances. This will imply a move away from "objective" quantitative inputs (more schools, more teachers, etc.) to more qualitative inputs, such as enlightened curriculum reform, flexible forms of schooling, gender-sensitisation programmes (given that the greatest educational inequality involves women and girls), and building on community knowledge and resources. Consultants will no longer be the carriers of "universal truth," but will be employed for well-specified and limited inputs; hence the overall volume of consultancy work will decline. To achieve this, expatriate consultants are likely to need training in culture sensitisation.

All this suggests smaller, more selective interventions, which donors with billions of dollars to spend annually dislike intensely. Therefore, the chances of there being a radical change in the way aid is disbursed is highly unlikely. Moreover, we need to remember that change is required well beyond the donor horizon. As Mikael Palme warns, radical change in the provision of schooling will require a change of world view among government officials in capital and regional cities who have a vested interest in seeing that the existing provision of schooling remains unchanged. This suggests that real change will only come about if donors are working with democratic governments, which are accountable to the people and to whom people can make their voices heard.

NOTES

[1] This, of course, suggests a certain contradiction, between, on the one hand, the trend towards internationalisation and uniformity through the creation of global economic, technological, and communication systems, which may also lead to demands for standardised educational provision and certification; and, on the other hand, the trend towards differentiation through the rejection of universal models and uniform solutions to localised problems, more specialised mar-

kets and forms of production, the disintegration of nation states, and more vocal demands by social groups outside the mainstream for greater autonomy and diversity, including in education. As we approach the millennium, these two dominant themes, globalisation and differentiation (as expressed through post-modernist writings), would appear to be pulling us in opposite directions.

[2] These are, of course, not strictly speaking aid agencies. However, the terms "aid" and "donor" are used very loosely in the development literature and will also be taken here to include the development banks.

[3] These terms "north" and "south" are also used very loosely, so much so that, along with "rich" and "poor," "developed" and "developing," they are acquiring a purely symbolic value. For example, the "south" would appear at the present time to include, for the purposes of aid, many countries in Eastern Europe, including those which were once part of the world's second superpower (the Soviet Union).

[4] During the 1970s and early 1980s a number of international agencies, led by the World Bank, gave enthusiastic support to initiatives to make education more practical and more relevant to the needs of young people in developing countries by introducing vocational subjects into a largely academic secondary school curriculum. The World Bank in its 1991 policy paper entitled *Vocational and Technical Education and Training* would appear to have conveniently forgotten this failed attempt at diversification, and the consequences for developing countries of having accepted the loans so readily offered.

[5] And, incidentally, so have developing country bureaucracies, which are now a parody of their 19th-century European model (Leach 1995; Reilly 1987).

[6] I would classify an expatriate as "long term" if he/she is resident in the host institution for a period of at least one year. A short-term consultant in contrast may make a number of visits; these could be as short as one week but are unlikely to exceed six months.

[7] Japan, now the world's largest bilateral donor, is a newcomer to the aid scene and has tended to concentrate on capital and financial aid, only coming recently to development project work. Almost no research exists into the Japanese aid programme, but one would assume that Japanese projects would reflect Japanese priorities and work practices.

REFERENCES

Arthur, L., and R. Preston with C. Ngahu, S. Shoaib le Breton, and D. Theobald. 1996. "Quality in Overseas Consultancy: Understanding the Issues." Manchester: British Council.

Berg, E.J. 1993. *Rethinking Technical Cooperation: Reforms for Capacity Building in Africa.* New York: UNDP.

Buchert, L., and K. King, eds. 1996. *Consultancy and Research in International Education: The New Dynamics.* Bonn: German Foundation for International Development.

Cassen, R., with associates.1994. *Does Aid Work? Report to an International Task Force,* 2nd ed. Oxford: Clarendon.

Fullan, M.G., with S. Stiegelbauer. 1991. *The New Meaning of Educational Change.* London: Cassell.

Handy, C. 1985. *Understanding Organisations,* 3rd ed. Harmondsworth: Penguin.

Inkeles, A., and D.H. Smith. 1974. *Becoming Modern.* London: Heinemann.

King, K. 1991. *Aid and Education in the Developing World.* Harlow: Longman

Leach, F. 1997. "International Aid to Education: Why Projects Fail." In *Education Dilemmas: Debate and Diversity,* K. Watson, C. Modgil, and S. Modgil., eds.Vol. 3. London: Cassell.

Leach, F. 1995. "Development Projects and Their Host Institutions: Are They Compatible?" *International Review of Education,* 41 (6): 459–479.

Leach, F. 1991. "Perception Gaps in Technical Assistance Projects: The Sudanese Case." In *Educational Innovation in Developing Countries: Case Studies of Changemakers,* K.M. Lewin with J.S. Stuart, eds. Basingstoke: Macmillan.

Lerner, D. 1958. *The Passing of Traditional Society: Modernizing the Middle East.* New York: Free Press.

Mazrui, A. 1980. *The African Condition.* London: Heinemann.

McClelland, D.C. 1961. *The Achieving Society.* Princeton: Van Nostrand.

OECD. 1996. *Development Cooperation Efforts and Policies of the Members of the DAC. 1996 Report.* Paris: OECD.

Reilly, W. 1987. "Management and Training for Development: The Hombe Thesis." *Public Administration and Development* 7 (1): 25–42.

Rogers, E.M., and L. Svenning. 1969. *Modernization Among Peasants.* New York: Holt, Rinehart and Winston.

Sachs, W. 1992. *The Development Dictionary.* London and Atlantic Highlands, NJ: Zed Books.

Stirrat, R.L. 1997. "Cultures of Consultancy." Unpublished Paper, Sussex University.

Street, B.V. 1990. *The Cultural Meanings of Literacy.* Geneva: UNESCO, International Bureau of Education.

Varghese, N.V. 1996. "Decentralisation of Educational Planning in India: The Case of the DPEP." *International Journal of Educational Development* 16 (4): 355–365.

World Bank. 1995. *Priorities and Strategies for Education: A World Bank Review.* Washington, DC: World Bank.

World Bank. 1991. *Technical and Vocational Education and Training: A World Bank Policy Paper.* Washington, DC: World Bank.

Index

Abernethy, D. B., 189
Africa, education in
  See also Ethiopia, language policy in; Mozambique, primary education in
  for adults, 130
  agrarian/economic, 126–127
  Bhutan, community financing in, 191–193
  in Cameroon, 210–215
  of children with disabilities, 121–124
  community-based rehabilitation (CBR), 123–124
  costs and benefits of restructuring, 132–134
  extracurricular activities, 127–130
  health education for mothers, 124–126
  home-based, 121–124
  human capital theory, 118–121
  Kenya, community financing in, 186–189
  Kenya, mathematics in, 301–312
  libraries in schools, 128
  local accountability, 130–132
  multiple roles in, 111–112
  narrowing staircase model of schooling, 115–121
  Nigeria, community financing in, 189–191
  parent–teacher associations, 129
  personal development, 112–115
  schools as community forums, 129–130
  in Uganda, 215–219
Ahai, N., 340
Aikman, Sheila, 20–21, 95–109, 361, 376
Alatas, A., 256
Ali, M. A., 229, 234
Amazon. *See* Madre de Dios region, education policy in
Anderson, J., 186, 198
Apter, D. E., 285
Argonauts of the Western Pacific (Malinowski), 34
Arthur, L., 388
Asad, Talal, 54–55
Australia-Pacific region, Indigenous cultures and higher education in
  background information, 241–243
  coconut palm model, 243–246

Australia-Pacific region (*cont.*)
doctoral thesis example, 254–255
effects of, 255–259
reestablishment and self-determination of Indigenous people, 246–249
teacher education example, 249–254

Bacchus, Kazim, 23–24, 225–235
Bangladesh Rural Advancement Committee (BRAC), 390
Banton, Michael, 50–51
Barros, R., 28, 328
Baumgratz, G., 350
Beare, H., 257
Bernstein, B., 24–25, 159
Bhutan, community financing in, 191–193
Bishop, A., 320, 339
Bochner, S., 365
Bourdieu, P., 24, 25, 159, 272
Bray, Mark, 23, 183–200
Brazil, aspirations in children
alternative forms of knowledge and impact on learning, 338–340
conclusions, 340–343
occupational identity and development in schools, 335–338
social representations of stratification, 330–335
Brislin, R., 364
Buchan, John, 52
Buchert, L., 389

Cameroon
parental attitudes toward the education of females, 214–215
private financing in, 212–214
public financing in, 210–212
Camilleri, C., 184
Camitta M., 62, 63
Cao, H. T., 295
"Capitalism and Rural Society in Germany" (Weber), 6–7
Carraher, D. W., 330, 335, 339
Carraher, T. N., 330, 335
Centre of Research on Multinational Corporations, 320
Cernea, M. M., 28–29
Chamie, M., 226
Chung, F., 196
Clarke, P., 262
Comenius, 115
Community-based rehabilitation (CBR), 123–124
Community financing of education
in Bhutan, 191–193
definition of terms, 184
extent of, 185
inefficiency, wastage, and poor quality issues, 197–199
inequality issues, 194–197
in Kenya, 186–189
in Nigeria, 189–191
reasons for, 184–185
Conrad, Joseph, 52
Conversations in Colombia (Gudeman), 36–37
Côte d'Ivoire. *See* Project management
"Cultural Endowments and Economic Development: What Can We Learn from Anthropology?" (Ruttan), 11
Culture
costs of, 22–24
economy and, 6–9, 14–15
goals of, debate over, 19–22
of knowledge and learning, 24–28
renewed interest in, 347
Culture and Practical Reason (Sahlins), 36
Culture in development, 49
concept of race, 50–53

concepts of culture, 53–56
literacy case example, 56–65

Darwin, Charles, 52
Davidson, A. L., 295
Davis, P. J., 304
De Abreu, G., 339, 340
Deinstitutionalization movement, 123
Delens, Michael, 29, 347–366, 383–384, 387
Dependency theory, 11
Development
See also Culture in development
alternatives to, 89–92
different views of, 15–17
education and, 3–4, 9–12
as a form of control, 83–88
goals of, debate over, 19–22
means and ends of, 17–19
modernization theory of, 10, 11, 118–119
Palestinian, 82–93
Dia, M., 363
Dickinson, J., 331
Disabled children, education for, 121–124
District Primary Education Project (DPEP), 380–381
Durkheim, Emile, 6

"East Asian Miracle" (World Bank), 39
Economics/economy
alternative models of, 41–42
anthropological approaches to, 33–45
as a cultural artifact, 36–41
culture and, 6–9, 14–15
formalists versus substantivists, 34–36
hegemonic role of, 34–36
Economics as Culture: Models and Metaphors of Livelihood (Gudeman), 36
Education
See also Rural communities, education in; *and under name of country/ location*
development and, 3–4, 9–12
home-based, 121–124
learning and, 12–14
Educational aid
See also Financing, community; Financing strategies
consultants, role of, 387–389
cross-cultural transfer, 384–386
dilemmas for, 28–30, 377–380
future of, 391–392
lessons learned, 390–391
projects as a means of, 380–384
Educational policy in Madre de Dios
conclusions, 108–109
cultural and geographical diversity, 96–98
cultural perceptions of the economy, 104–106
development in, 98–99
human resources, 100–101
indigenous peoples (Arakmbut), 103–104
mestizos, 101–102
need for new, 95–96
serranos, 102–103
views toward, 106–107
Ellis, G., 363
Emler, N., 331
End of Economics, The (Perelman), 15
English language teaching (ELT), project management and
conclusions, 365–366
cultural conflicts, 352–353
cultural interfaces, 351–352
curriculum development for indigenous minorities, 360–361
false impressions, 353–354

English language teaching (*cont.*)
implications for planners, 363–365
intercultural education, 362–363
native versus nonnative rules, 347–349
project planning, 349–351
strategic management, 358–360
systems theory approach, 355–358
Ernest, P., 318
Ethiopia, language policy in
changes in the education system, 144–146
conclusions, 155–157
costs of implementing multilanguage textbook policy, 151–155
diversity of languages, problems with, 146–149
in the 1990s, 144
textbook provisions, 149–151
Evans-Pritchard, E. E., 159
Evolution, 52

Faraclas, N., 340
Farah, Iffat, 23–24, 225–235
Fasheh, Munir, 19–20, 81–93, 322–323, 371, 372
Female education, in Pakistan
availability of, 227
conclusions, 234–235
economic versus cultural issues, 228–232
purdah, impact of, 228
school locations and, 232–233
school quality and, 233
social and cultural norms, 227–228
Female education, parental attitudes toward
in Cameroon, 214–215
in Uganda, 218–219
Fennema, E., 304
Financing, community
See also Educational aid
in Bhutan, 191–193
definition of terms, 184
extent of, 185
inefficiency, wastage, and poor quality issues, 197–199
inequality issues, 194–197
in Kenya, 186–189
in Nigeria, 189–191
reasons for, 184–185
Financing strategies
See also Educational aid
in Cameroon, 210–215
crisis in sub-Saharan Africa, 204–206
cultural issues, 208–210
decline of government role, effects of, 219–220
economic costs and benefits, 206–208
rate-of-return studies, 207–208
recommendations, 220–221
in Uganda, 215–219
Formalists versus substantivists, 34–36
Frank, Andre Gunder, 11
Fullan, M., 358, 386
Fuller, B., 262
Furnham, A., 365

Gale, P., 257
Galtung, J., 11, 15
Geertz, Clifford, 39
Gender differences, 209–210
See also Female education
mathematics and, 318, 321–324
mathematics in Kenya and, 307
usefulness of science education in the Solomon Islands and, 289–290
workplaces and, 319–320, 321–323
Gilbreath, R., 353
Gilroy, Paul, 53, 54
Gokalp, A., 363

Goldsmith, E., 70
Grameen Bank, 390
Great Didactic (Comenius), 115
Great Transformation, The (Polanyi), 8
Gudeman, Stephen, 15, 36–37, 41

Hagerstrand, 60
Haggard, Rider, 52
Halsey, A. H., 330, 331
Handy, C., 350, 351, 366, 383
Han-Siu Chow, I., 350
Harris, Mary, 27–28, 315–324, 371, 385
Havelock, R., 357
Health education for mothers, 124–126
Helu-Thaman, Konai, 8–9, 69–76, 257, 371
Hersh, R., 304
Heyneman, S., 15, 205
Hill, M. A., 225–226
Hill, M. J. D., 187–189
Hillery, G. A., 184
Himmelweit, H., 330, 331
Hofstede, G., 349, 350, 351, 352, 354, 365–366
Home-based education, 121–124
Horton, Robin, 276
Howson, G., 316
Huberman, A., 357
Hui, C., 357
Human capital theory, 3, 10–11, 17, 118–121, 376

Igwe, S. O., 189–191
Inkeles, A., 10
Institutionalized public basic schooling (IPBS), 115–121
Intelligence tests, 327
Iran, literacy in, 56–60

Jevons, W., 37

Kennan, George, 83–84
Kenya
  community financing in, 186–189
  cultural conflicts, 302–303
  8-4-4 program, 301–302
Kenya, mathematics in
  appropriateness of, and for whom, 307–310
  conclusions, 311–312
  costs of, 310–311
  cultural views on, 304–307
  definition of mathematics, 303–304
  gender differences, 307
King, E. M., 225–226
King, K., 389
Kipling, Rudyard, 52
Klein, G. K., 228
Knowledge, culture of, 24–28
Kulick, D., 61–62

Lam, D., 28, 328
Landau, M., 307
Language policies, in Ethiopia
  changes in the education system, 144–146
  conclusions, 155–157
  costs of implementing multilanguage textbook policy, 151–155
  diversity of languages, problems with, 146–149
  in the 1990s, 144
  textbook provisions, 149–151
Language policies, in Mauritius, 163–169
Lankshear, Colin, 59
Leach, Fiona, 29–30, 351, 352, 366, 371–393
Learning
  culture of, 24–28
  education and, 12–14
Lesh, R., 307
Lewin, Keith, 22–23, 159–181, 374

Literacy
ideological model of, 61, 63
in Iran, 56–60
in New Guinea, 61–62
in Philadelphia, 62–63
Social Uses of Literacy project in South Africa, 63–65
Literacy, Schooling, and Revolution (Lankshear), 59
Little, Angela, 3–30, 374, 376
Lowe, John, 27, 283–297, 374

MacLaughlin, J., 350
Madre de Dios region, education policy in
conclusions, 108–109
cultural and geographical diversity, 96–98
cultural perceptions of the economy, 104–106
development in, 98–99
human resources, 100–101
indigenous peoples (Arakmbut), 103–104
mestizos, 101–102
need for new, 95–96
serranos, 102–103
views toward, 106–107
Mahaweli Authority of Sri Lanka (MASL), 42–44
Malinowski, Bronislaw, 34
Markoff, John, 34, 39, 40
Marx, Karl, 6
Mathematics
females and, 318, 321–324
schools and, 316–318
social context, 320–321
special role of, 315–316
in the workplace, 319
Mathematics, in Kenya
appropriateness of, and for whom, 307–310
conclusions, 311–312
costs of, 310–311
cultural views on, 304–307
definition of mathematics, 303–304
gender differences, 307
Mauritius, educational dilemmas in
cultural concepts, 160–162
language issues, 163–169
repeating grades, 169–174
work and organizational practices, 174–180
Mazrui, Ali, 372
Mbithi, M., 187, 197
McClelland, D., 10
McGavin, P., 208
McNab, Christine, 22, 143–157, 374, 391
Mel, M. A., 242
Mill, John Stuart, 19
Miller, J. D., 296
Modernization theory of development, 10, 11, 118–119
science education and, 283–288
Montecinos, Veronica, 34, 39, 40
Mozambique, primary education in
classroom activities, quality and type of, 262–265
future outlook, 277–279
influences on learning, 265–268
matrilineal society, role of, 268–272
negative impact of education, 272
ritualistic teaching, 263–265
teachers, role of, 272–277
Musgrove, F., 159

Nabobo, U., 250, 257
Narrowing staircase model of schooling, 115–121
age-by-grade matching, 115–118
National Federation of Women's Institutes (NFWI), 323
Nestvogel, R., 228
New Guinea, literacy in, 61–62

Nigeria, community financing in, 189–191
Nunes, Terezinha, 28, 327–342
Nyamu, Florence Kiragu, 27

Ocho, L., 194
Ogbu, J., 340
Ogunniyi, M., 297
Olembo, J. O., 198
Opolot, J. A., 196
Ozigi, A., 194

Pakistan, female education in
  availability of, 227
  conclusions, 234–235
  economic versus cultural issues, 228–232
  purdah, impact of, 228
  school locations and, 232–233
  school quality and, 233
  social and cultural norms, 227–228
Palestinians, 82–93
Palme, Mikael, 24, 26–27, 261–280, 373, 392
Pappas, T., 303, 308
Pasacharopoulos, G., 208
Passeron, J. P., 24, 25
Patkar, A., 226
Perelman, M., 15
Phelan, P., 295
Philadelphia, literacy in, 62–63
Polanyi, Karl, 8, 35
Pompeu, G., 339
Preston, P., 38
Preston, R., 388
Project management
  conclusions, 365–366
  cultural conflicts, 352–353
  cultural interfaces, 351–352
  curriculum development for indigenous minorities, 360–361
  false impressions, 353–354
  implications for planners, 363–365
  intercultural education, 362–363
  native versus non-native rules, 347–349
  project planning, 349–351
  strategic management, 358–360
  systems theory approach, 355–358
Protestant Ethic and the Spirit of Capitalism (Weber), 7

Race, concept of, 50–53
Radcliffe-Brown, A. R., 159
Rasmusson, R., 187, 197
Reimers, F., 232, 233
"Religion as a Cultural System" (Geertz), 39
Religious beliefs, role of, 209–210
Rhodes, Cecil, 160
Roazzi, Antonio, 28, 327–342
Rondinelli, D., 358
Rural communities, education in
  for adults, 130
  agrarian/economic, 126–127
  of children with disabilities, 121–124
  community-based rehabilitation (CBR), 123–124
  costs and benefits of restructuring, 132–134
  extracurricular activities, 127–130
  health education for mothers, 124–126
  home-based, 121–124
  human capital theory, 118–121
  libraries in schools, 128
  local accountability, 130–132
  multiple roles in, 111–112
  narrowing staircase model of schooling, 115–121
  parent–teacher associations, 129
  personal development, 112–115
  schools as community forums, 129–130

Ruskin, John, 160
Ruttan, V. W., 11

Sahlins, Marshall, 35, 36, 257
Said, Edward, 50
Schliemann, A. D., 339
Schultz, Theodore W., 17, 19
Science education, modernization theory and expectation for, 283–288
Science education, Solomon Island students and
  customs versus modernization, 293–297
  gender differences, 289–290
  impact of, 288–293
Scientific literacy, use of term, 284
Scribner, S., 319
Self-Employed Women's Association (SEWA), 390
Serpell, Robert, 21–22, 111–134, 268, 273, 302, 303, 371, 391
Shultz, T. P., 225
Shuman, A., 62, 63
Slaughter, R., 257
Smith, Adam, 19
Smith, D., 10
Social reproduction theory, 3
Social Uses of Literacy project in South Africa, 63–65
Socioeconomic status (SES)
  conclusions, 340–343
  occupational identity and development in schools, 335–338
  social representations of stratification, 330–335
Solomon Island students, science education and
  customs versus modernization, 293–297
  gender differences, 289–290
  impact of, 288–293
South Africa, Social Uses of Literacy project in, 63–65
Stairs, A., 360–361, 363, 365
Stevenson, H. W., 305
Stigler, J. W., 305
Stirrat, R. L., 8, 14–17, 33–45, 375–376, 384–385, 388
Stoye, Peter, 22, 143–157, 374, 391
Strategic management, 358–360
Street, Brian V., 11–12, 49–65, 372, 375, 384
Stroud, C., 61–62
Substantivists, formalists versus, 34–36
Systems theory, 355–358

Tamer Institute, 92
Taunton Report, 317, 318
Teasdale, G. R., 26, 241–259, 371
Teasdale, J. I., 26, 241–259, 371
Tembon, Mercy, 23–24, 203–221, 373
Tonga
  ako, 72–73, 74–76
  economic development and affects of formal education, 70–71
  educational goals, views of, 71–72
  foreign schooling and affects on Tonga culture, 70
  'ilo, 72, 73, 74–76
  notions of education, 72–74
  poto, 72, 74–76
Triandis, H., 359

Uganda, 215
  parental attitudes toward the education of females, 218–219
  private financing in, 218
  public financing in, 216–218

Vygotsky, L. S., 121

Ware, S. A., 283
Warwick, D., 232, 233

Weber, Max, 6–7
Whitaker, P., 358
White, L., 286, 297
White, R., 347–348, 354
Willis, P., 340
Wilson, B., 316
Wilson, G. M., 308
Woodhall, M., 208
Workplaces
  gender differences, 319–320, 321–323
  mathematics in, 319
World Bank, 82, 83
  "East Asian Miracle," 39
  Mahaweli Authority of Sri Lanka (MASL) and, 42–44
World Declaration on Education For All, 118
Wrong, D. H., 228

ZIMCARE, 124
Zone of proximal development (ZPD), 121–122
Zulus, 55–56

Reference Books in International Education
Edward R. Beauchamp, *Series Editor*

Education in the People's Republic of China, Past and Present
An Annotated Bibliography
by Franklin Parker
and Betty June Parker

Education in South Asia
A Select Annotated Bibliography
by Philip G. Altbach, Denzil Saldanha, and Jeanne Weiler

Textbooks in the Third World
Policy, Content, and Context
by Philip G. Altbach
and Gail P. Kelly

Teachers and Teaching in the Developing World
by Val D. Rust and Per Dalin

Russian and Soviet Education, 1731–1989
A Multilingual Annotated Bibliography
by William W. Brickman
and John T. Zepper

Education in the Arab Gulf States and the Arab World
An Annotated Bibliographic Guide
by Nagat El-Sanabary

Education in England and Wales
An Annotated Bibliography
by Franklin Parker
and Betty June Parker

Understanding Educational Reform in Global Context
Economy, Ideology, and the State
edited by Mark B. Ginsburg

Education and Social Change in Korea
by Don Adams
and Esther E. Gottlieb

Three Decades of Peace Education Around the World
An Anthology
edited by Robin J. Burns
and Robert Aspeslagh

Education and Disability in Cross-Cultural Perspective
edited by Susan J. Peters

Russian Education
Tradition and Transition
by Brian Holmes, Gerald H. Read, and Natalya Voskresenskaya

Learning to Teach in Two Cultures
Japan and the United States
by Nobuo K. Shimahara
and Akira Sakai

Educating Immigrant Children
Schools and Language Minorities in Twelve Nations
by Charles L. Glenn
with Ester J. de Jong

Teacher Education in Industrialized Nations
Issues in Changing Social Contexts
edited by Nobuo K. Shimahara
and Ivan Z. Holowinsky

Education and Development in East Asia
edited by Paul Morris
and Anthony Sweeting

The Unification of German Education
by Val D. Rust and Diane Rust

Women, Education, and Development in Asia
Cross-National Perspectives
edited by Grace C.L. Mak

QUALITATIVE EDUCATIONAL RESEARCH IN DEVELOPING COUNTRIES
Current Perspectives
edited by Michael Crossley and Graham Vulliamy

SOCIAL CARTOGRAPHY
Mapping Ways of Seeing Social and Educational Change
edited by Rolland G. Paulston

SOCIAL JUSTICE AND THIRD WORLD EDUCATION
edited by Timothy J. Scrase

QUALITY EDUCATION FOR ALL
Community-Oriented Approaches
edited by H. Dean Nielsen and William K. Cummings

EDUCATION AND THE SCANDINAVIAN WELFARE STATE IN THE YEAR 2000
Equality, Policy, and Reform
edited by Arild Tjeldvoll

POLITICS OF CLASSROOM LIFE
Classroom Management in International Perspective
edited by Nobuo K. Shimahara

SCHOOLING IN SUB-SAHARAN AFRICA
Contemporary Issues and Future Concerns
edited by Cynthia Szymanski Sunal

GENDER ISSUES IN INTERNATIONAL EDUCATION
Beyond Policy and Practice
edited by Maggie Wilson and Sheena Erskine

CHINA'S NATIONAL MINORITY EDUCATION
Culture, Schooling, and Development
edited by Gerard A. Postiglione